Shojo Beat

STROBE EDGE

Vol. 2

Story & Art by
Io Sakisaka

STROBE EDGE

Volume 2
CONTENTS

Chapter 5......3
Chapter 6......57
Chapter 7......101
Strobe Edge ~Another Light~ 145

Story Thus Far

Ninako is a down-to-earth high school freshman who doesn't really know how it feels to be in love. So when her friends tell her that her affection for Daiki, a boy she's known since middle school, means she's in love with him, she believes it...until she meets the school idol, Ren Ichinose. As Ninako gets to know Ren, who's in another class, she realizes that she's falling in love with him.

When Daiki tells Ninako that he's in love with her, she runs away. Her own feelings for Ren are impossible to ignore, even after she finds out that Ren is dating Daiki's older sister. After Ninako finally admits to Daiki that she's not in love with him, her friend Sayuri tells him that *she's* in love with him. And Ninako decides it's time to tell Ren the truth about her feelings...

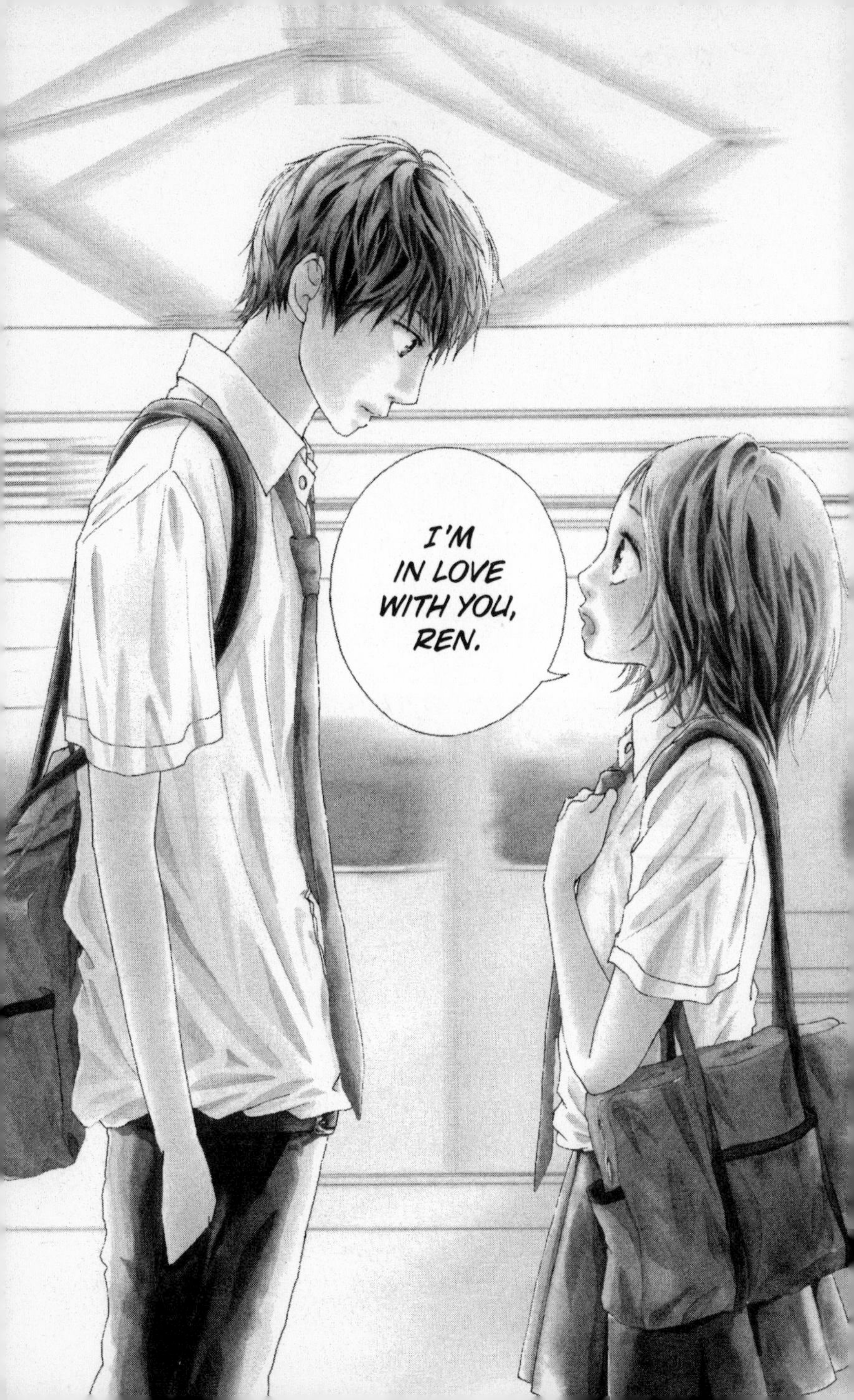
I'M IN LOVE WITH YOU, REN.

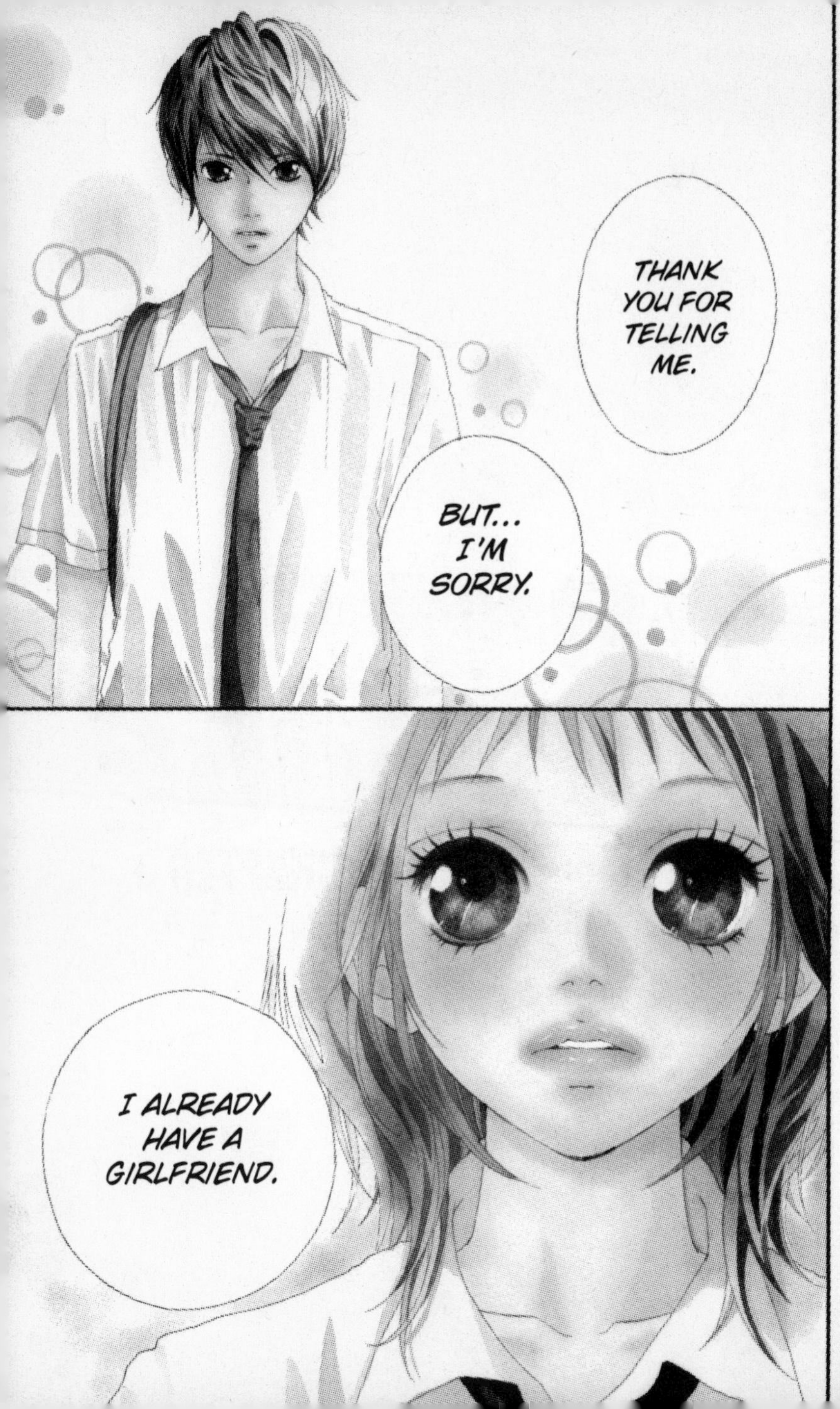
THANK YOU FOR TELLING ME.
BUT... I'M SORRY.
I ALREADY HAVE A GIRLFRIEND.

STROBE EDGE
CHAPTER 5

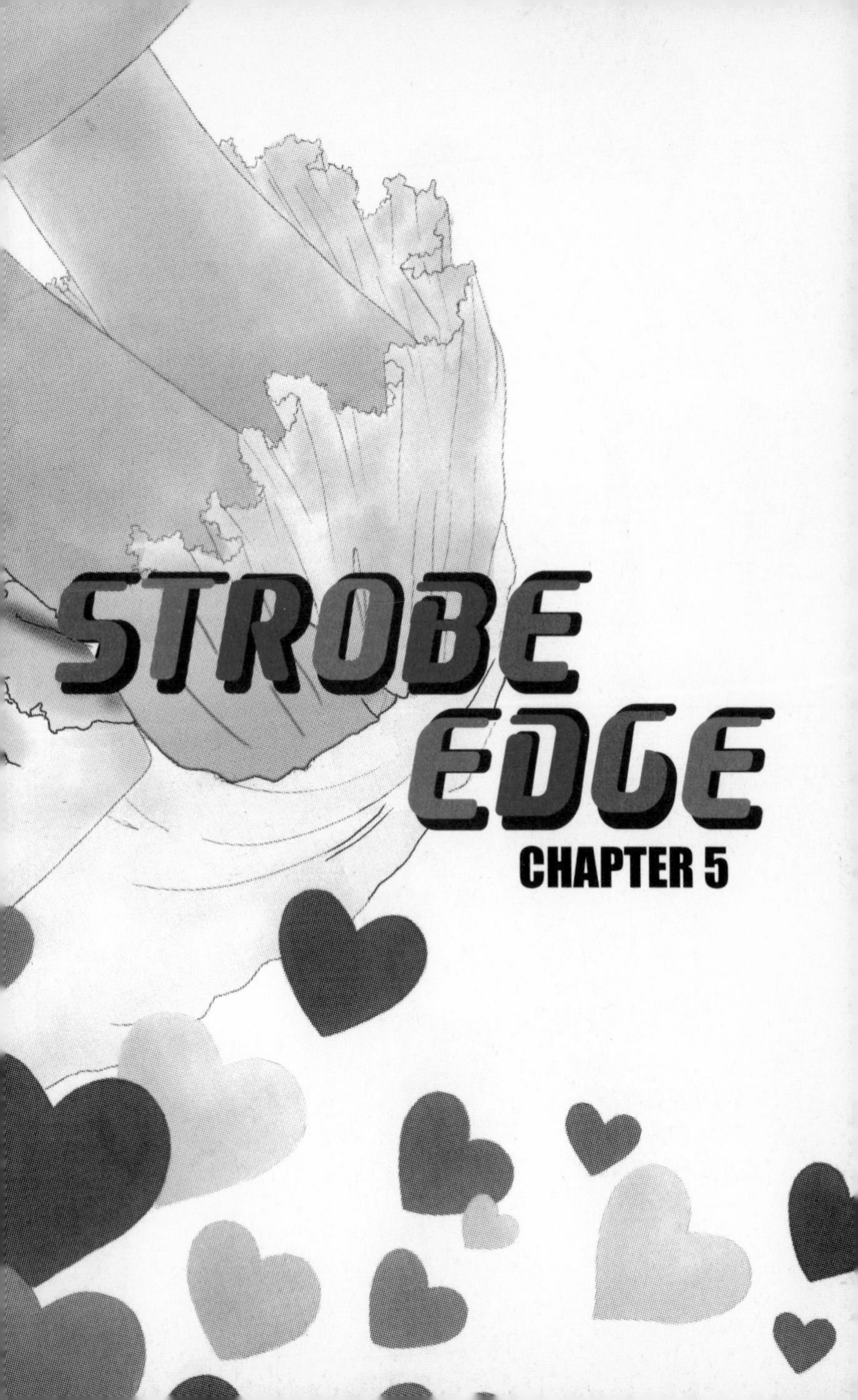

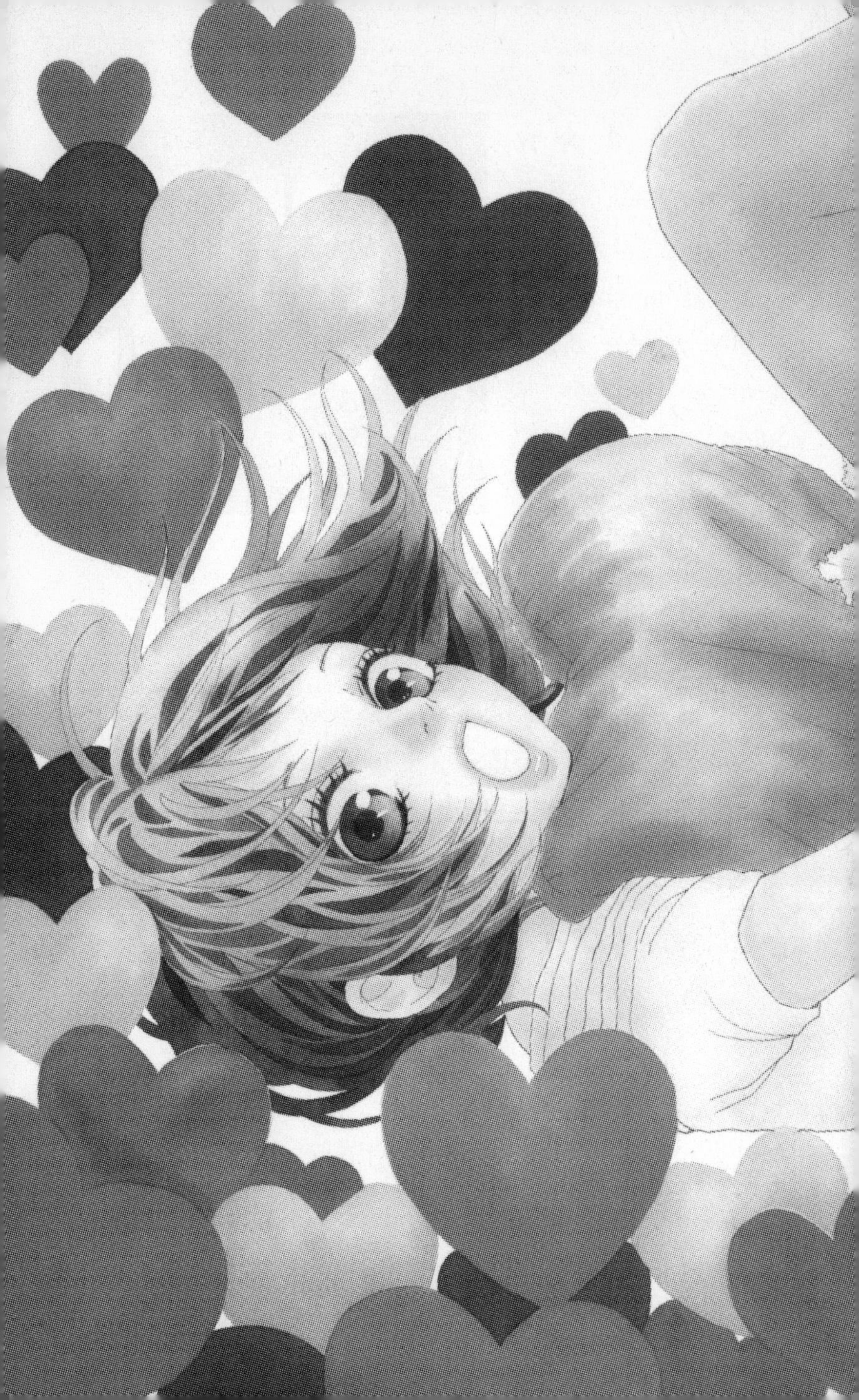

Hello! Io Sakisaka here! Thank you for checking out *Strobe Edge* volume 2. This book wouldn't exist without readers like you. Thank you so much!

I always think that the "sparkles" of everyday life—those precious moments—are incredibly beautiful, so I want to capture as many of them as possible. But those fleeting moments are usually well hidden, so unless I really make sure to have my feelers out, I can miss them entirely. So it's very exciting when I do notice one! Yes!

With *Strobe Edge*, I'm hoping to portray those "sparkles" and share the thrill of discovering them—that moment of "Yes!"—with all of you.

And now, on to *Strobe Edge 2*...

 Io Sakisaka

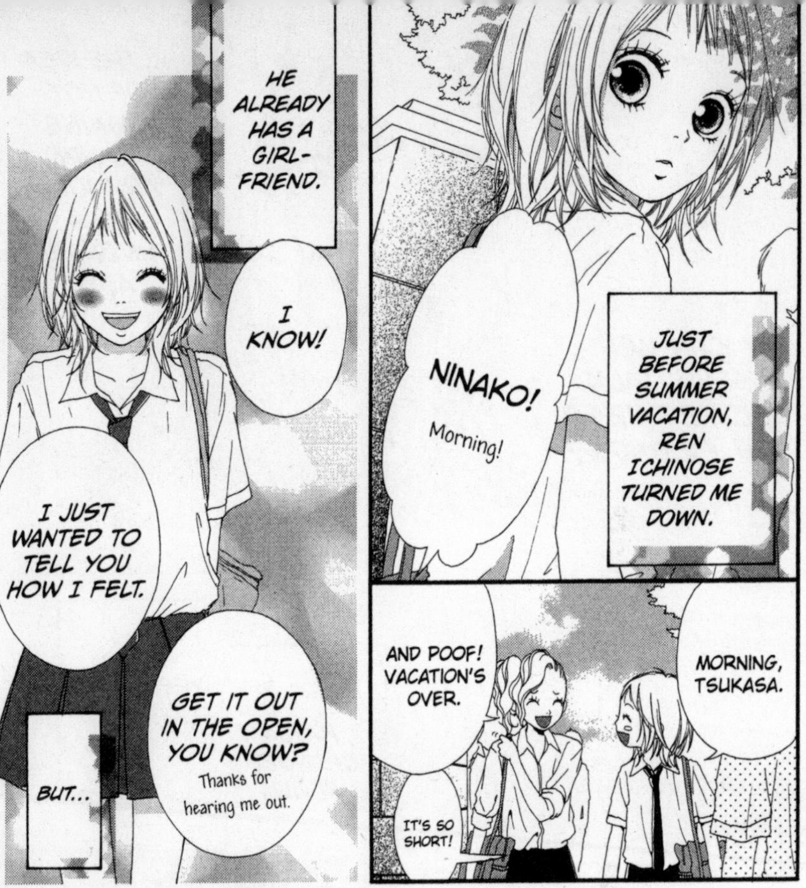
JUST BEFORE SUMMER VACATION, REN ICHINOSE TURNED ME DOWN.
NINAKO!
Morning!
MORNING, TSUKASA.
AND POOF! VACATION'S OVER.
IT'S SO SHORT!
HE ALREADY HAS A GIRL-FRIEND.
I KNOW!
I JUST WANTED TO TELL YOU HOW I FELT.
GET IT OUT IN THE OPEN, YOU KNOW?
Thanks for hearing me out.
BUT...

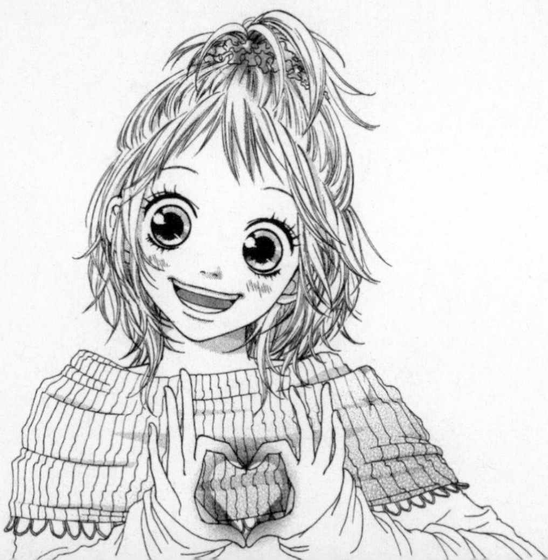

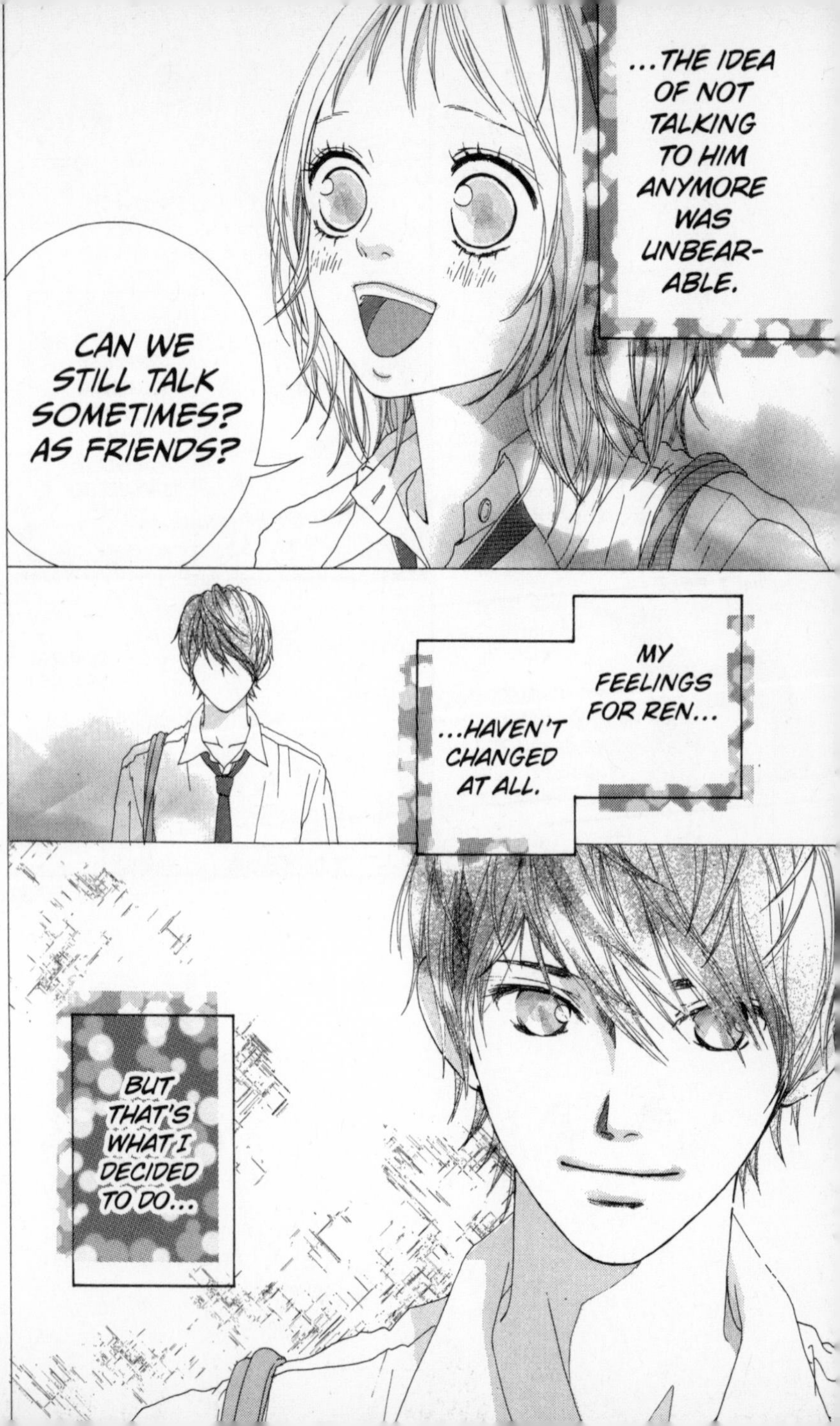
...THE IDEA OF NOT TALKING TO HIM ANYMORE WAS UNBEAR-ABLE.
CAN WE STILL TALK SOMETIMES? AS FRIENDS?
MY FEELINGS FOR REN...
...HAVEN'T CHANGED AT ALL.
BUT THAT'S WHAT I DECIDED TO DO...

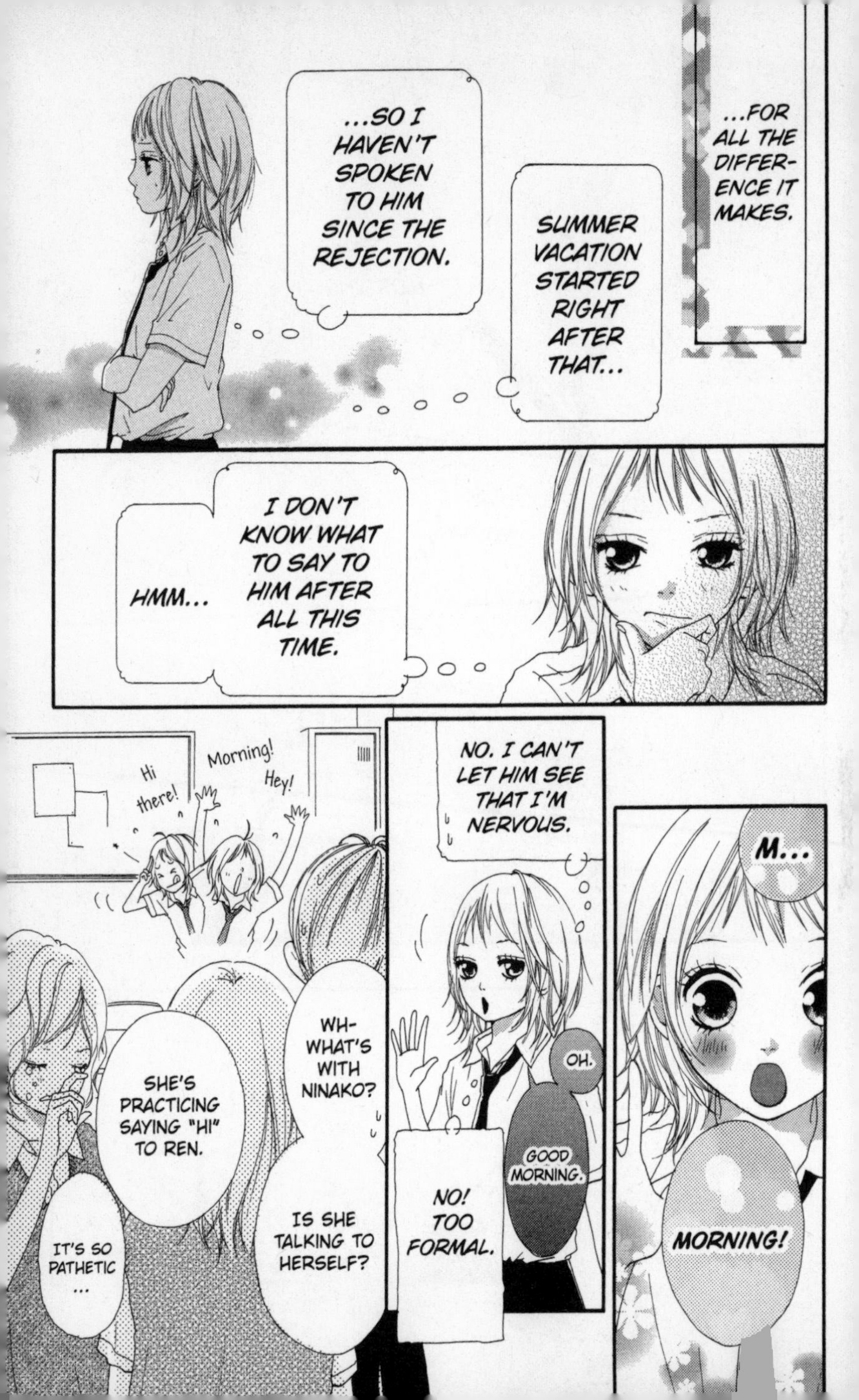
...FOR ALL THE DIFFERENCE IT MAKES.
SUMMER VACATION STARTED RIGHT AFTER THAT...
...SO I HAVEN'T SPOKEN TO HIM SINCE THE REJECTION.
I DON'T KNOW WHAT TO SAY TO HIM AFTER ALL THIS TIME.
HMM...
M...
MORNING!
NO. I CAN'T LET HIM SEE THAT I'M NERVOUS.
OH.
GOOD MORNING.
NO! TOO FORMAL.
Morning!
Hey!
Hi there!
WH- WHAT'S WITH NINAKO?
SHE'S PRACTICING SAYING "HI" TO REN.
IS SHE TALKING TO HERSELF?
IT'S SO PATHETIC ...

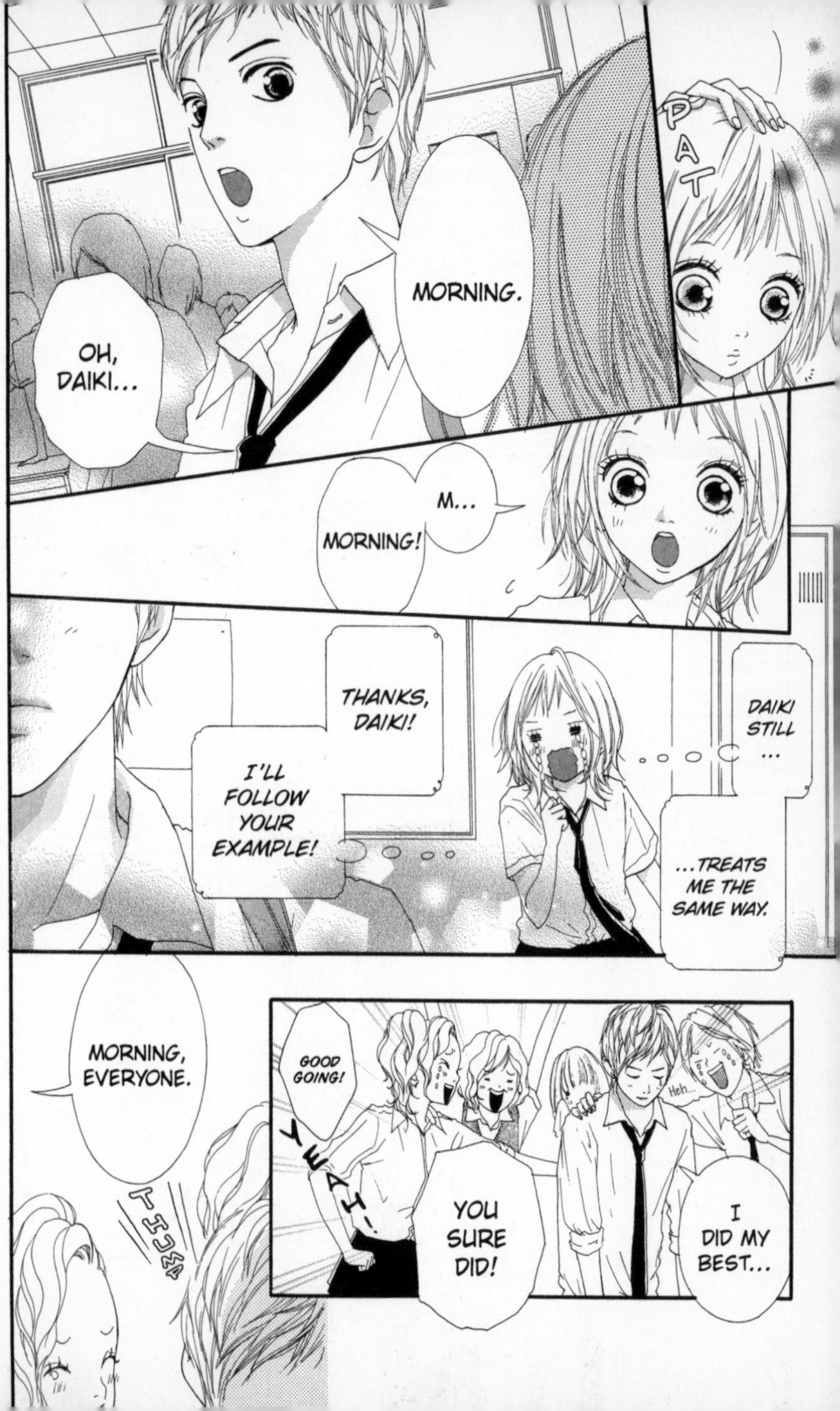
PAT
MORNING.
OH, DAIKI...
M...
MORNING!
DAIKI STILL ...
...TREATS ME THE SAME WAY.
THANKS, DAIKI!
I'LL FOLLOW YOUR EXAMPLE!
Heh...
I DID MY BEST...
YOU SURE DID!
GOOD GOING!
YEAH!
MORNING, EVERYONE.
THUMP

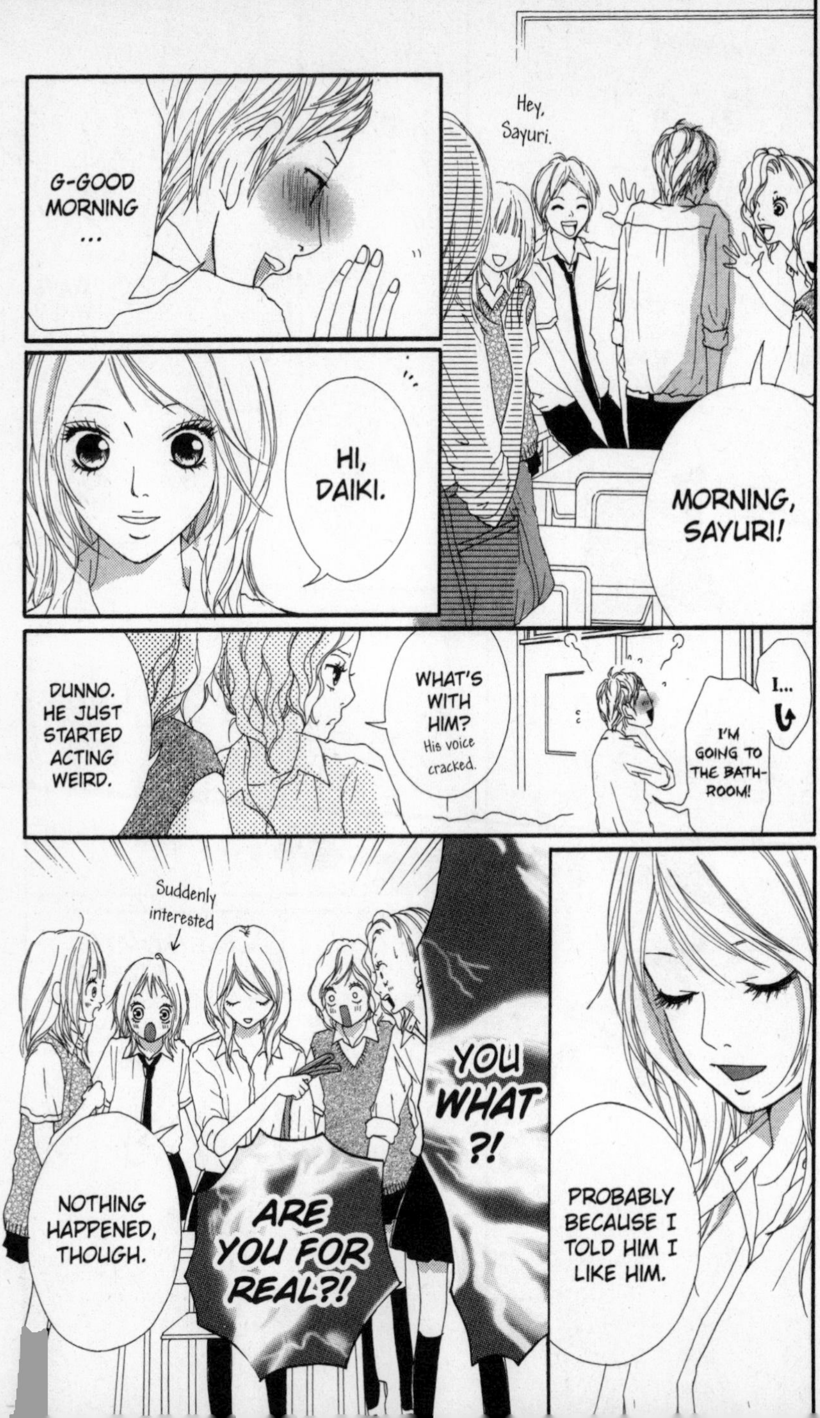
Hey, Sayuri.
MORNING, SAYURI!
G-GOOD MORNING ...
HI, DAIKI.
I...
I'M GOING TO THE BATH-ROOM!
WHAT'S WITH HIM? His voice cracked.
DUNNO. HE JUST STARTED ACTING WEIRD.
PROBABLY BECAUSE I TOLD HIM I LIKE HIM.
YOU WHAT?!
ARE YOU FOR REAL?!
Suddenly interested
NOTHING HAPPENED, THOUGH.

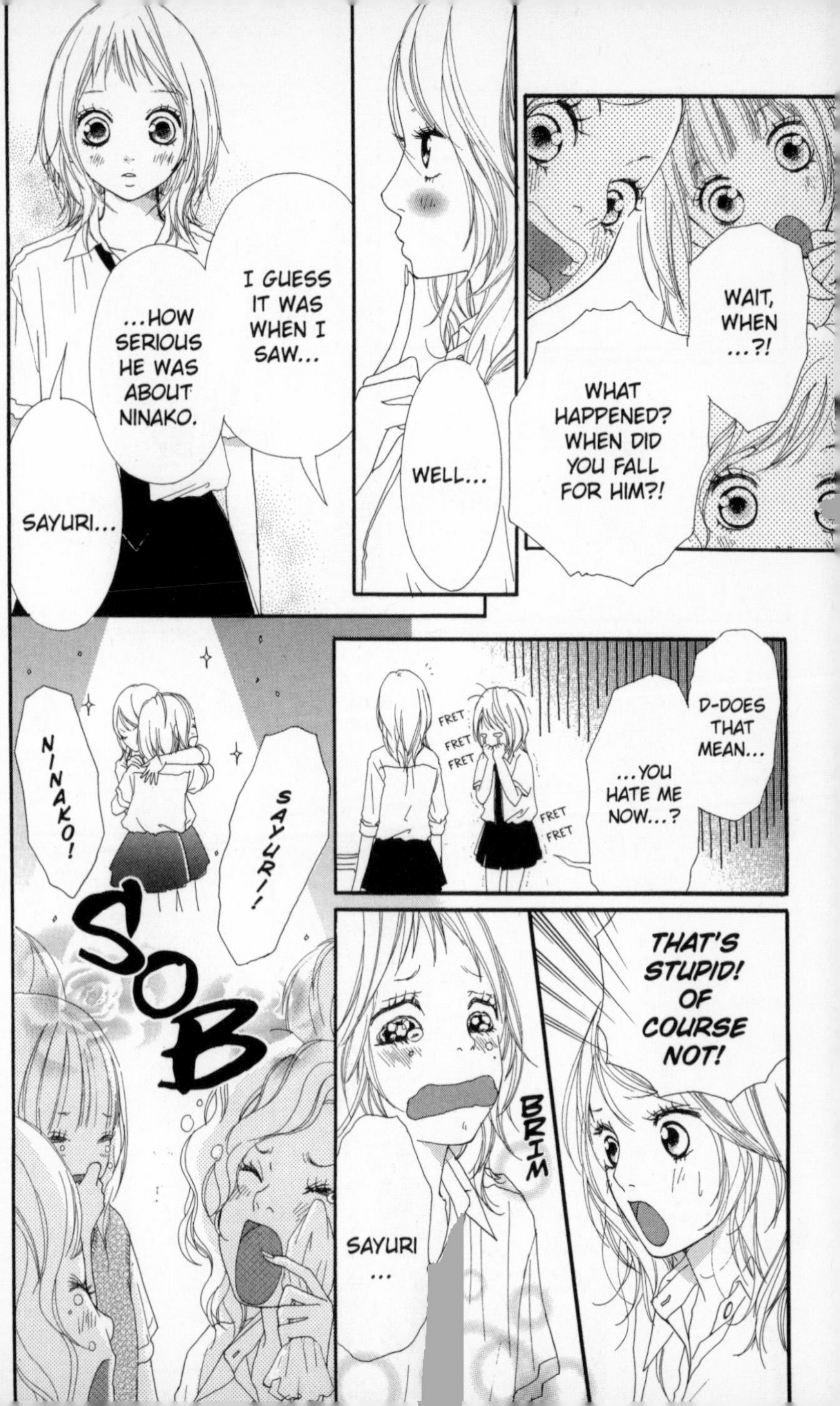
WAIT, WHEN ...?!
WHAT HAPPENED? WHEN DID YOU FALL FOR HIM?!
WELL...
I GUESS IT WAS WHEN I SAW...
...HOW SERIOUS HE WAS ABOUT NINAKO.
SAYURI...
D-DOES THAT MEAN...
...YOU HATE ME NOW...?
FRET FRET FRET
FRET FRET
THAT'S STUPID! OF COURSE NOT!
BRIM
SAYURI ...
SAYURI!!
NINAKO!
SOB

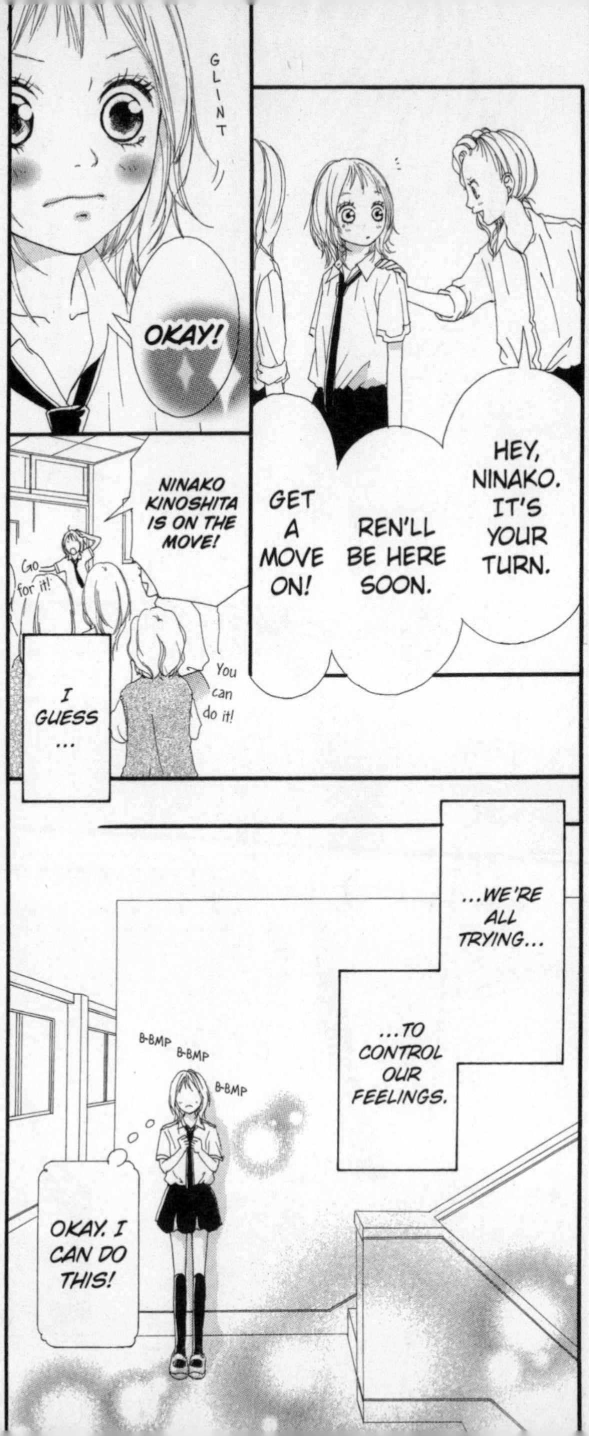
HEY, NINAKO. IT'S YOUR TURN.
REN'LL BE HERE SOON.
GET A MOVE ON!
GLINT
OKAY!
NINAKO KINOSHITA IS ON THE MOVE!
Go for it!
You can do it!
I GUESS...
...WE'RE ALL TRYING...
...TO CONTROL OUR FEELINGS.
B-BMP
B-BMP
B-BMP
OKAY. I CAN DO THIS!

WANNA GO FOR A DRIVE? 1

I got my license about a year ago. All of my friends already have theirs, and I started thinking how convenient it'd be to be able to drive to my parents' house.

I decided to take driving lessons, and I chose a driving school that was a bit out of the way because its practice route was basically the same as the route to my parents' place. I was determined to pass the written test in one try, so I studied hard.

After I finished the test, I was feeling confident as I waited for the numbers of the students who'd passed to light up on the electric bulletin board. But when the numbers appeared, mine wasn't there! I was shocked! I'd studied so much!

So needless to say, I was pretty depressed about it. But later on I found out that one section of the electric board was broken, so my number just happened to not light up. I passed! Whew!

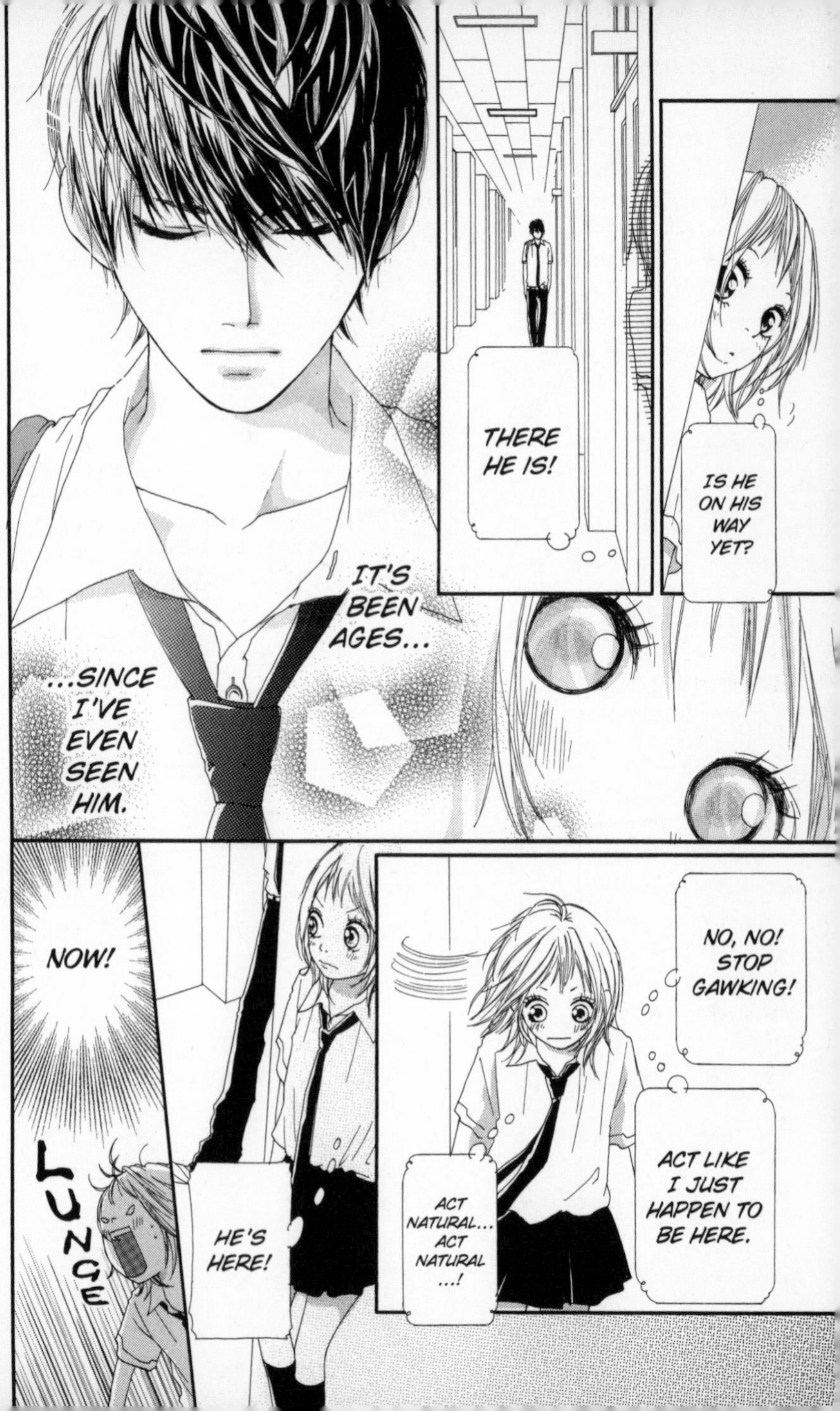
IS HE ON HIS WAY YET?
THERE HE IS!
IT'S BEEN AGES...
...SINCE I'VE EVEN SEEN HIM.
NO, NO! STOP GAWKING!
ACT LIKE I JUST HAPPEN TO BE HERE.
ACT NATURAL... ACT NATURAL ...!
HE'S HERE!
NOW!
LUNGE

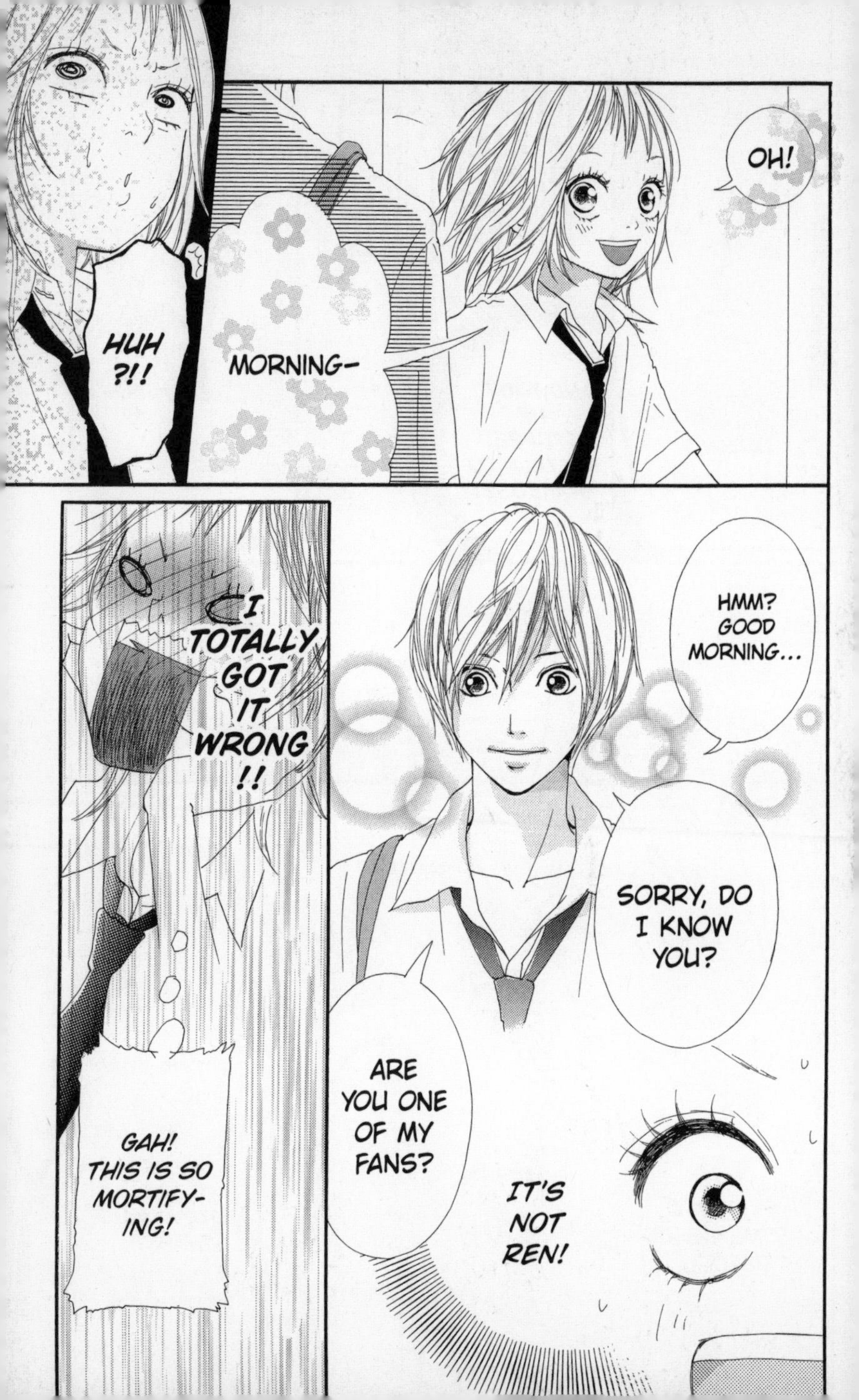
OH!
MORNING-
HUH ?!!
HMM? GOOD MORNING...
SORRY, DO I KNOW YOU?
ARE YOU ONE OF MY FANS?
IT'S NOT REN!
I TOTALLY GOT IT WRONG!!
GAH! THIS IS SO MORTIFY-ING!

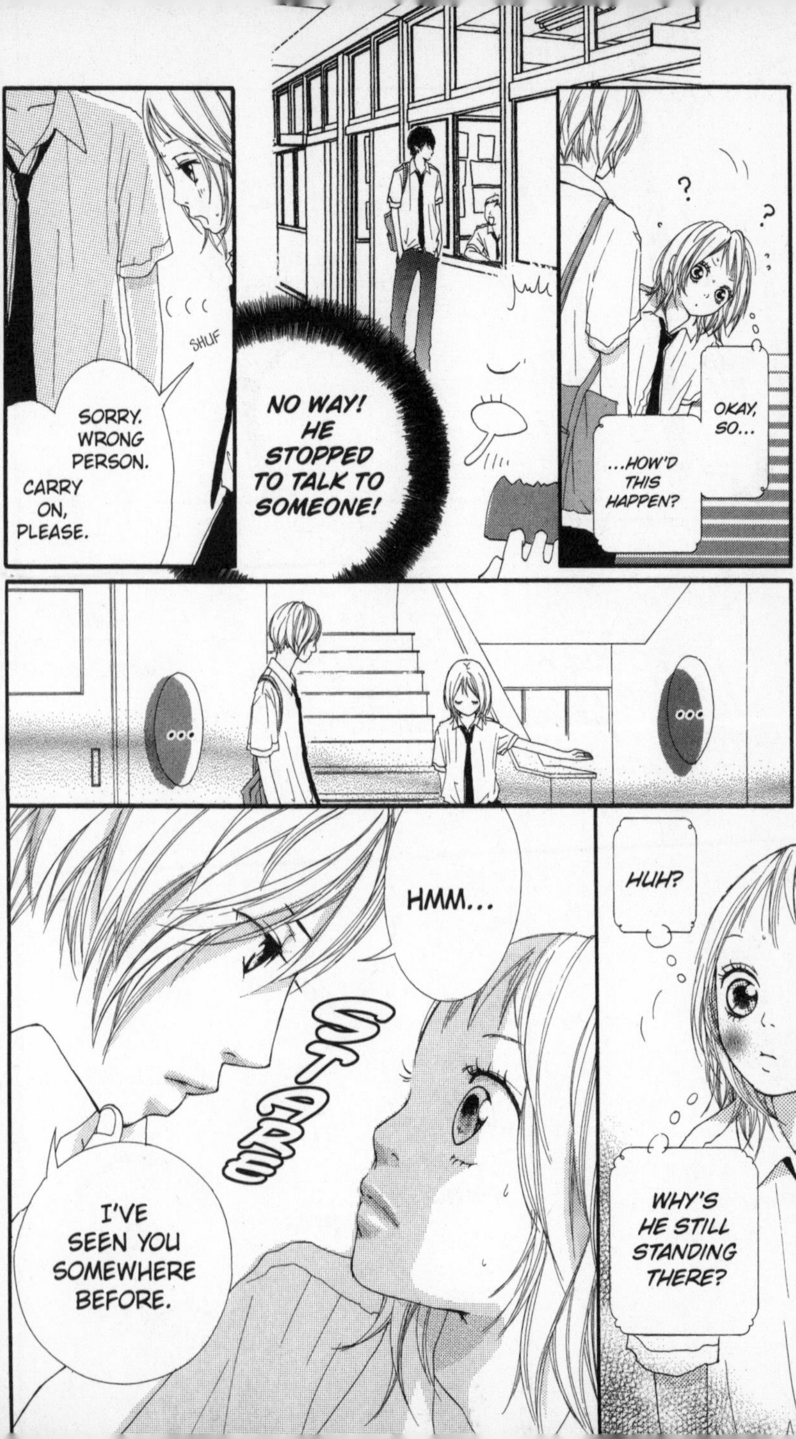
OKAY, SO...
...HOW'D THIS HAPPEN?
NO WAY! HE STOPPED TO TALK TO SOMEONE!
SHUF
SORRY. WRONG PERSON. CARRY ON, PLEASE.
HUH?
WHY'S HE STILL STANDING THERE?
HMM...
I'VE SEEN YOU SOMEWHERE BEFORE.

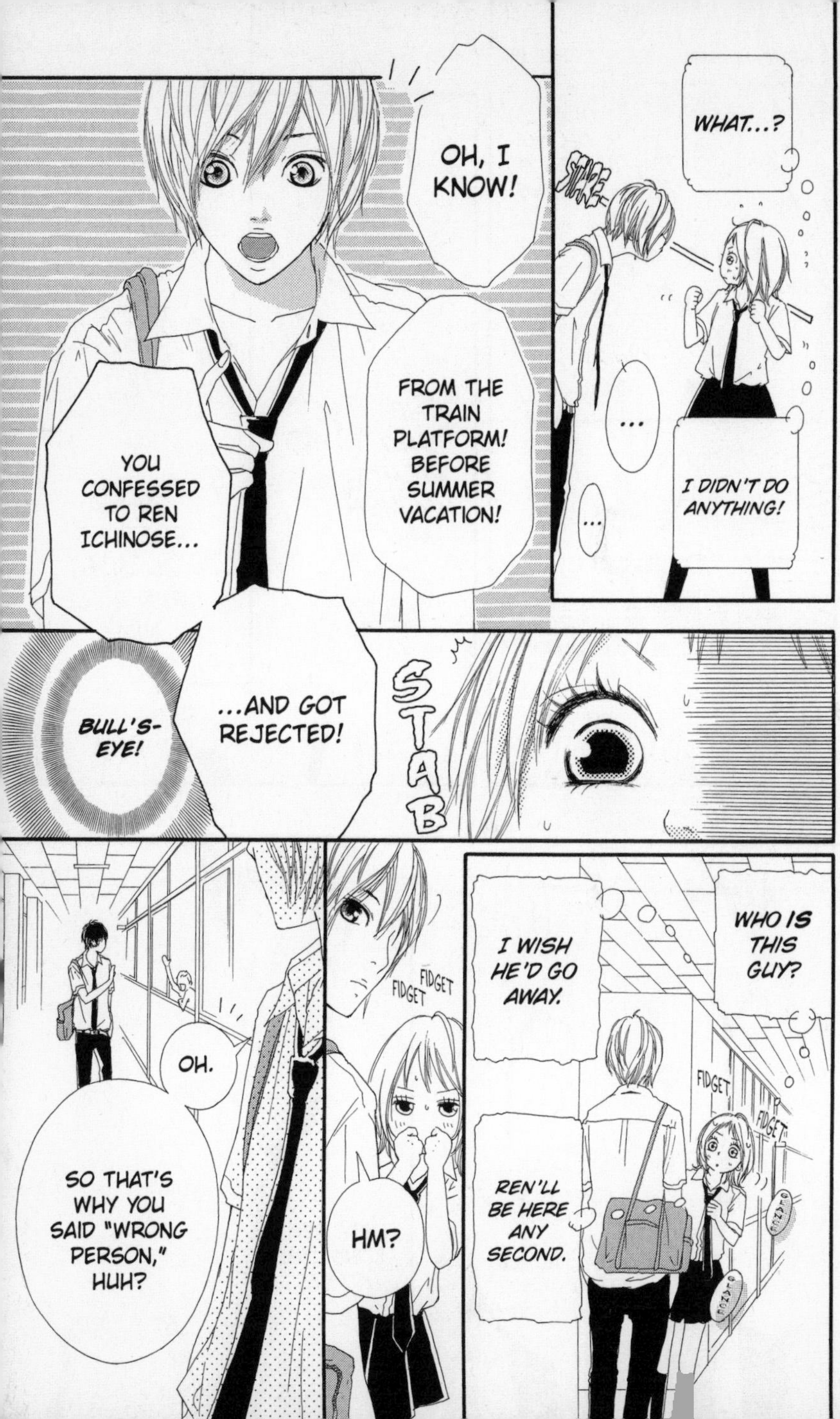
WHAT...?
STARE
...
...
I DIDN'T DO ANYTHING!
OH, I KNOW!
FROM THE TRAIN PLATFORM! BEFORE SUMMER VACATION!
YOU CONFESSED TO REN ICHINOSE...
STAB
...AND GOT REJECTED!
BULL'S-EYE!
WHO IS THIS GUY?
I WISH HE'D GO AWAY.
FIDGET
FIDGET
GLANCE
GLANCE
REN'LL BE HERE ANY SECOND.
FIDGET
FIDGET
HM?
OH.
SO THAT'S WHY YOU SAID "WRONG PERSON," HUH?

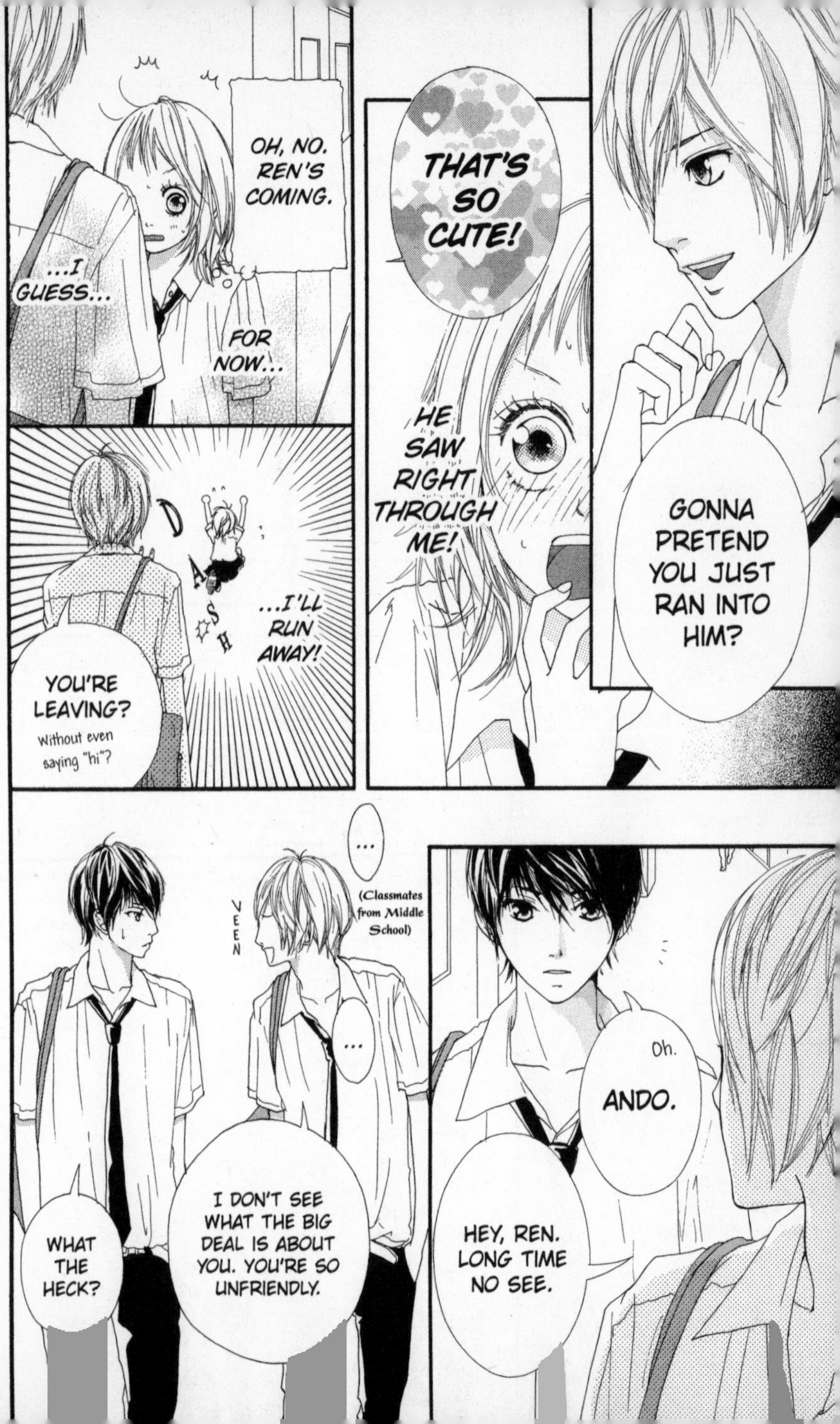

GONNA PRETEND YOU JUST RAN INTO HIM?
THAT'S SO CUTE!
HE SAW RIGHT THROUGH ME!
OH, NO. REN'S COMING.
...I GUESS...
FOR NOW...
...I'LL RUN AWAY!
DASH
YOU'RE LEAVING? Without even saying "hi"?
Oh.
ANDO.
HEY, REN. LONG TIME NO SEE.
...
(Classmates from Middle School)
VEEN
...
I DON'T SEE WHAT THE BIG DEAL IS ABOUT YOU. YOU'RE SO UNFRIENDLY.
WHAT THE HECK?

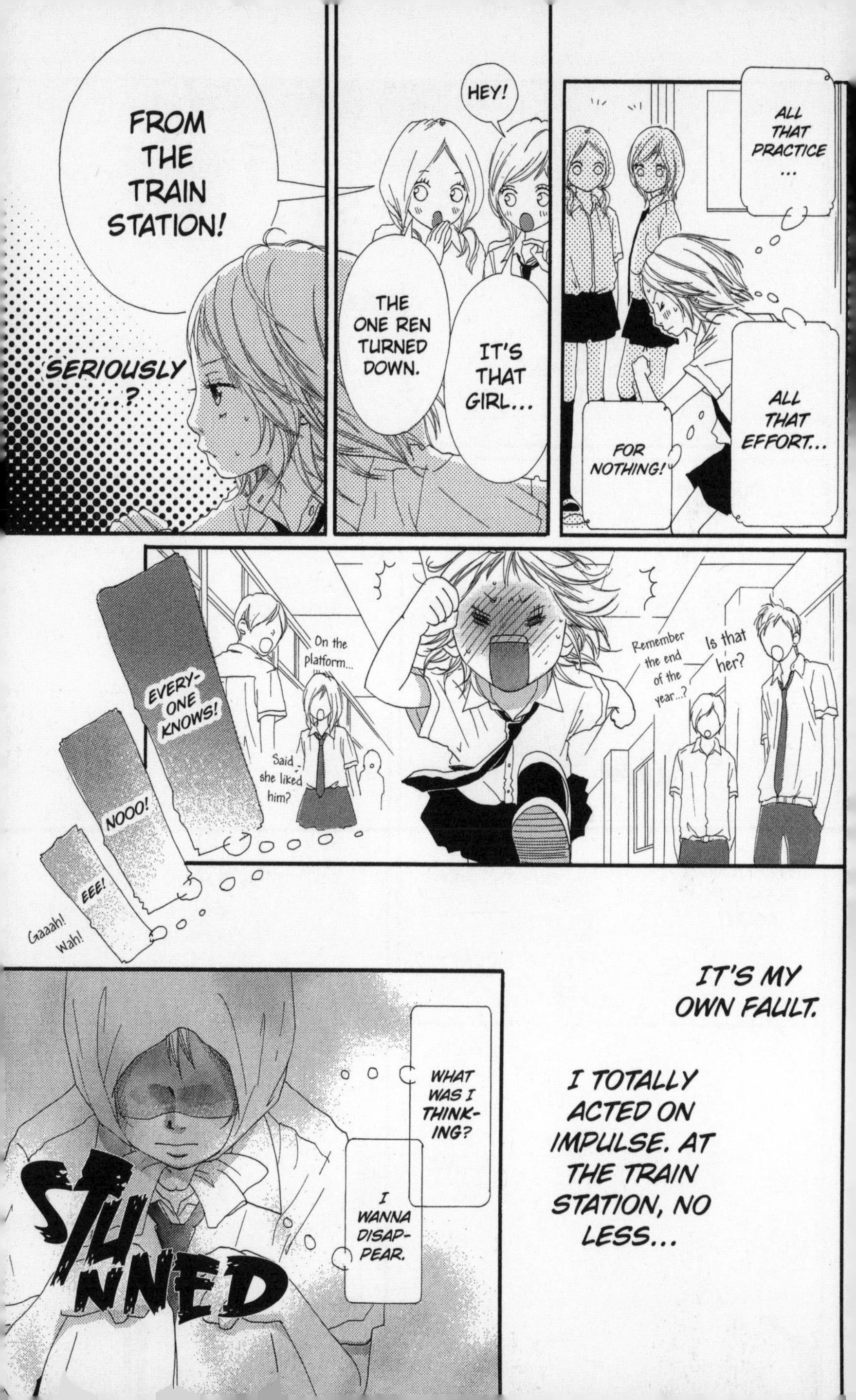
ALL THAT PRACTICE...
ALL THAT EFFORT...
FOR NOTHING!
HEY!
IT'S THAT GIRL...
THE ONE REN TURNED DOWN.
FROM THE TRAIN STATION!
SERIOUSLY...?
Is that her?
Remember the end of the year...?
On the platform...
Said she liked him?
EVERY-ONE KNOWS!
NOOO!
EEE!
Gaaah! Wah!
IT'S MY OWN FAULT.
I TOTALLY ACTED ON IMPULSE. AT THE TRAIN STATION, NO LESS...
WHAT WAS I THINKING?
I WANNA DISAP-PEAR.
STUNNED

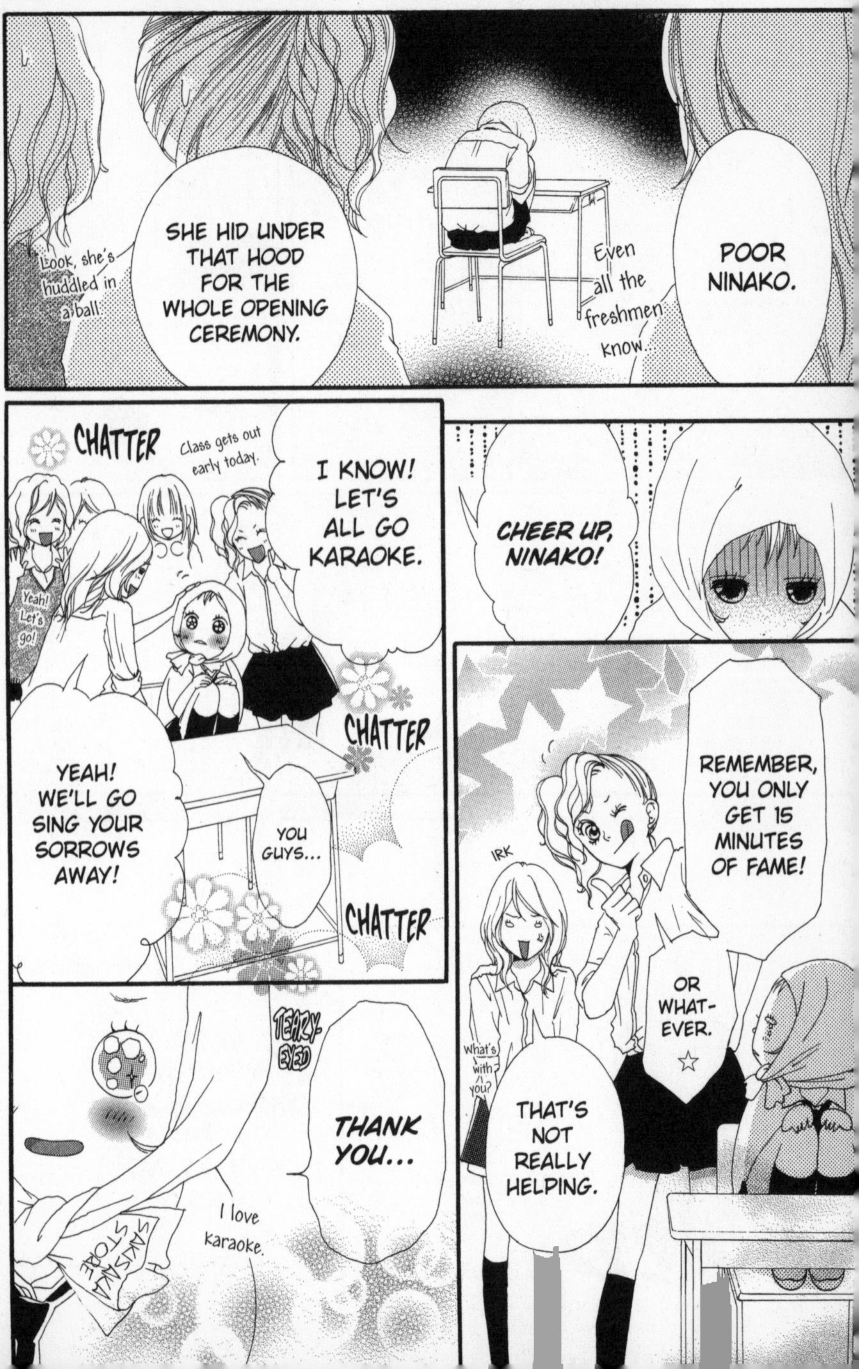
POOR NINAKO.
Even all the freshmen know...
SHE HID UNDER THAT HOOD FOR THE WHOLE OPENING CEREMONY.
Look, she's huddled in a ball.
CHEER UP, NINAKO!
I KNOW! LET'S ALL GO KARAOKE.
Class gets out early today.
CHATTER
Yeah! Let's go!
YEAH! WE'LL GO SING YOUR SORROWS AWAY!
YOU GUYS...
CHATTER
CHATTER
REMEMBER, YOU ONLY GET 15 MINUTES OF FAME!
OR WHAT-EVER. ☆
IRK
THAT'S NOT REALLY HELPING.
What's with you?
TEARY-EYED
THANK YOU...
I love karaoke.
SAKISAKA STORE

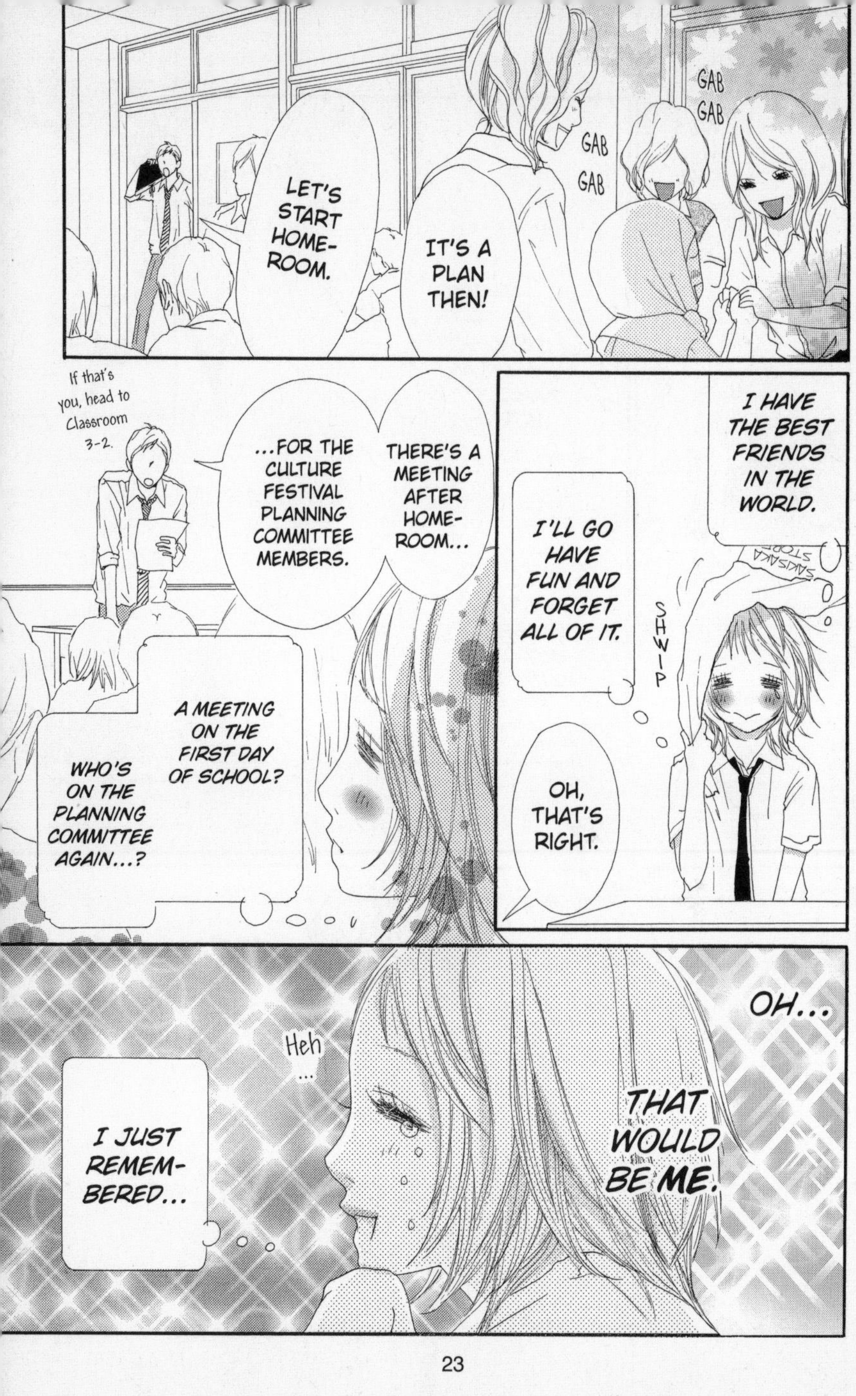
GAB GAB
GAB GAB
IT'S A PLAN THEN!
LET'S START HOME-ROOM.
I HAVE THE BEST FRIENDS IN THE WORLD.
SHWIP
I'LL GO HAVE FUN AND FORGET ALL OF IT.
OH, THAT'S RIGHT.
THERE'S A MEETING AFTER HOME-ROOM...
...FOR THE CULTURE FESTIVAL PLANNING COMMITTEE MEMBERS.
If that's you, head to Classroom 3-2.
A MEETING ON THE FIRST DAY OF SCHOOL?
WHO'S ON THE PLANNING COMMITTEE AGAIN...?
OH...
THAT WOULD BE ME.
Heh...
I JUST REMEMBERED...

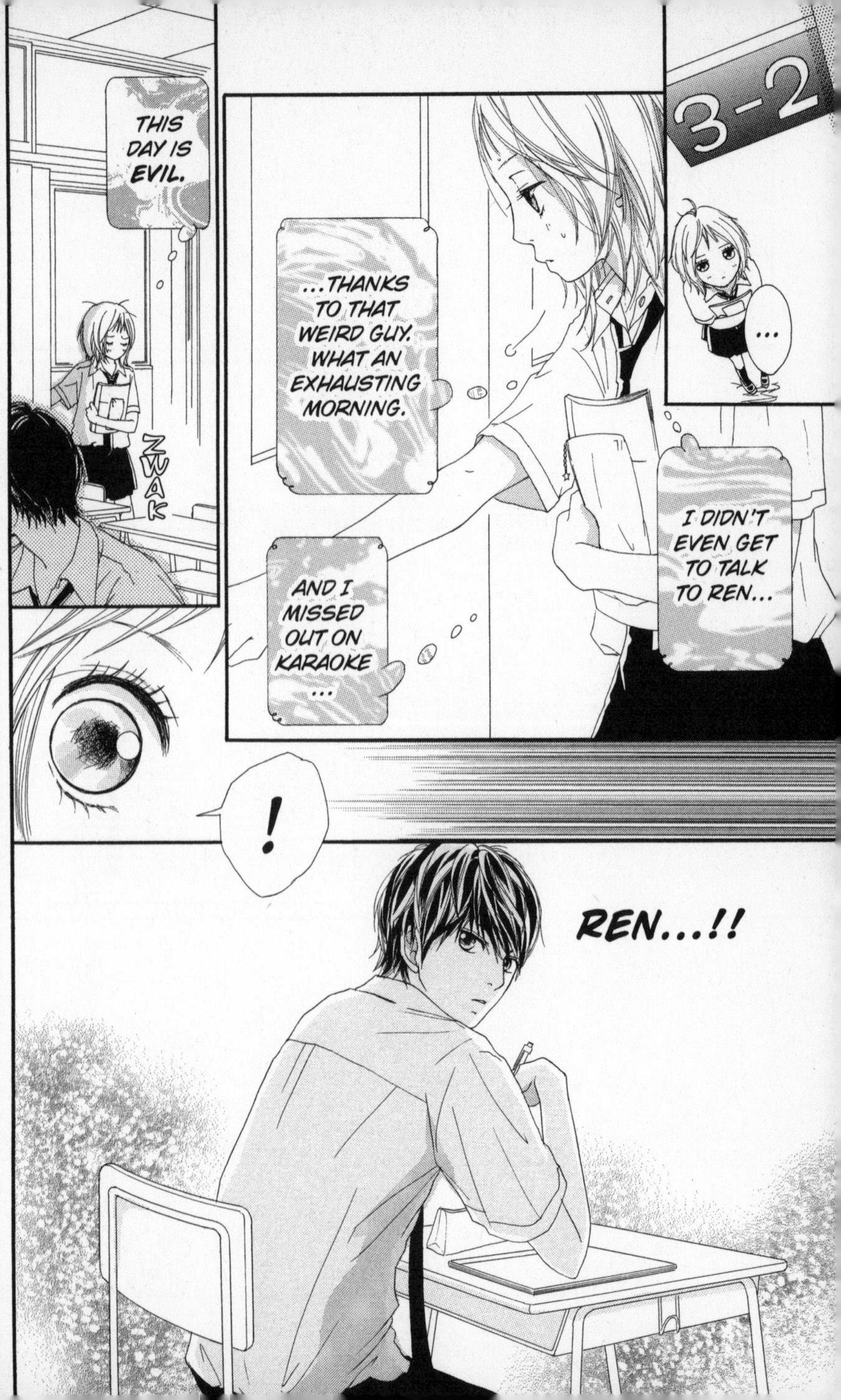
3-2
...
...THANKS TO THAT WEIRD GUY. WHAT AN EXHAUSTING MORNING.
I DIDN'T EVEN GET TO TALK TO REN...
AND I MISSED OUT ON KARAOKE ...
THIS DAY IS EVIL.
ZWAK
!
REN...!!

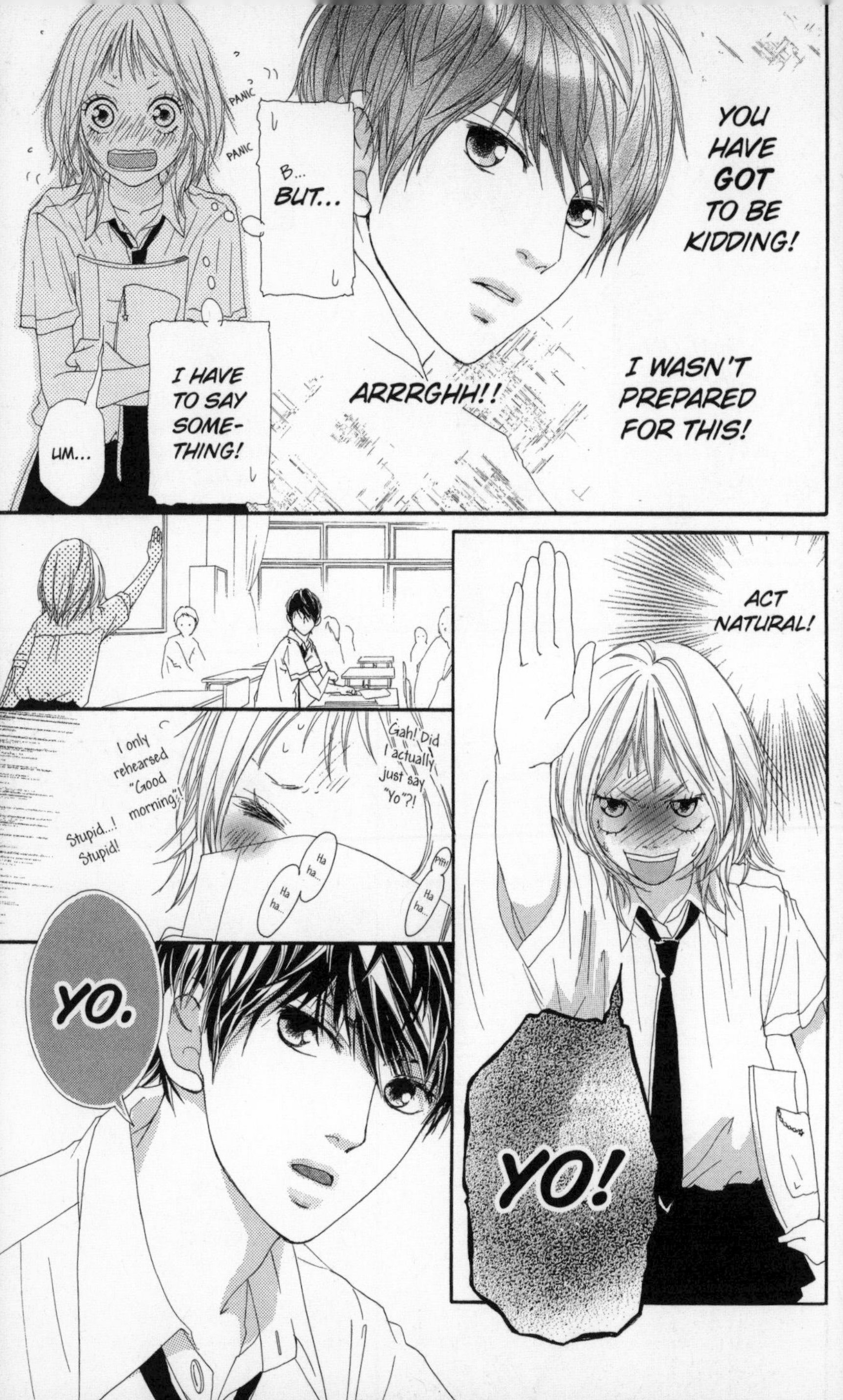
YOU HAVE GOT TO BE KIDDING!
I WASN'T PREPARED FOR THIS!
B... BUT...
PANIC
PANIC
ARRRGHH!!
I HAVE TO SAY SOME-THING!
UM...
ACT NATURAL!
YO!
Gah! Did I actually just say "Yo"?!
I only rehearsed "Good morning"!
Stupid...! Stupid!
Ha ha...
Ha ha...
Ha ha...
YO.

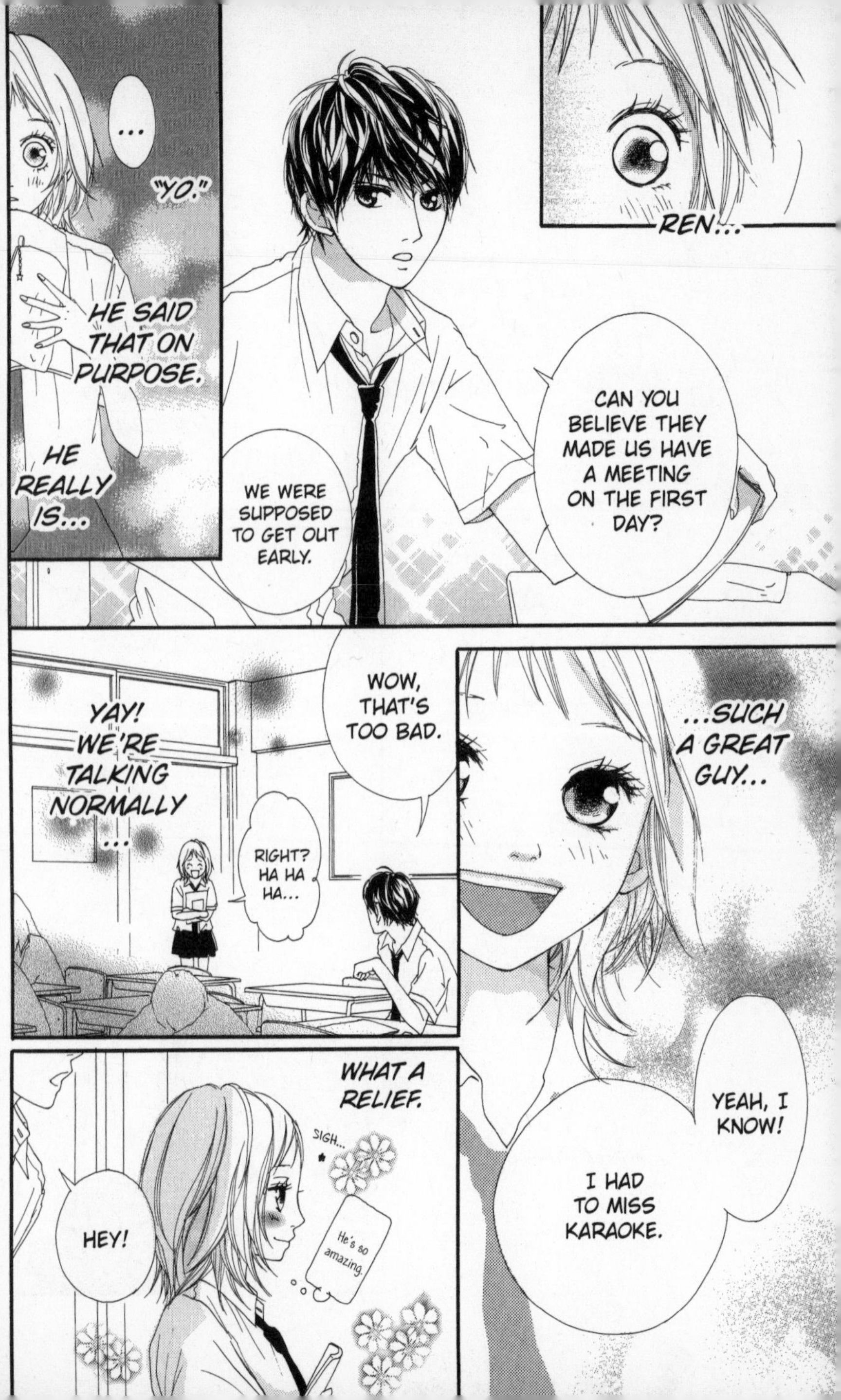
REN...
CAN YOU BELIEVE THEY MADE US HAVE A MEETING ON THE FIRST DAY?
WE WERE SUPPOSED TO GET OUT EARLY.
...
"YO."
HE SAID THAT ON PURPOSE.
HE REALLY IS...
...SUCH A GREAT GUY...
YEAH, I KNOW!
I HAD TO MISS KARAOKE.
WOW, THAT'S TOO BAD.
YAY! WE'RE TALKING NORMALLY...
RIGHT? HA HA HA...
WHAT A RELIEF.
SIGH...
He's so amazing.
HEY!

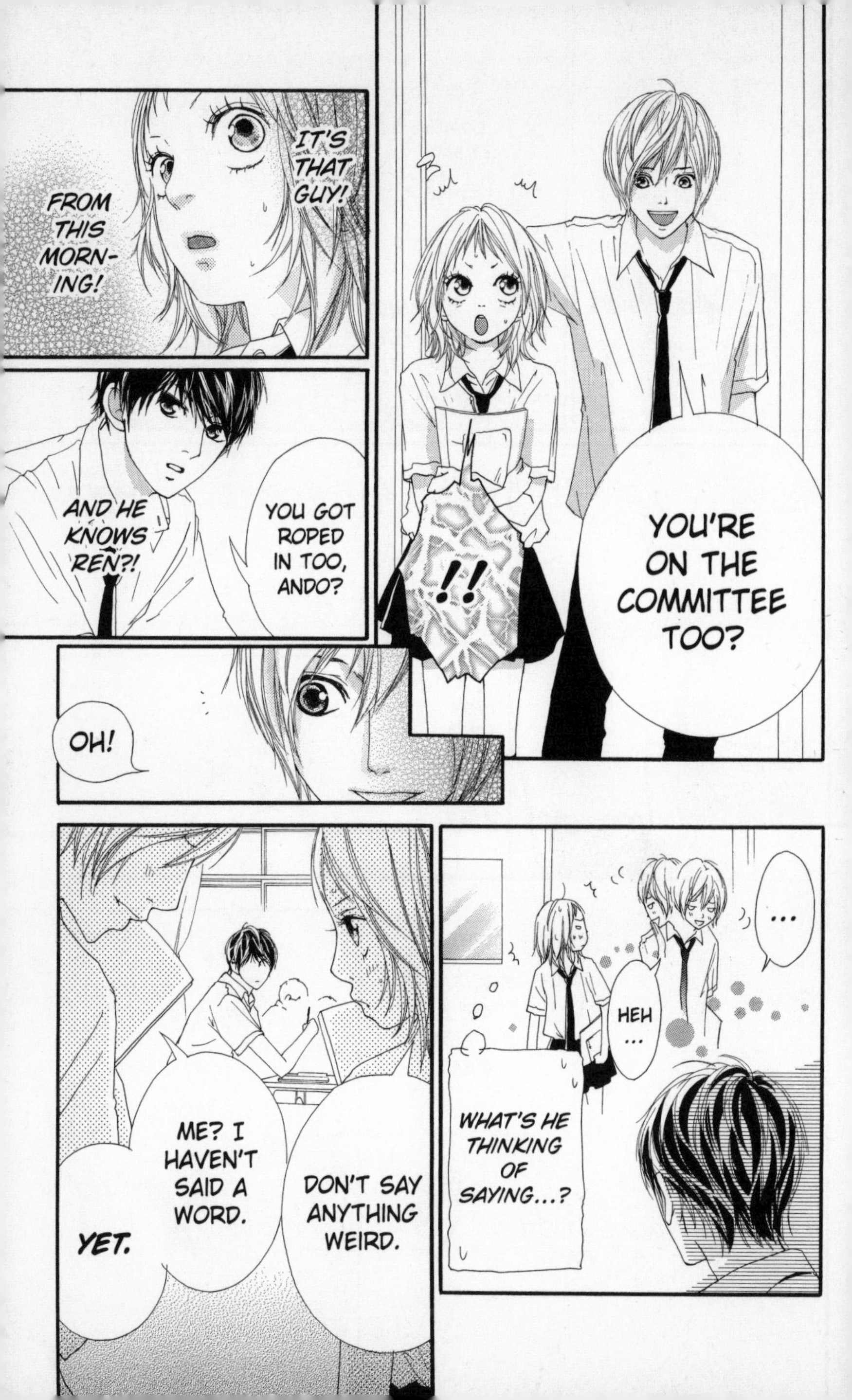
YOU'RE ON THE COMMITTEE TOO?
!!
IT'S THAT GUY!
FROM THIS MORNING!
YOU GOT ROPED IN TOO, ANDO?
AND HE KNOWS REN?!
OH!
...
HEH...
WHAT'S HE THINKING OF SAYING...?
DON'T SAY ANYTHING WEIRD.
ME? I HAVEN'T SAID A WORD.
YET.

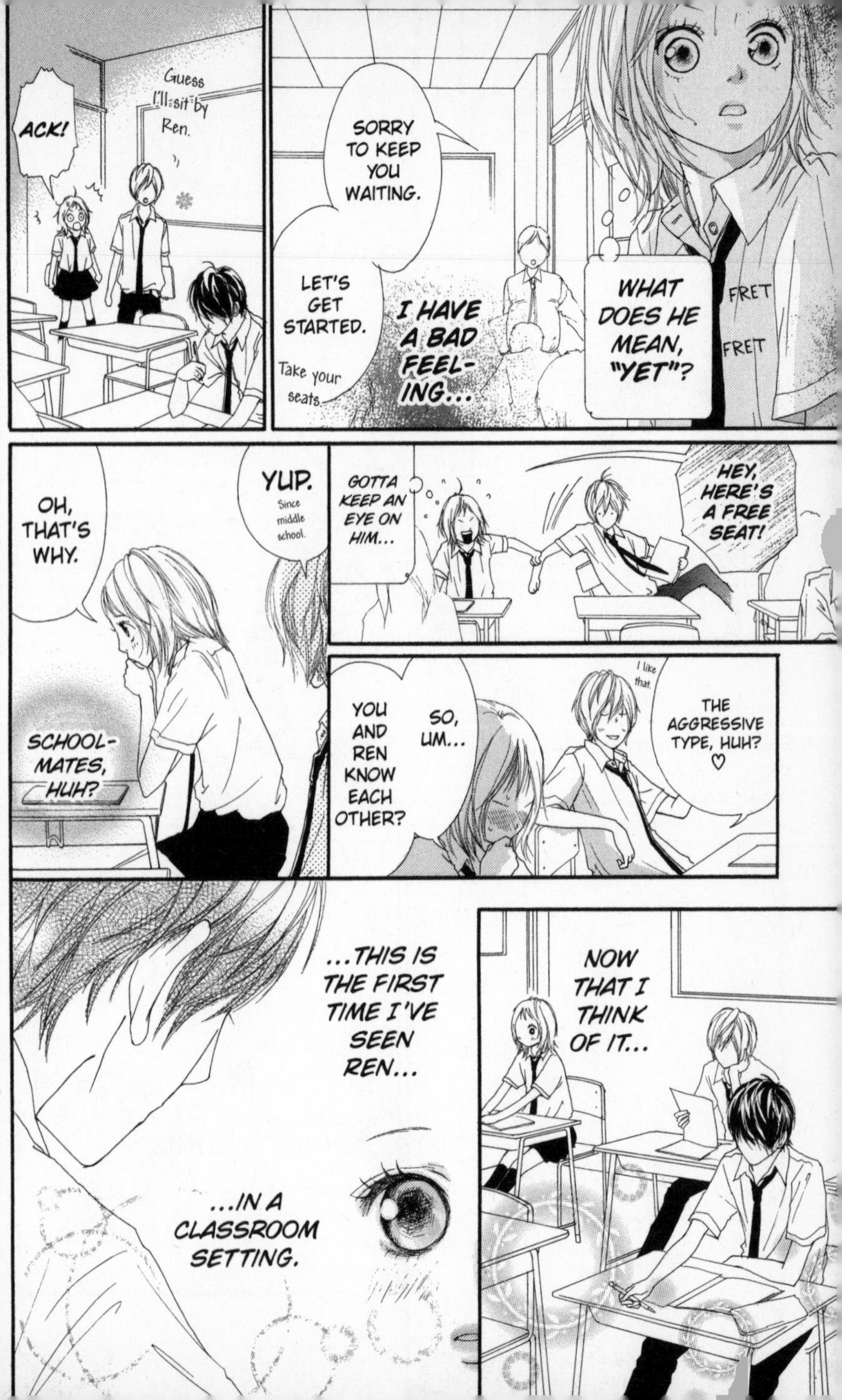
WHAT DOES HE MEAN, "YET"?
FRET FRET
SORRY TO KEEP YOU WAITING.
I HAVE A BAD FEELING...
LET'S GET STARTED.
Take your seats.
Guess I'll sit by Ren.
ACK!
HEY, HERE'S A FREE SEAT!
GOTTA KEEP AN EYE ON HIM...
THE AGGRESSIVE TYPE, HUH? ♡
I like that.
SO, UM...
YOU AND REN KNOW EACH OTHER?
YUP.
Since middle school.
OH, THAT'S WHY.
SCHOOLMATES, HUH?
NOW THAT I THINK OF IT...
...THIS IS THE FIRST TIME I'VE SEEN REN...
...IN A CLASSROOM SETTING.

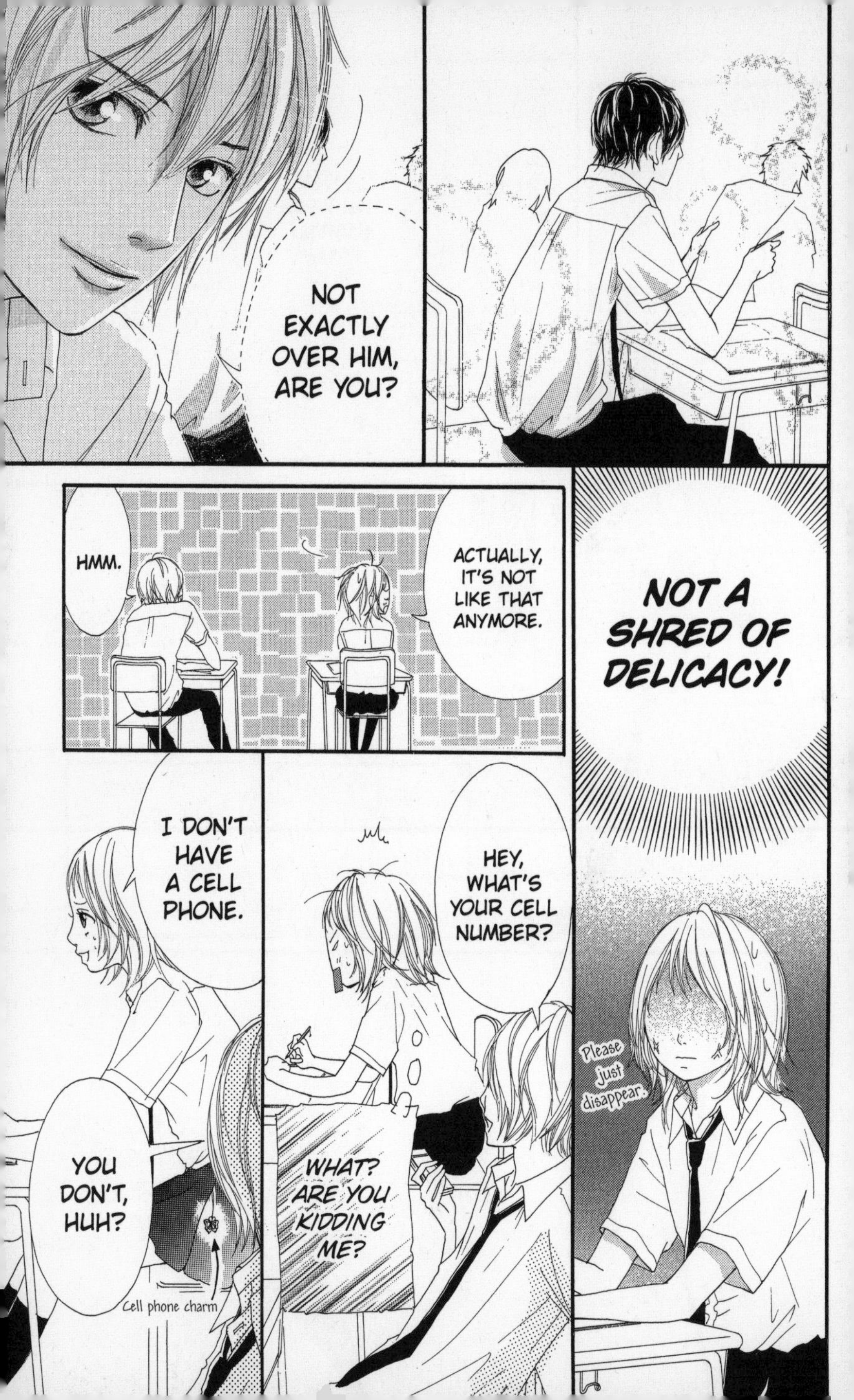
NOT EXACTLY OVER HIM, ARE YOU?
NOT A SHRED OF DELICACY!
Please just disappear.
ACTUALLY, IT'S NOT LIKE THAT ANYMORE.
HMM.
HEY, WHAT'S YOUR CELL NUMBER?
WHAT? ARE YOU KIDDING ME?
I DON'T HAVE A CELL PHONE.
YOU DON'T, HUH?
Cell phone charm

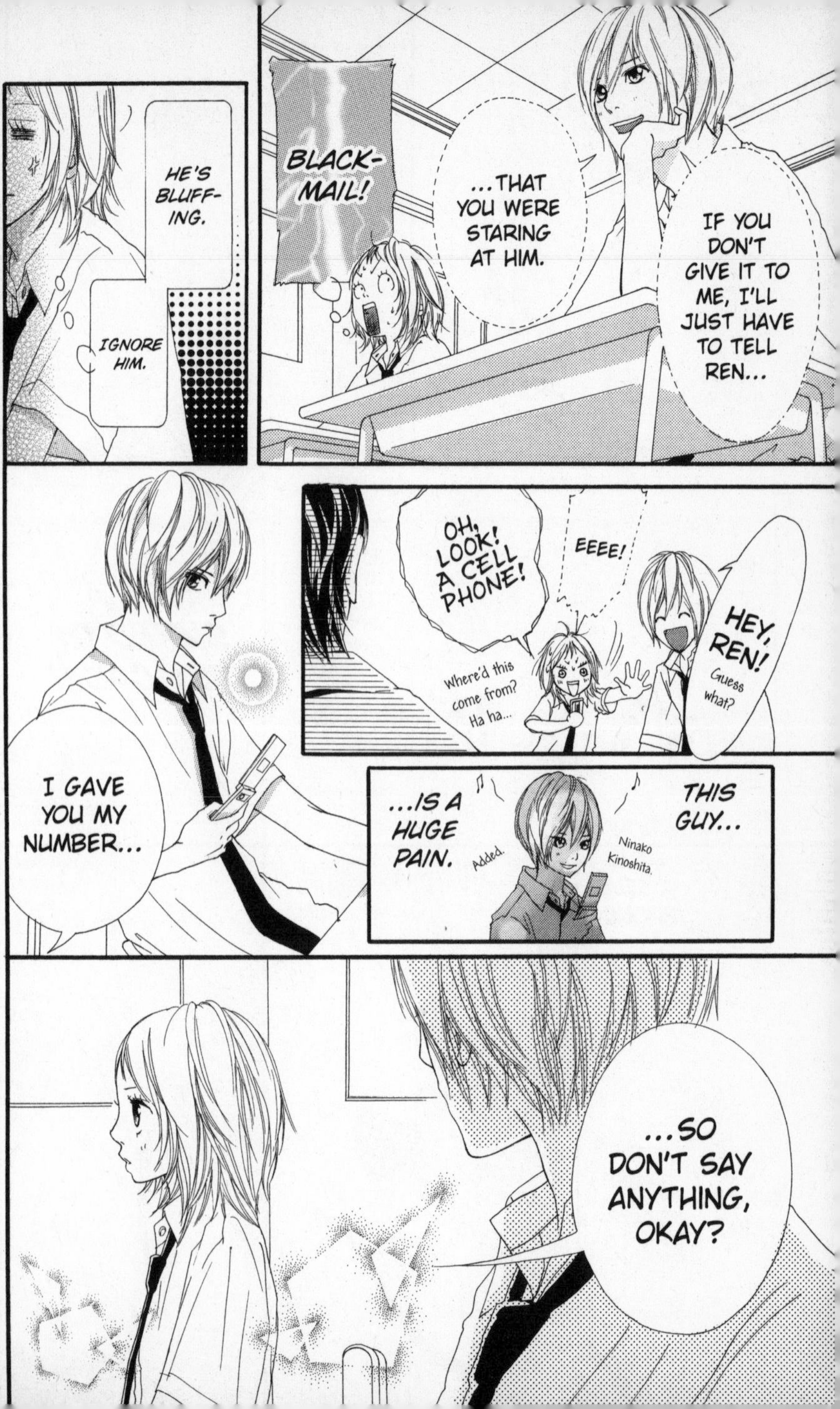
IF YOU DON'T GIVE IT TO ME, I'LL JUST HAVE TO TELL REN...
...THAT YOU WERE STARING AT HIM.
BLACK-MAIL!
HE'S BLUFF-ING.
IGNORE HIM.
HEY, REN!
Guess what?
EEEE!
OH, LOOK! A CELL PHONE!
Where'd this come from? Ha ha...
THIS GUY...
Ninako Kinoshita.
Added.
...IS A HUGE PAIN.
I GAVE YOU MY NUMBER...
...SO DON'T SAY ANYTHING, OKAY?

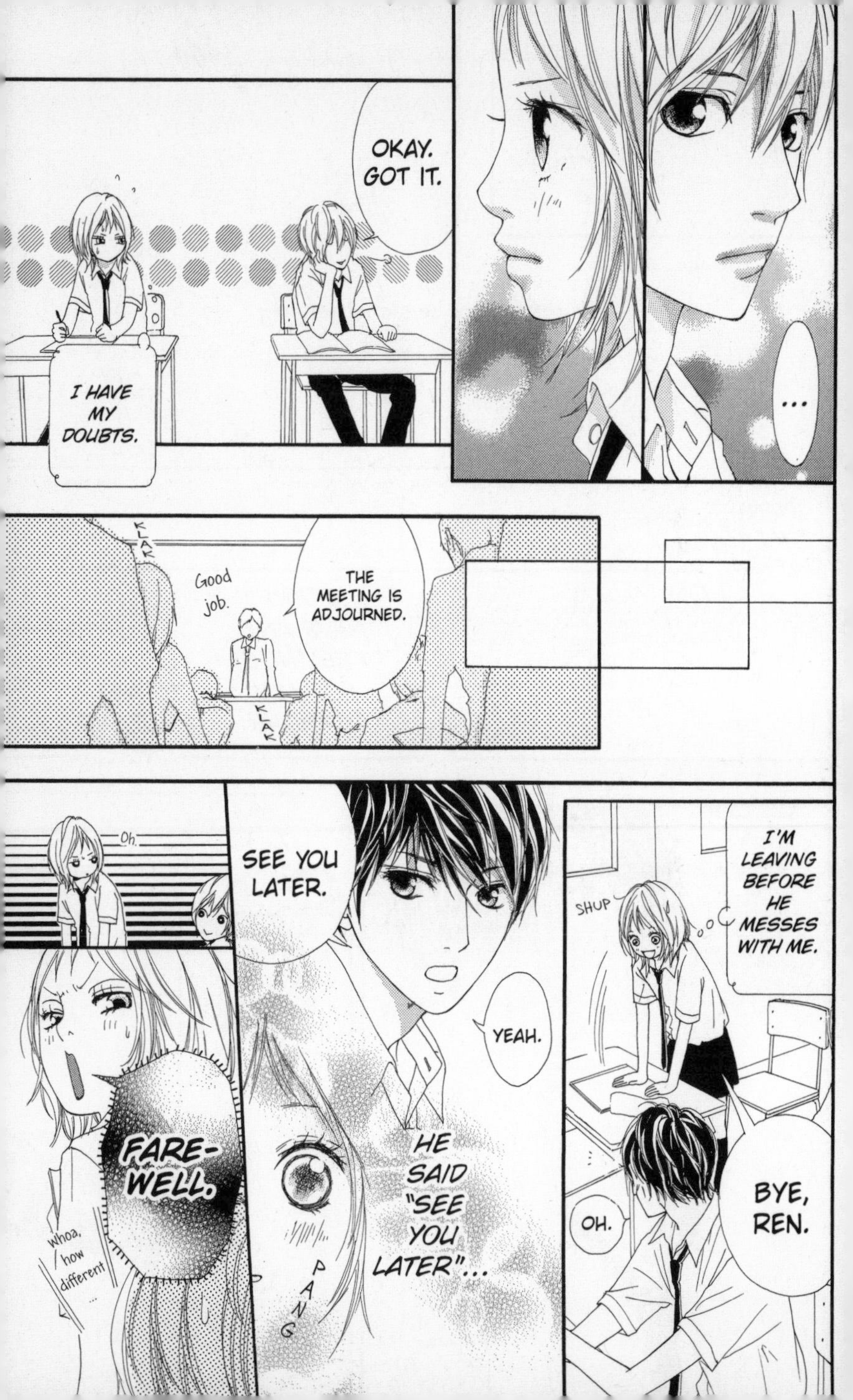
...
OKAY. GOT IT.
I HAVE MY DOUBTS.
KLAK
THE MEETING IS ADJOURNED.
Good job.
KLAK
I'M LEAVING BEFORE HE MESSES WITH ME.
SHUP
BYE, REN.
OH.
SEE YOU LATER.
YEAH.
HE SAID "SEE YOU LATER"...
PANG
Oh.
FARE-WELL.
whoa, how different...

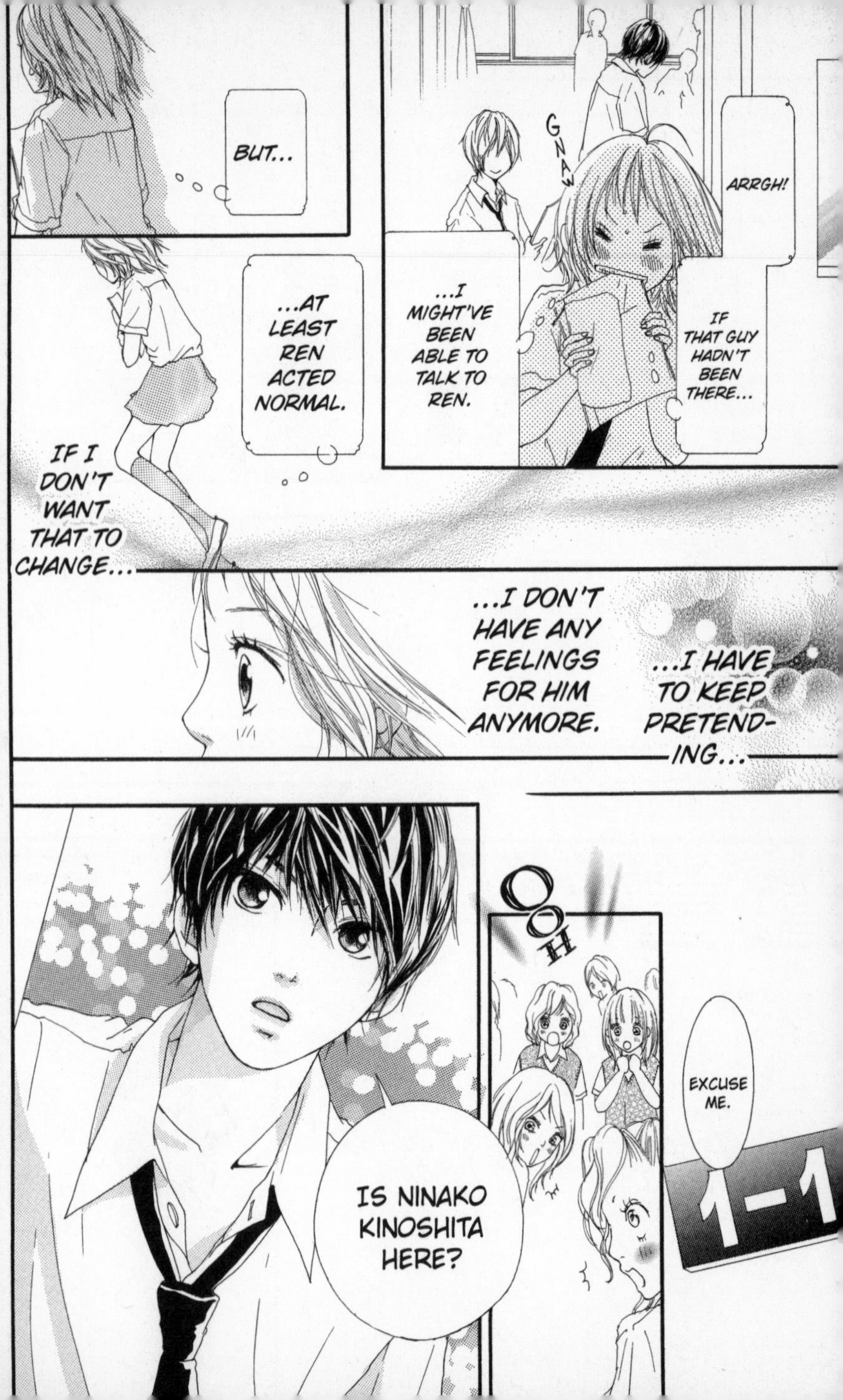

ARRGH!
GNAW
IF THAT GUY HADN'T BEEN THERE...
...I MIGHT'VE BEEN ABLE TO TALK TO REN.
BUT...
...AT LEAST REN ACTED NORMAL.
IF I DON'T WANT THAT TO CHANGE...
...I HAVE TO KEEP PRETEND-ING...
...I DON'T HAVE ANY FEELINGS FOR HIM ANYMORE.
OOOH
1-1
EXCUSE ME.
IS NINAKO KINOSHITA HERE?

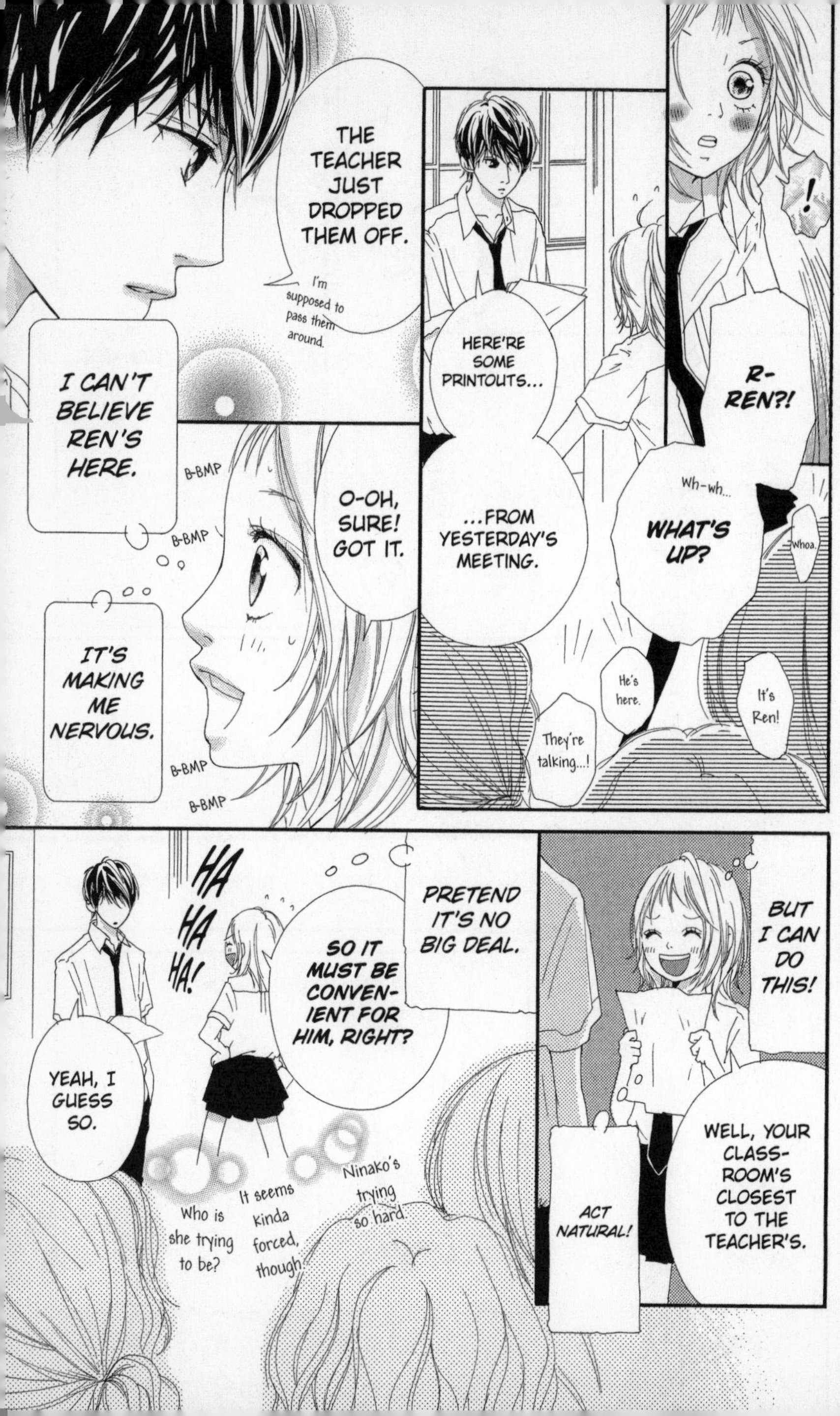
!
R-REN?!
HERE'RE SOME PRINTOUTS...
...FROM YESTERDAY'S MEETING.
Wh-wh...
WHAT'S UP?
Whoa.
It's Ren!
He's here.
They're talking...!
THE TEACHER JUST DROPPED THEM OFF.
I'm supposed to pass them around.
I CAN'T BELIEVE REN'S HERE.
O-OH, SURE! GOT IT.
B-BMP
B-BMP
B-BMP
B-BMP
IT'S MAKING ME NERVOUS.
BUT I CAN DO THIS!
WELL, YOUR CLASSROOM'S CLOSEST TO THE TEACHER'S.
ACT NATURAL!
PRETEND IT'S NO BIG DEAL.
SO IT MUST BE CONVENIENT FOR HIM, RIGHT?
HA HA HA HA!
YEAH, I GUESS SO.
Ninako's trying so hard.
It seems kinda forced, though.
Who is she trying to be?

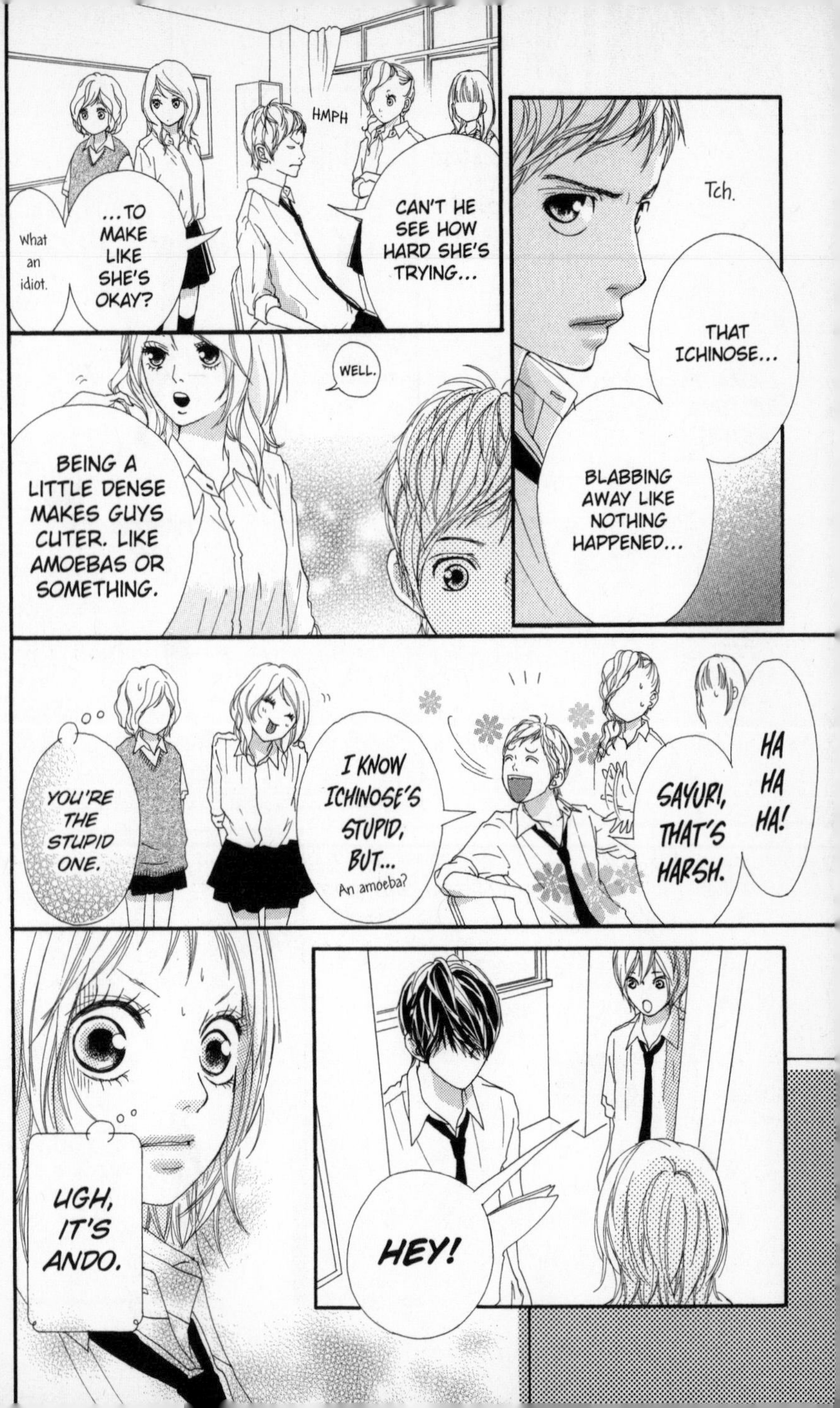
Tch.
THAT ICHINOSE...
BLABBING AWAY LIKE NOTHING HAPPENED...
HMPH
CAN'T HE SEE HOW HARD SHE'S TRYING...
...TO MAKE LIKE SHE'S OKAY?
What an idiot.
WELL.
BEING A LITTLE DENSE MAKES GUYS CUTER. LIKE AMOEBAS OR SOMETHING.
HA HA HA!
SAYURI, THAT'S HARSH.
I KNOW ICHINOSE'S STUPID, BUT...
An amoeba?
YOU'RE THE STUPID ONE.
HEY!
UGH, IT'S ANDO.

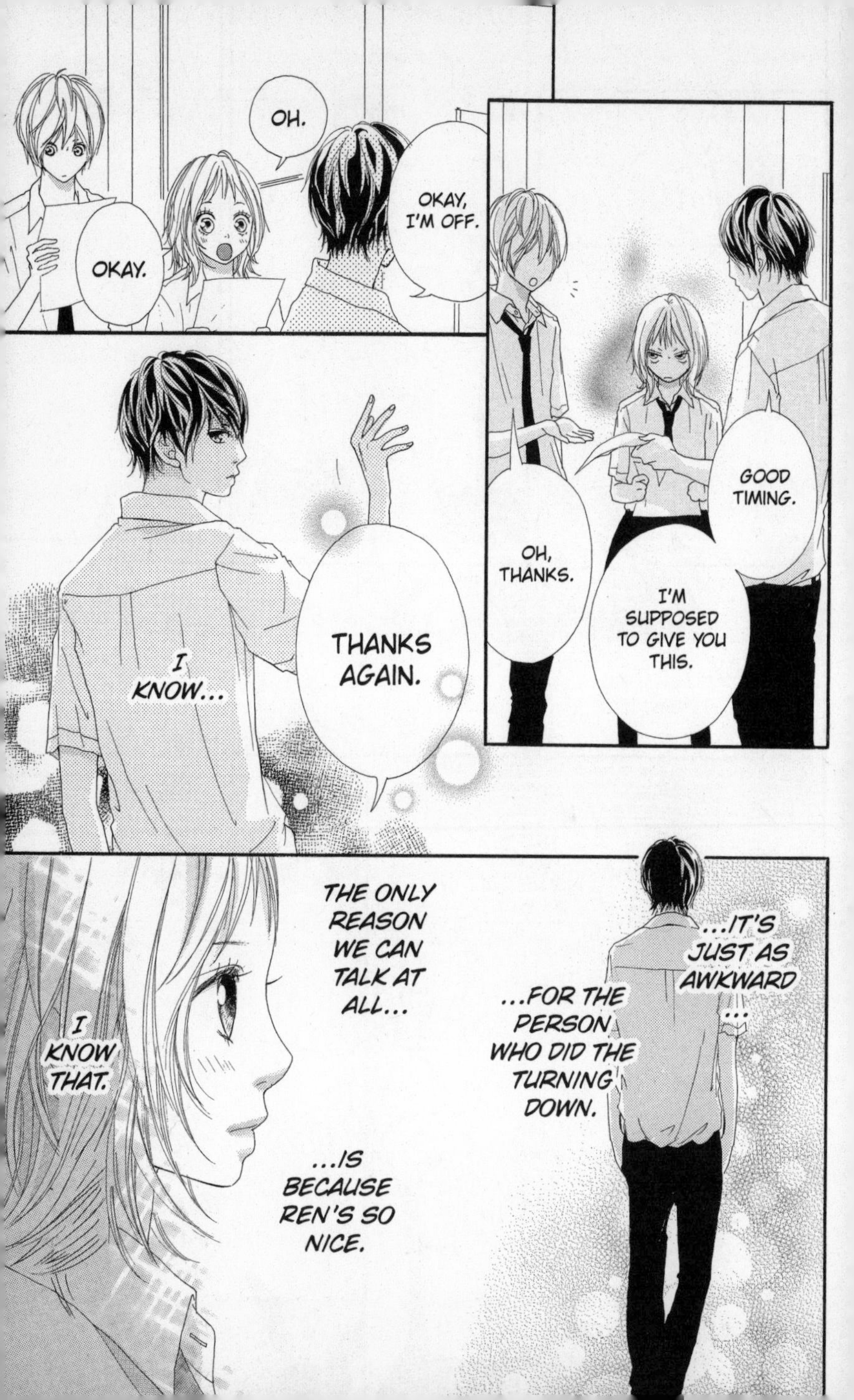
OKAY, I'M OFF.
OH.
OKAY.
GOOD TIMING.
I'M SUPPOSED TO GIVE YOU THIS.
OH, THANKS.
THANKS AGAIN.
I KNOW...
...IT'S JUST AS AWKWARD...
...FOR THE PERSON WHO DID THE TURNING DOWN.
THE ONLY REASON WE CAN TALK AT ALL...
...IS BECAUSE REN'S SO NICE.
I KNOW THAT.

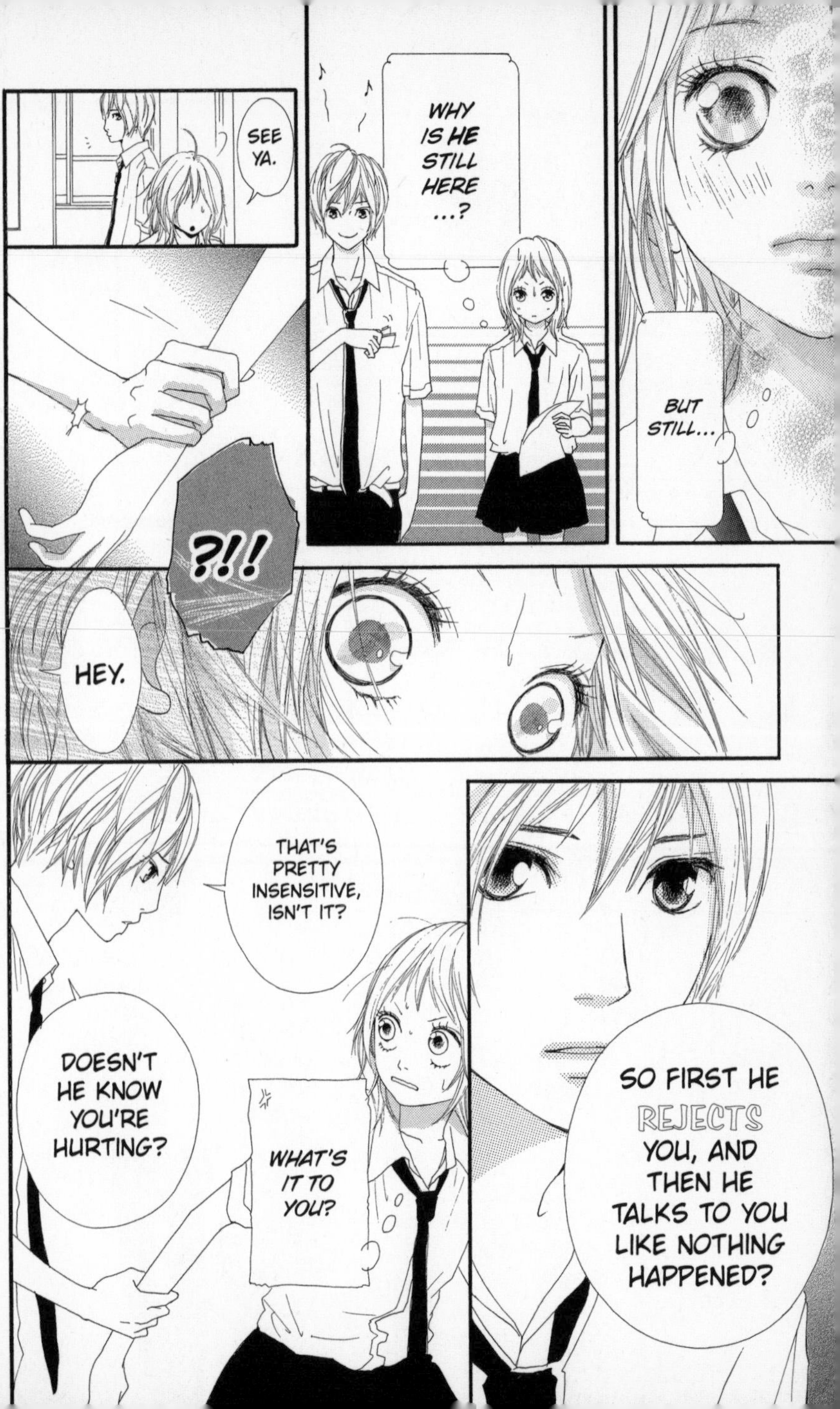
BUT STILL...
WHY IS HE STILL HERE ...?
SEE YA.
?!!
HEY.
SO FIRST HE REJECTS YOU, AND THEN HE TALKS TO YOU LIKE NOTHING HAPPENED?
THAT'S PRETTY INSENSITIVE, ISN'T IT?
DOESN'T HE KNOW YOU'RE HURTING?
WHAT'S IT TO YOU?

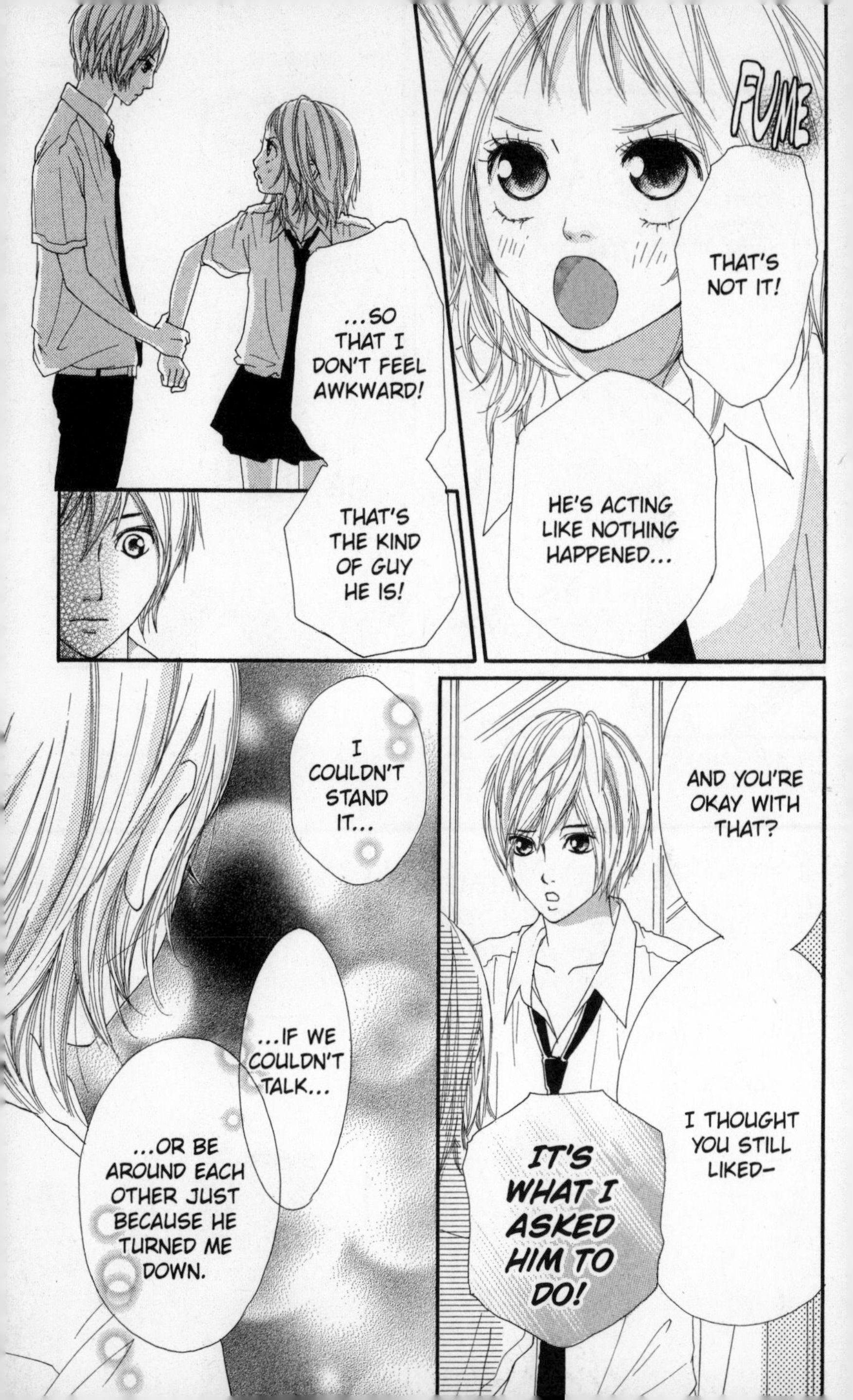
FUME
THAT'S NOT IT!
HE'S ACTING LIKE NOTHING HAPPENED...
...SO THAT I DON'T FEEL AWKWARD!
THAT'S THE KIND OF GUY HE IS!
AND YOU'RE OKAY WITH THAT?
I THOUGHT YOU STILL LIKED—
IT'S WHAT I ASKED HIM TO DO!
I COULDN'T STAND IT...
...IF WE COULDN'T TALK...
...OR BE AROUND EACH OTHER JUST BECAUSE HE TURNED ME DOWN.

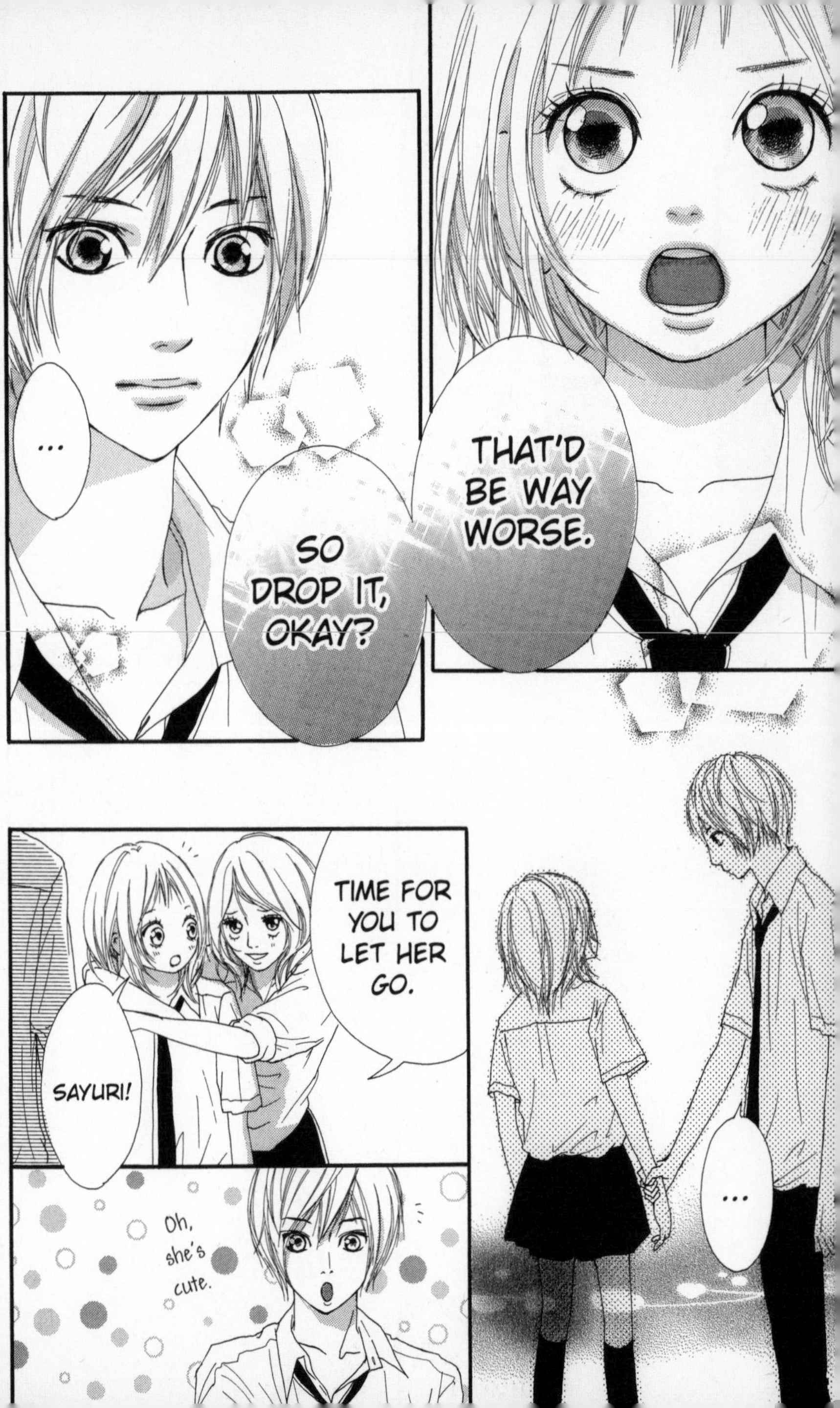
THAT'D BE WAY WORSE.
SO DROP IT, OKAY?
...
...
TIME FOR YOU TO LET HER GO.
SAYURI!
Oh, she's cute.

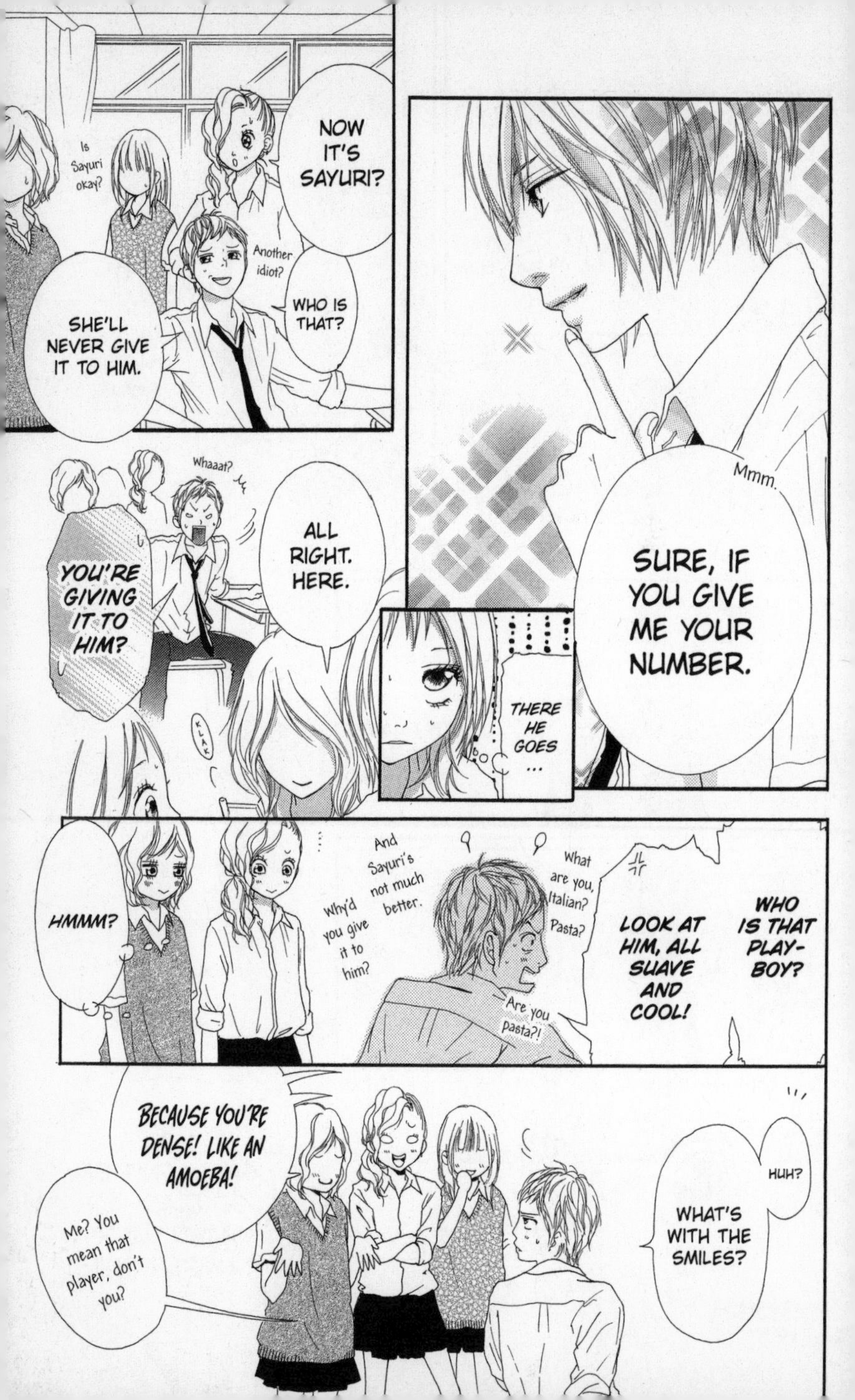
NOW IT'S SAYURI?
Is Sayuri okay?
Another idiot?
WHO IS THAT?
SHE'LL NEVER GIVE IT TO HIM.
Mmm.
SURE, IF YOU GIVE ME YOUR NUMBER.
ALL RIGHT. HERE.
Whaaat?
YOU'RE GIVING IT TO HIM?
KLAK
THERE HE GOES ...
WHO IS THAT PLAY-BOY?
LOOK AT HIM, ALL SUAVE AND COOL!
What are you, Italian? Pasta?
Are you pasta?!
And Sayuri's not much better.
Why'd you give it to him?
HMMM?
HUH?
WHAT'S WITH THE SMILES?
BECAUSE YOU'RE DENSE! LIKE AN AMOEBA!
Me? You mean that player, don't you?

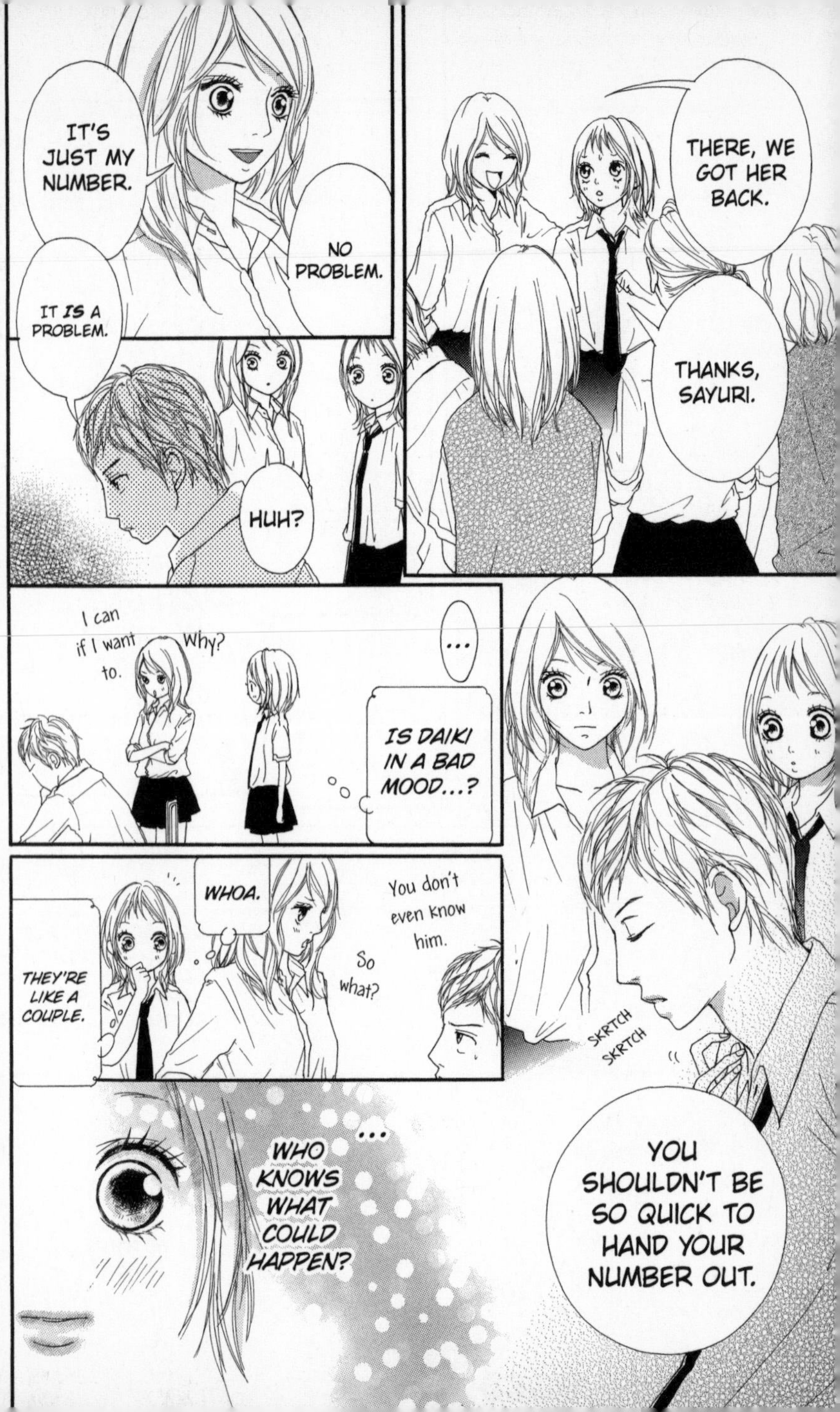
THERE, WE GOT HER BACK.
THANKS, SAYURI.
IT'S JUST MY NUMBER.
NO PROBLEM.
IT IS A PROBLEM.
HUH?
SKRTCH SKRTCH
YOU SHOULDN'T BE SO QUICK TO HAND YOUR NUMBER OUT.
...
Why?
I can if I want to.
IS DAIKI IN A BAD MOOD...?
You don't even know him.
So what?
WHOA.
THEY'RE LIKE A COUPLE.
...WHO KNOWS WHAT COULD HAPPEN?

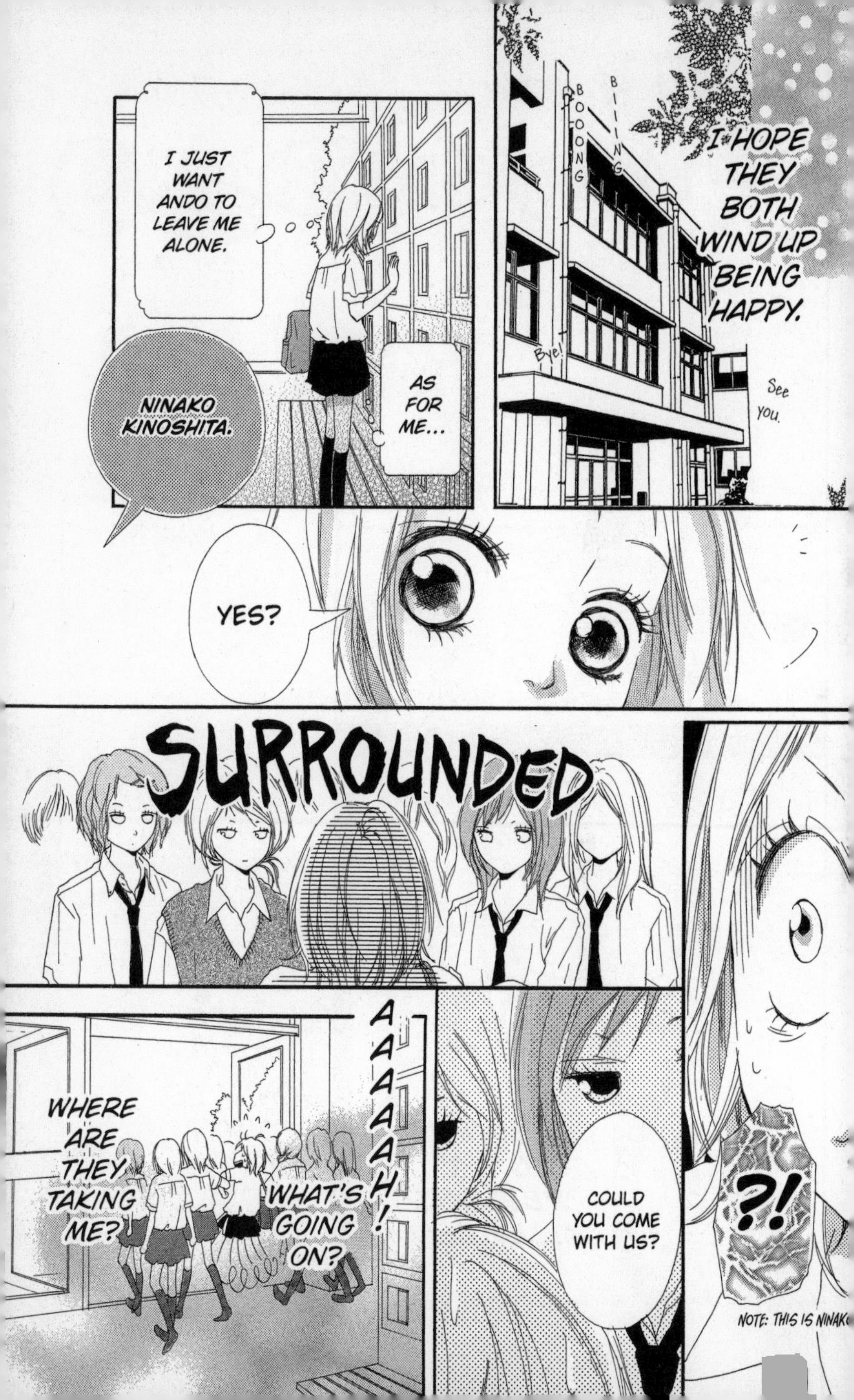

BIIING
BOOONG
I HOPE THEY BOTH WIND UP BEING HAPPY.
Bye!
See you.
I JUST WANT ANDO TO LEAVE ME ALONE.
AS FOR ME...
NINAKO KINOSHITA.
YES?
?!
NOTE: THIS IS NINAKO
SURROUNDED
COULD YOU COME WITH US?
AAAAAAH!
WHAT'S GOING ON?
WHERE ARE THEY TAKING ME?

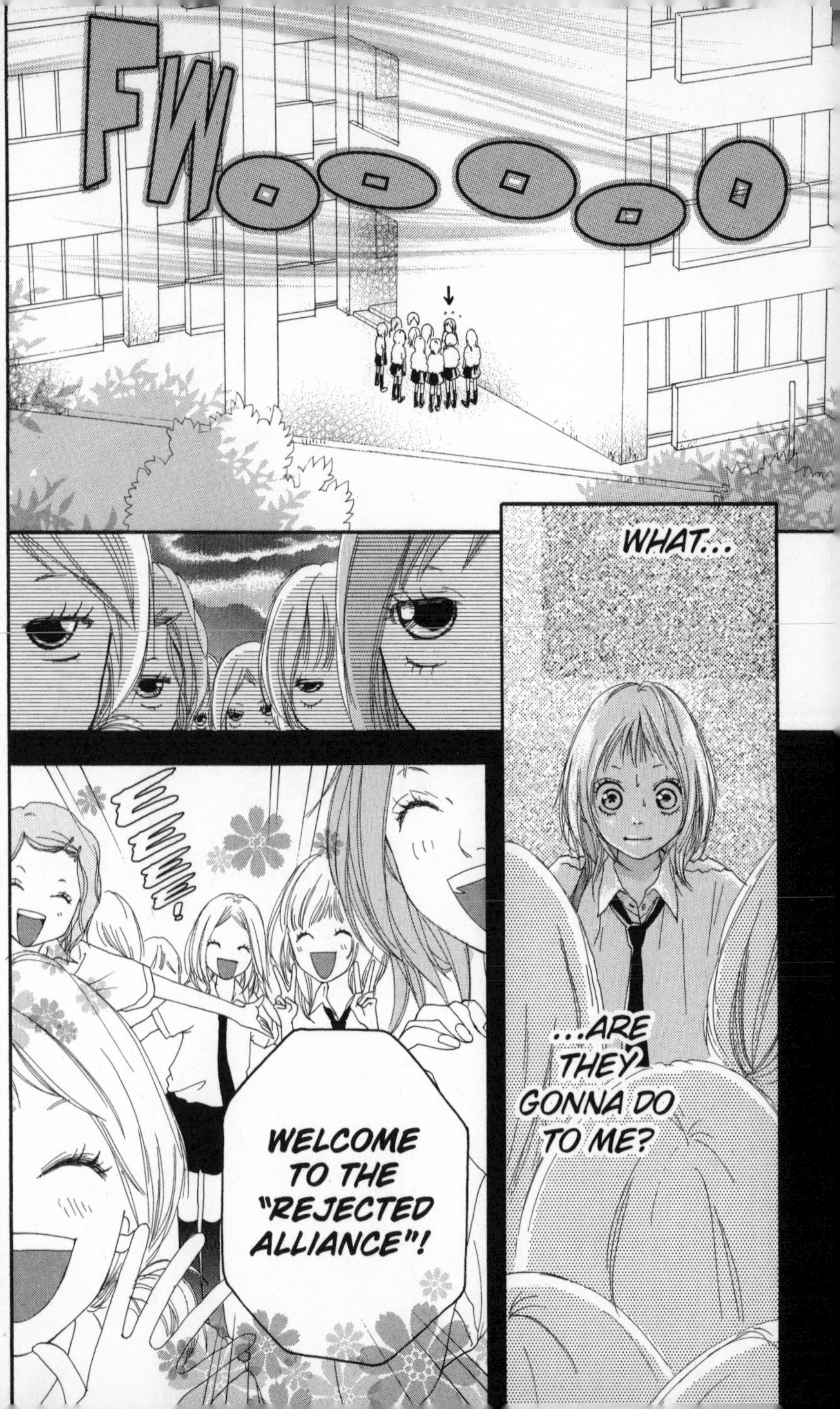
FWOOOOO
WHAT...
...ARE THEY GONNA DO TO ME?
WELCOME TO THE "REJECTED ALLIANCE"!

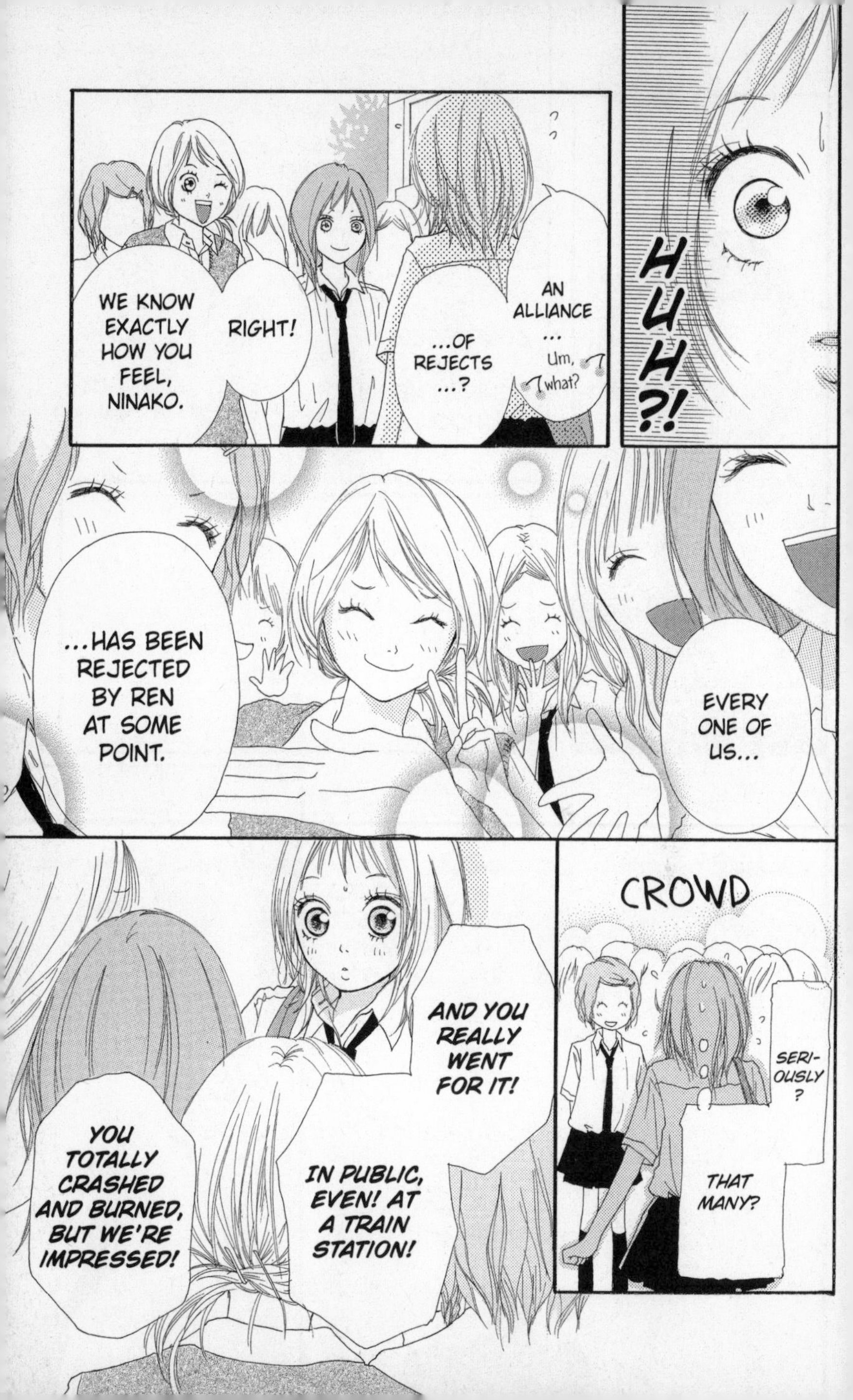
HUH?!
AN ALLIANCE...
Um, what?
...OF REJECTS...?
RIGHT!
WE KNOW EXACTLY HOW YOU FEEL, NINAKO.
EVERY ONE OF US...
...HAS BEEN REJECTED BY REN AT SOME POINT.
CROWD
SERI-OUSLY?
THAT MANY?
AND YOU REALLY WENT FOR IT!
IN PUBLIC, EVEN! AT A TRAIN STATION!
YOU TOTALLY CRASHED AND BURNED, BUT WE'RE IMPRESSED!

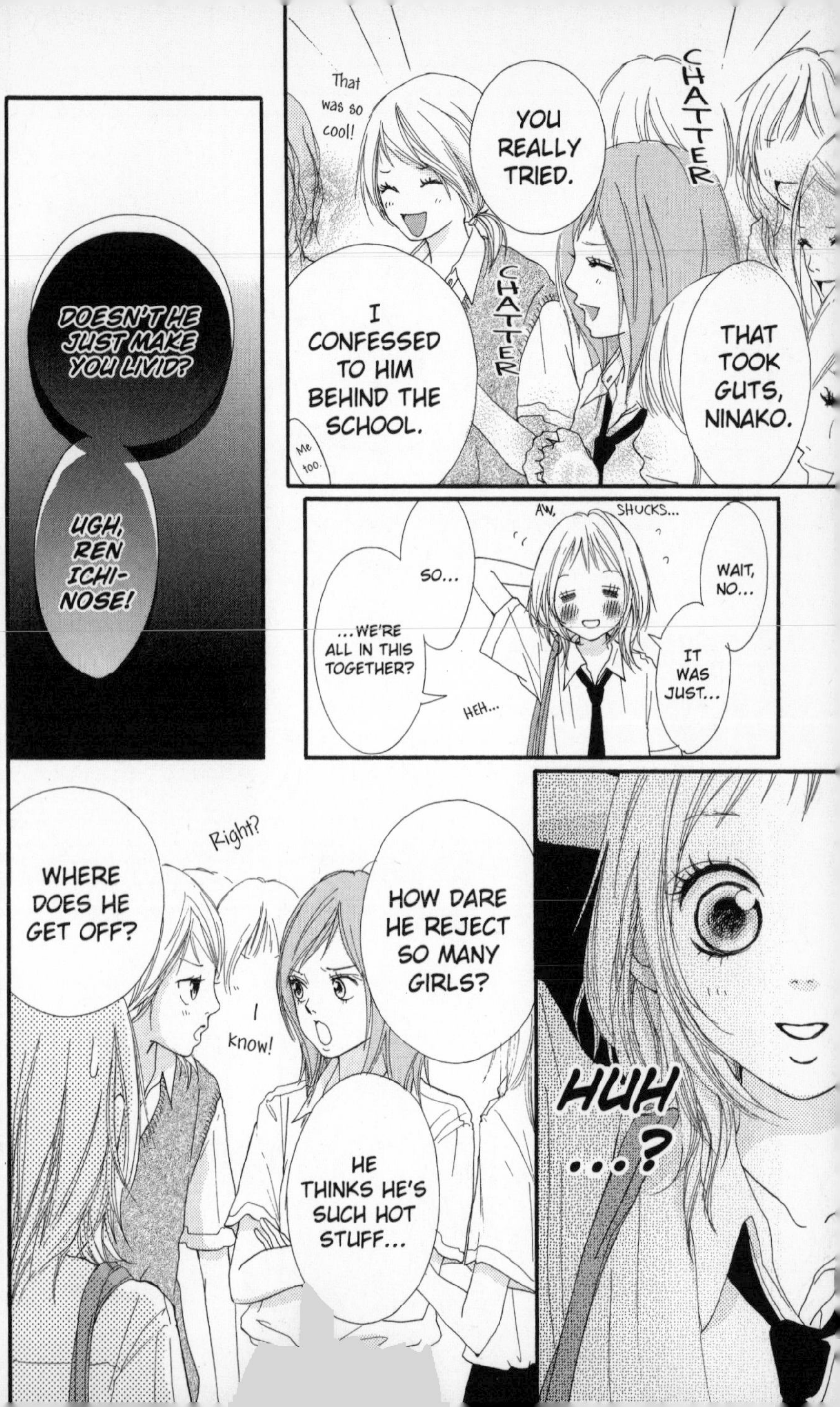
CHATTER
YOU REALLY TRIED.
That was so cool!
THAT TOOK GUTS, NINAKO.
CHATTER
I CONFESSED TO HIM BEHIND THE SCHOOL.
Me too.
WAIT, NO...
IT WAS JUST...
AW, SHUCKS...
SO...
...WE'RE ALL IN THIS TOGETHER?
HEH...
DOESN'T HE JUST MAKE YOU LIVID?
UGH, REN ICHINOSE!
HUH ...?
HOW DARE HE REJECT SO MANY GIRLS?
HE THINKS HE'S SUCH HOT STUFF...
I know!
Right?
WHERE DOES HE GET OFF?

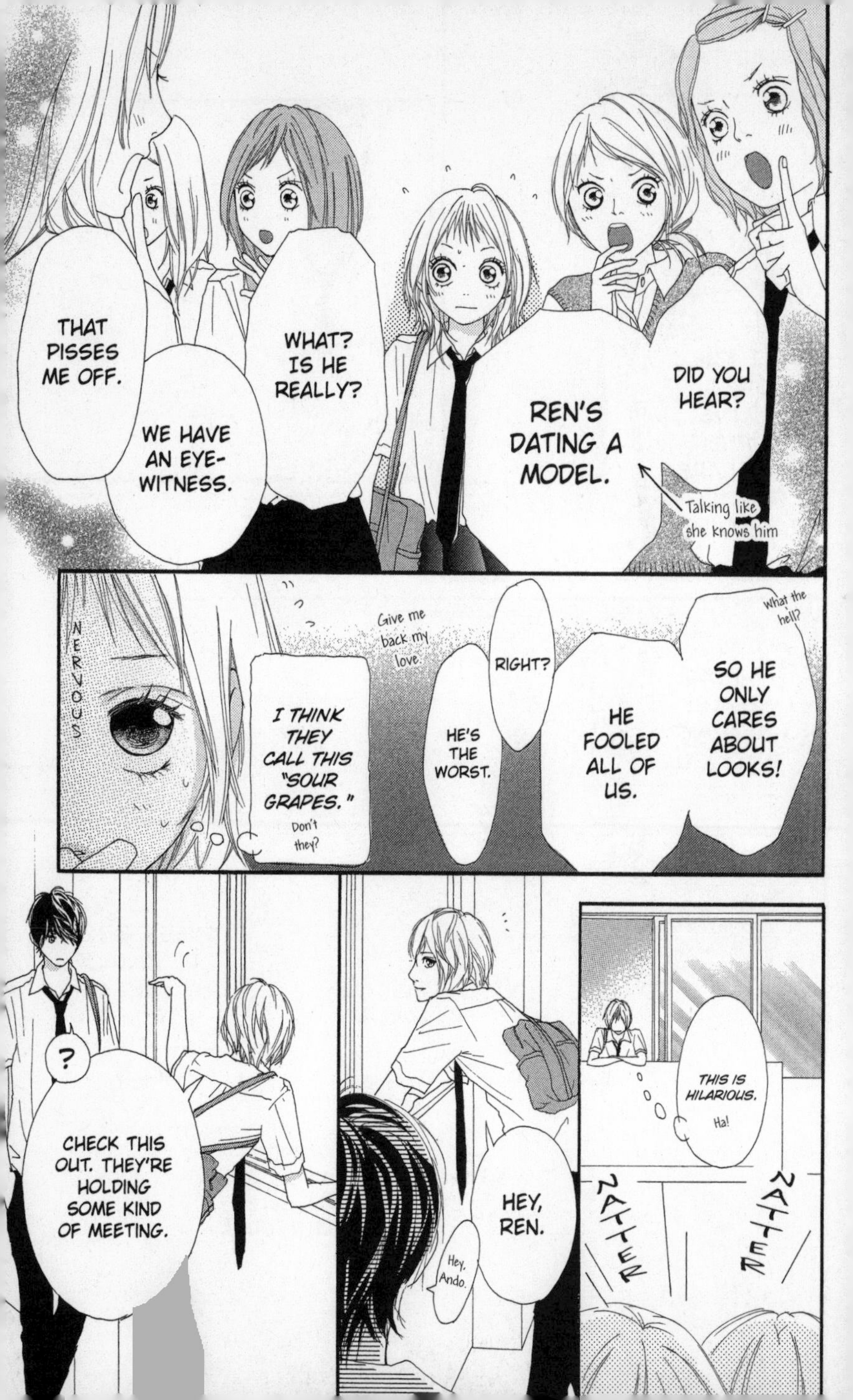

DID YOU HEAR?
REN'S DATING A MODEL.
Talking like she knows him
WHAT? IS HE REALLY?
THAT PISSES ME OFF.
WE HAVE AN EYE-WITNESS.
what the hell?
SO HE ONLY CARES ABOUT LOOKS!
HE FOOLED ALL OF US.
RIGHT?
HE'S THE WORST.
Give me back my love.
I THINK THEY CALL THIS "SOUR GRAPES."
Don't they?
NERVOUS
THIS IS HILARIOUS.
Ha!
NATTER
NATTER
HEY, REN.
Hey, Ando.
?
CHECK THIS OUT. THEY'RE HOLDING SOME KIND OF MEETING.

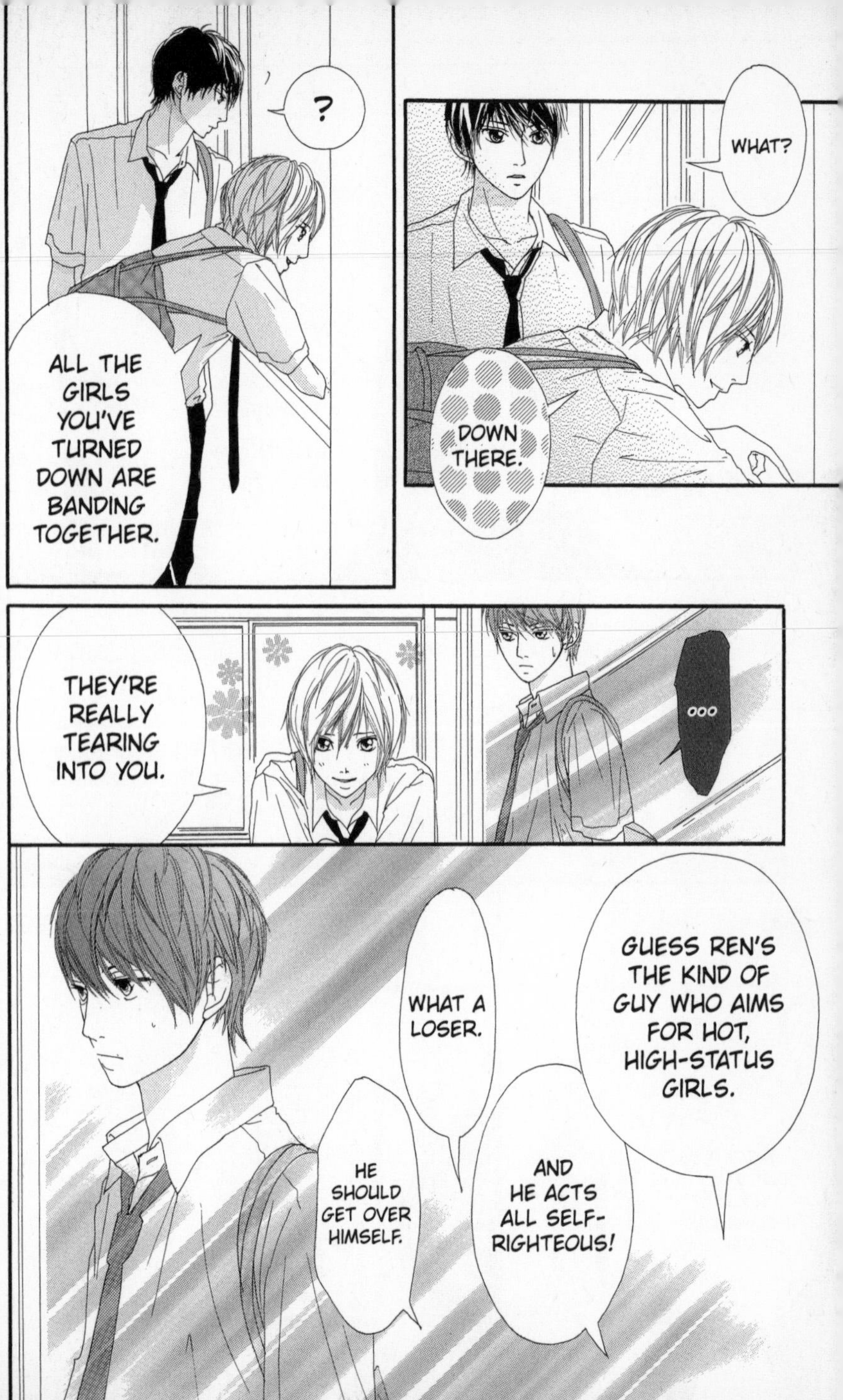
WHAT?
DOWN THERE.
?
ALL THE GIRLS YOU'VE TURNED DOWN ARE BANDING TOGETHER.
THEY'RE REALLY TEARING INTO YOU.
GUESS REN'S THE KIND OF GUY WHO AIMS FOR HOT, HIGH-STATUS GIRLS.
WHAT A LOSER.
AND HE ACTS ALL SELF-RIGHTEOUS!
HE SHOULD GET OVER HIMSELF.

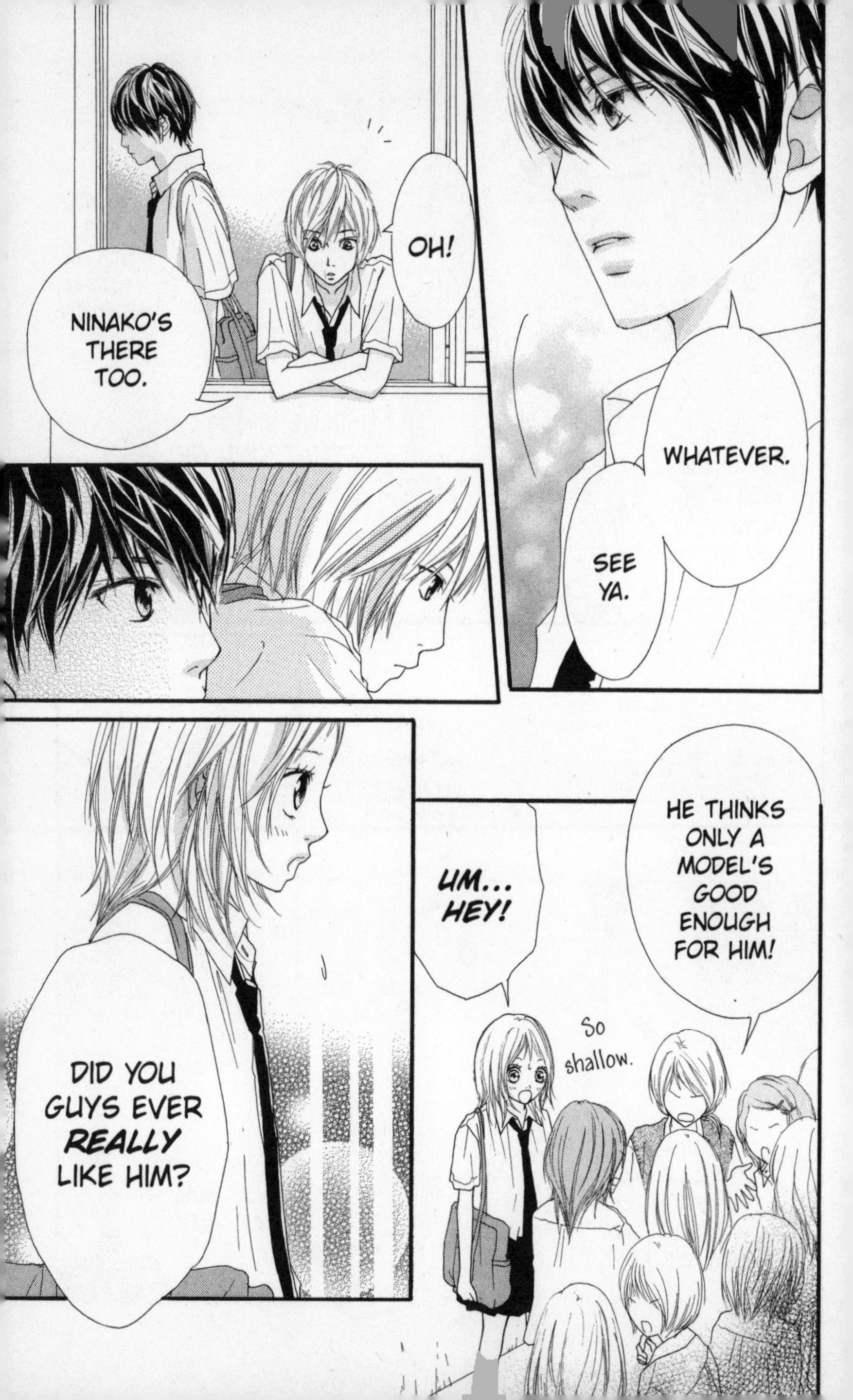
WHATEVER.
SEE YA.
OH!
NINAKO'S THERE TOO.
HE THINKS ONLY A MODEL'S GOOD ENOUGH FOR HIM!
So shallow.
UM... HEY!
DID YOU GUYS EVER REALLY LIKE HIM?

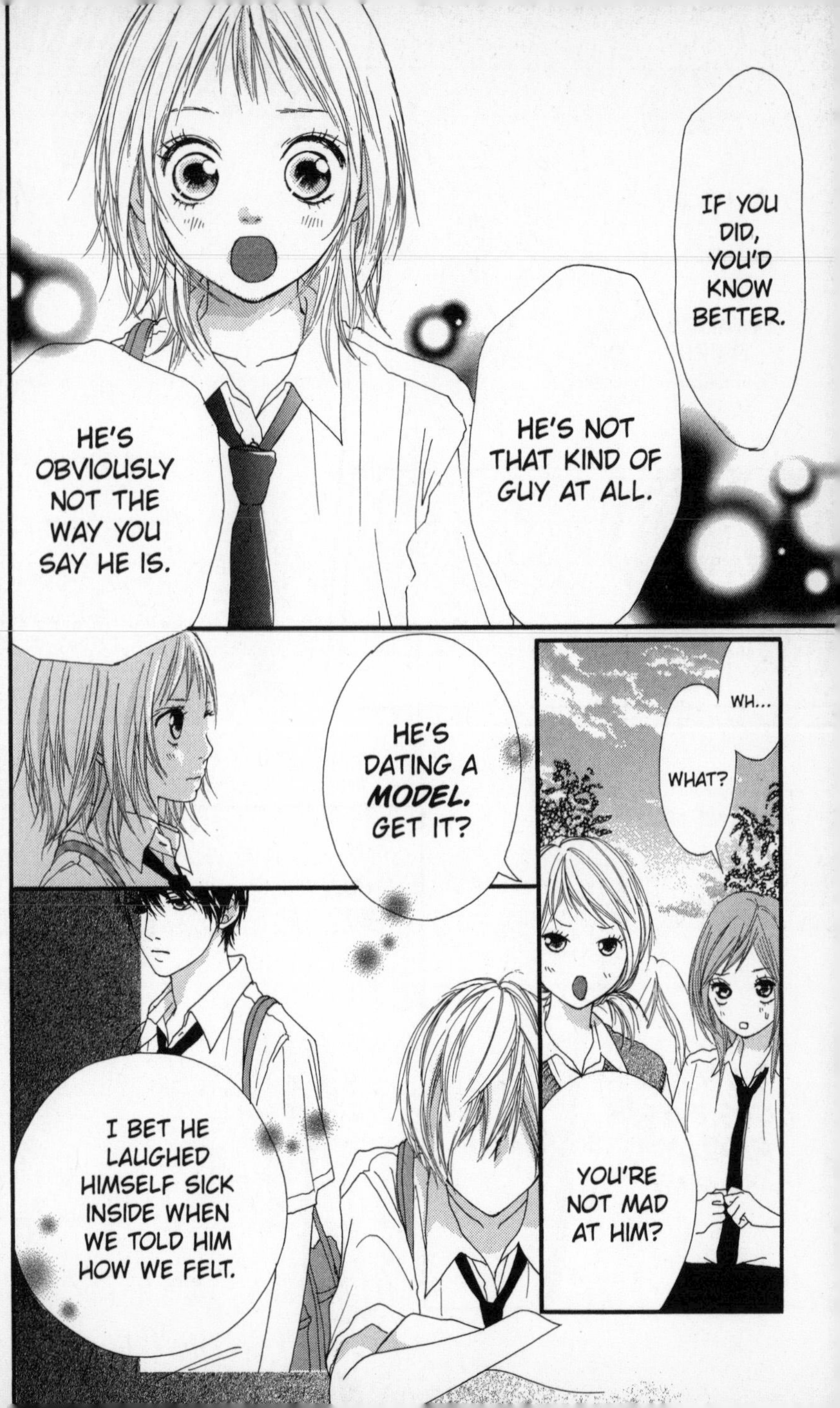
IF YOU DID, YOU'D KNOW BETTER.
HE'S NOT THAT KIND OF GUY AT ALL.
HE'S OBVIOUSLY NOT THE WAY YOU SAY HE IS.
WH...
WHAT?
YOU'RE NOT MAD AT HIM?
HE'S DATING A *MODEL.* GET IT?
I BET HE LAUGHED HIMSELF SICK INSIDE WHEN WE TOLD HIM HOW WE FELT.

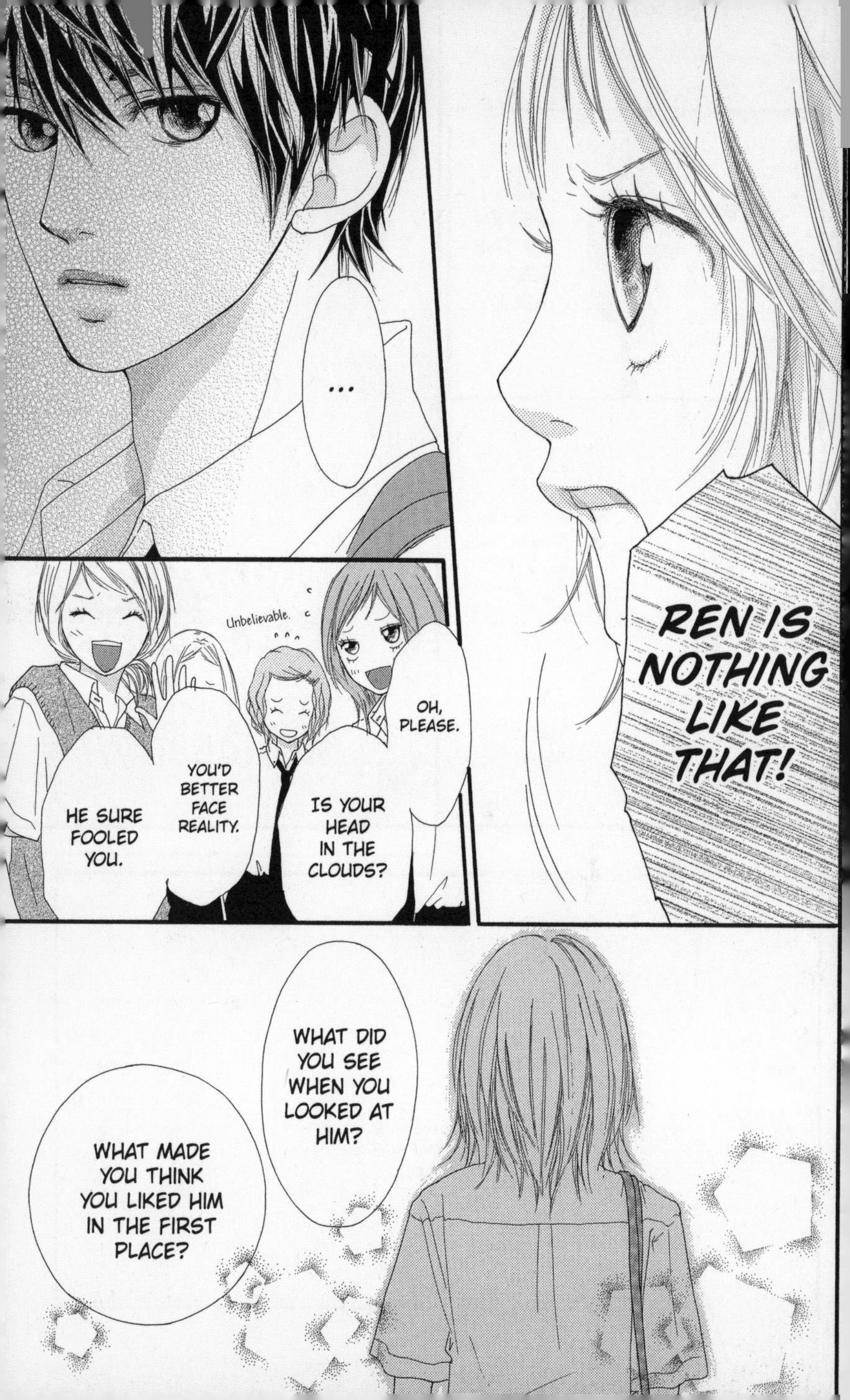
REN IS NOTHING LIKE THAT!
...
OH, PLEASE.
Unbelievable.
IS YOUR HEAD IN THE CLOUDS?
YOU'D BETTER FACE REALITY.
HE SURE FOOLED YOU.
WHAT DID YOU SEE WHEN YOU LOOKED AT HIM?
WHAT MADE YOU THINK YOU LIKED HIM IN THE FIRST PLACE?

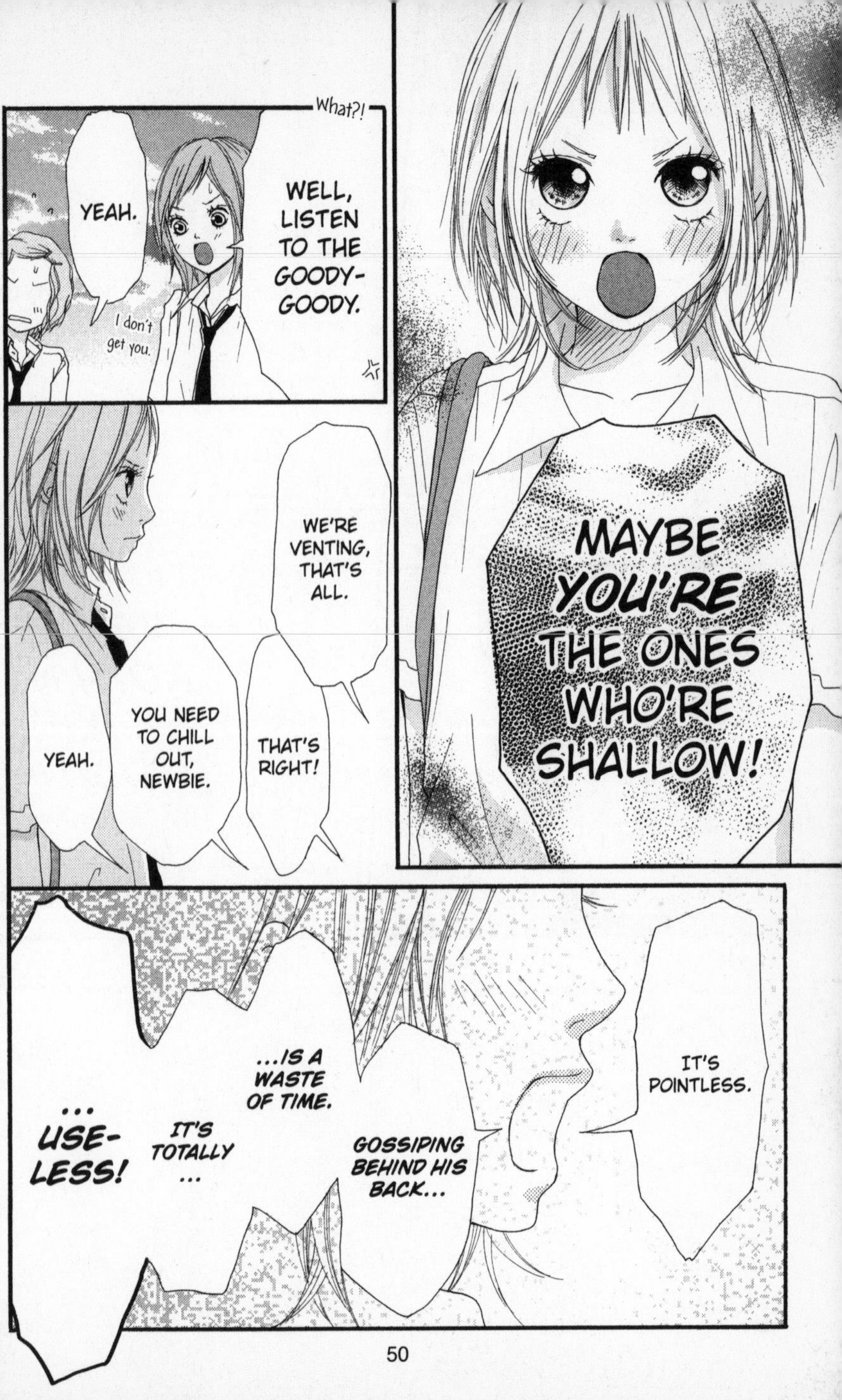
MAYBE YOU'RE THE ONES WHO'RE SHALLOW!
What?!
WELL, LISTEN TO THE GOODY-GOODY.
YEAH.
I don't get you.
WE'RE VENTING, THAT'S ALL.
THAT'S RIGHT!
YOU NEED TO CHILL OUT, NEWBIE.
YEAH.
IT'S POINTLESS.
GOSSIPING BEHIND HIS BACK...
...IS A WASTE OF TIME.
IT'S TOTALLY ...
... USE-LESS!

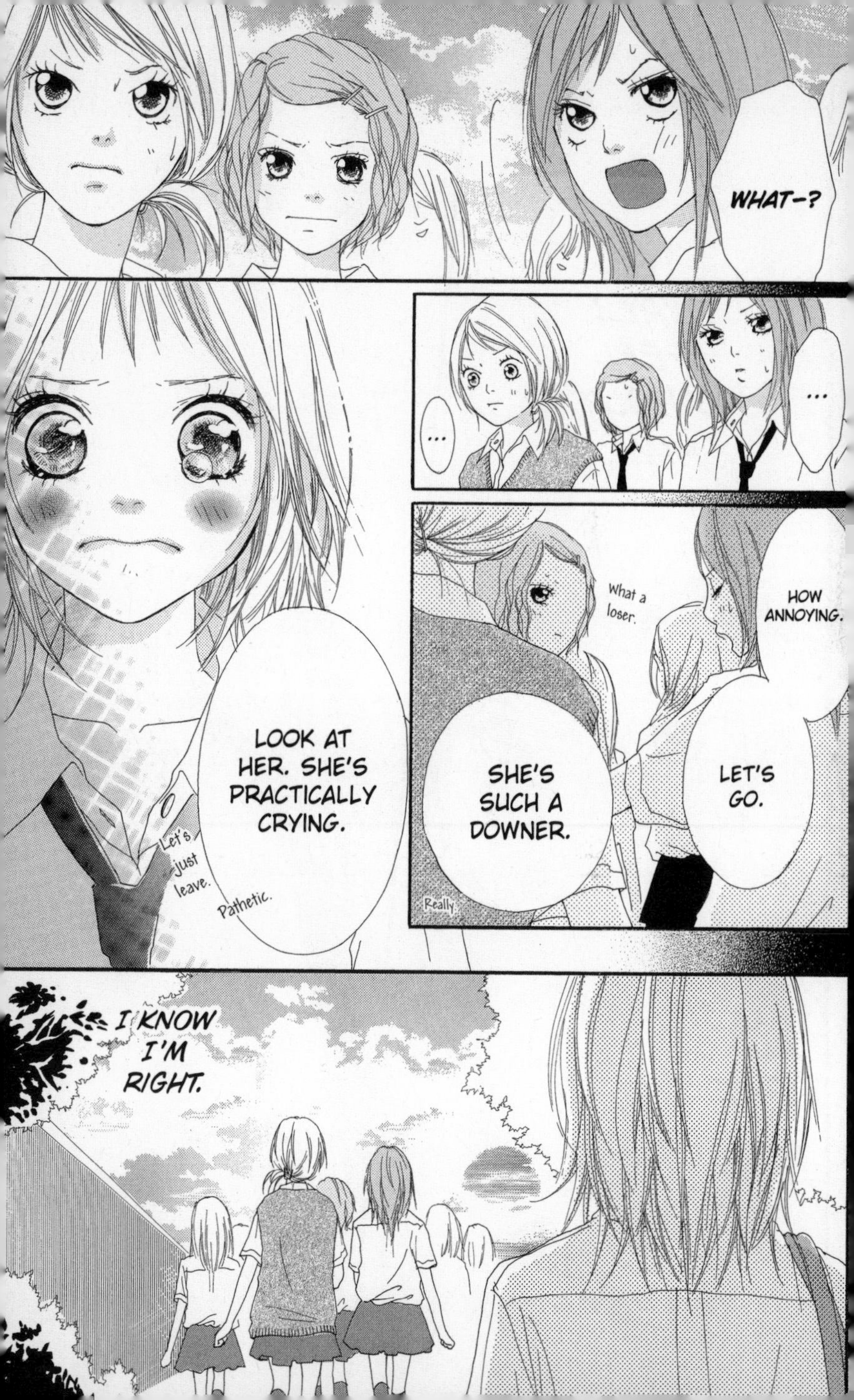
WHAT-?
...
...
HOW ANNOYING.
What a loser.
LET'S GO.
SHE'S SUCH A DOWNER.
Really.
LOOK AT HER. SHE'S PRACTICALLY CRYING.
Let's just leave.
Pathetic.
I KNOW I'M RIGHT.

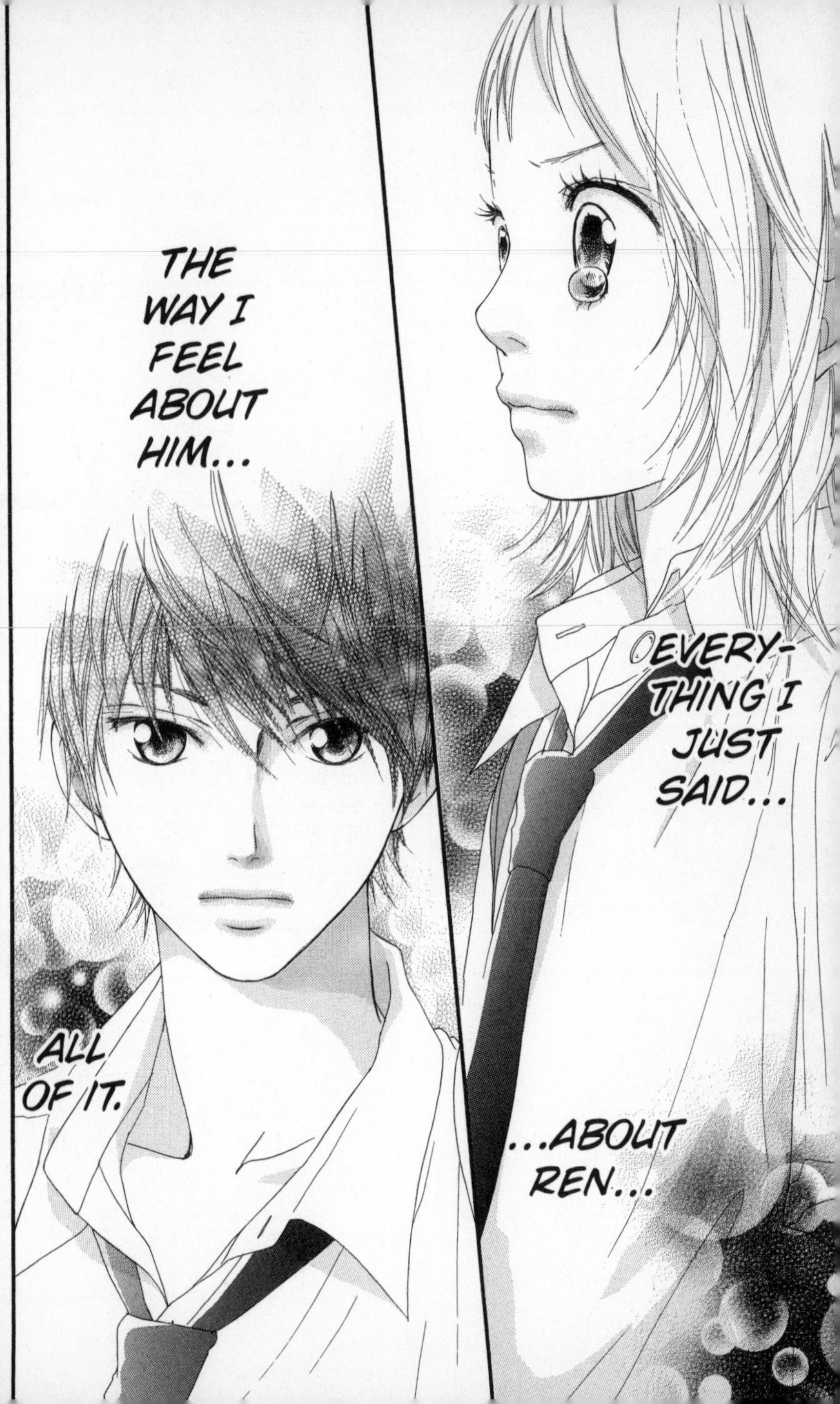
EVERY-THING I JUST SAID...
...ABOUT REN...
THE WAY I FEEL ABOUT HIM...
ALL OF IT.

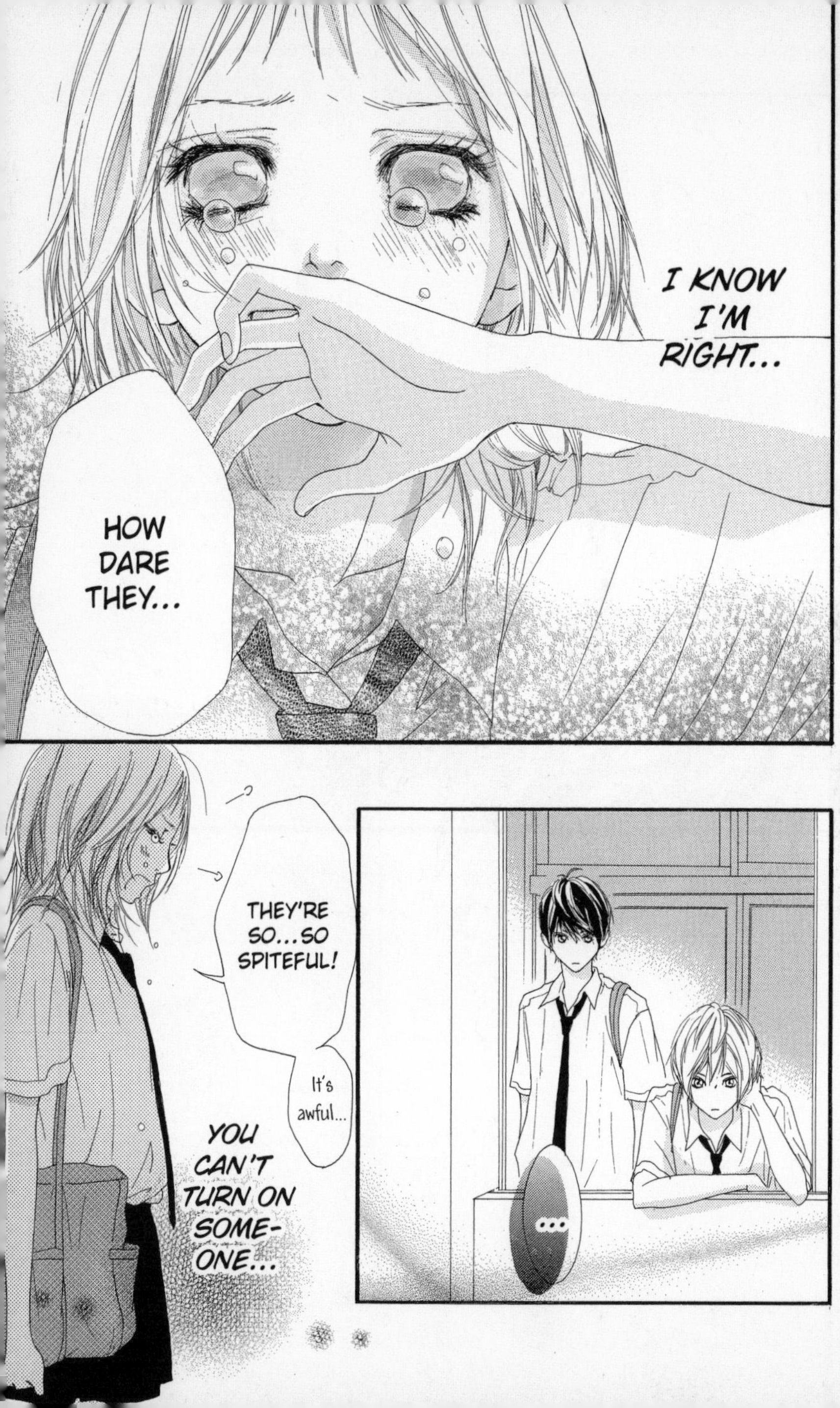
I KNOW I'M RIGHT...
HOW DARE THEY...
...
THEY'RE SO...SO SPITEFUL!
It's awful...
YOU CAN'T TURN ON SOME-ONE...

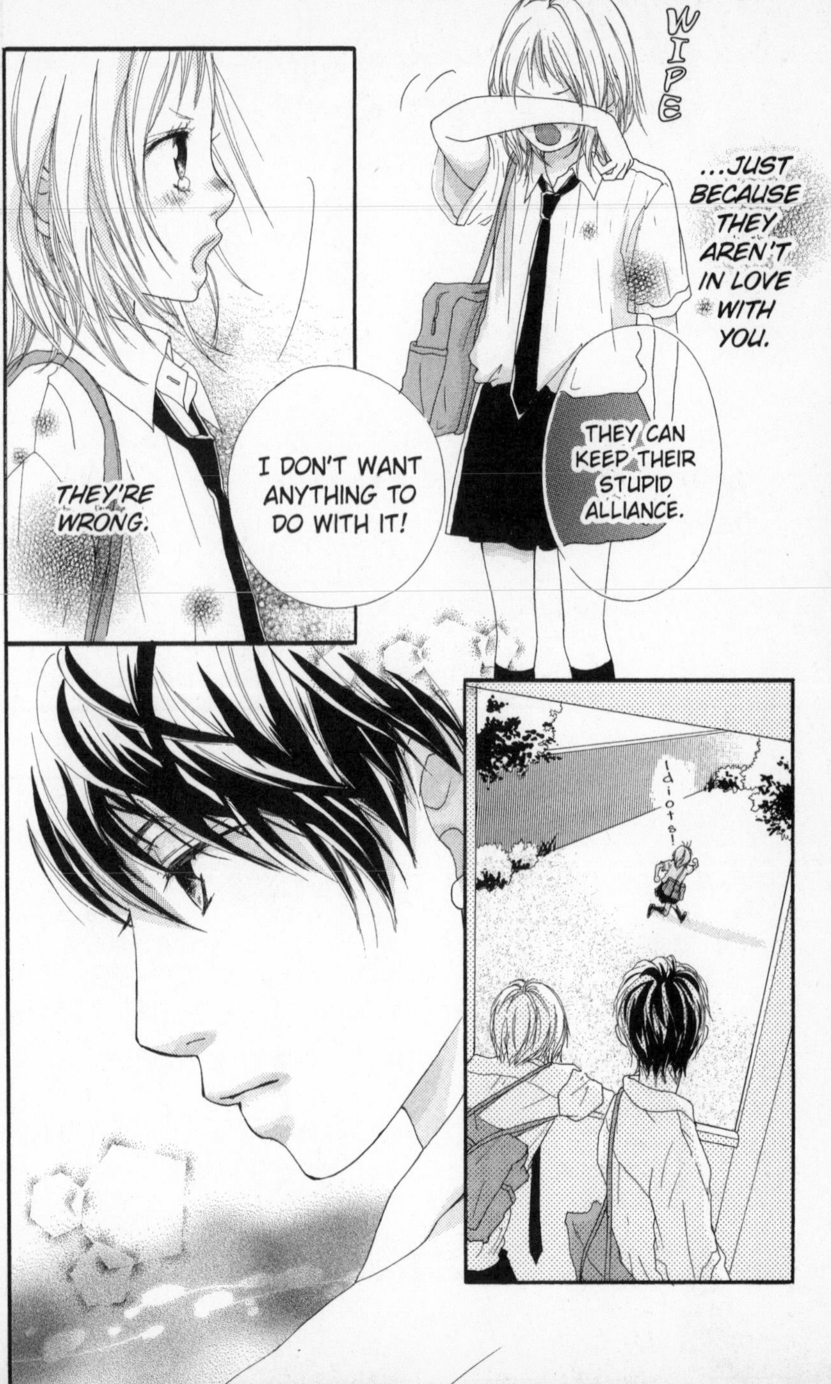
WIPE
...JUST BECAUSE THEY AREN'T IN LOVE WITH YOU.
THEY CAN KEEP THEIR STUPID ALLIANCE.
I DON'T WANT ANYTHING TO DO WITH IT!
THEY'RE WRONG.
Idiots!

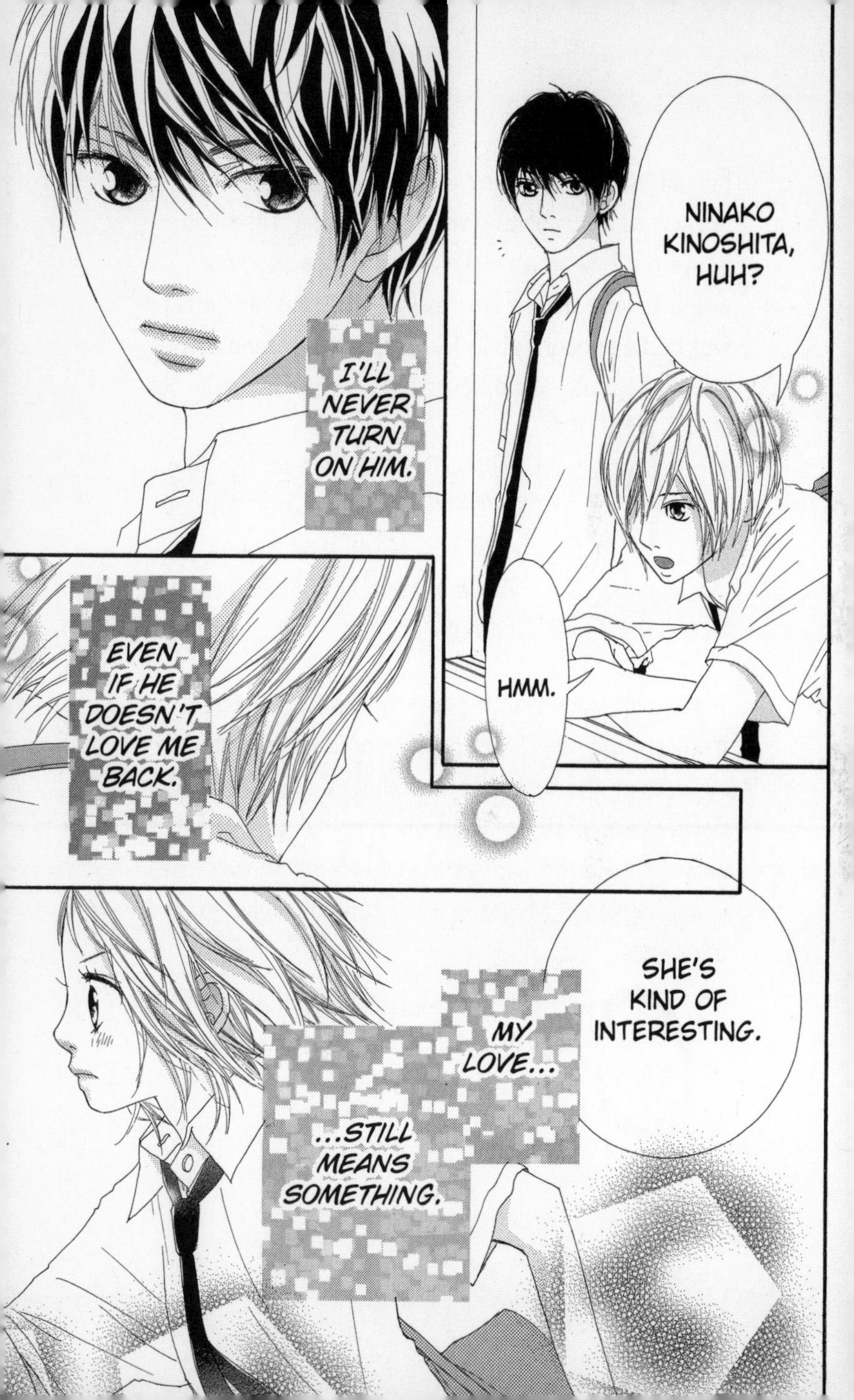
NINAKO KINOSHITA, HUH?
HMM.
I'LL NEVER TURN ON HIM.
EVEN IF HE DOESN'T LOVE ME BACK.
SHE'S KIND OF INTERESTING.
MY LOVE...
...STILL MEANS SOMETHING.

For all of Strobe Edge 1, I worked solo. I'm a slow worker, so my schedule was pretty tiring. I tried to figure out how to go faster, so first I decided not to sleep. To help myself stay awake, I decided not to eat. But oddly enough, when I worked without food or sleep, I basically keeled over.

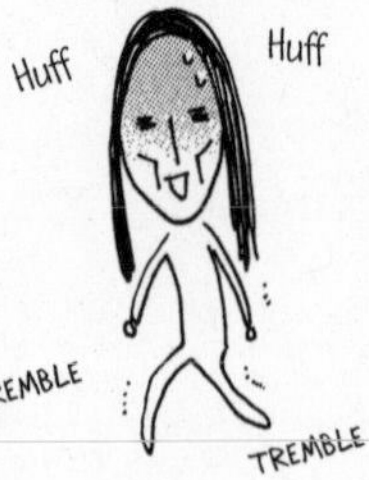
Huff
Huff
TREMBLE
TREMBLE

I thought, "I can't go on like this." So I decided to get some help on volume 2. Now I have Naomi Minamoto and Umi Ayase helping me out.

These girls work fast. I love it. It's so fun to have them around, and I feel much more stable emotionally. Warm and fuzzy. So thankfully, I could eat and sleep again, and I regained my stamina! Yay! Yay! But before I knew it, I was getting rounder than ever. This is unacceptable! My jeans are too tight! I have to rethink this...

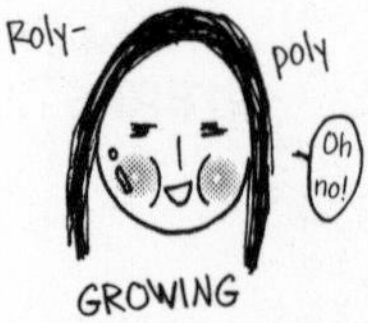
Roly-
poly
Oh no!
GROWING

Naomi Minamoto, Umi Ayase, thank you so much for helping me!!

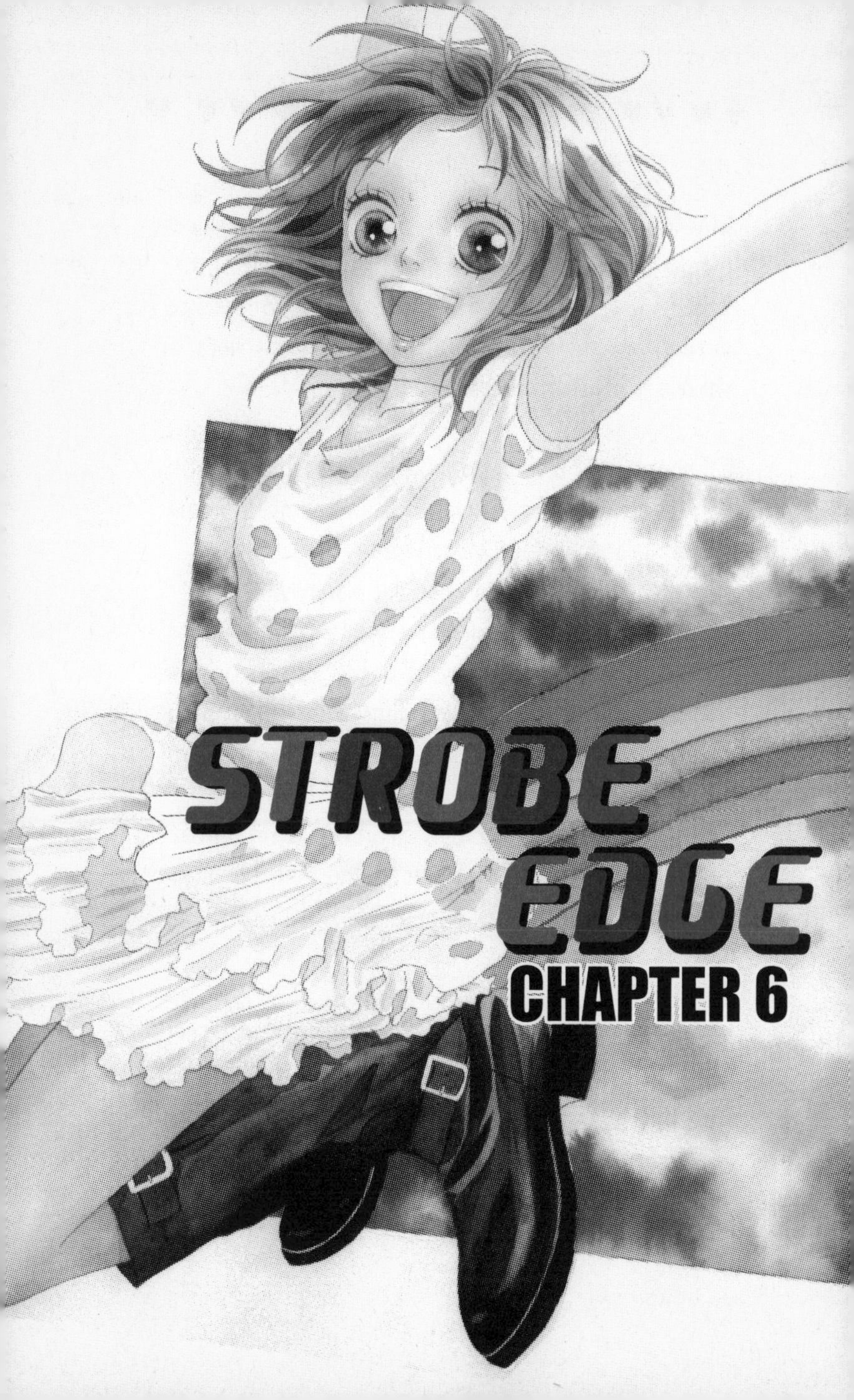
STROBE EDGE
CHAPTER 6

♥ ♥ ♥ ♥ ♥ ♥ ♥ ♥ ♥ ♥ ♥ ♥ ♥ ♥ ♥ ♥ ♥

In volume 1, I wrote that I'd never been able to witness my pet chinchilla giving birth. But the other day, I finally saw it! I thought it was about time, so I peeked in early one morning after finishing up some work, and she'd already had one baby. ♥ ♥ ♥

I thought she'd give birth to at least one more, but I had no idea how far apart they would come. Mommy chinchilla's expression looked sleepy as usual, and I had no way of knowing when she was having a contraction, so I just watched. I watched and watched, but the mommy didn't move. But just as I thought she was only having one baby this time, a face peeked out. She was giving birth! With such a poker face?!

In any case, well done! Good girl. She wound up having two babies. It was my first time seeing a newborn! I was so happy!

 The baby's fur was still damp and kind of wavy. So cute! It started playing right away.

♥ ♥ ♥ ♥ ♥ ♥ ♥ ♥ ♥ ♥ ♥ ♥ ♥ ♥ ♥ ♥ ♥

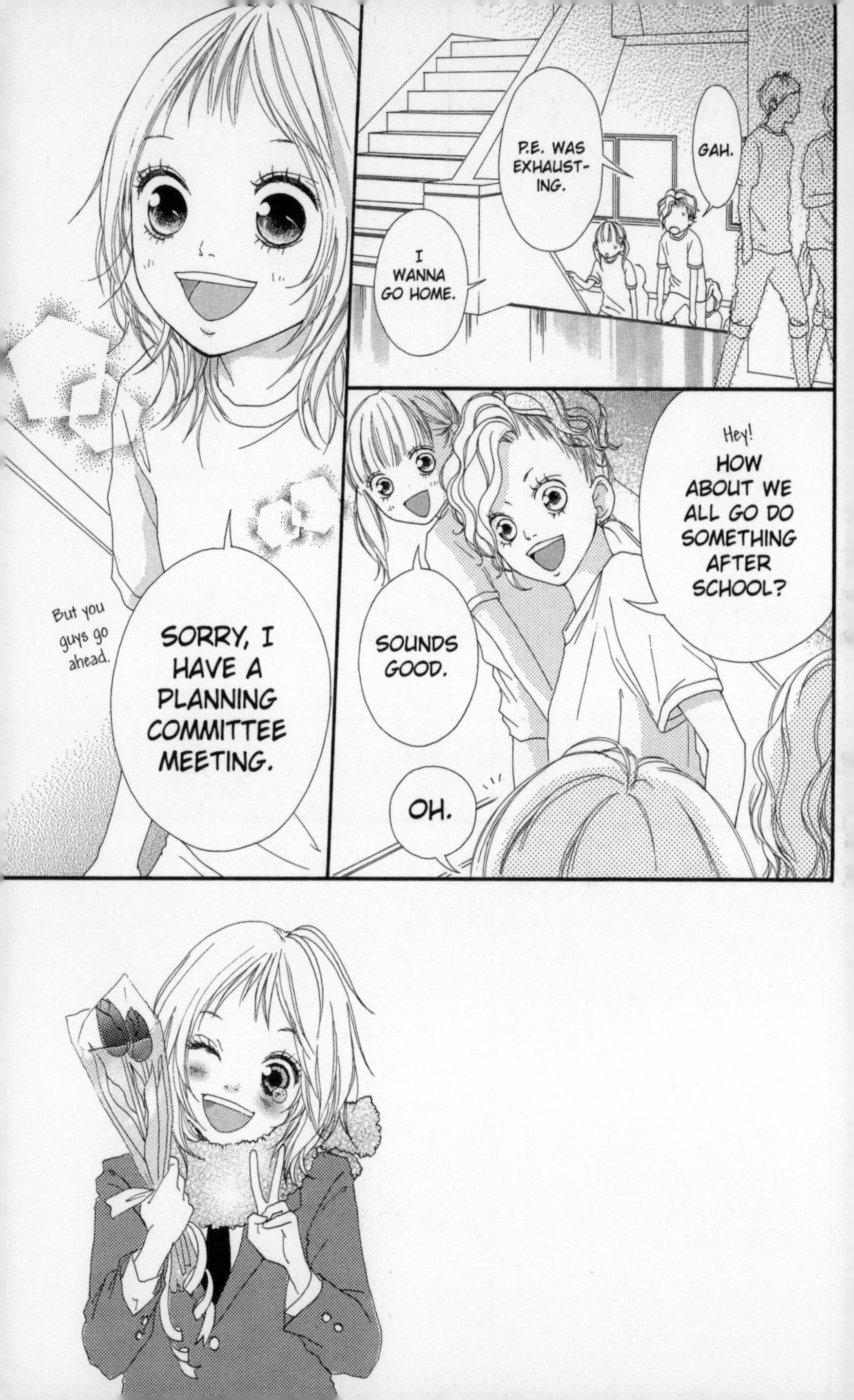
GAH.
P.E. WAS EXHAUST-ING.
I WANNA GO HOME.
Hey! HOW ABOUT WE ALL GO DO SOMETHING AFTER SCHOOL?
SOUNDS GOOD.
OH.
SORRY, I HAVE A PLANNING COMMITTEE MEETING.
But you guys go ahead.

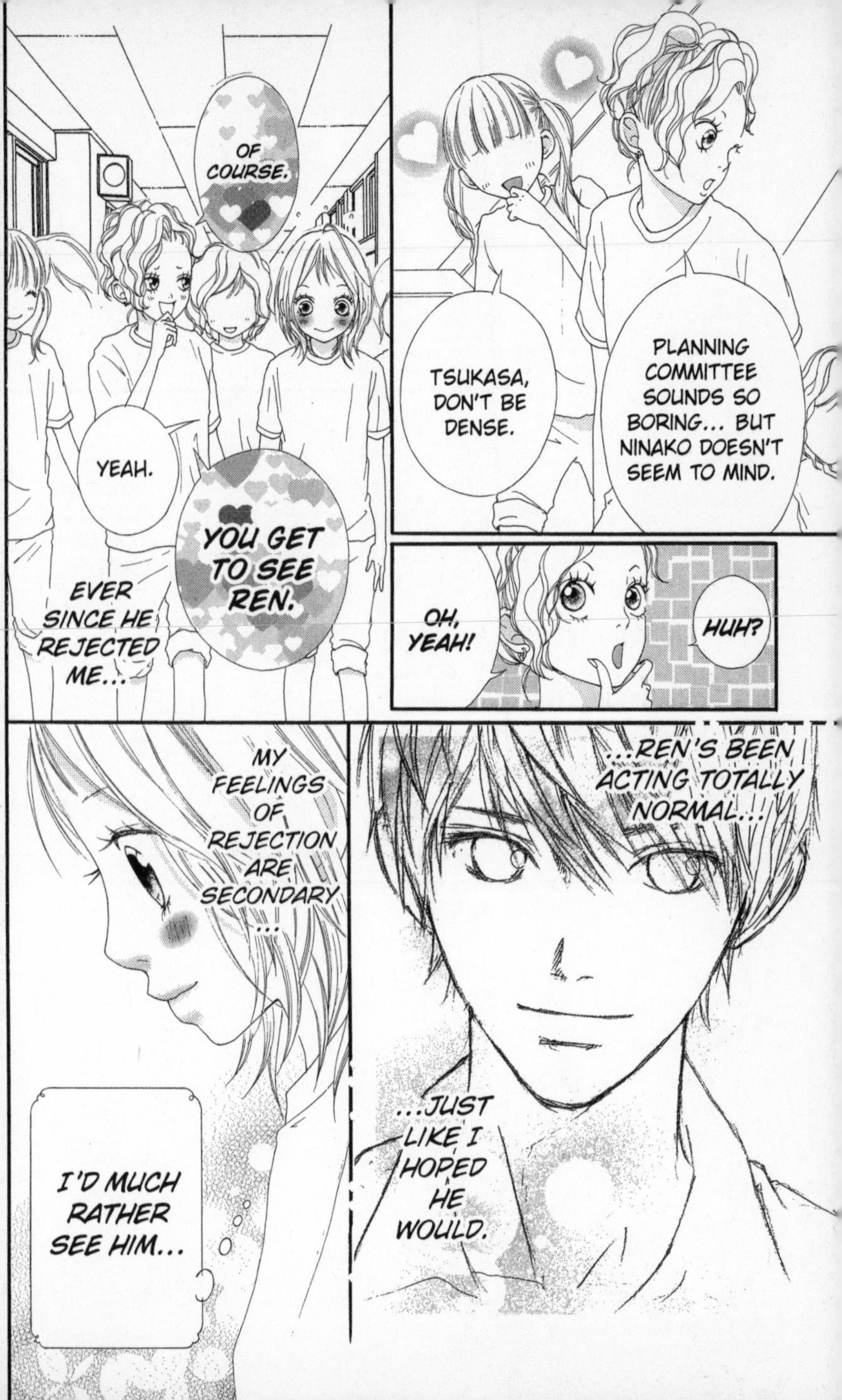
PLANNING COMMITTEE SOUNDS SO BORING... BUT NINAKO DOESN'T SEEM TO MIND.
TSUKASA, DON'T BE DENSE.
HUH?
OH, YEAH!
OF COURSE.
YOU GET TO SEE REN.
YEAH.
EVER SINCE HE REJECTED ME...
...REN'S BEEN ACTING TOTALLY NORMAL...
...JUST LIKE I HOPED HE WOULD.
MY FEELINGS OF REJECTION ARE SECONDARY...
I'D MUCH RATHER SEE HIM...

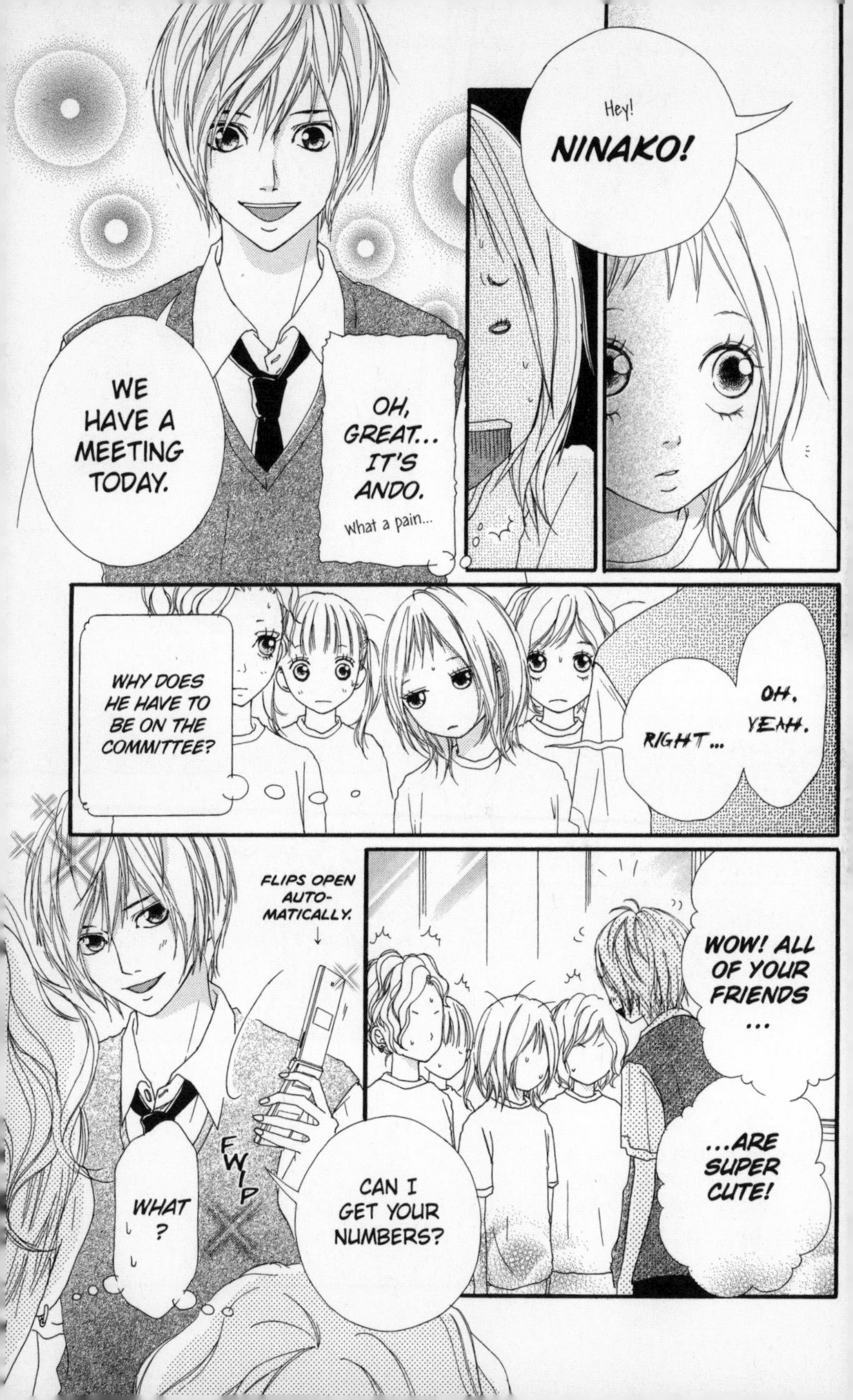
Hey!
NINAKO!
WE HAVE A MEETING TODAY.
OH, GREAT... IT'S ANDO.
What a pain...
OH. YEAH.
RIGHT...
WHY DOES HE HAVE TO BE ON THE COMMITTEE?
WOW! ALL OF YOUR FRIENDS ...
...ARE SUPER CUTE!
FLIPS OPEN AUTO-MATICALLY.
CAN I GET YOUR NUMBERS?
FWIP
WHAT ?

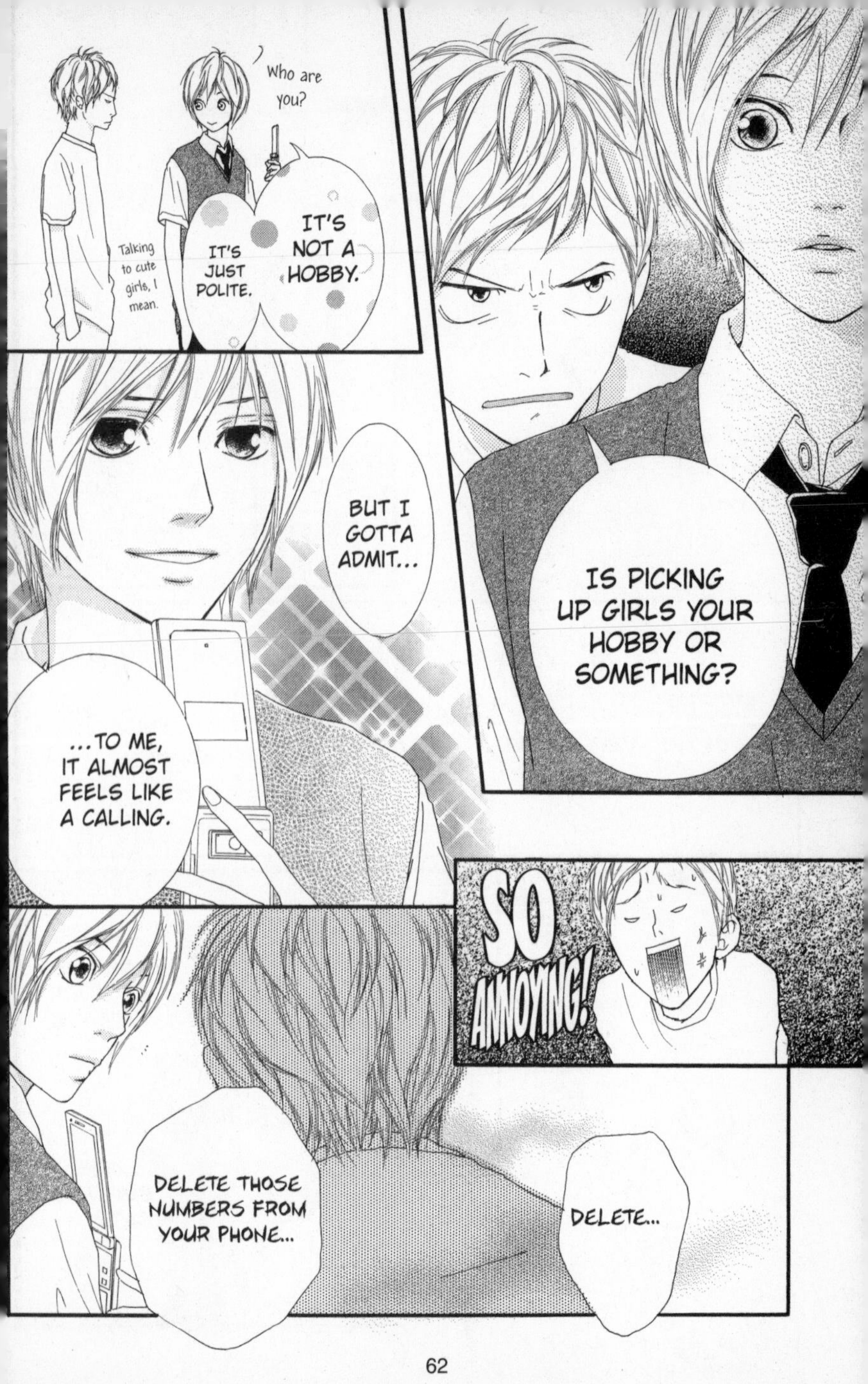
IS PICKING UP GIRLS YOUR HOBBY OR SOMETHING?
IT'S NOT A HOBBY.
IT'S JUST POLITE.
Talking to cute girls, I mean.
Who are you?
BUT I GOTTA ADMIT...
...TO ME, IT ALMOST FEELS LIKE A CALLING.
SO ANNOYING!
DELETE...
DELETE THOSE NUMBERS FROM YOUR PHONE...

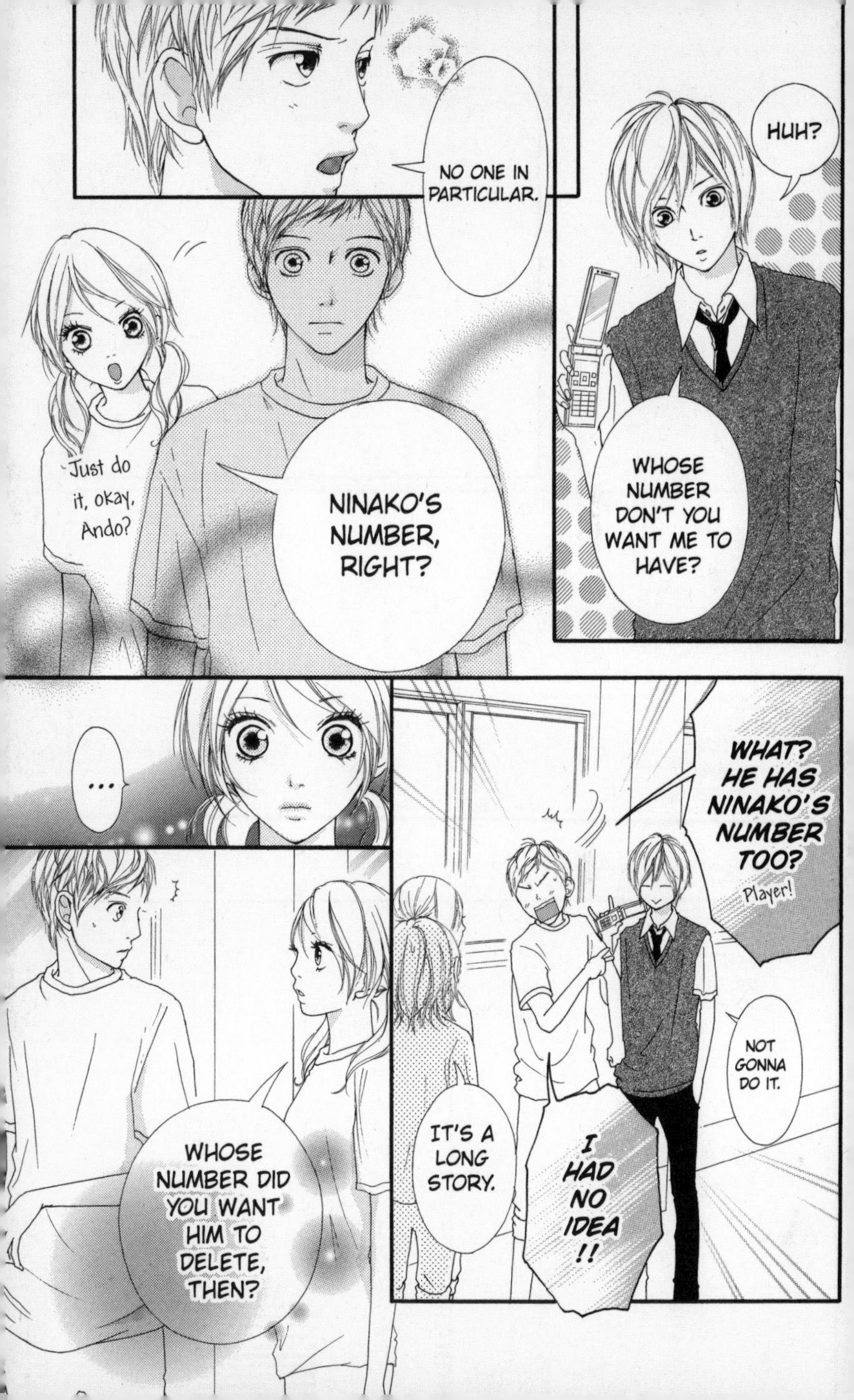
HUH?
WHOSE NUMBER DON'T YOU WANT ME TO HAVE?
NO ONE IN PARTICULAR.
NINAKO'S NUMBER, RIGHT?
Just do it, okay, Ando?
WHAT? HE HAS NINAKO'S NUMBER TOO?
Player!
NOT GONNA DO IT.
I HAD NO IDEA!!
IT'S A LONG STORY.
...
WHOSE NUMBER DID YOU WANT HIM TO DELETE, THEN?

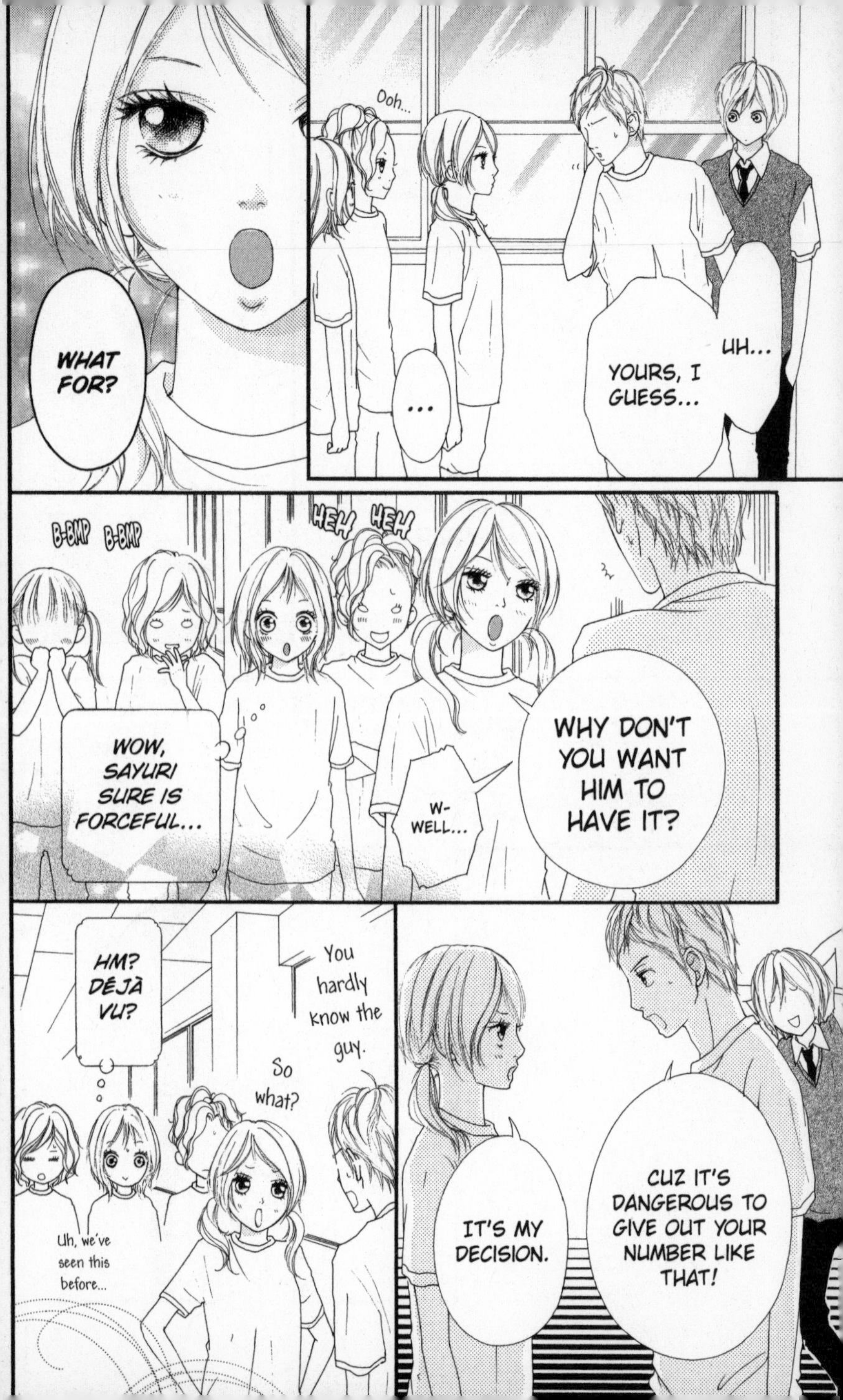
UH... YOURS, I GUESS...
Ooh...
...
WHAT FOR?
HEH HEH
B-BMP B-BMP
WHY DON'T YOU WANT HIM TO HAVE IT?
W-WELL...
WOW, SAYURI SURE IS FORCEFUL...
CUZ IT'S DANGEROUS TO GIVE OUT YOUR NUMBER LIKE THAT!
IT'S MY DECISION.
You hardly know the guy.
So what?
HM? DÉJÀ VU?
Uh, we've seen this before...

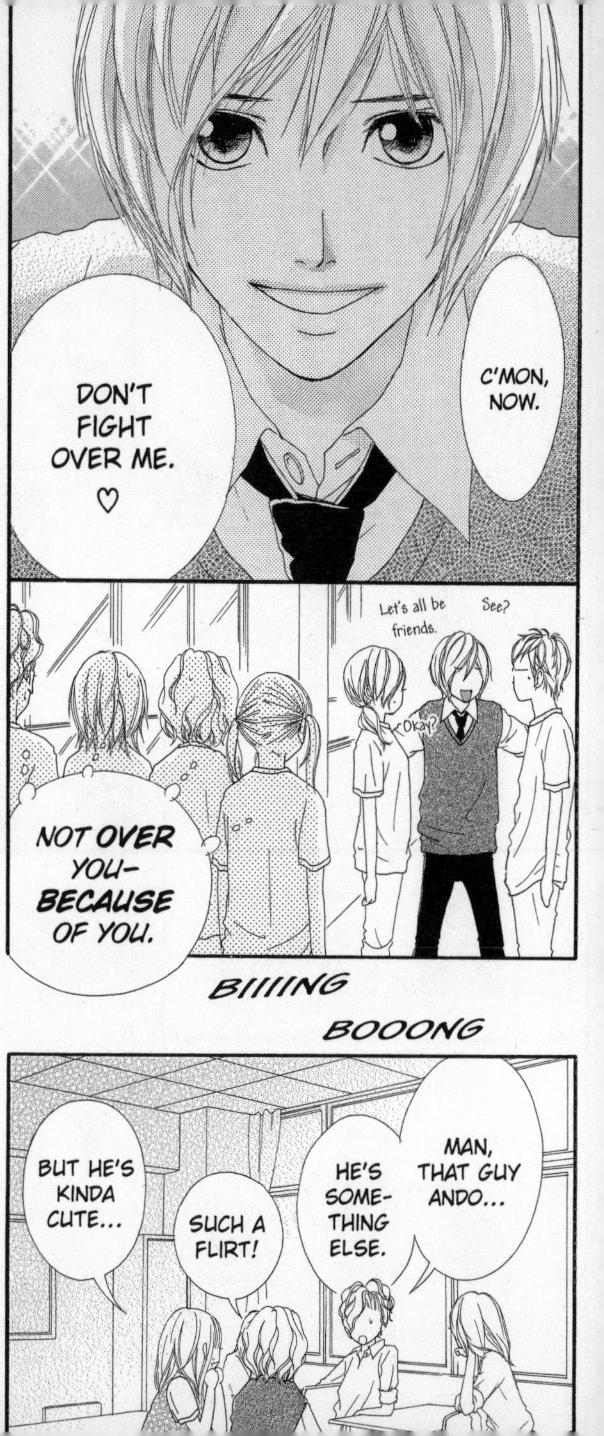
C'MON, NOW.
DON'T FIGHT OVER ME. ♡
See?
Let's all be friends.
Okay?
NOT OVER YOU— BECAUSE OF YOU.
BIIIING
BOOONG
MAN, THAT GUY ANDO...
HE'S SOMETHING ELSE.
SUCH A FLIRT!
BUT HE'S KINDA CUTE...

WANNA GO FOR A DRIVE? ②

Despite appearances, I'm actually pretty timid. After I got my permit and had to sit behind the wheel and learn to drive, I was so scared I thought my heart was going to explode.

Drive in some steel contraption? At that speed? **Me?** That's terrifying. My instructor always tells me to speed up, but I'm too scared. One time, he sighed and said, "You sure don't drive the way you look." I thought, "Who drives the way they look?" but all I said was "I'm sorry."

He must be sick and tired of teaching people like me day after day, but still, that was so rude. He didn't have to rub it in...! *Sniff...* Why do I always seem to get that instructor? I don't ever want to go back.

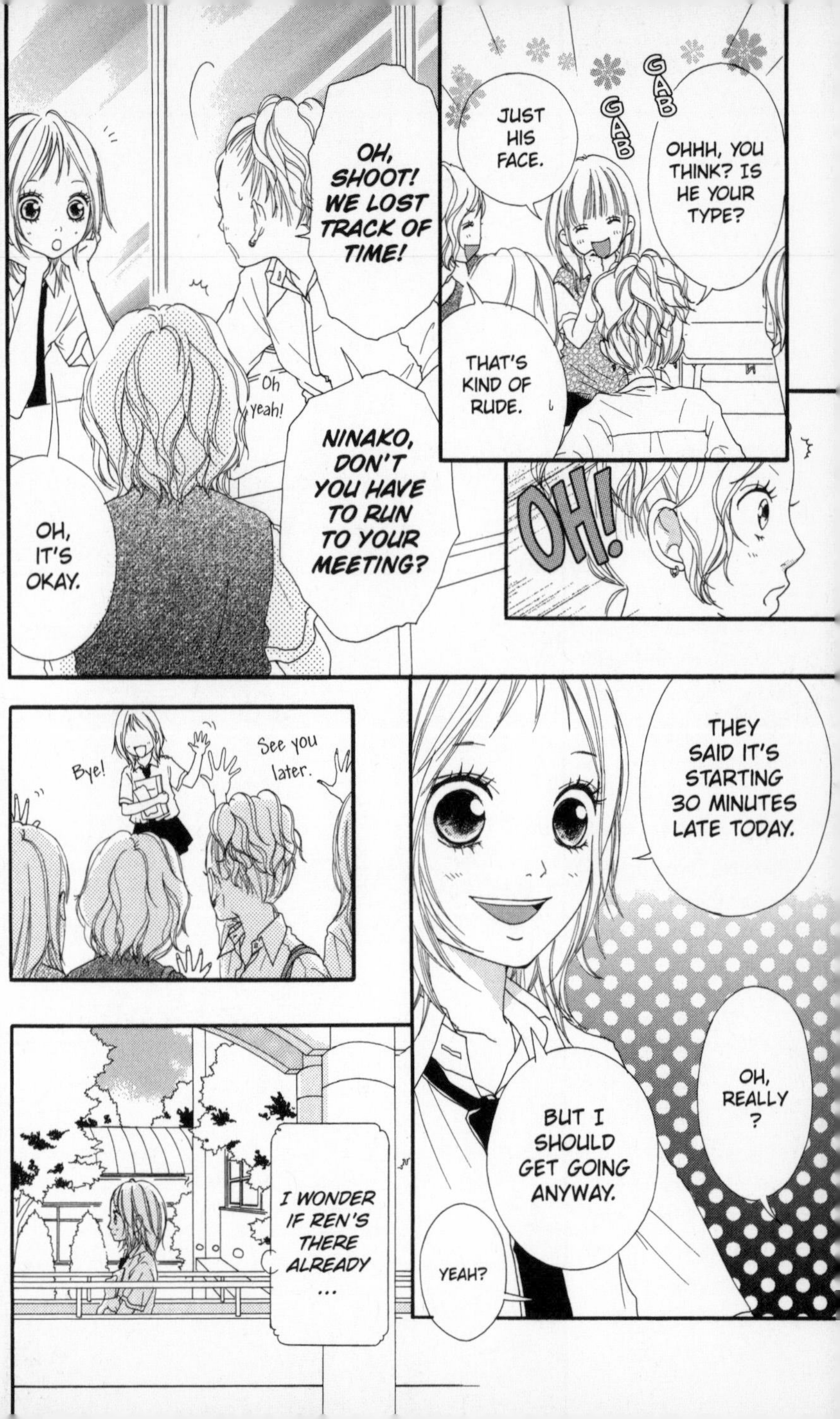
OHHH, YOU THINK? IS HE YOUR TYPE?
GAB GAB
JUST HIS FACE.
THAT'S KIND OF RUDE.
OH!
OH, SHOOT! WE LOST TRACK OF TIME!
NINAKO, DON'T YOU HAVE TO RUN TO YOUR MEETING?
Oh yeah!
OH, IT'S OKAY.
THEY SAID IT'S STARTING 30 MINUTES LATE TODAY.
OH, REALLY?
BUT I SHOULD GET GOING ANYWAY.
YEAH?
See you later.
Bye!
I WONDER IF REN'S THERE ALREADY ...

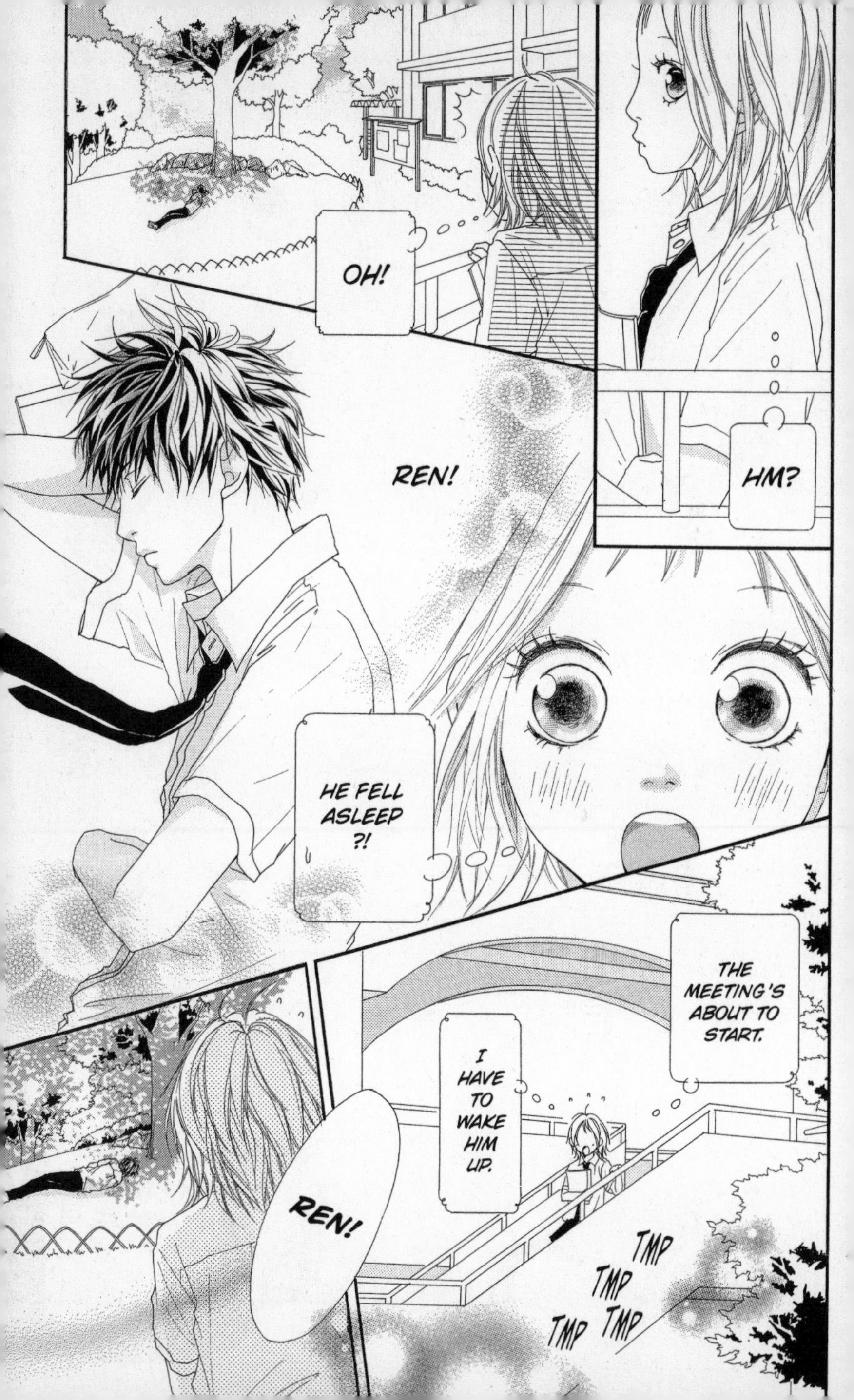
HM?
OH!
REN!
HE FELL ASLEEP ?!
THE MEETING'S ABOUT TO START.
I HAVE TO WAKE HIM UP.
TMP TMP TMP TMP TMP
REN!

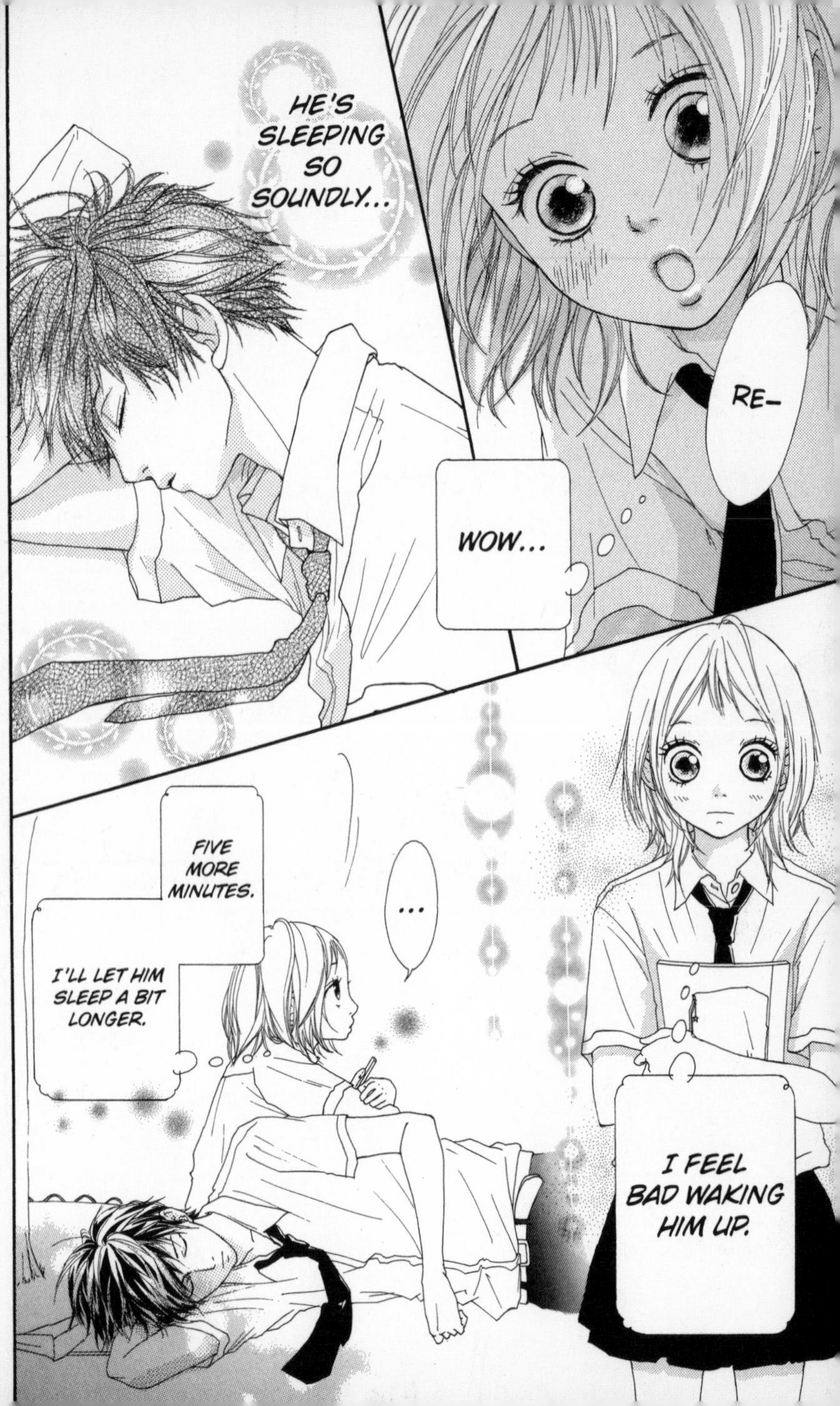
RE-
WOW...
HE'S SLEEPING SO SOUNDLY...
I FEEL BAD WAKING HIM UP.
...
FIVE MORE MINUTES.
I'LL LET HIM SLEEP A BIT LONGER.

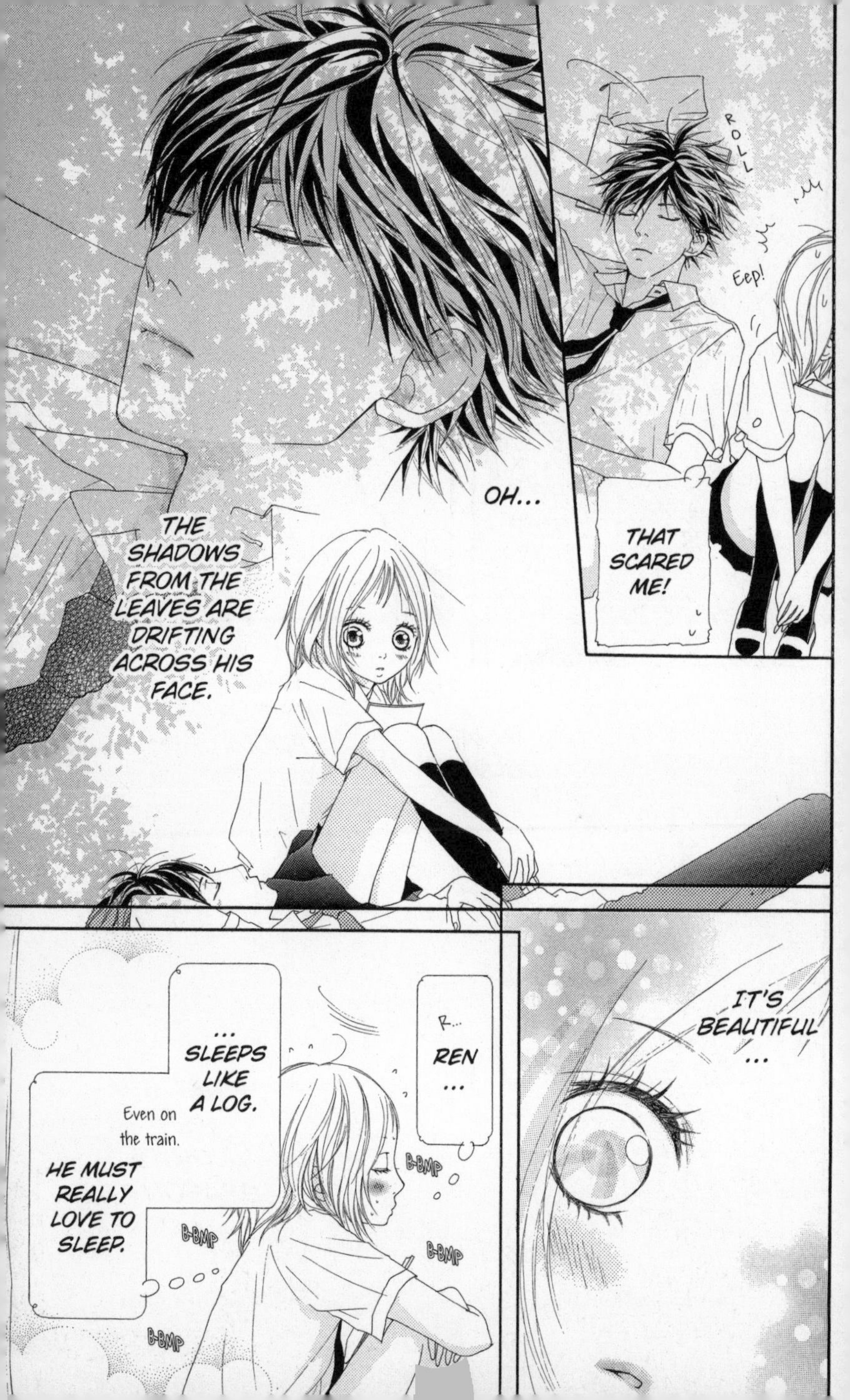
ROLL
Eep!
THAT SCARED ME!
OH...
THE SHADOWS FROM THE LEAVES ARE DRIFTING ACROSS HIS FACE.
IT'S BEAUTIFUL...
R... REN...
... SLEEPS LIKE A LOG.
Even on the train.
HE MUST REALLY LOVE TO SLEEP.
B-BMP
B-BMP
B-BMP
B-BMP

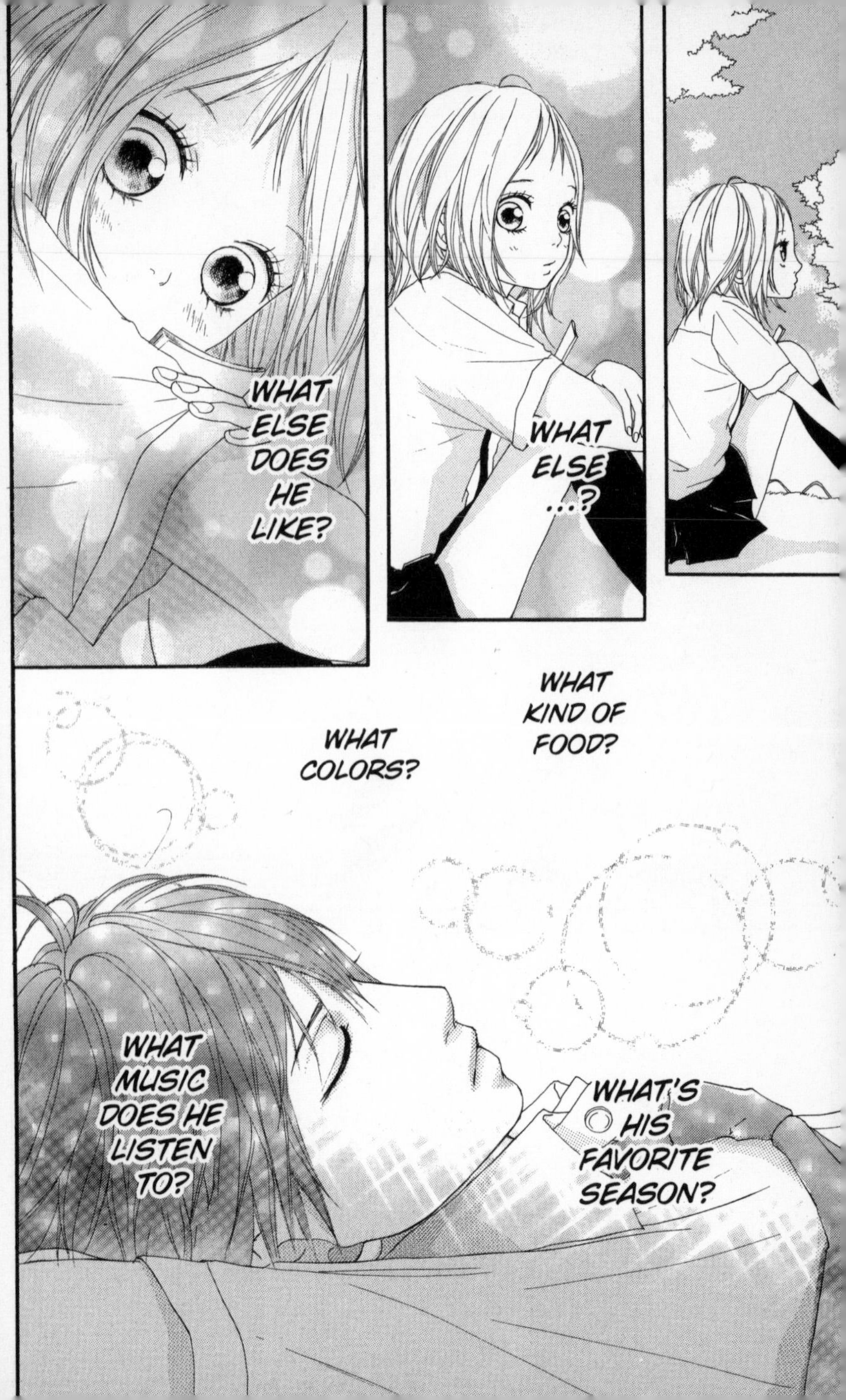
WHAT ELSE ...?
WHAT ELSE DOES HE LIKE?
WHAT KIND OF FOOD?
WHAT COLORS?
WHAT'S HIS FAVORITE SEASON?
WHAT MUSIC DOES HE LISTEN TO?

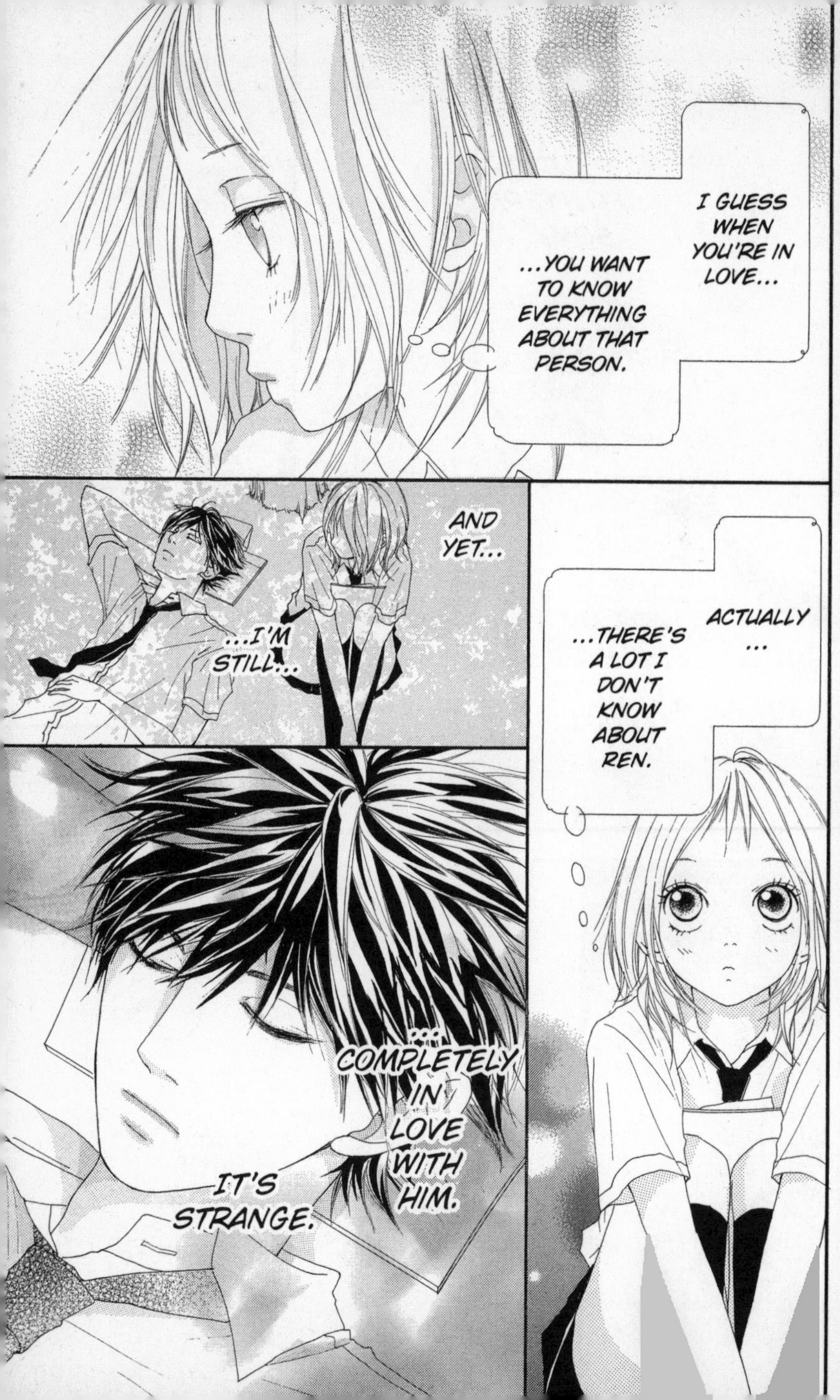
I GUESS WHEN YOU'RE IN LOVE...
...YOU WANT TO KNOW EVERYTHING ABOUT THAT PERSON.
ACTUALLY...
...THERE'S A LOT I DON'T KNOW ABOUT REN.
AND YET...
...I'M STILL...
...COMPLETELY IN LOVE WITH HIM.
IT'S STRANGE.

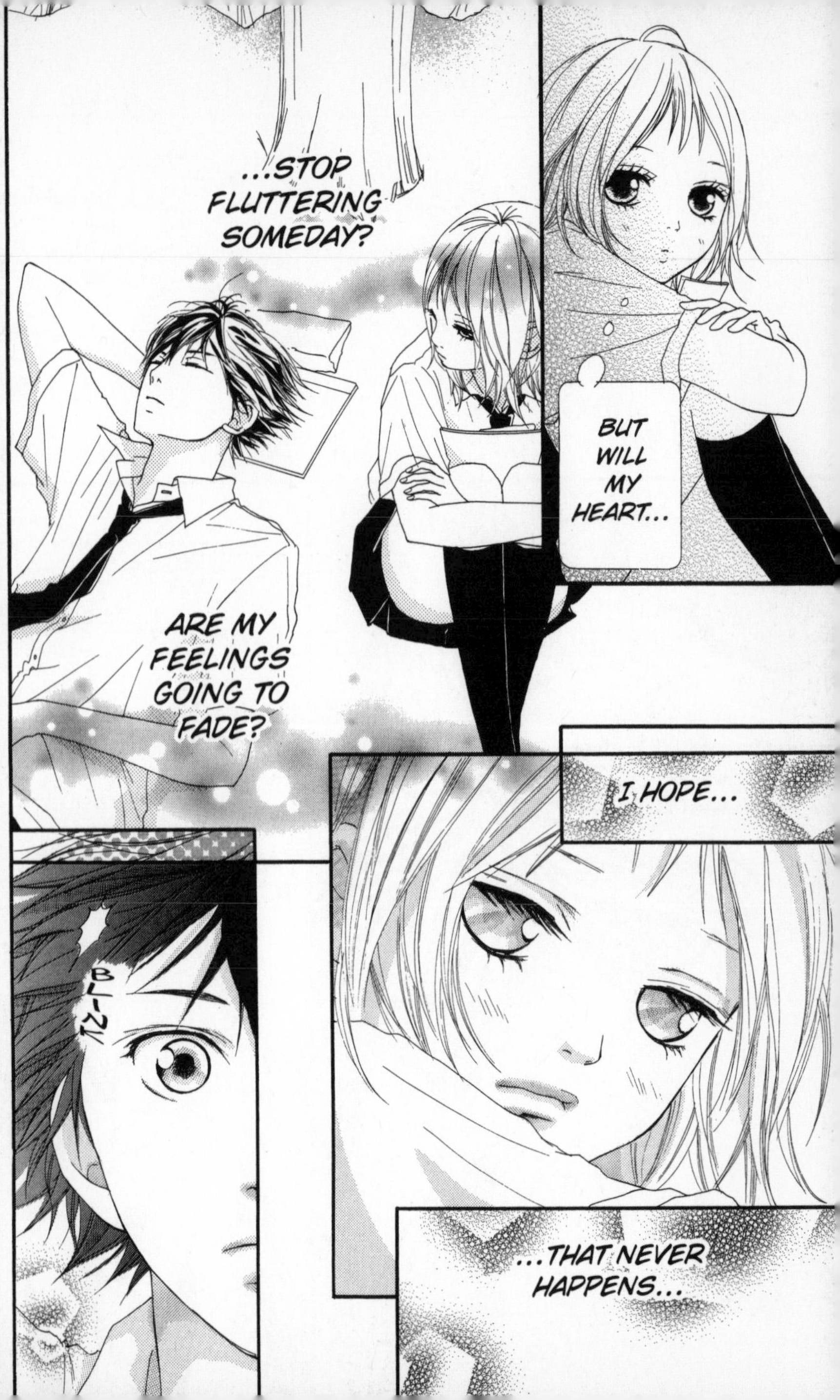
BUT WILL MY HEART...
...STOP FLUTTERING SOMEDAY?
ARE MY FEELINGS GOING TO FADE?
I HOPE...
...THAT NEVER HAPPENS...
BLINK

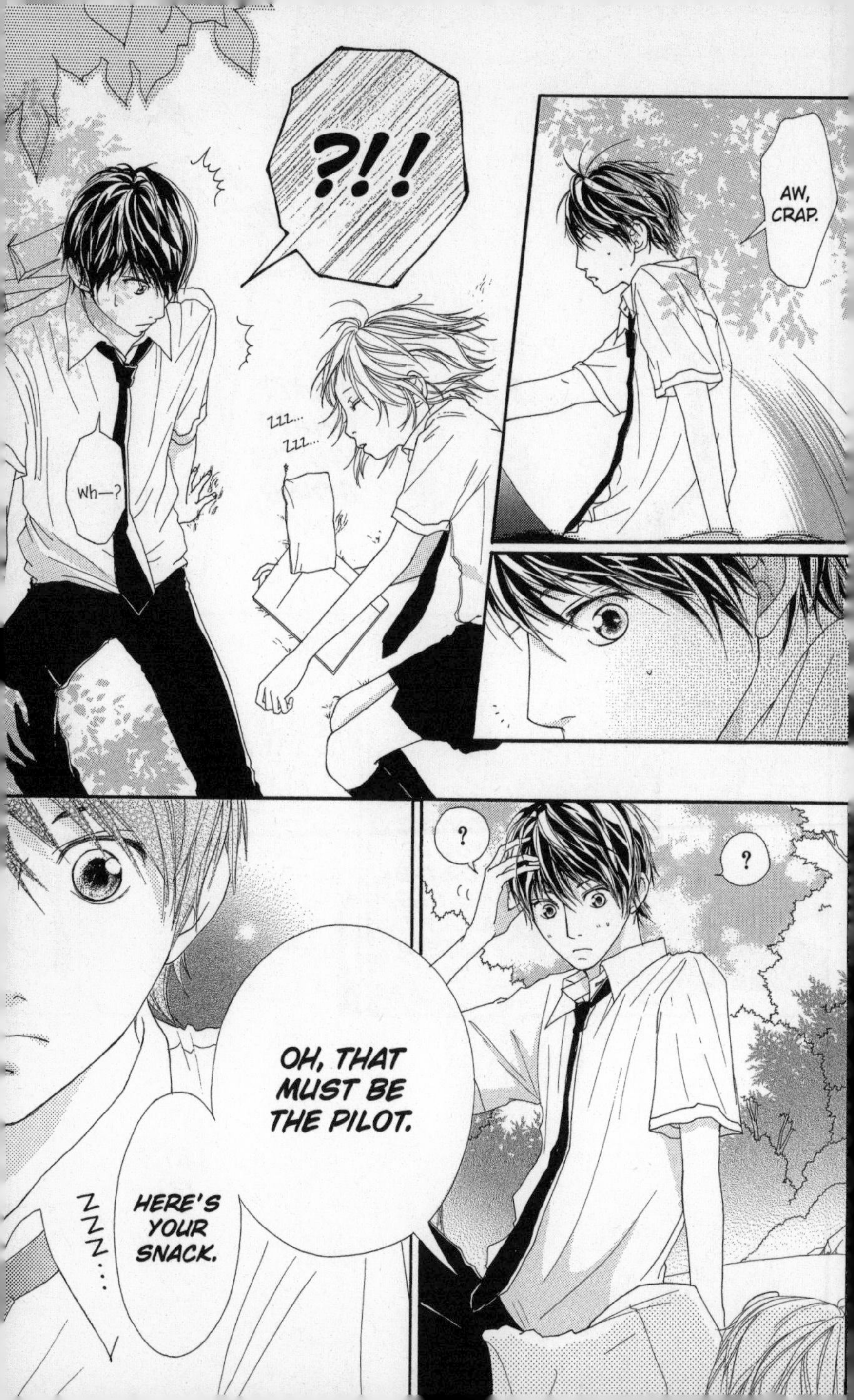
AW, CRAP.
?!!
ZZZ...
ZZZ...
Wh—?
?
?
OH, THAT MUST BE THE PILOT.
HERE'S YOUR SNACK.
ZZZ...

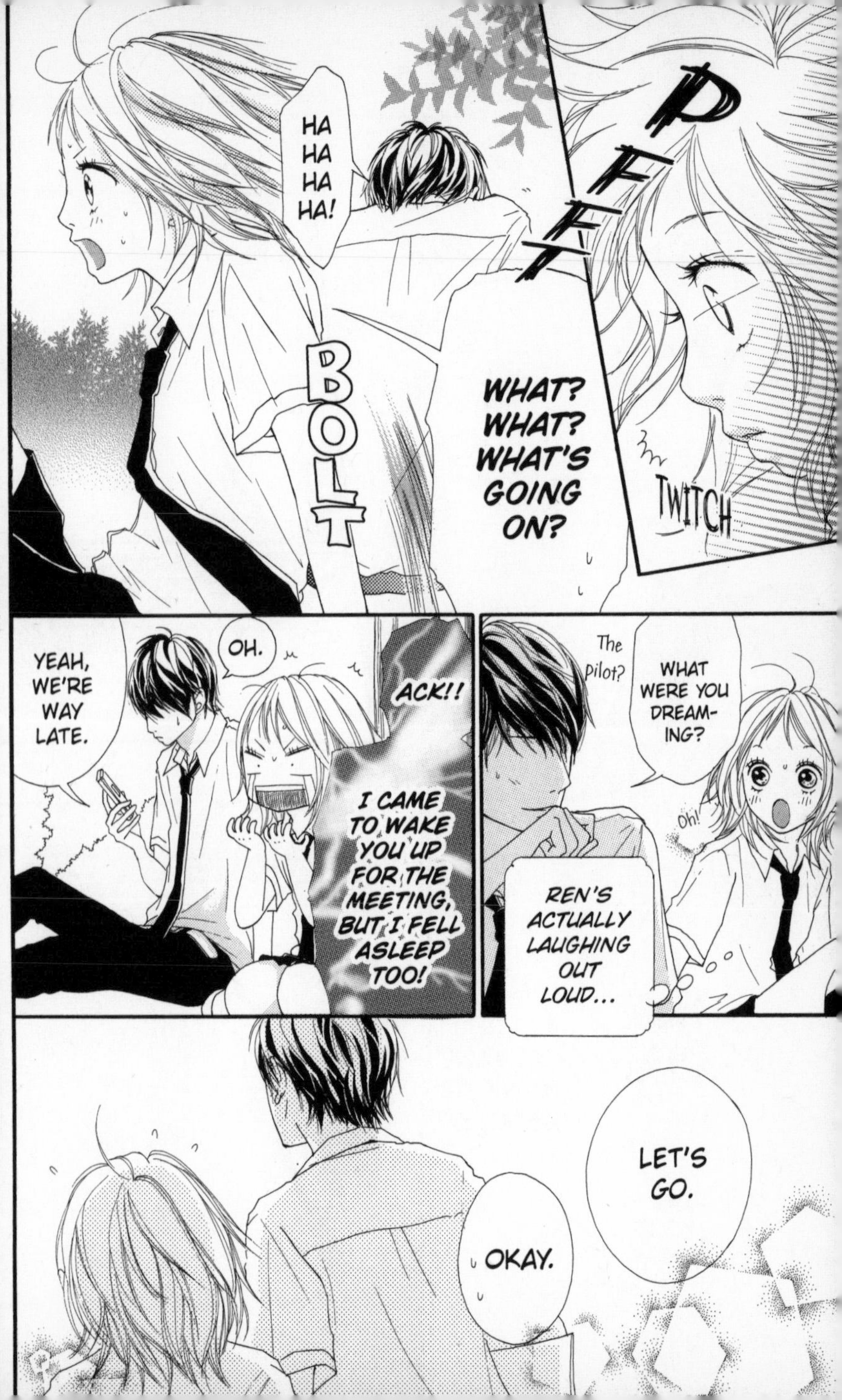
PFFT
TWITCH
HA HA HA HA!
BOLT
WHAT? WHAT? WHAT'S GOING ON?
WHAT WERE YOU DREAM-ING?
The pilot?
Oh!
REN'S ACTUALLY LAUGHING OUT LOUD...
ACK!!
I CAME TO WAKE YOU UP FOR THE MEETING, BUT I FELL ASLEEP TOO!
OH.
YEAH, WE'RE WAY LATE.
LET'S GO.
OKAY.

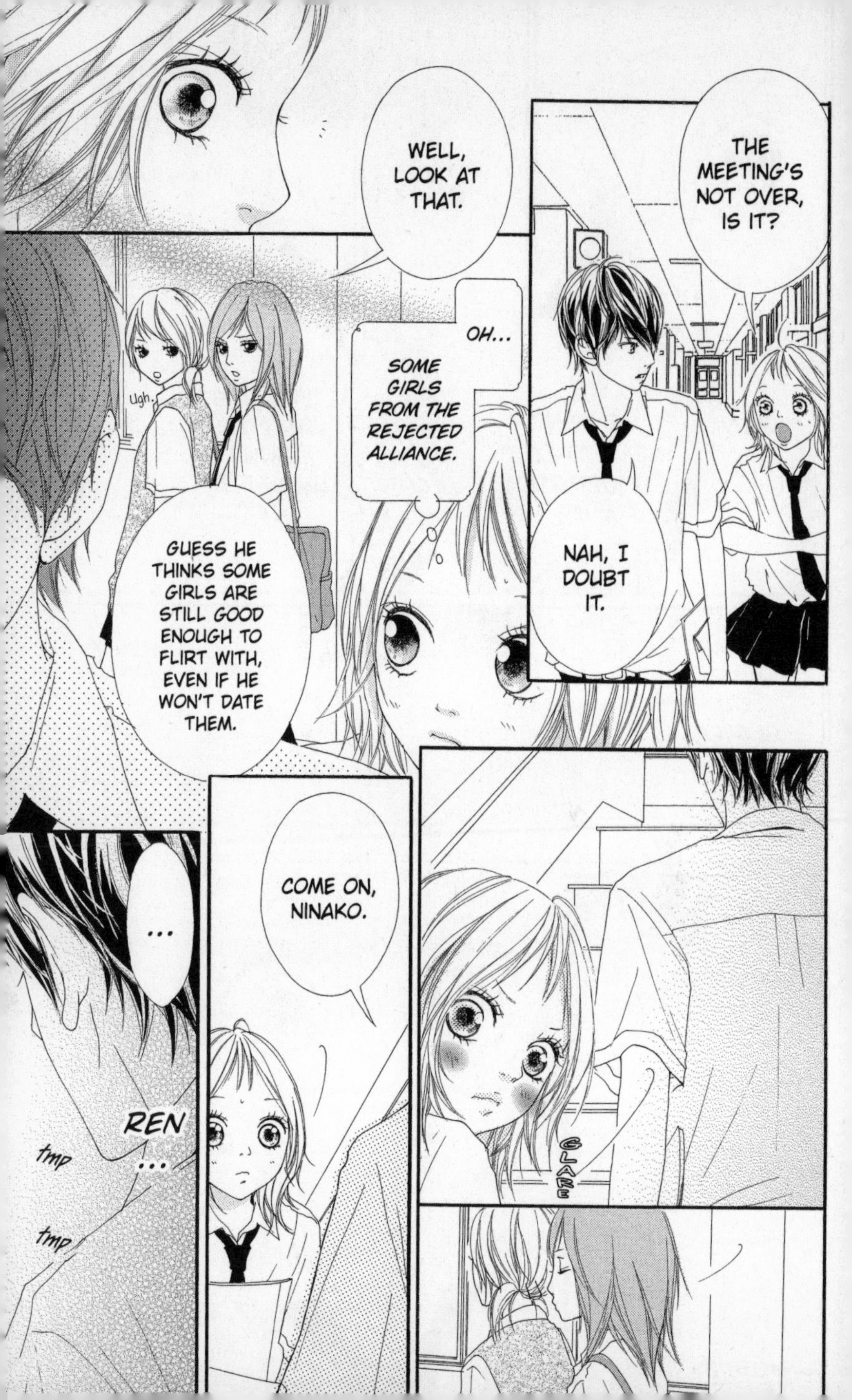
THE MEETING'S NOT OVER, IS IT?
NAH, I DOUBT IT.
WELL, LOOK AT THAT.
OH...
SOME GIRLS FROM THE REJECTED ALLIANCE.
Ugh.
GUESS HE THINKS SOME GIRLS ARE STILL GOOD ENOUGH TO FLIRT WITH, EVEN IF HE WON'T DATE THEM.
GLARE
COME ON, NINAKO.
...
REN...
tmp
tmp

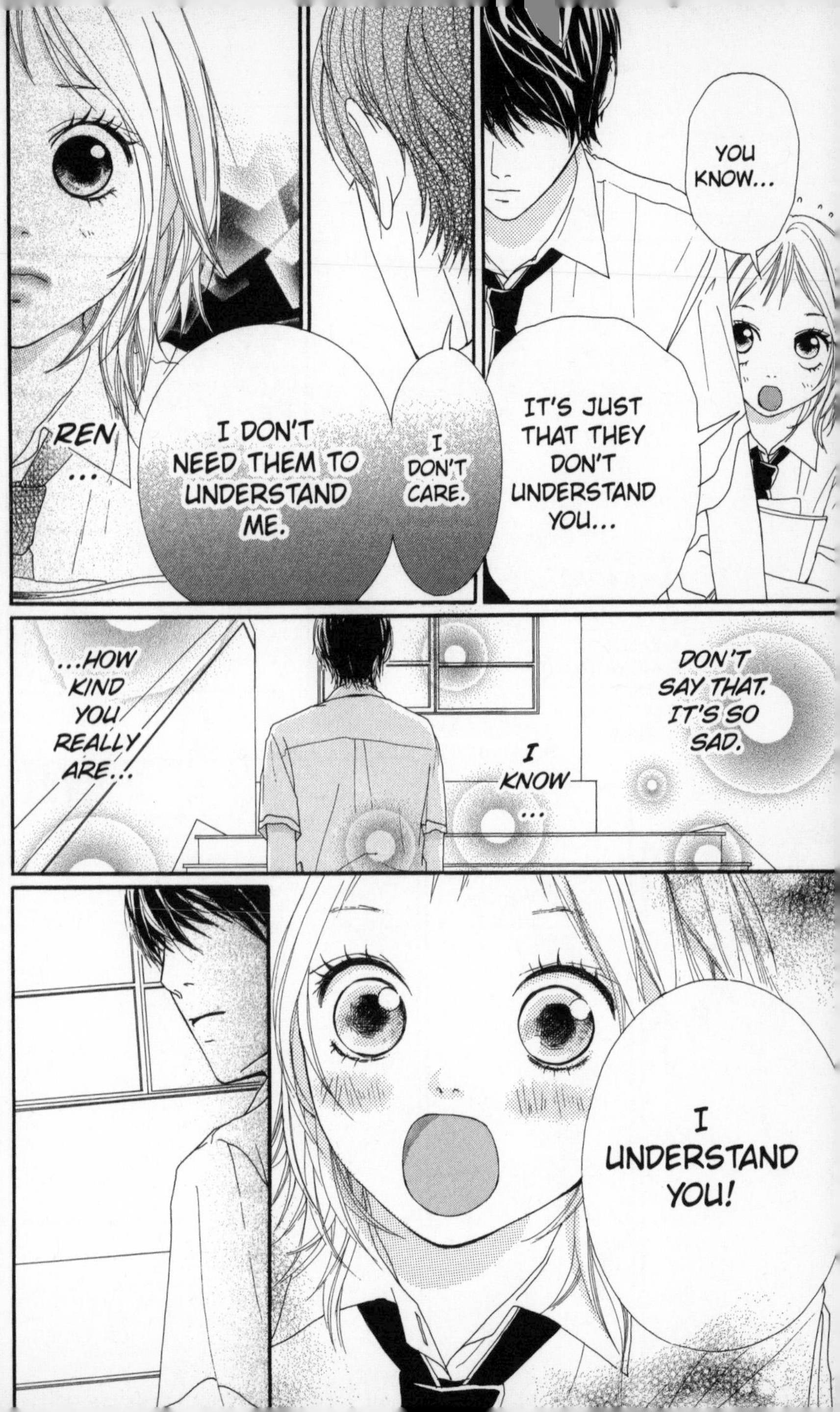
YOU KNOW...
IT'S JUST THAT THEY DON'T UNDERSTAND YOU...
I DON'T CARE.
I DON'T NEED THEM TO UNDERSTAND ME.
REN...
DON'T SAY THAT. IT'S SO SAD.
I KNOW...
...HOW KIND YOU REALLY ARE...
I UNDERSTAND YOU!

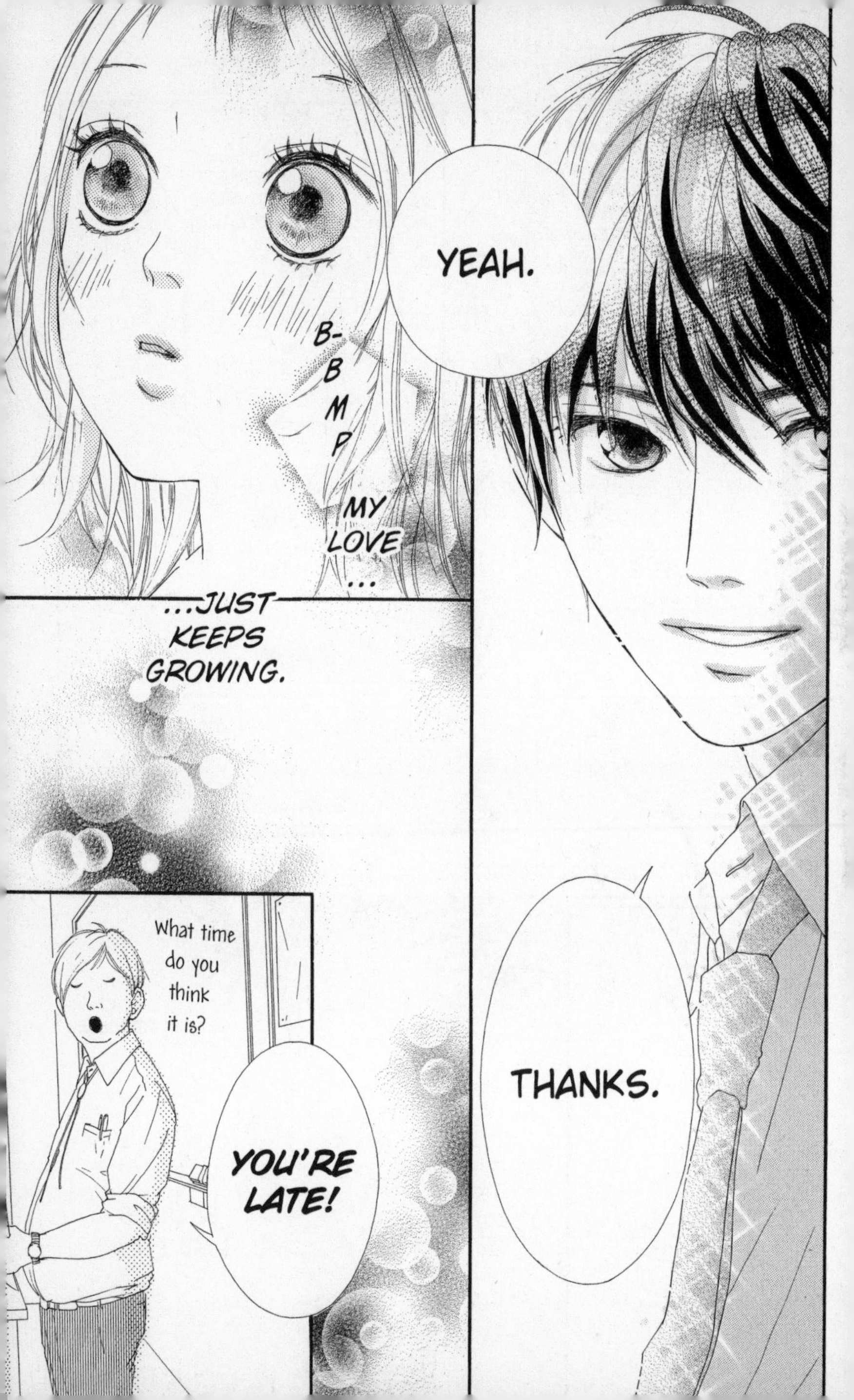
YEAH.
THANKS.
B-BMP
MY LOVE...
...JUST KEEPS GROWING.
YOU'RE LATE!
What time do you think it is?

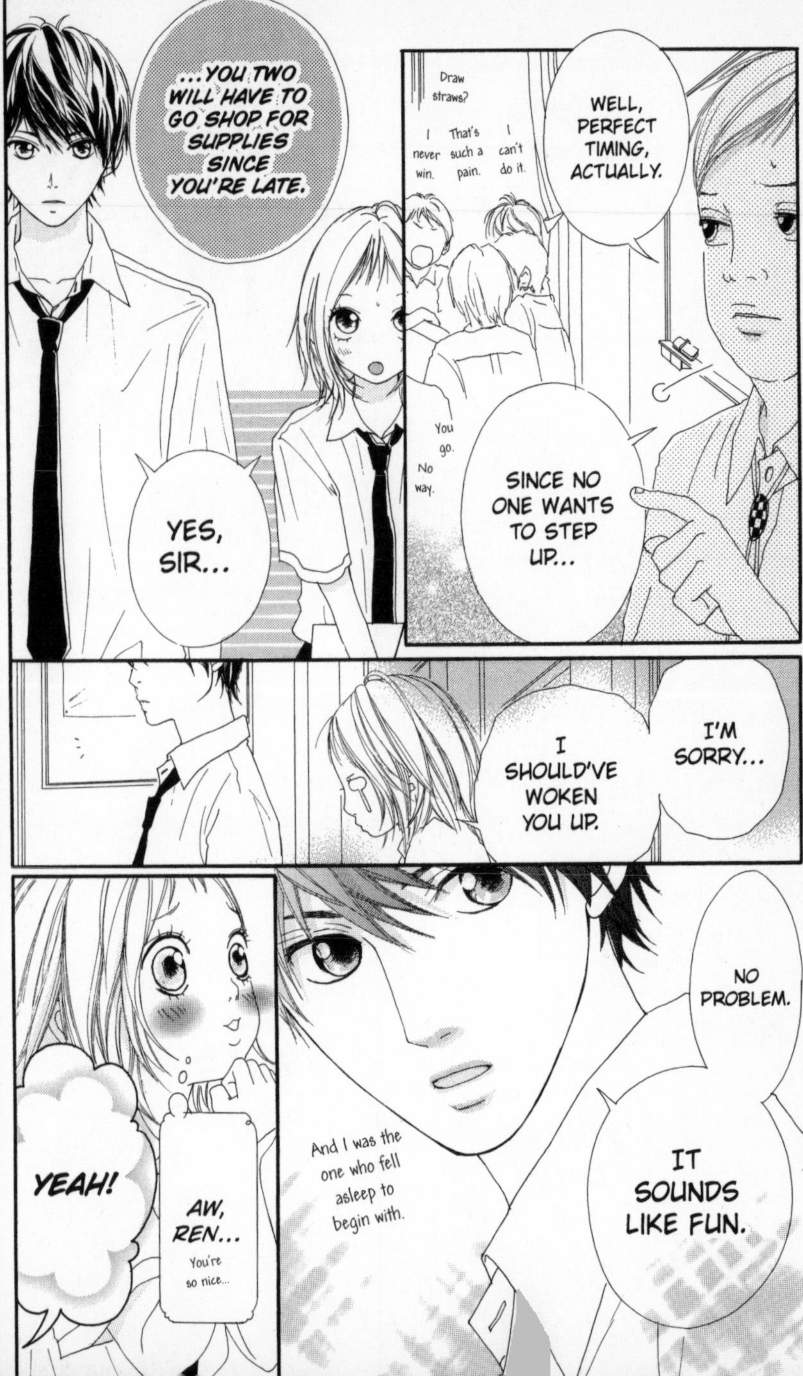
Draw straws?
I can't do it.
That's such a pain.
I never win.
WELL, PERFECT TIMING, ACTUALLY.
SINCE NO ONE WANTS TO STEP UP...
You go.
No way.
...YOU TWO WILL HAVE TO GO SHOP FOR SUPPLIES SINCE YOU'RE LATE.
YES, SIR...
I'M SORRY...
I SHOULD'VE WOKEN YOU UP.
NO PROBLEM.
IT SOUNDS LIKE FUN.
And I was the one who fell asleep to begin with.
AW, REN...
You're so nice...
YEAH!

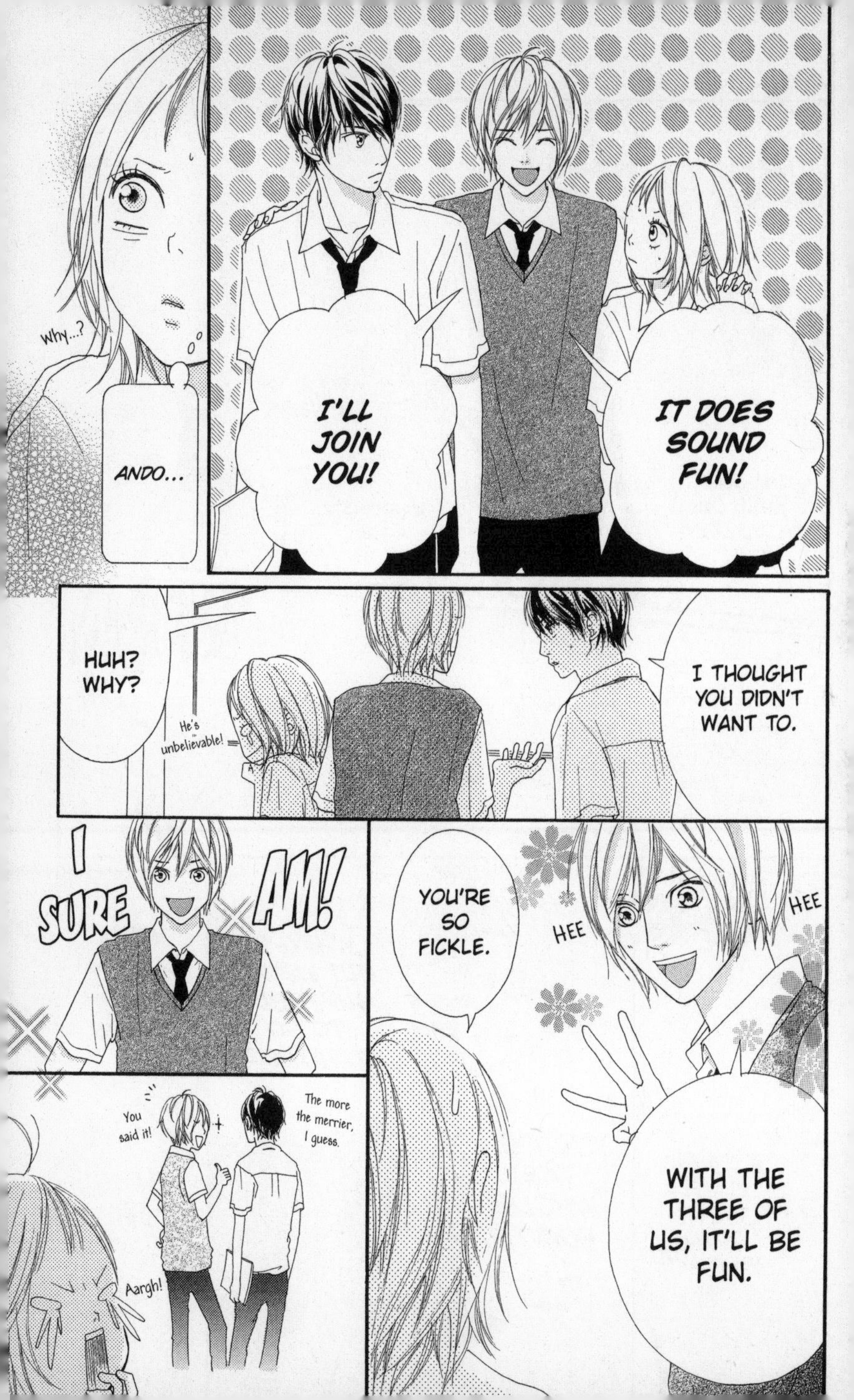
IT DOES SOUND FUN!
I'LL JOIN YOU!
Why...?
ANDO...
I THOUGHT YOU DIDN'T WANT TO.
HUH? WHY?
He's unbelievable!
HEE
YOU'RE SO FICKLE.
HEE
WITH THE THREE OF US, IT'LL BE FUN.
I SURE AM!
The more the merrier, I guess.
You said it!
Aargh!

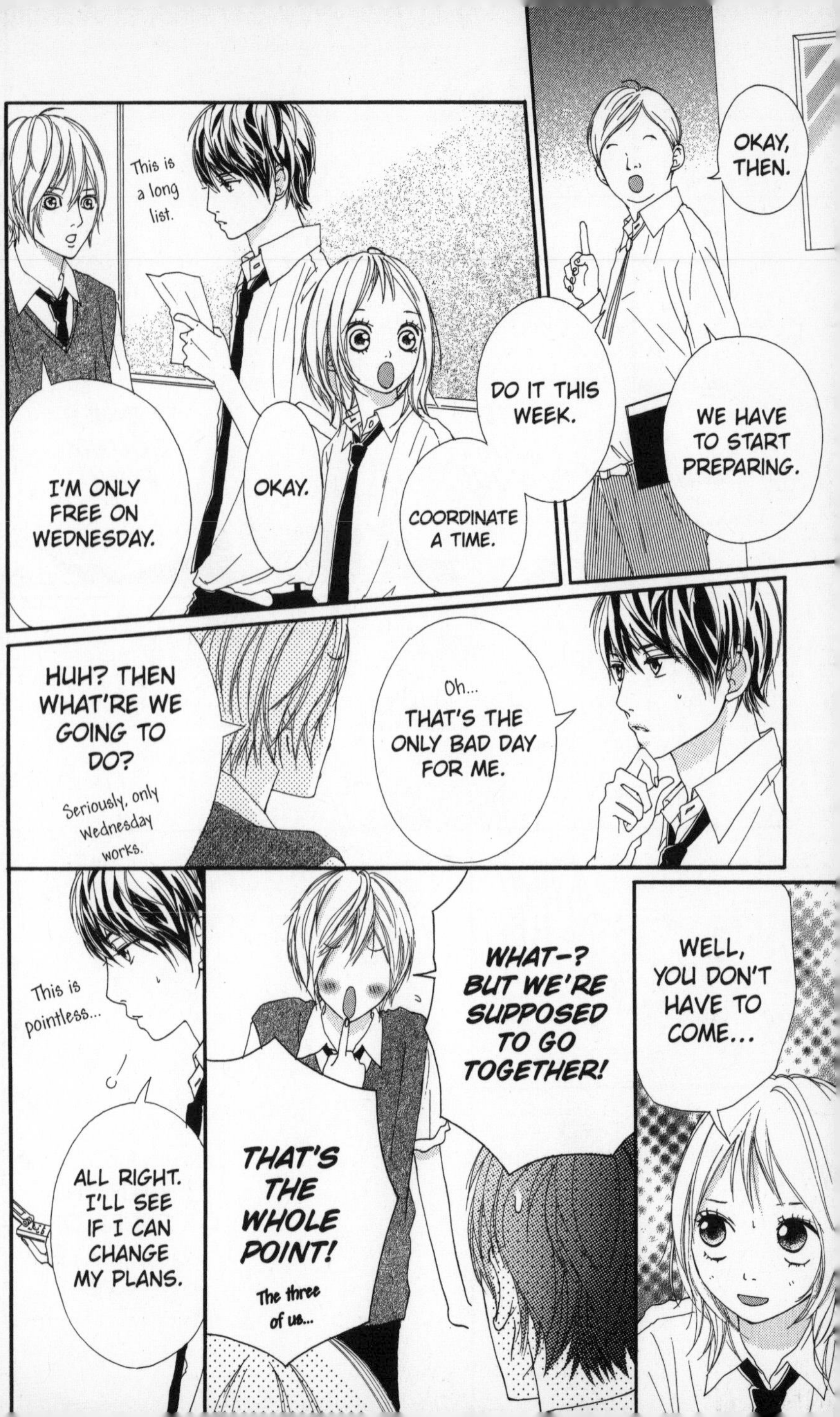
OKAY, THEN.
WE HAVE TO START PREPARING.
DO IT THIS WEEK.
COORDINATE A TIME.
OKAY.
This is a long list.
I'M ONLY FREE ON WEDNESDAY.
Oh...
THAT'S THE ONLY BAD DAY FOR ME.
HUH? THEN WHAT'RE WE GOING TO DO?
Seriously, only Wednesday works.
WELL, YOU DON'T HAVE TO COME...
WHAT-? BUT WE'RE SUPPOSED TO GO TOGETHER!
THAT'S THE WHOLE POINT!
The three of us...
This is pointless...
ALL RIGHT. I'LL SEE IF I CAN CHANGE MY PLANS.

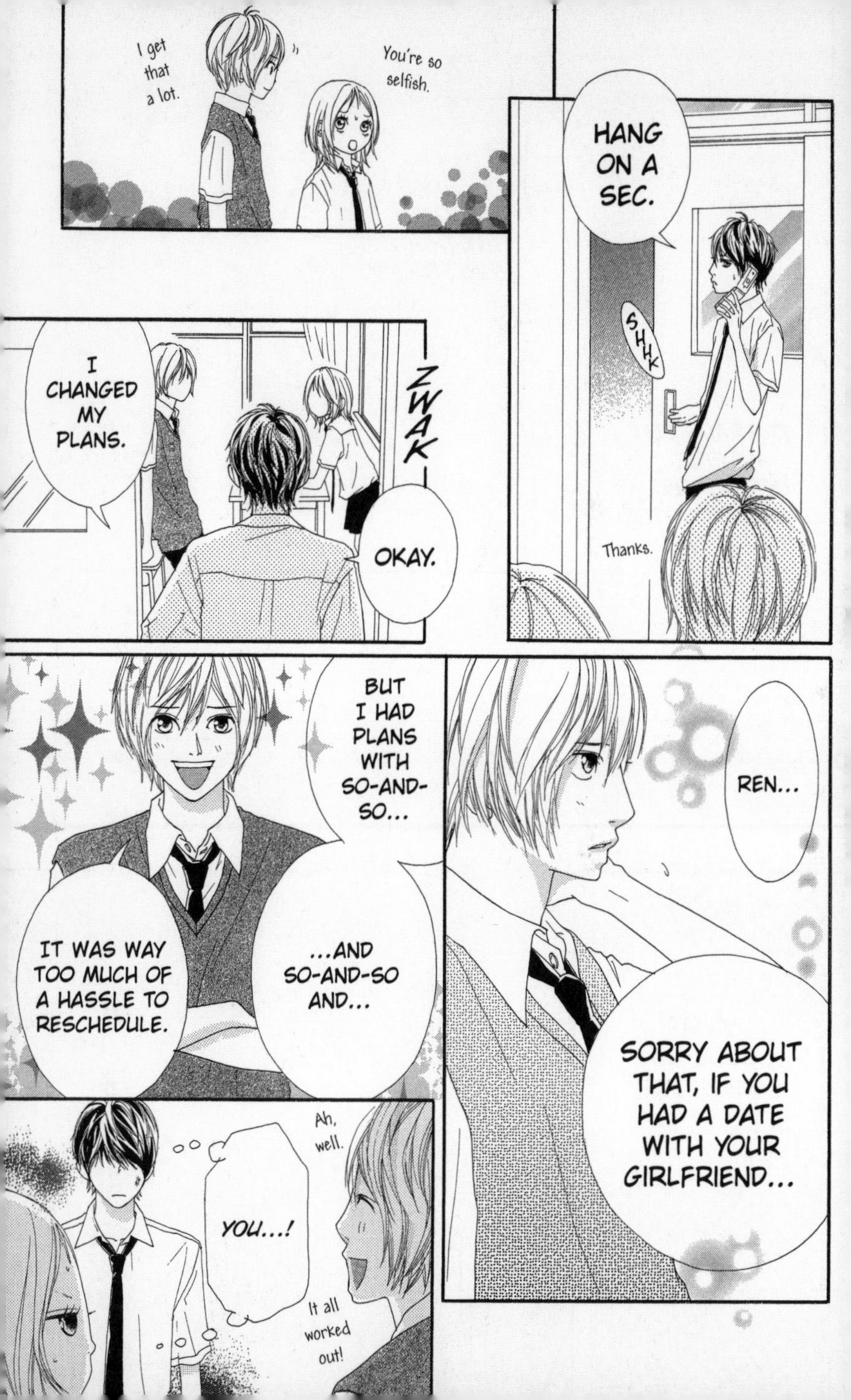
You're so selfish.
I get that a lot.
HANG ON A SEC.
SHHK
Thanks.
I CHANGED MY PLANS.
ZWAK
OKAY.
REN...
SORRY ABOUT THAT, IF YOU HAD A DATE WITH YOUR GIRLFRIEND...
BUT I HAD PLANS WITH SO-AND-SO...
...AND SO-AND-SO AND...
IT WAS WAY TOO MUCH OF A HASSLE TO RESCHEDULE.
Ah, well.
It all worked out!
YOU...!

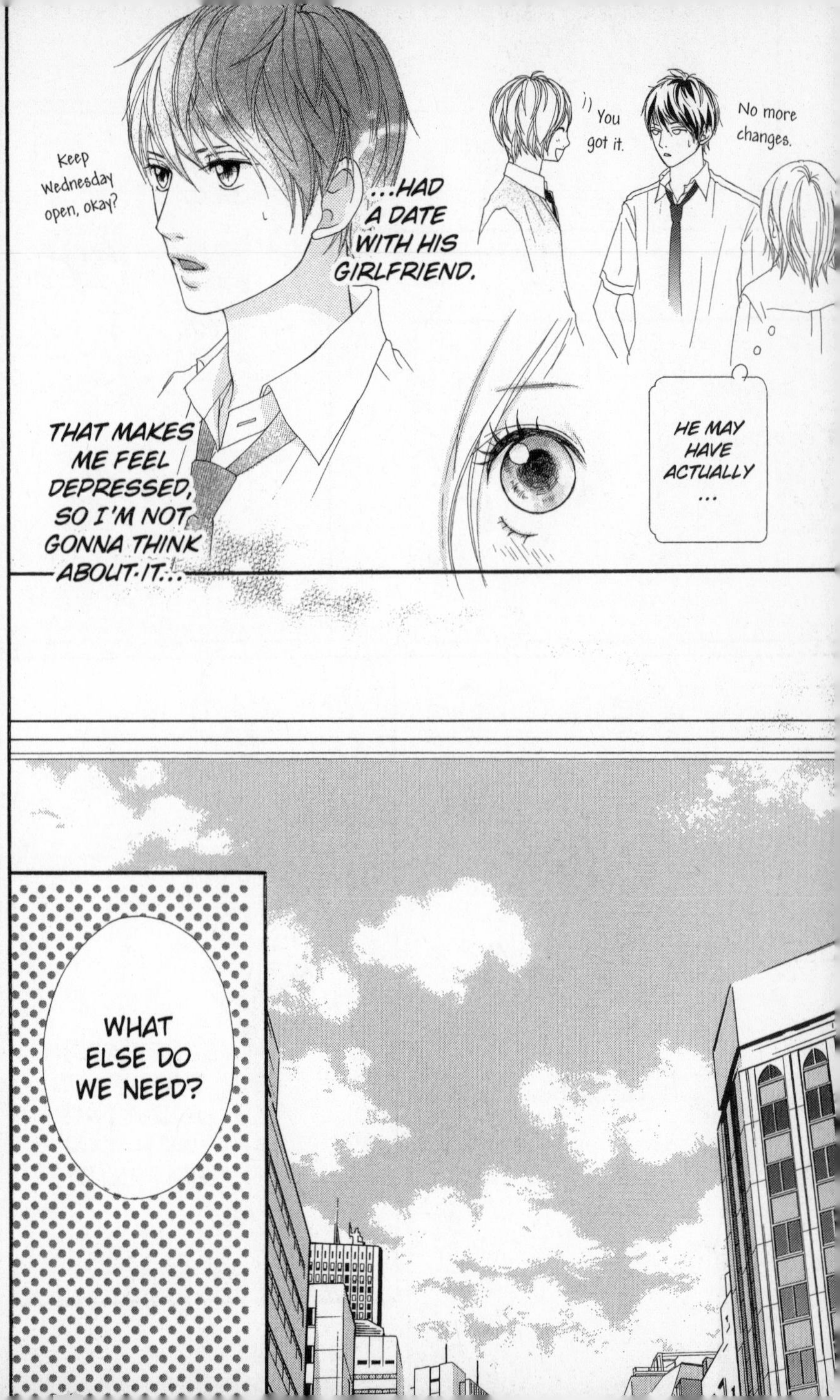
No more changes.
You got it.
HE MAY HAVE ACTUALLY ...
...HAD A DATE WITH HIS GIRLFRIEND.
Keep Wednesday open, okay?
THAT MAKES ME FEEL DEPRESSED, SO I'M NOT GONNA THINK ABOUT IT...
WHAT ELSE DO WE NEED?

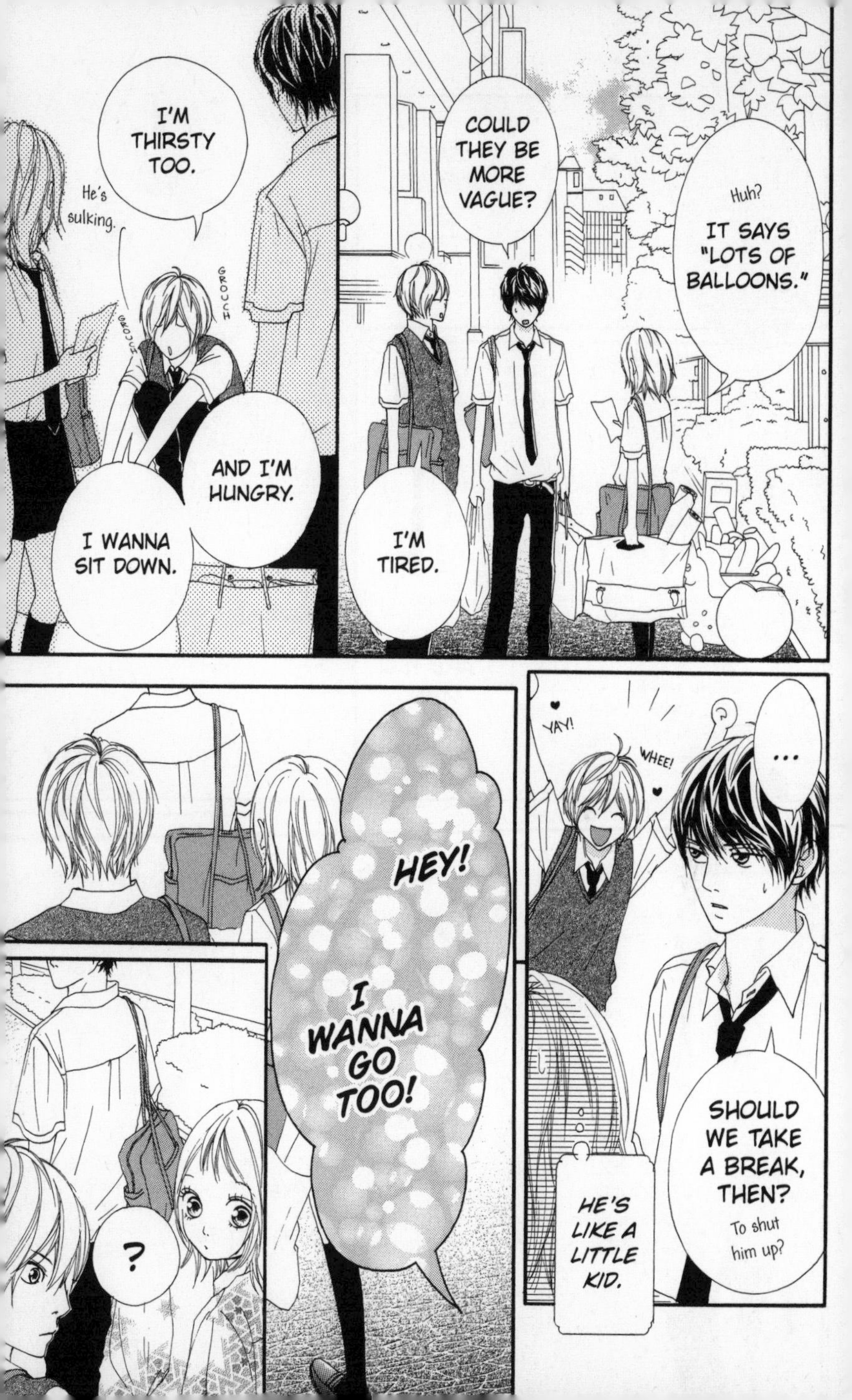
Huh?
IT SAYS "LOTS OF BALLOONS."
COULD THEY BE MORE VAGUE?
I'M TIRED.
I'M THIRSTY TOO.
He's sulking.
GROUCH
GROUCH
AND I'M HUNGRY.
I WANNA SIT DOWN.
YAY!
WHEE!
...
SHOULD WE TAKE A BREAK, THEN?
To shut him up?
HE'S LIKE A LITTLE KID.
HEY!
I WANNA GO TOO!
?

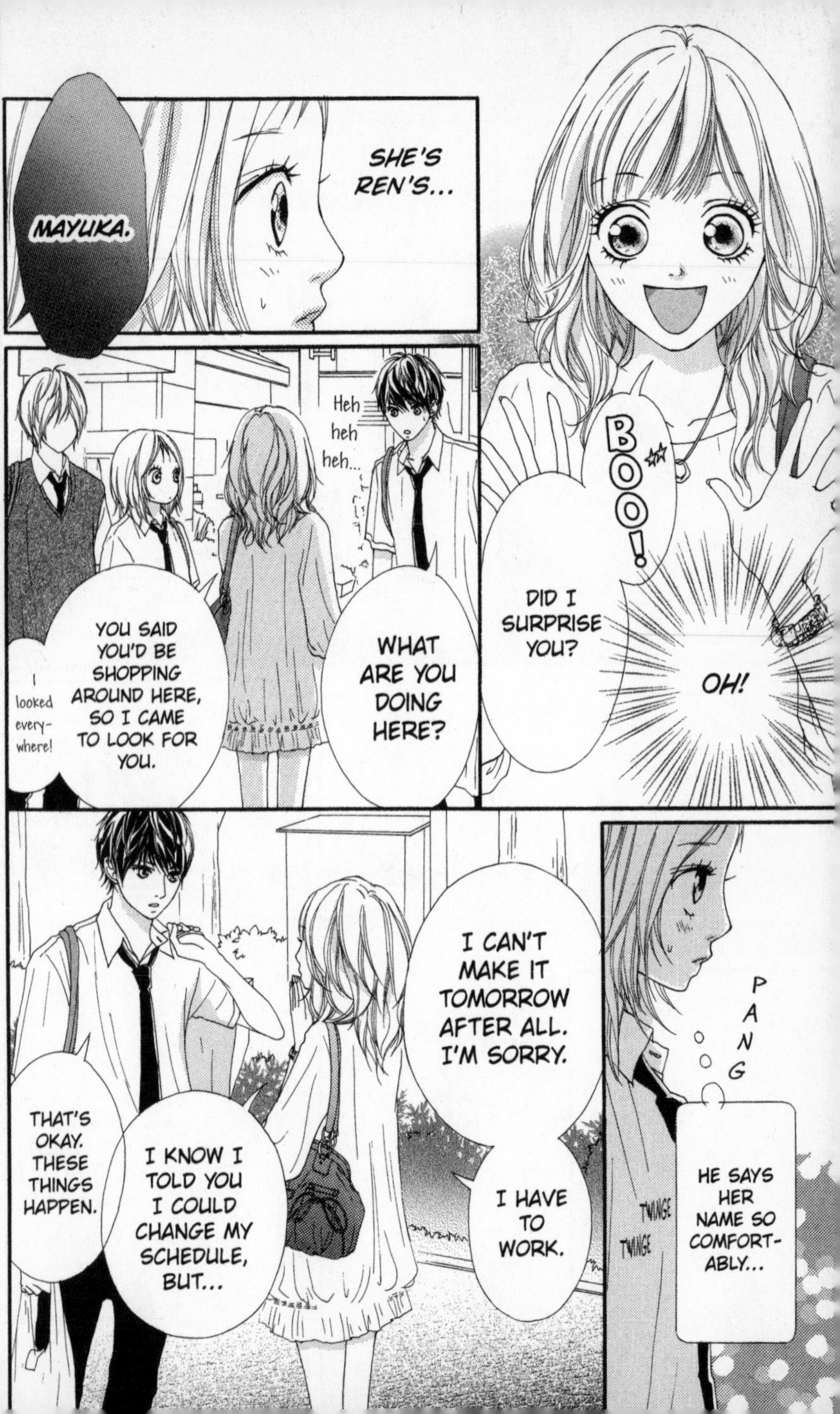
BOO!
DID I SURPRISE YOU?
OH!
SHE'S REN'S...
MAYUKA.
Heh heh heh...
WHAT ARE YOU DOING HERE?
YOU SAID YOU'D BE SHOPPING AROUND HERE, SO I CAME TO LOOK FOR YOU.
I looked every-where!
PANG
HE SAYS HER NAME SO COMFORT-ABLY...
TWINGE
TWINGE
I CAN'T MAKE IT TOMORROW AFTER ALL. I'M SORRY.
I HAVE TO WORK.
I KNOW I TOLD YOU I COULD CHANGE MY SCHEDULE, BUT...
THAT'S OKAY. THESE THINGS HAPPEN.

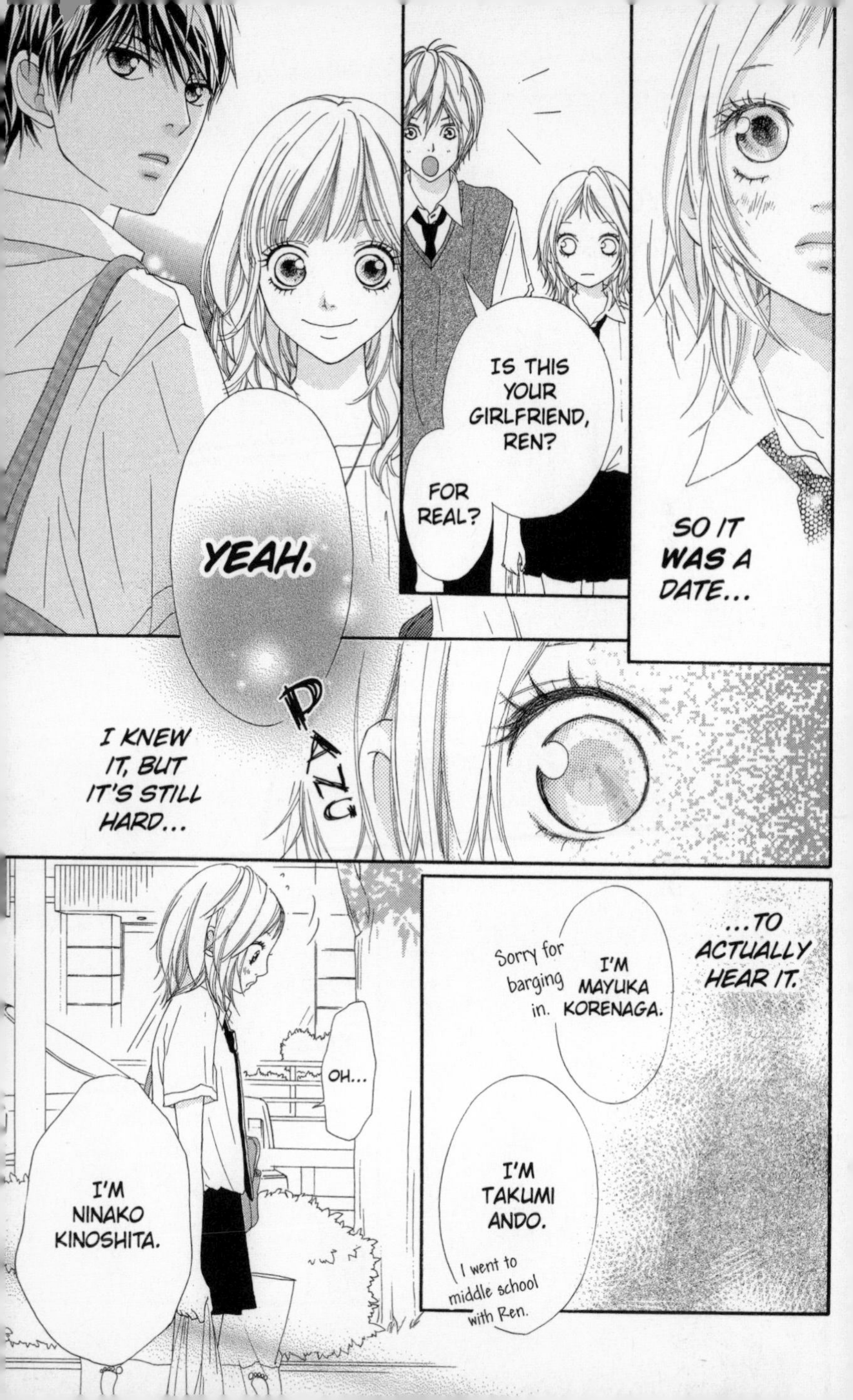
SO IT WAS A DATE...
IS THIS YOUR GIRLFRIEND, REN?
FOR REAL?
YEAH.
PAZU
I KNEW IT, BUT IT'S STILL HARD...
...TO ACTUALLY HEAR IT.
I'M MAYUKA KORENAGA.
Sorry for barging in.
I'M TAKUMI ANDO.
I went to middle school with Ren.
OH...
I'M NINAKO KINOSHITA.

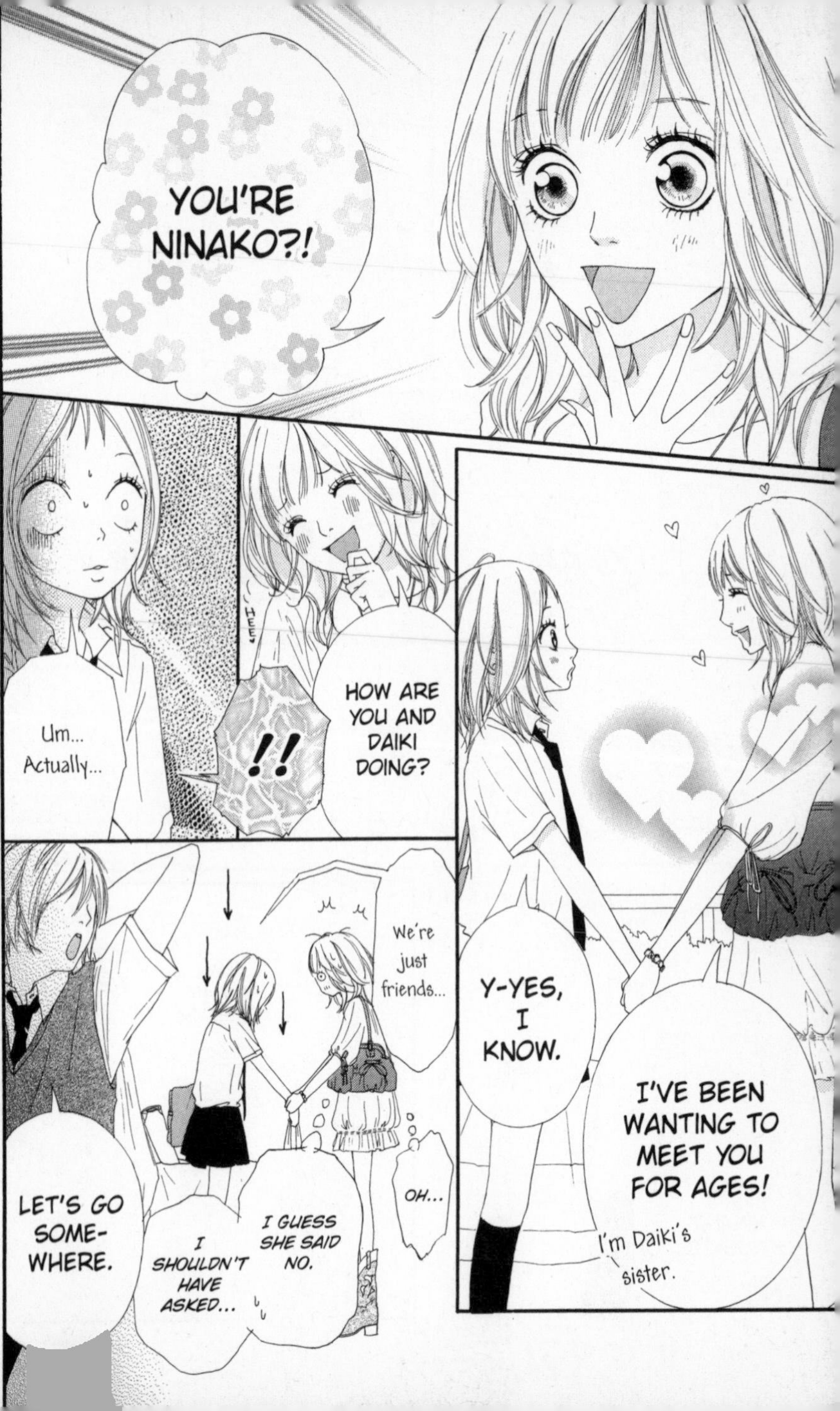
YOU'RE NINAKO?!
I'VE BEEN WANTING TO MEET YOU FOR AGES!
I'm Daiki's sister.
Y-YES, I KNOW.
HEE
HOW ARE YOU AND DAIKI DOING?
!!
Um... Actually...
We're just friends...
OH...
I GUESS SHE SAID NO.
I SHOULDN'T HAVE ASKED...
LET'S GO SOME-WHERE.

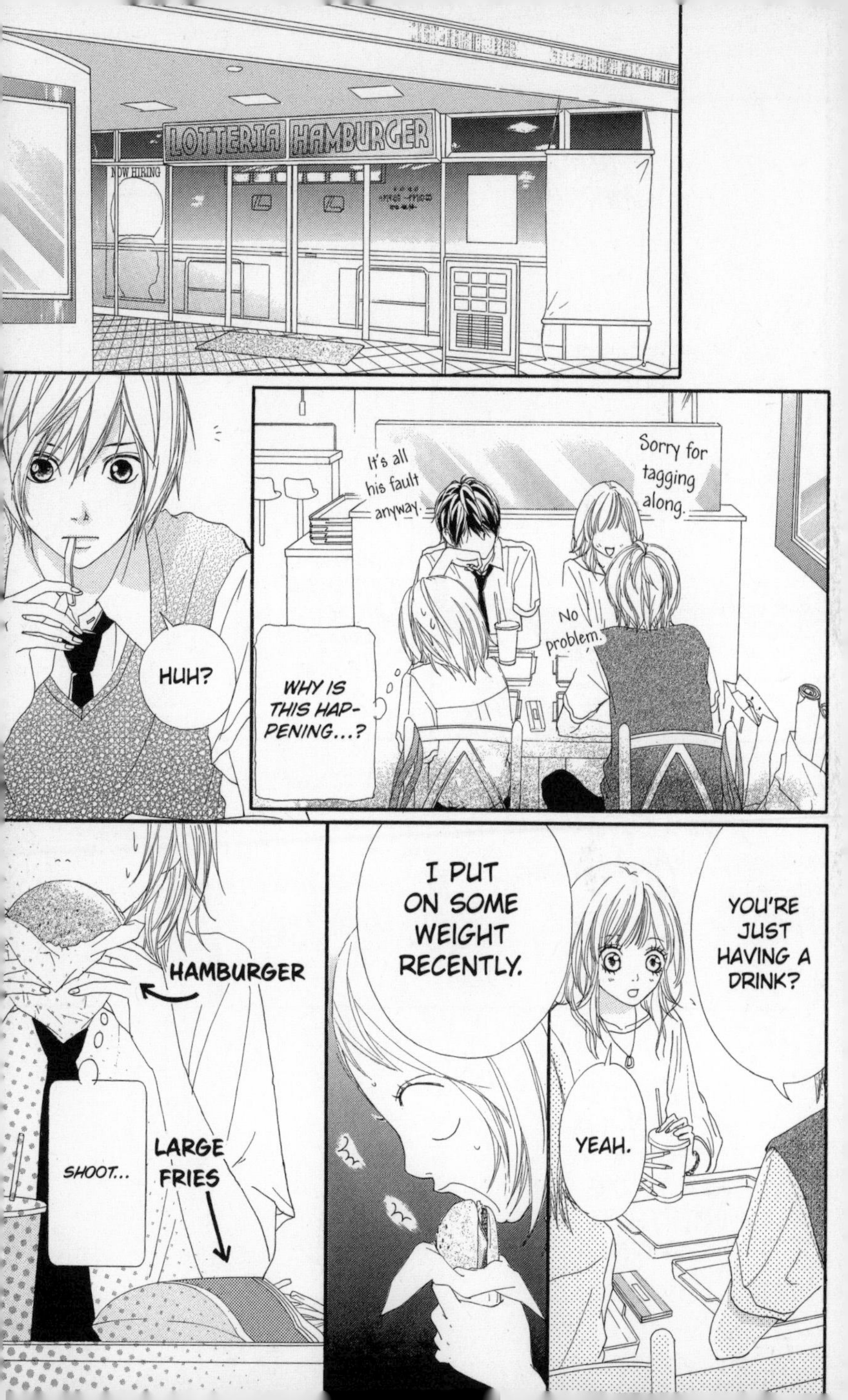
LOTTERIA HAMBURGER
NOW HIRING
Sorry for tagging along.
No problem.
It's all his fault anyway.
WHY IS THIS HAP-PENING...?
HUH?
YOU'RE JUST HAVING A DRINK?
YEAH.
I PUT ON SOME WEIGHT RECENTLY.
HAMBURGER
LARGE FRIES
SHOOT...

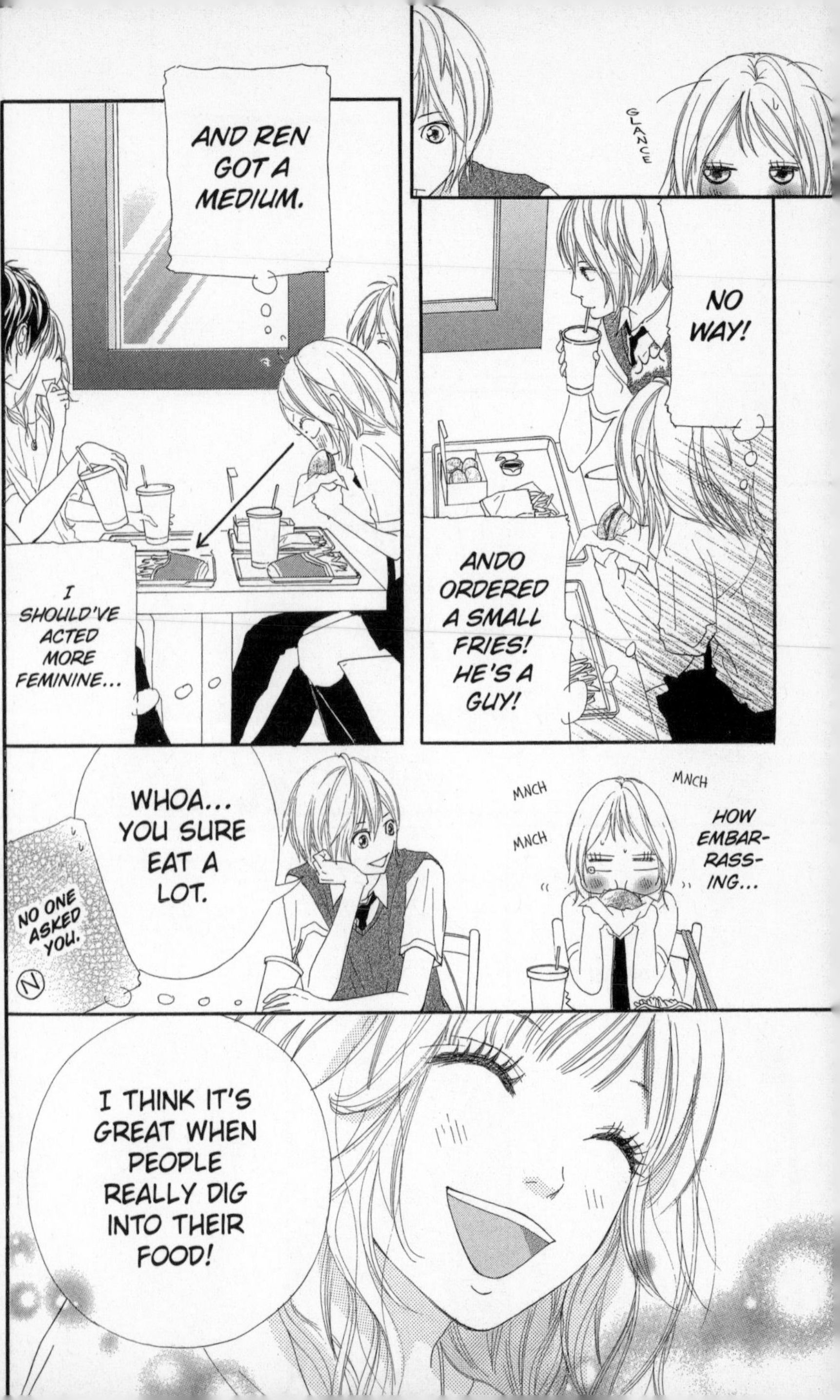

GLANCE
NO WAY!
ANDO ORDERED A SMALL FRIES! HE'S A GUY!
AND REN GOT A MEDIUM.
I SHOULD'VE ACTED MORE FEMININE...
MNCH
HOW EMBAR-RASS-ING...
MNCH
MNCH
WHOA... YOU SURE EAT A LOT.
NO ONE ASKED YOU.
I THINK IT'S GREAT WHEN PEOPLE REALLY DIG INTO THEIR FOOD!

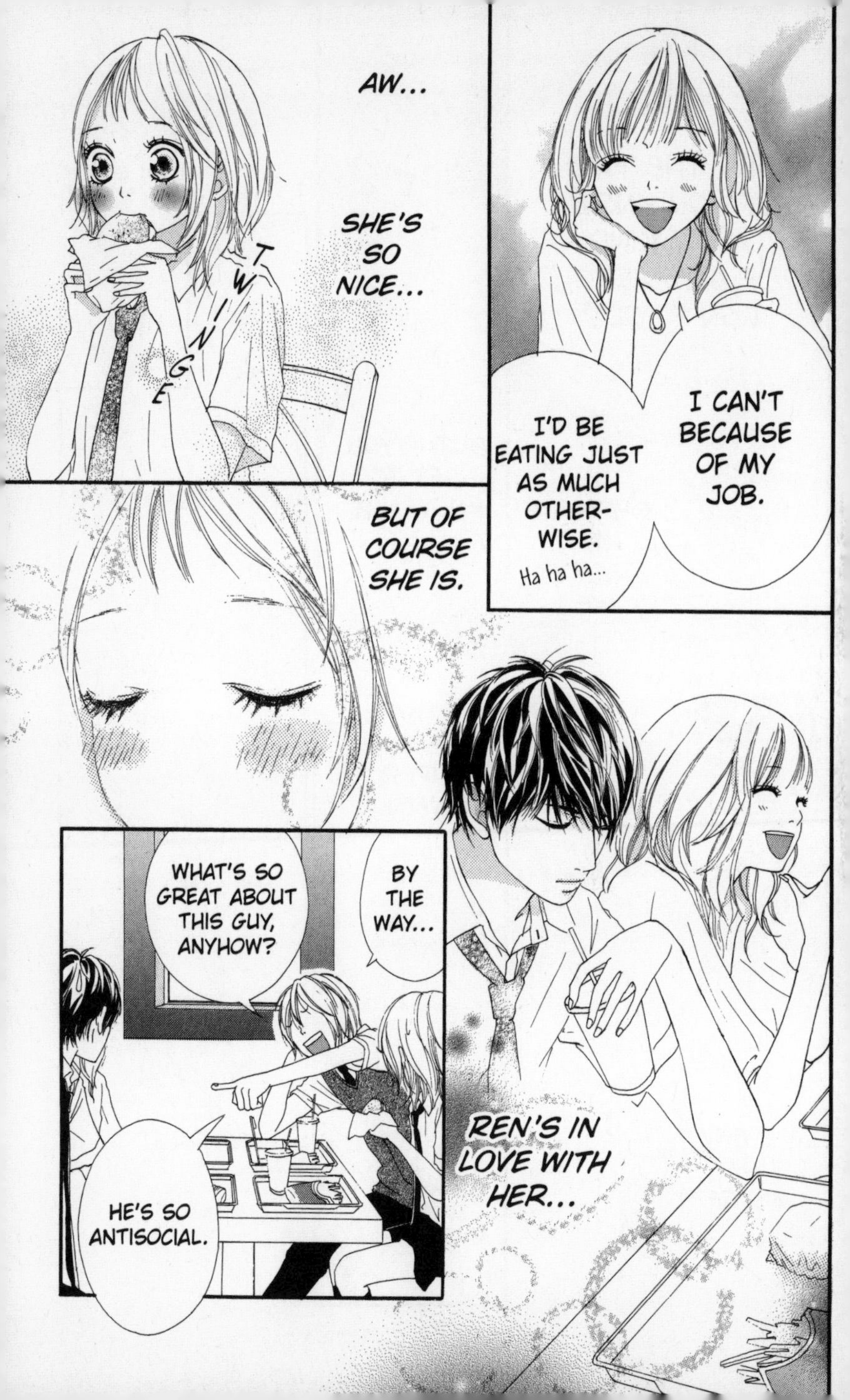
I CAN'T BECAUSE OF MY JOB.
I'D BE EATING JUST AS MUCH OTHERWISE.
Ha ha ha...
AW...
SHE'S SO NICE...
TWINGE
BUT OF COURSE SHE IS.
REN'S IN LOVE WITH HER...
BY THE WAY...
WHAT'S SO GREAT ABOUT THIS GUY, ANYHOW?
HE'S SO ANTISOCIAL.

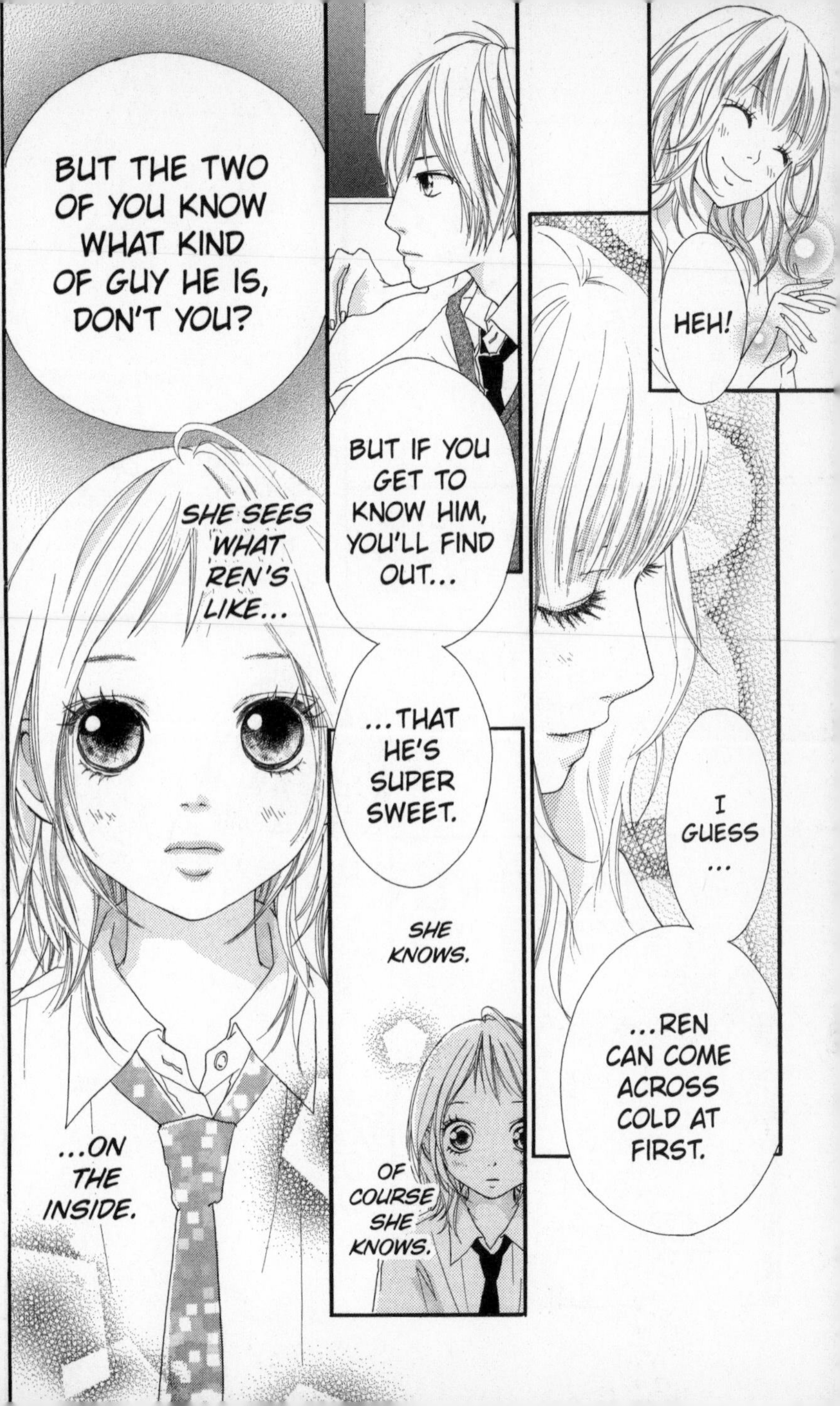
HEH!
I GUESS...
...REN CAN COME ACROSS COLD AT FIRST.
BUT IF YOU GET TO KNOW HIM, YOU'LL FIND OUT...
...THAT HE'S SUPER SWEET.
BUT THE TWO OF YOU KNOW WHAT KIND OF GUY HE IS, DON'T YOU?
SHE KNOWS.
OF COURSE SHE KNOWS.
SHE SEES WHAT REN'S LIKE...
...ON THE INSIDE.

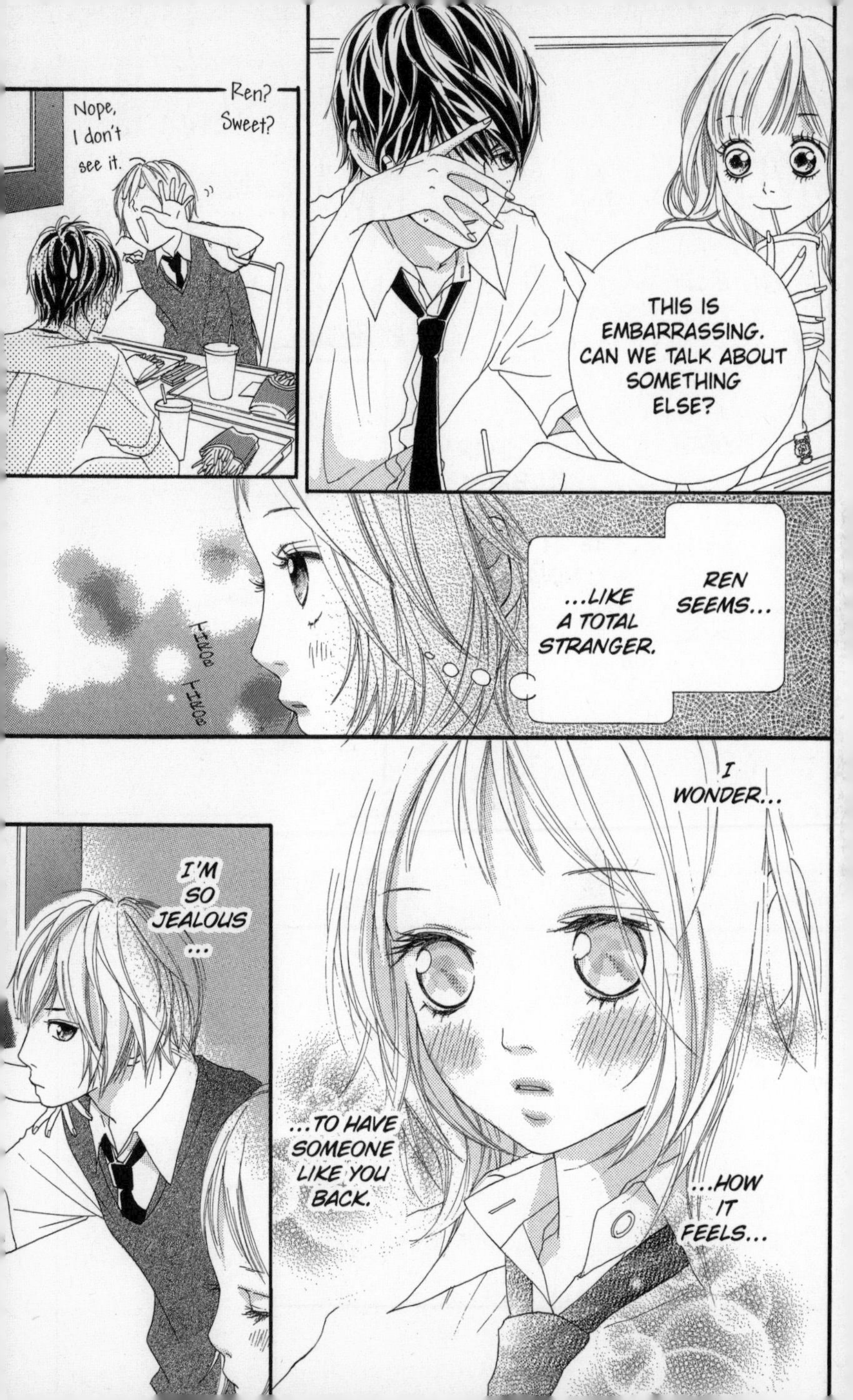
THIS IS EMBARRASSING. CAN WE TALK ABOUT SOMETHING ELSE?
Ren? Sweet?
Nope, I don't see it.
REN SEEMS...
...LIKE A TOTAL STRANGER.
I WONDER...
...HOW IT FEELS...
I'M SO JEALOUS...
...TO HAVE SOMEONE LIKE YOU BACK.

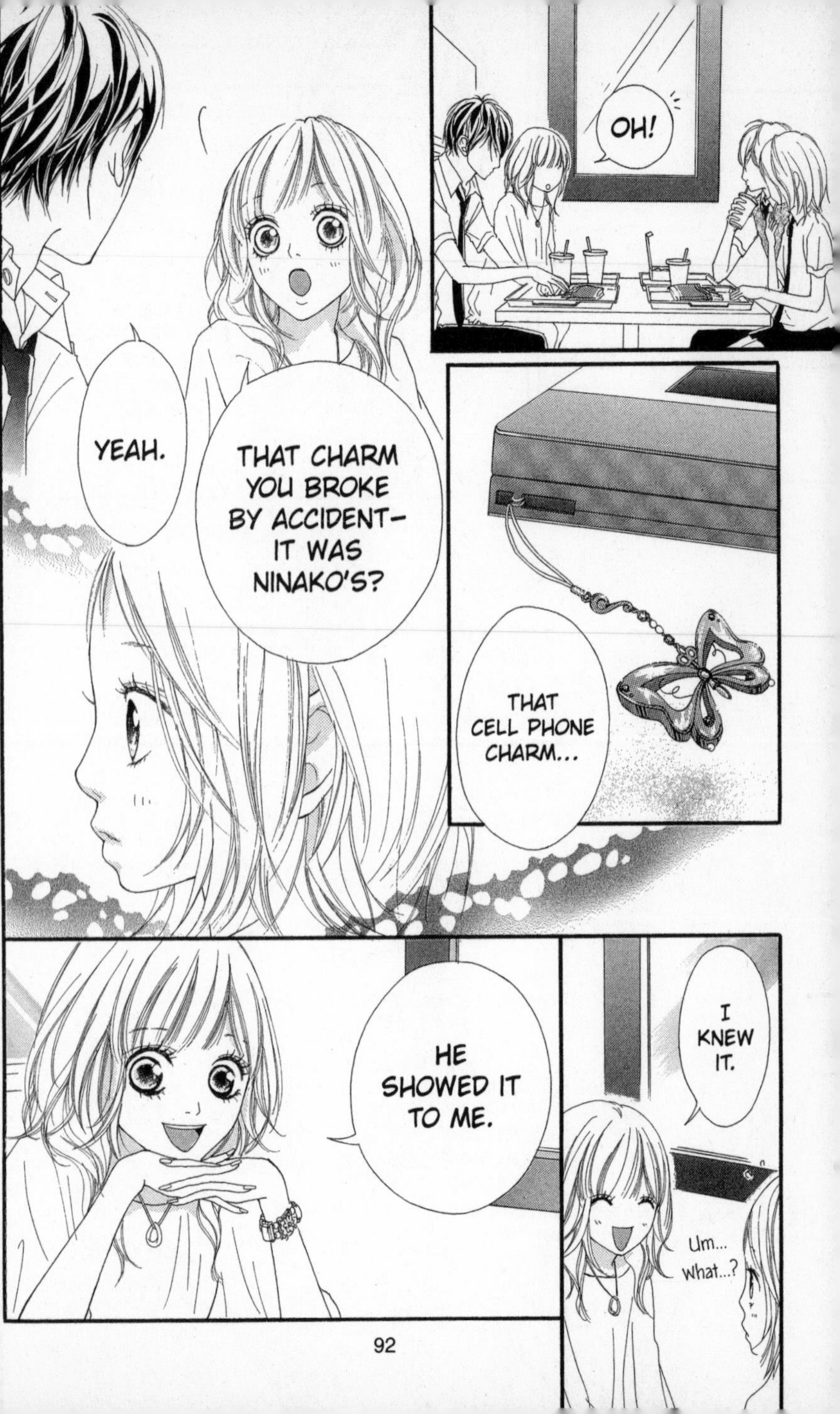
OH!
THAT CELL PHONE CHARM...
THAT CHARM YOU BROKE BY ACCIDENT-IT WAS NINAKO'S?
YEAH.
I KNEW IT.
Um... what...?
HE SHOWED IT TO ME.

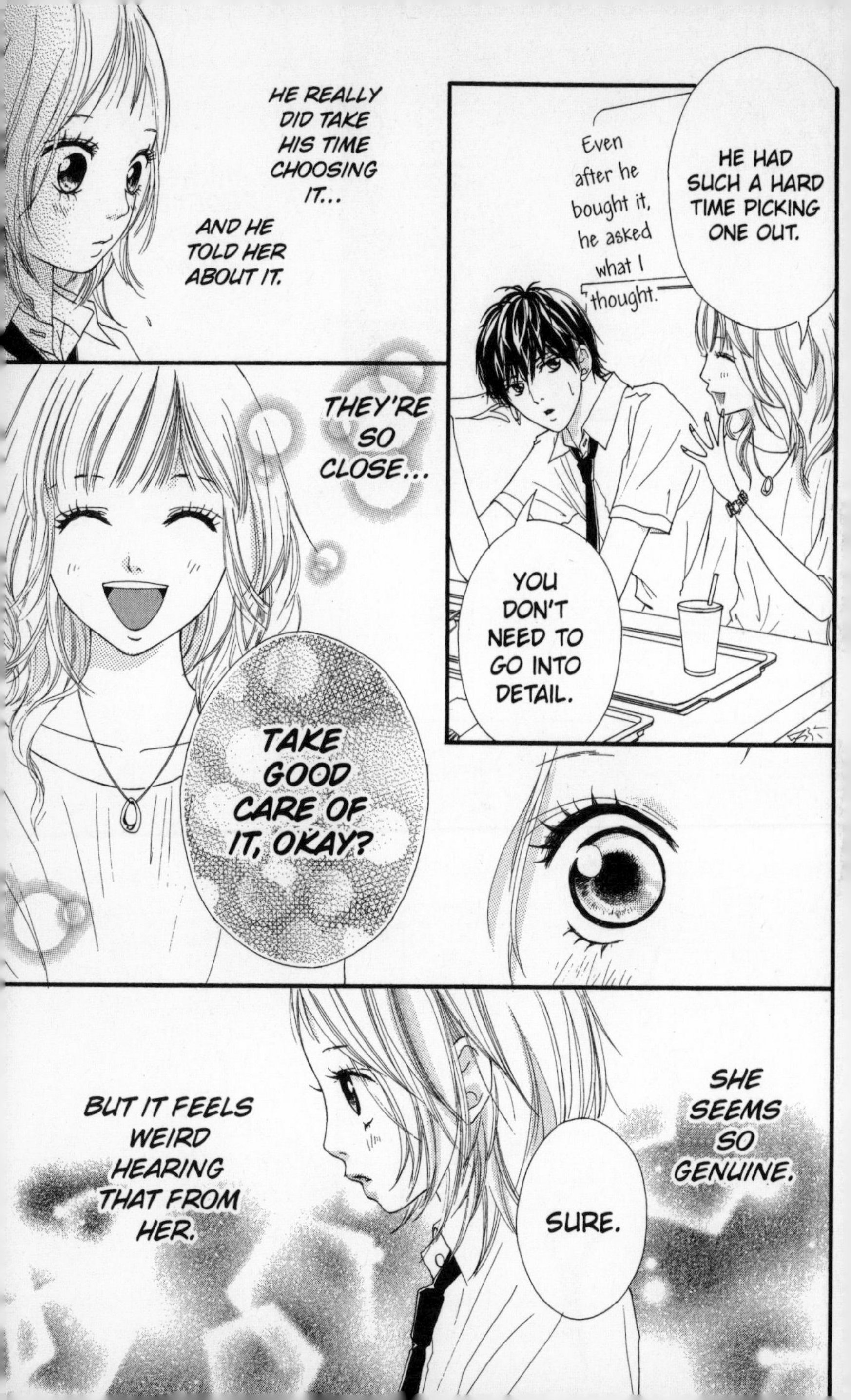
HE HAD SUCH A HARD TIME PICKING ONE OUT.
Even after he bought it, he asked what I thought.
YOU DON'T NEED TO GO INTO DETAIL.
HE REALLY DID TAKE HIS TIME CHOOSING IT...
AND HE TOLD HER ABOUT IT.
THEY'RE SO CLOSE...
TAKE GOOD CARE OF IT, OKAY?
SHE SEEMS SO GENUINE.
SURE.
BUT IT FEELS WEIRD HEARING THAT FROM HER.

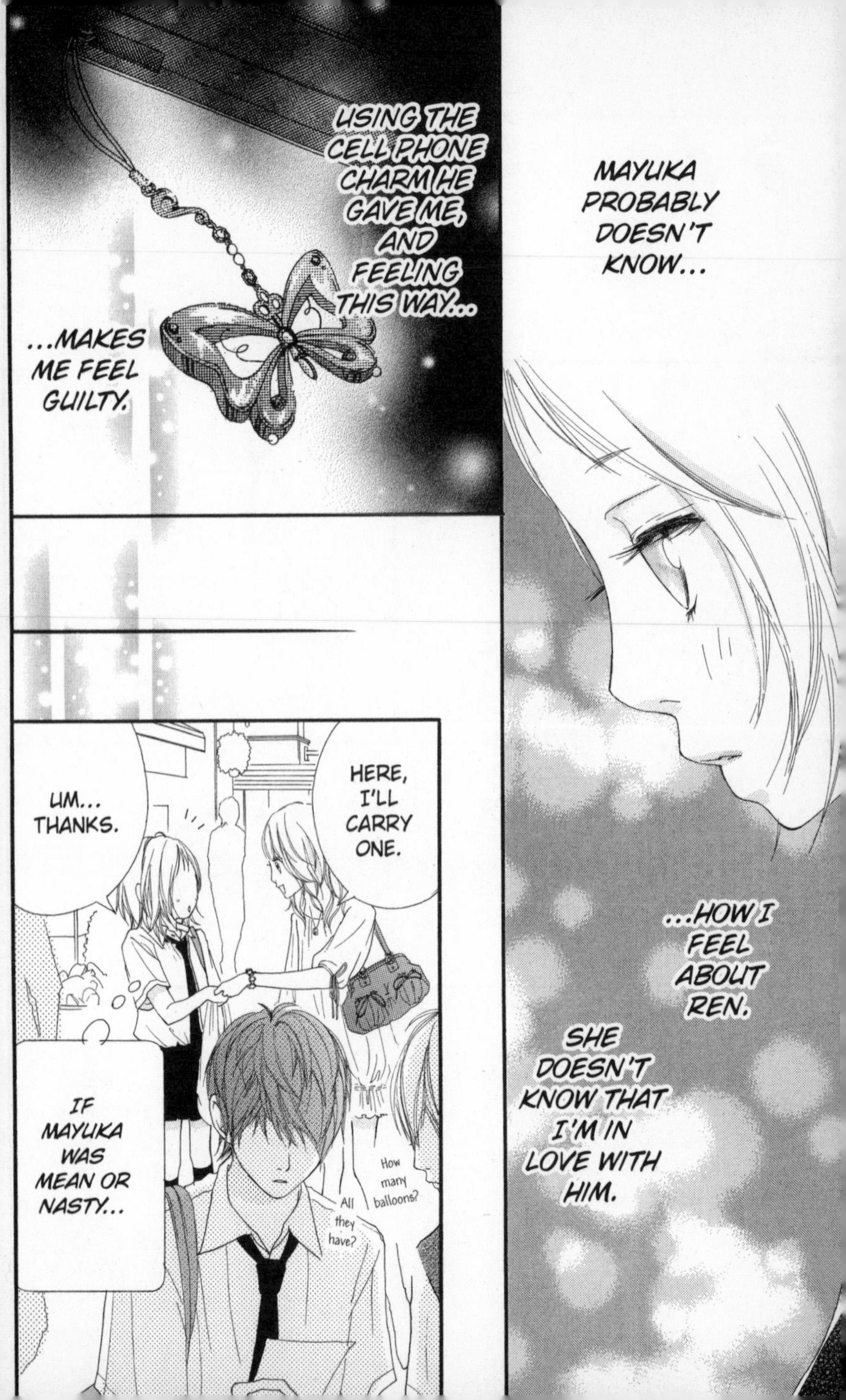
MAYUKA PROBABLY DOESN'T KNOW...
...HOW I FEEL ABOUT REN.
SHE DOESN'T KNOW THAT I'M IN LOVE WITH HIM.
USING THE CELL PHONE CHARM HE GAVE ME, AND FEELING THIS WAY...
...MAKES ME FEEL GUILTY.
HERE, I'LL CARRY ONE.
UM... THANKS.
IF MAYUKA WAS MEAN OR NASTY...
How many balloons?
All they have?

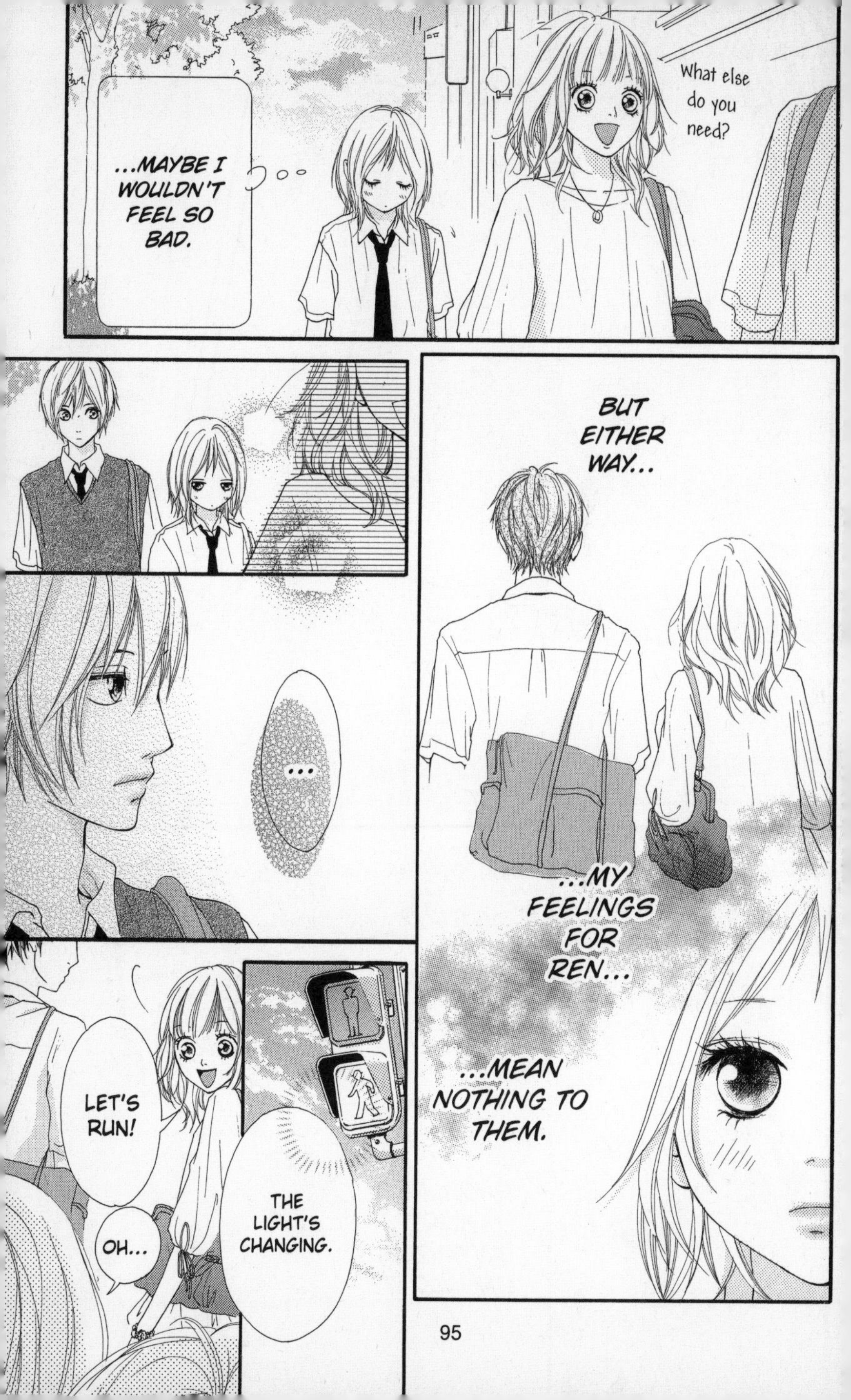
What else do you need?
...MAYBE I WOULDN'T FEEL SO BAD.
BUT EITHER WAY...
...MY FEELINGS FOR REN...
...MEAN NOTHING TO THEM.
...
THE LIGHT'S CHANGING.
LET'S RUN!
OH...

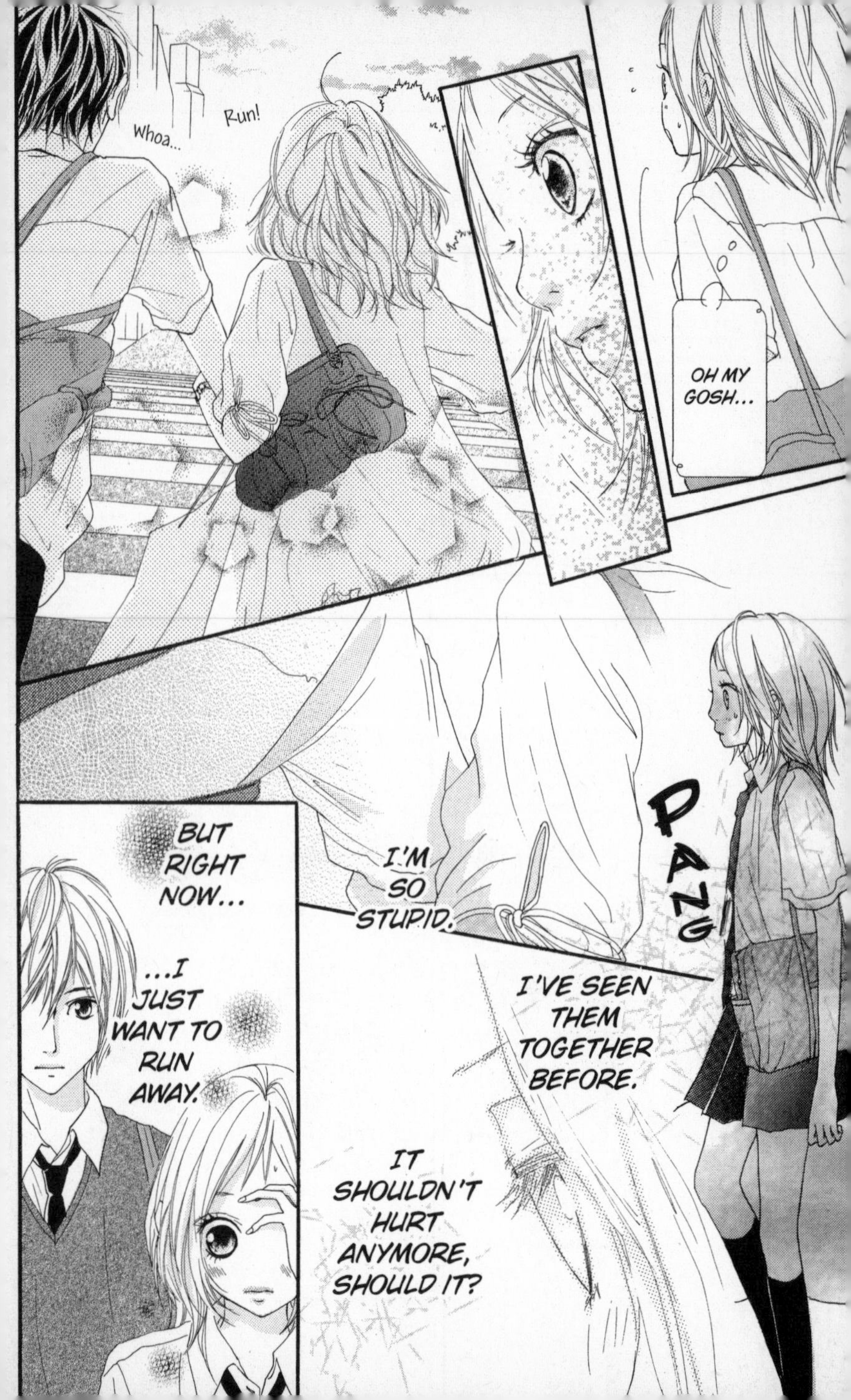
OH MY GOSH...
Run!
Whoa...
PANG
I'M SO STUPID.
I'VE SEEN THEM TOGETHER BEFORE.
IT SHOULDN'T HURT ANYMORE, SHOULD IT?
BUT RIGHT NOW...
...I JUST WANT TO RUN AWAY.

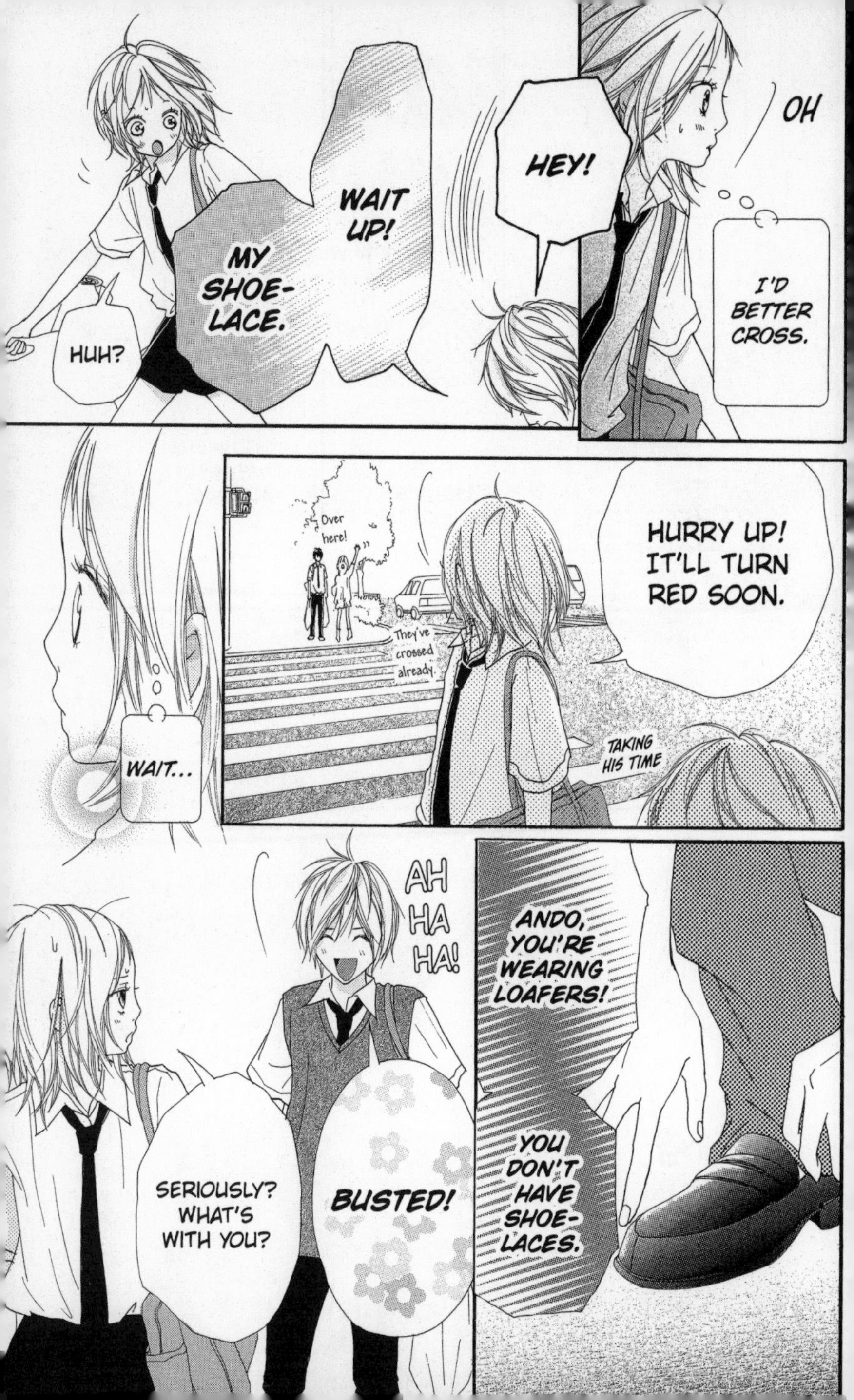
OH
I'D BETTER CROSS.
HEY!
WAIT UP!
MY SHOE-LACE.
HUH?
HURRY UP! IT'LL TURN RED SOON.
Over here!
They've crossed already.
TAKING HIS TIME
WAIT...
ANDO, YOU'RE WEARING LOAFERS!
YOU DON'T HAVE SHOE-LACES.
AH HA HA!
BUSTED!
SERIOUSLY? WHAT'S WITH YOU?

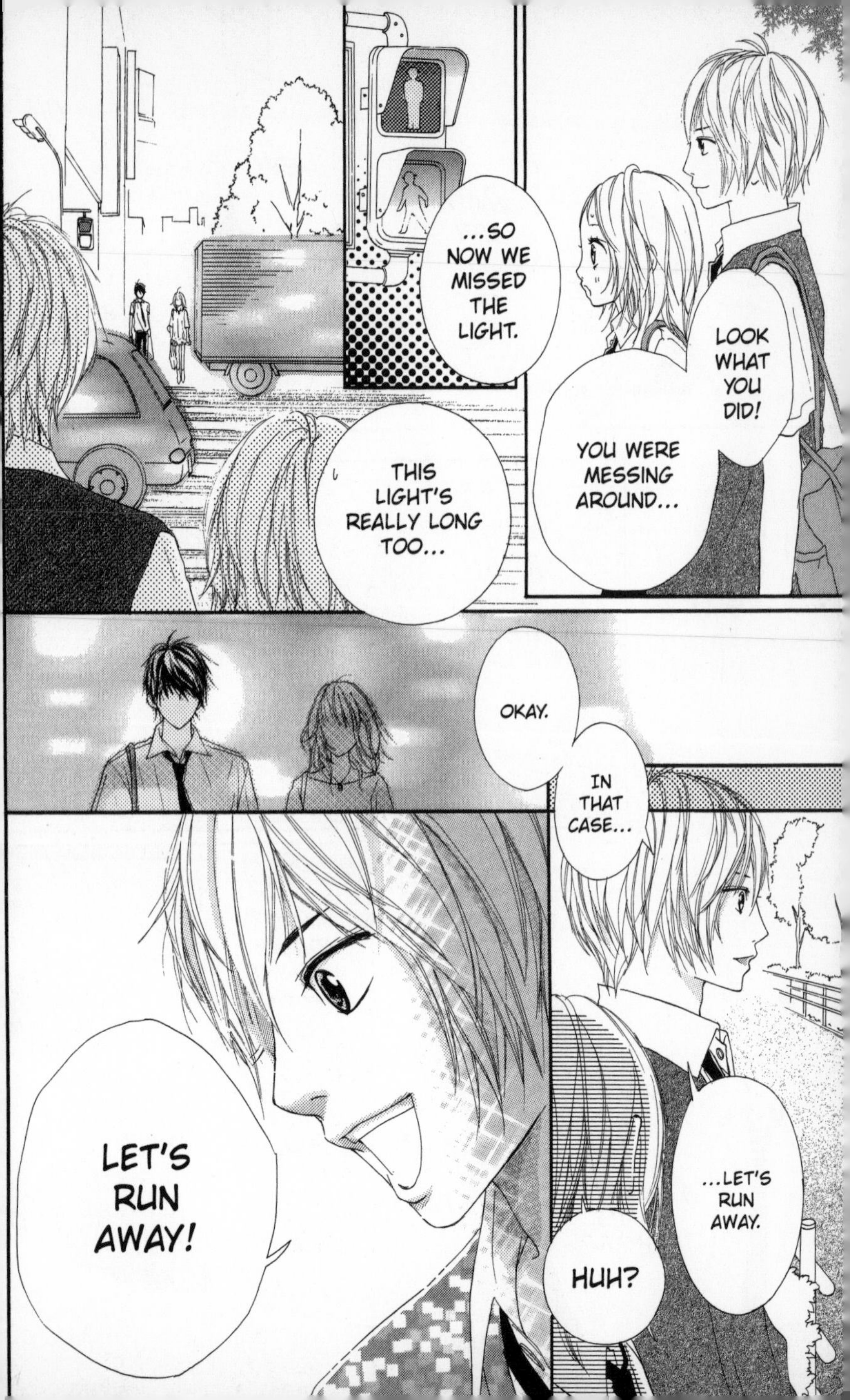
LOOK WHAT YOU DID!
YOU WERE MESSING AROUND...
...SO NOW WE MISSED THE LIGHT.
THIS LIGHT'S REALLY LONG TOO...
OKAY.
IN THAT CASE...
...LET'S RUN AWAY.
HUH?
LET'S RUN AWAY!

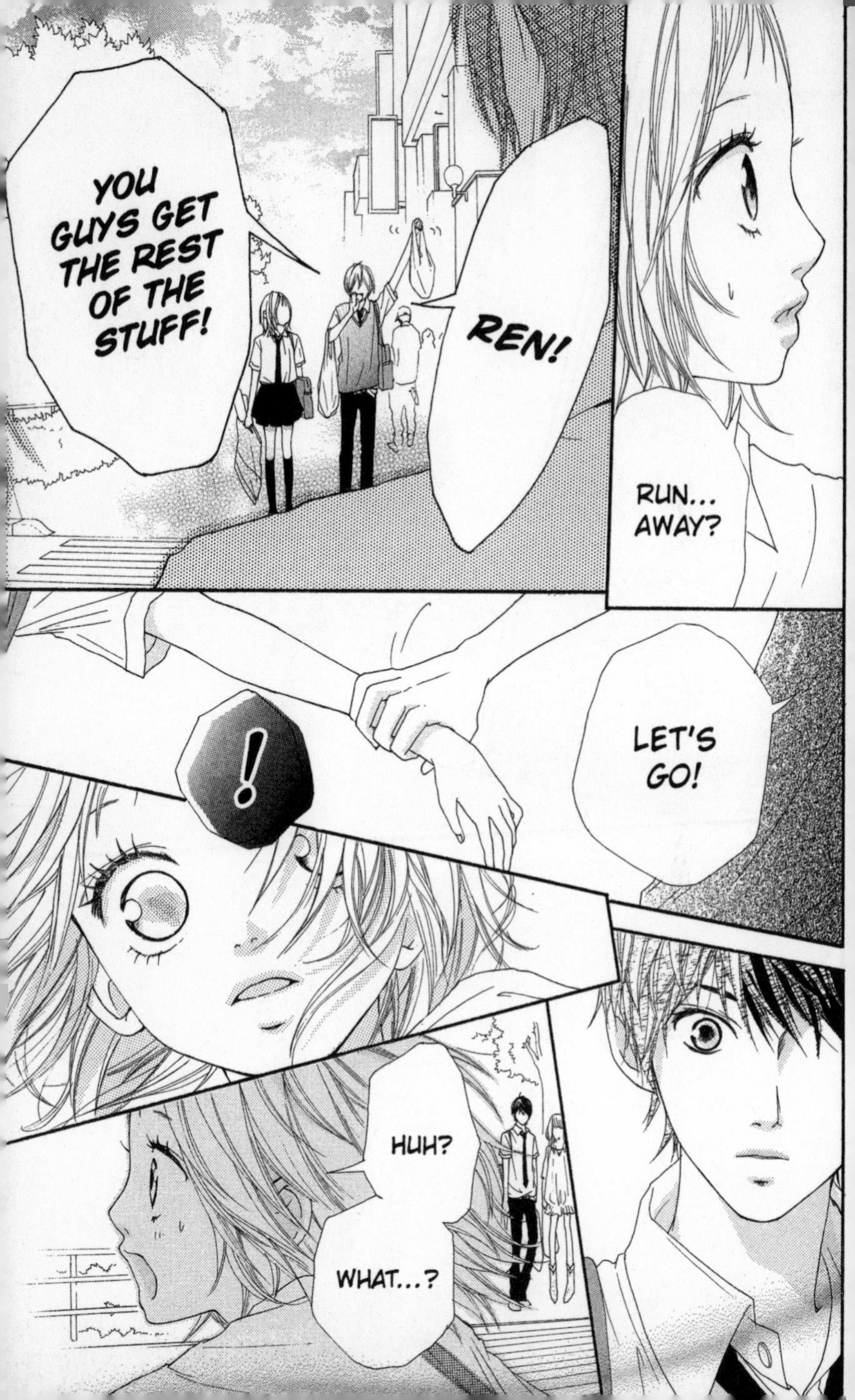
RUN... AWAY?
REN!
YOU GUYS GET THE REST OF THE STUFF!
LET'S GO!
!
HUH?
WHAT...?

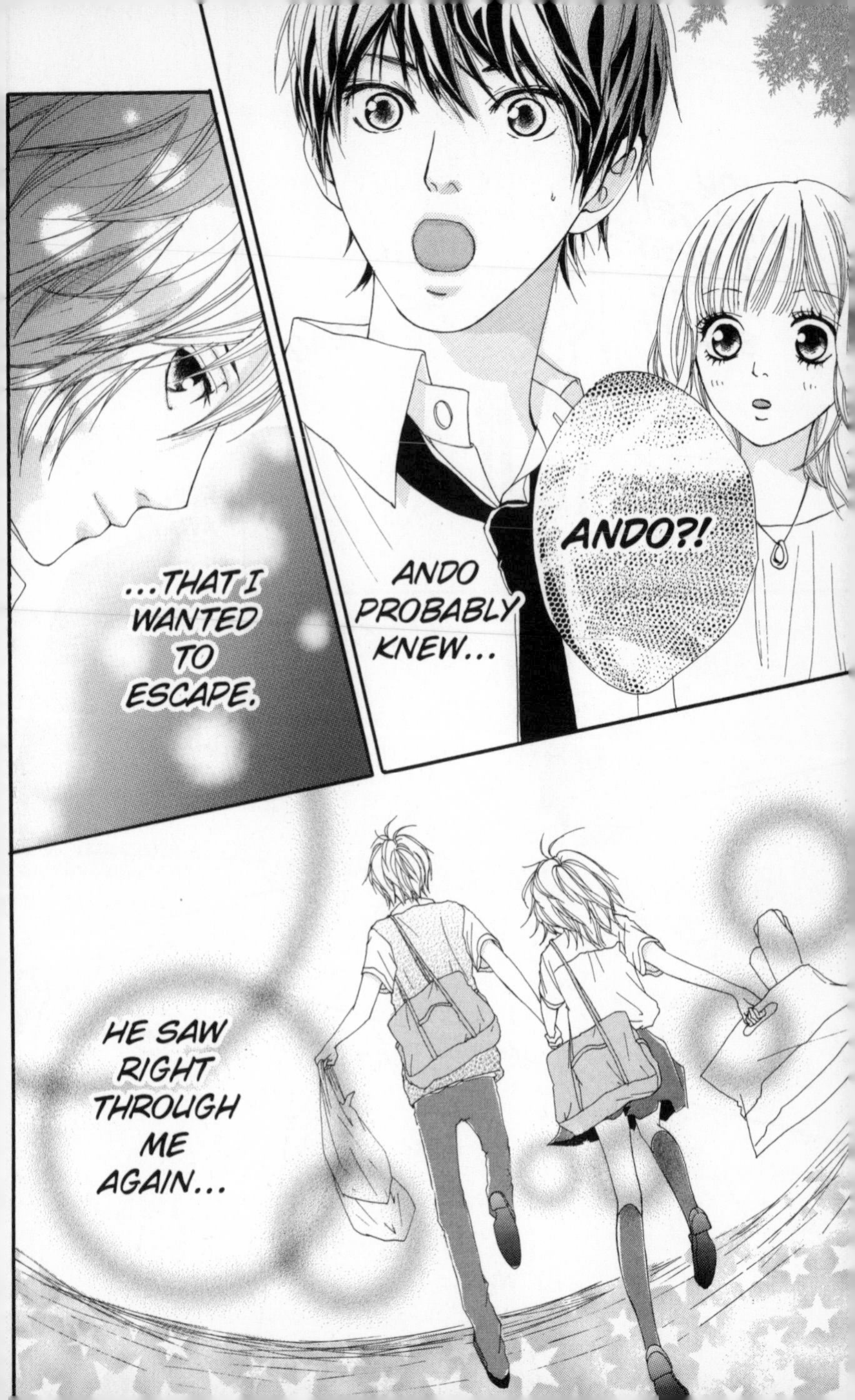
ANDO?!
ANDO PROBABLY KNEW...
...THAT I WANTED TO ESCAPE.
HE SAW RIGHT THROUGH ME AGAIN...

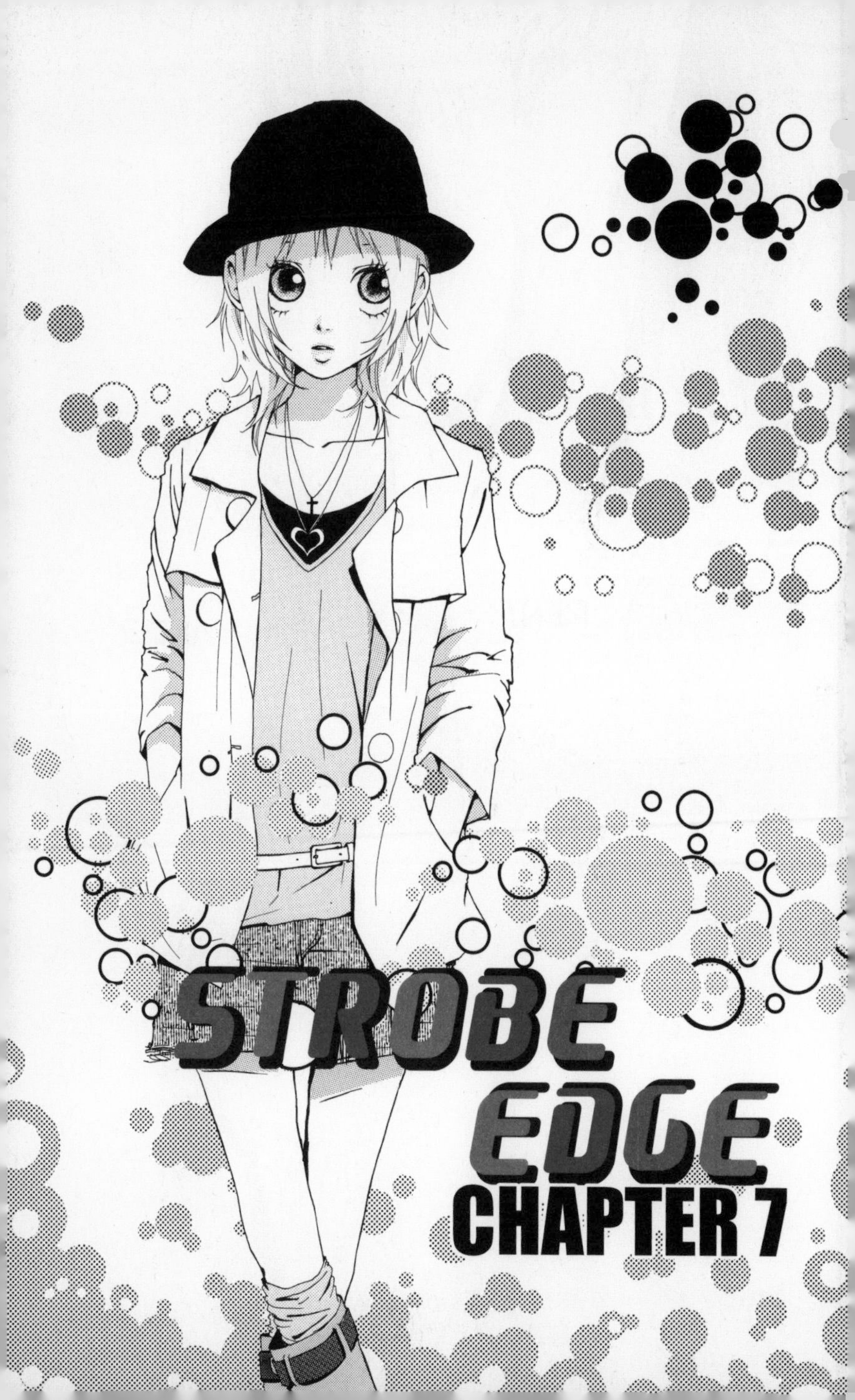
STROBE EDGE
CHAPTER 7

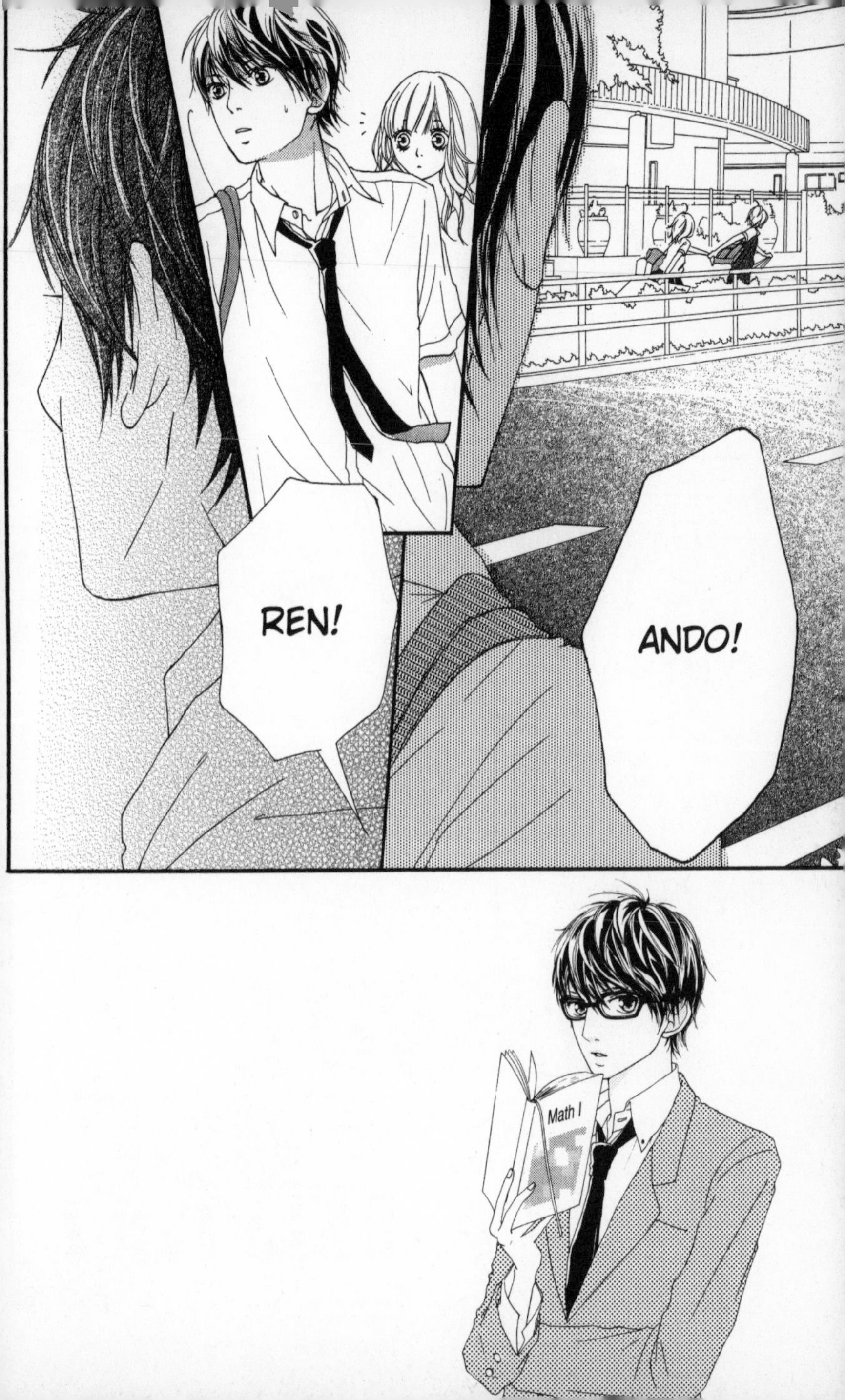
ANDO!
REN!
Math I

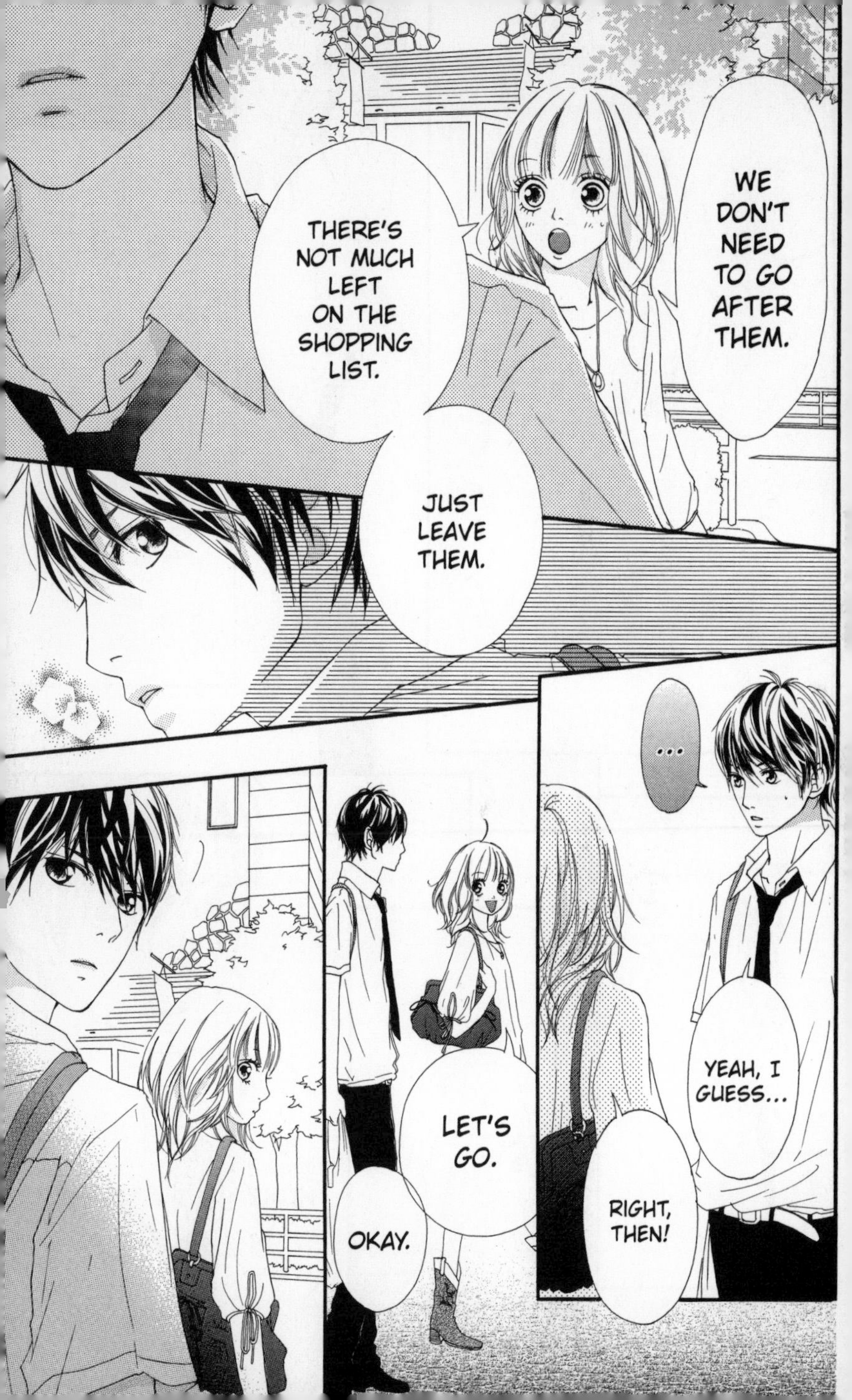
WE DON'T NEED TO GO AFTER THEM.
THERE'S NOT MUCH LEFT ON THE SHOPPING LIST.
JUST LEAVE THEM.
...
YEAH, I GUESS...
RIGHT, THEN!
LET'S GO.
OKAY.

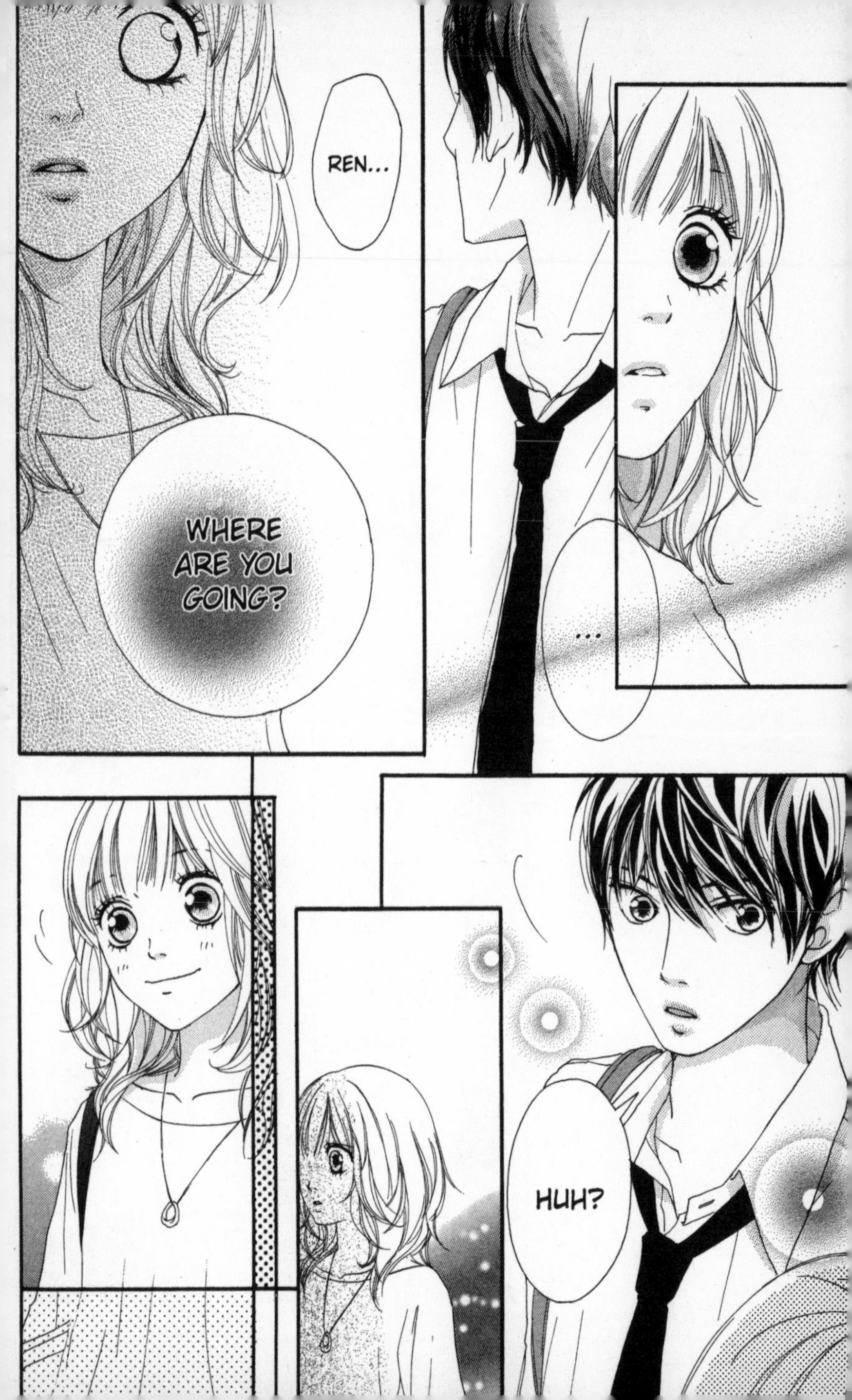
...
REN...
WHERE ARE YOU GOING?
HUH?

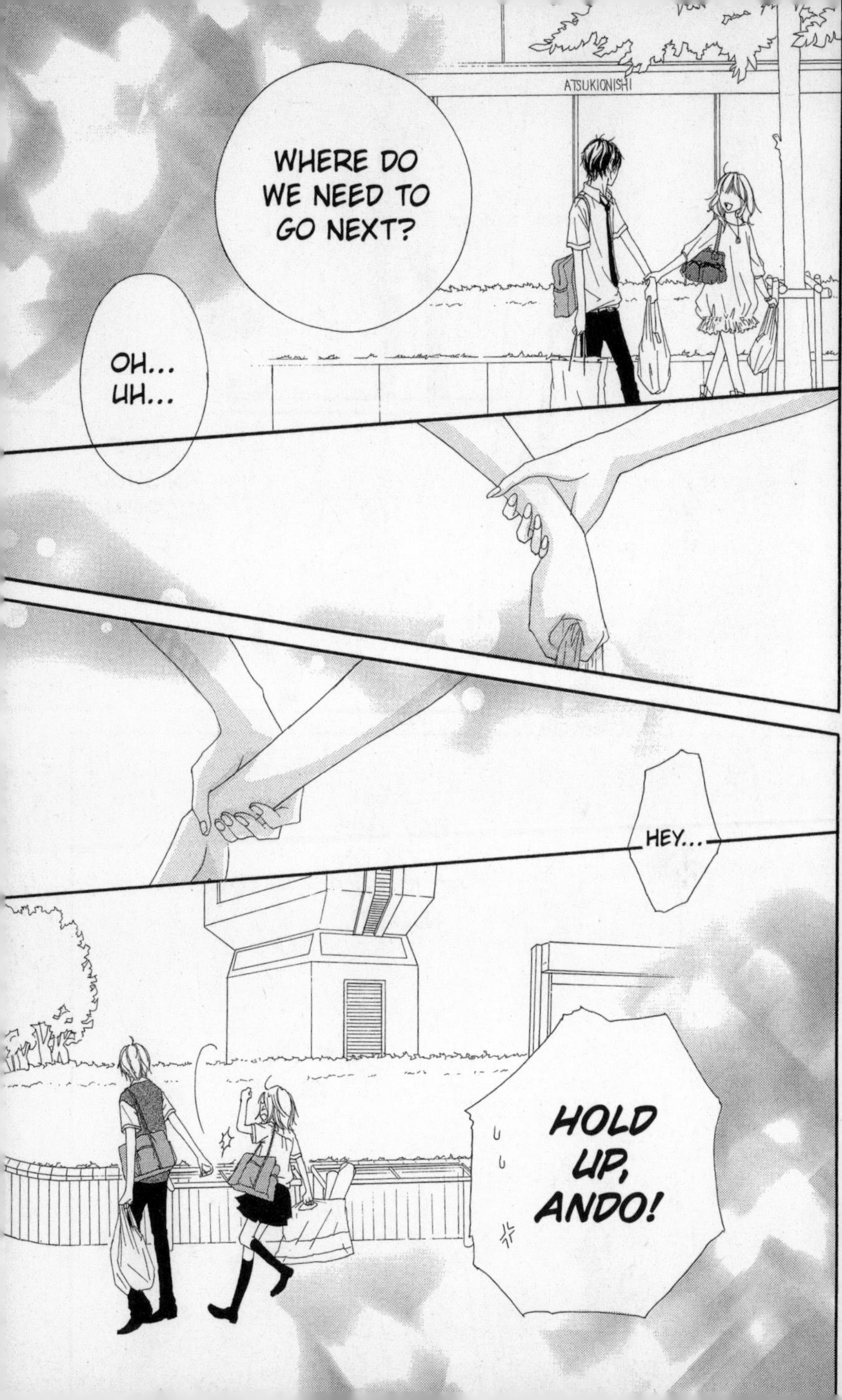
ATSUKIONISHI
WHERE DO WE NEED TO GO NEXT?
OH... UH...
HEY...
HOLD UP, ANDO!

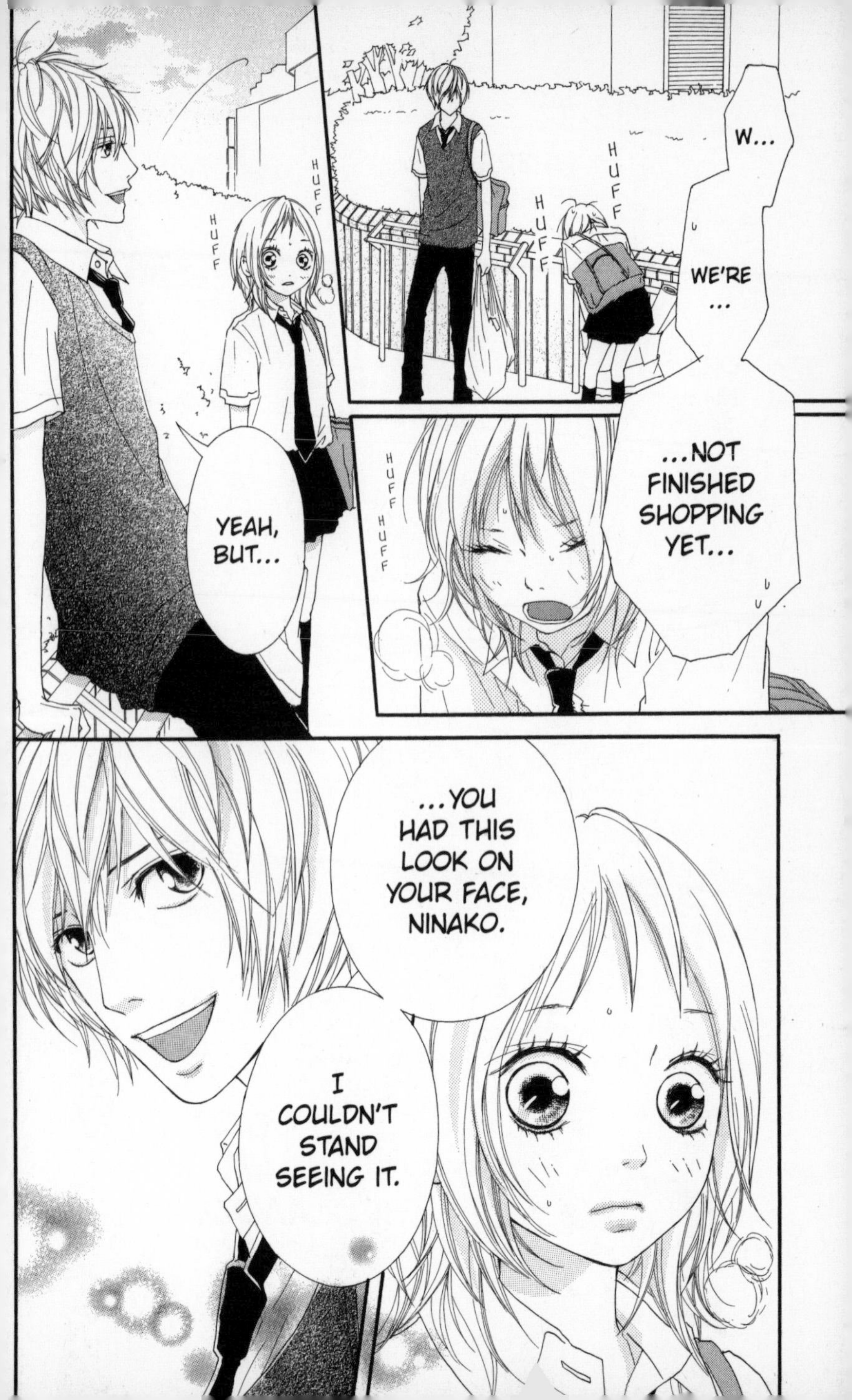
HUFF
HUFF
W...
WE'RE ...
HUFF HUFF
...NOT FINISHED SHOPPING YET...
HUFF
HUFF
YEAH, BUT...
...YOU HAD THIS LOOK ON YOUR FACE, NINAKO.
I COULDN'T STAND SEEING IT.

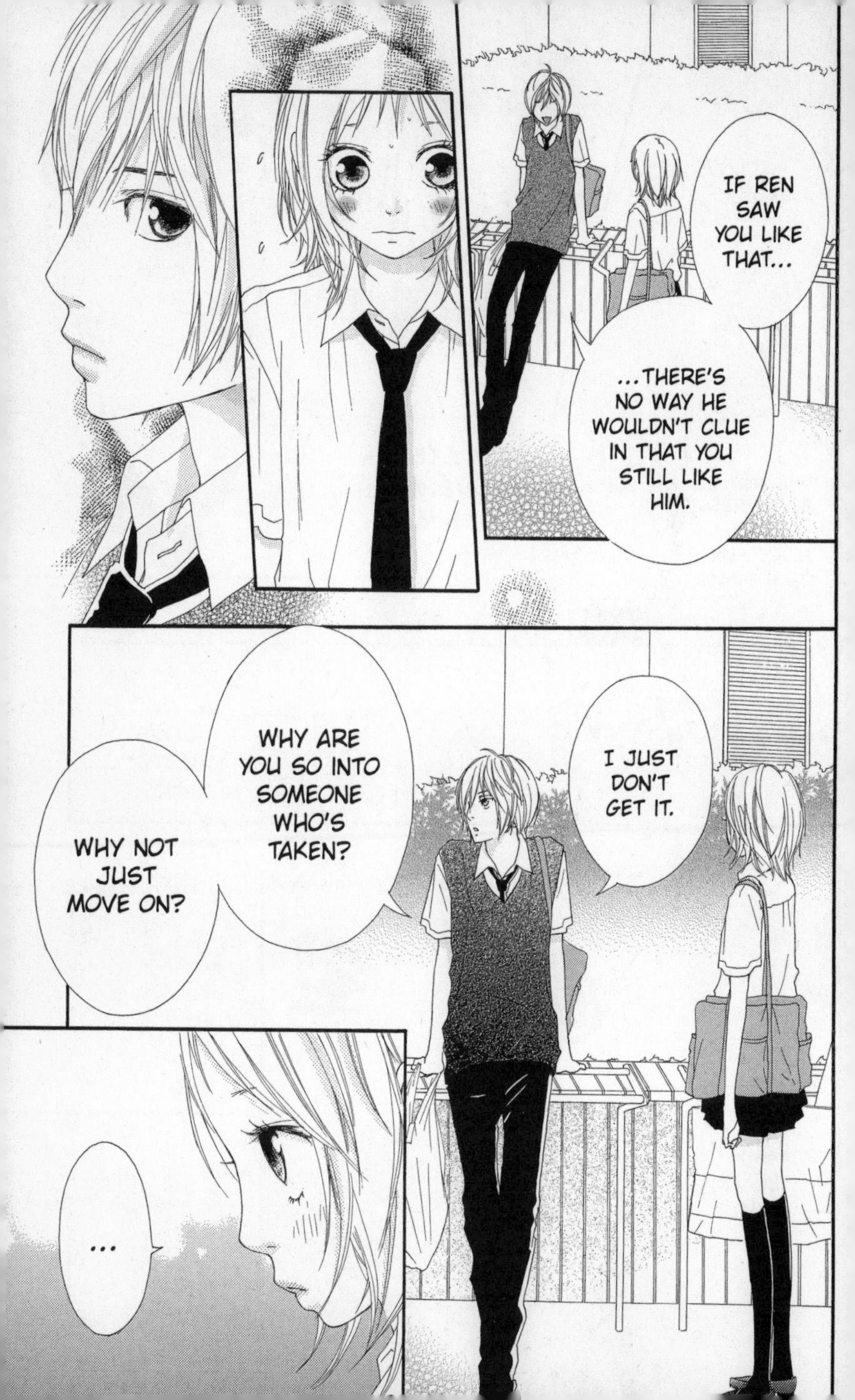
IF REN SAW YOU LIKE THAT...
...THERE'S NO WAY HE WOULDN'T CLUE IN THAT YOU STILL LIKE HIM.
I JUST DON'T GET IT.
WHY ARE YOU SO INTO SOMEONE WHO'S TAKEN?
WHY NOT JUST MOVE ON?
...

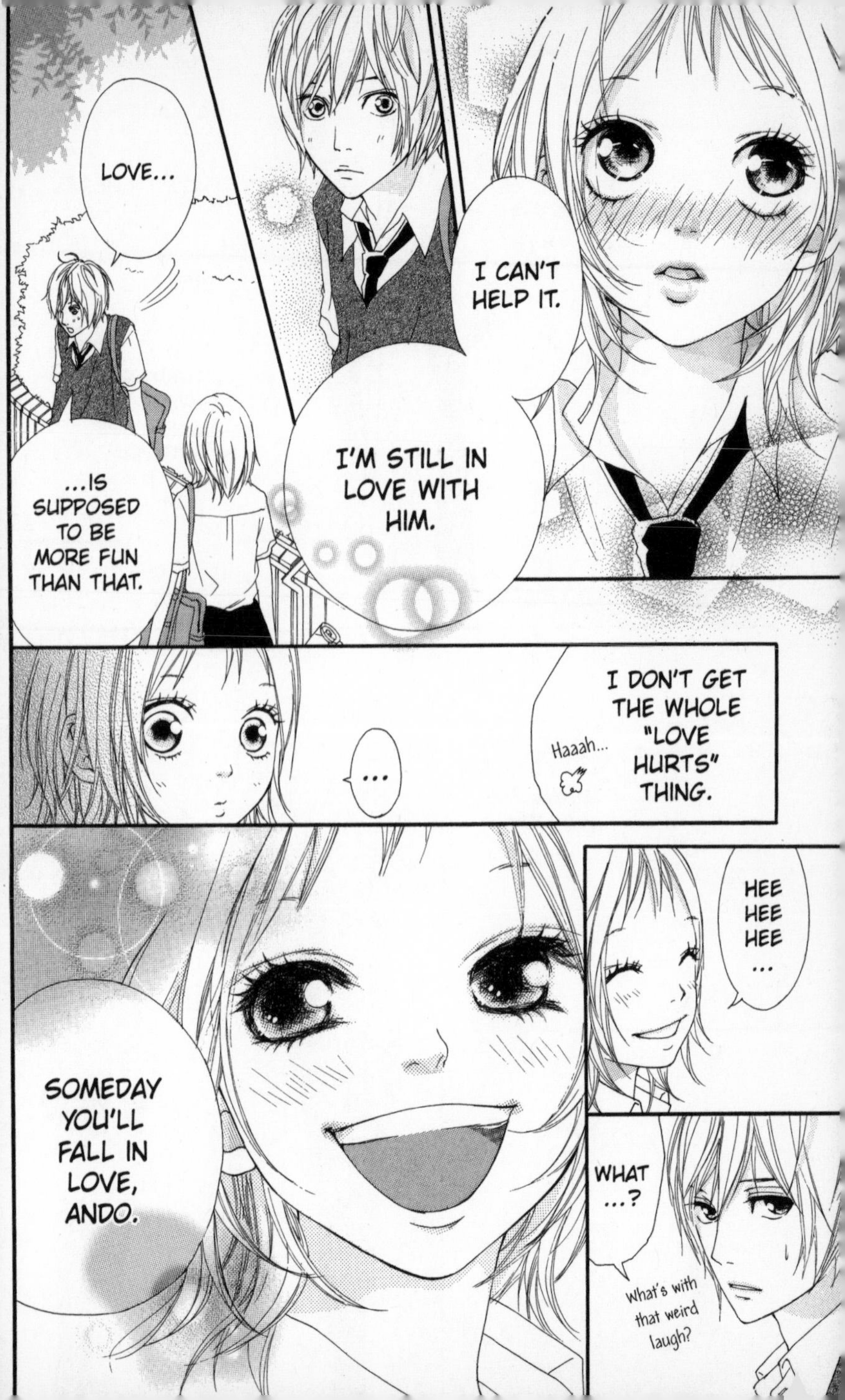
I CAN'T HELP IT.
I'M STILL IN LOVE WITH HIM.
LOVE...
...IS SUPPOSED TO BE MORE FUN THAN THAT.
I DON'T GET THE WHOLE "LOVE HURTS" THING.
Haaah...
...
HEE HEE HEE...
WHAT...?
What's with that weird laugh?
SOMEDAY YOU'LL FALL IN LOVE, ANDO.

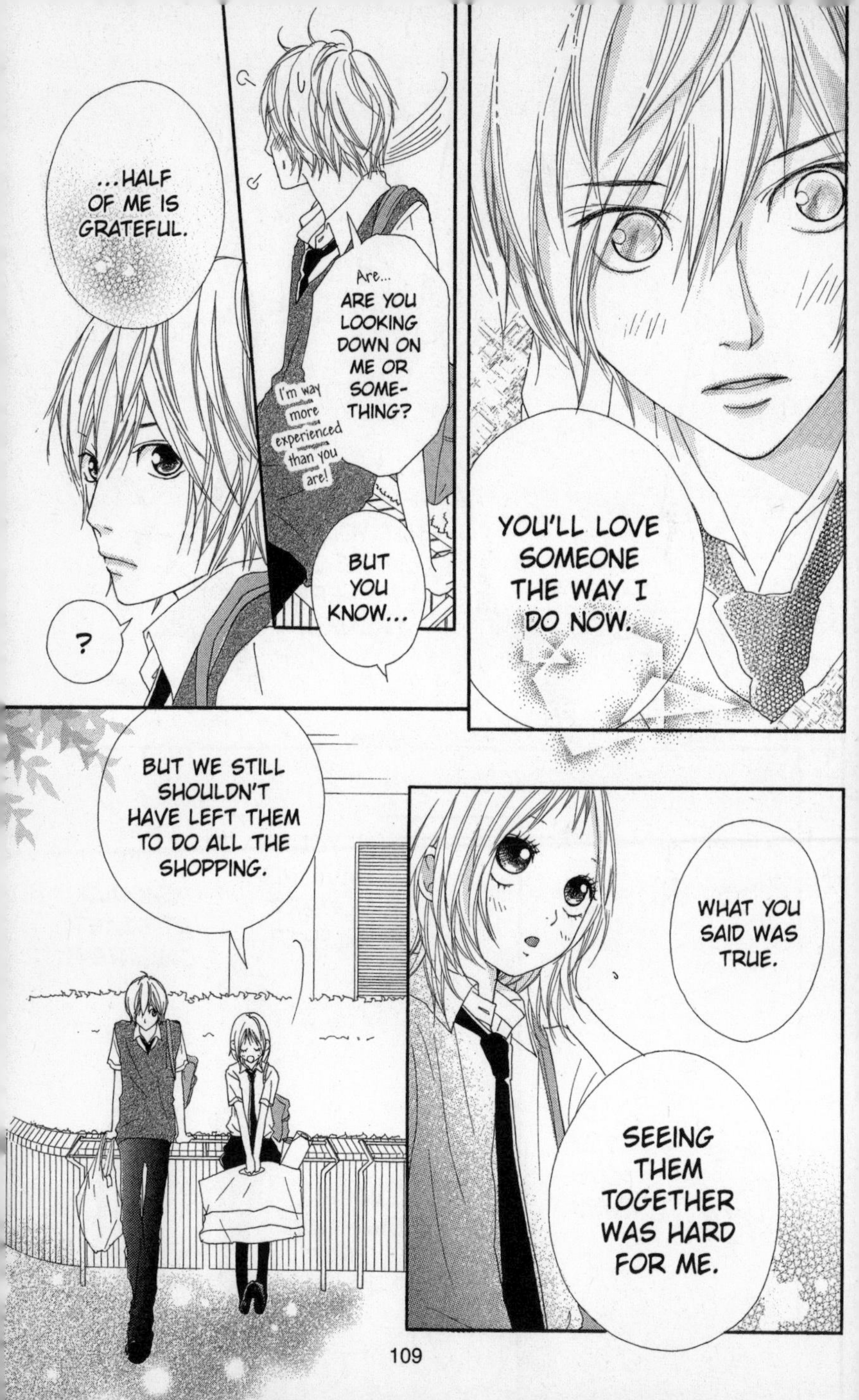

YOU'LL LOVE SOMEONE THE WAY I DO NOW.
Are... ARE YOU LOOKING DOWN ON ME OR SOME-THING?
I'm way more experienced than you are!
BUT YOU KNOW...
...HALF OF ME IS GRATEFUL.
?
WHAT YOU SAID WAS TRUE.
SEEING THEM TOGETHER WAS HARD FOR ME.
BUT WE STILL SHOULDN'T HAVE LEFT THEM TO DO ALL THE SHOPPING.

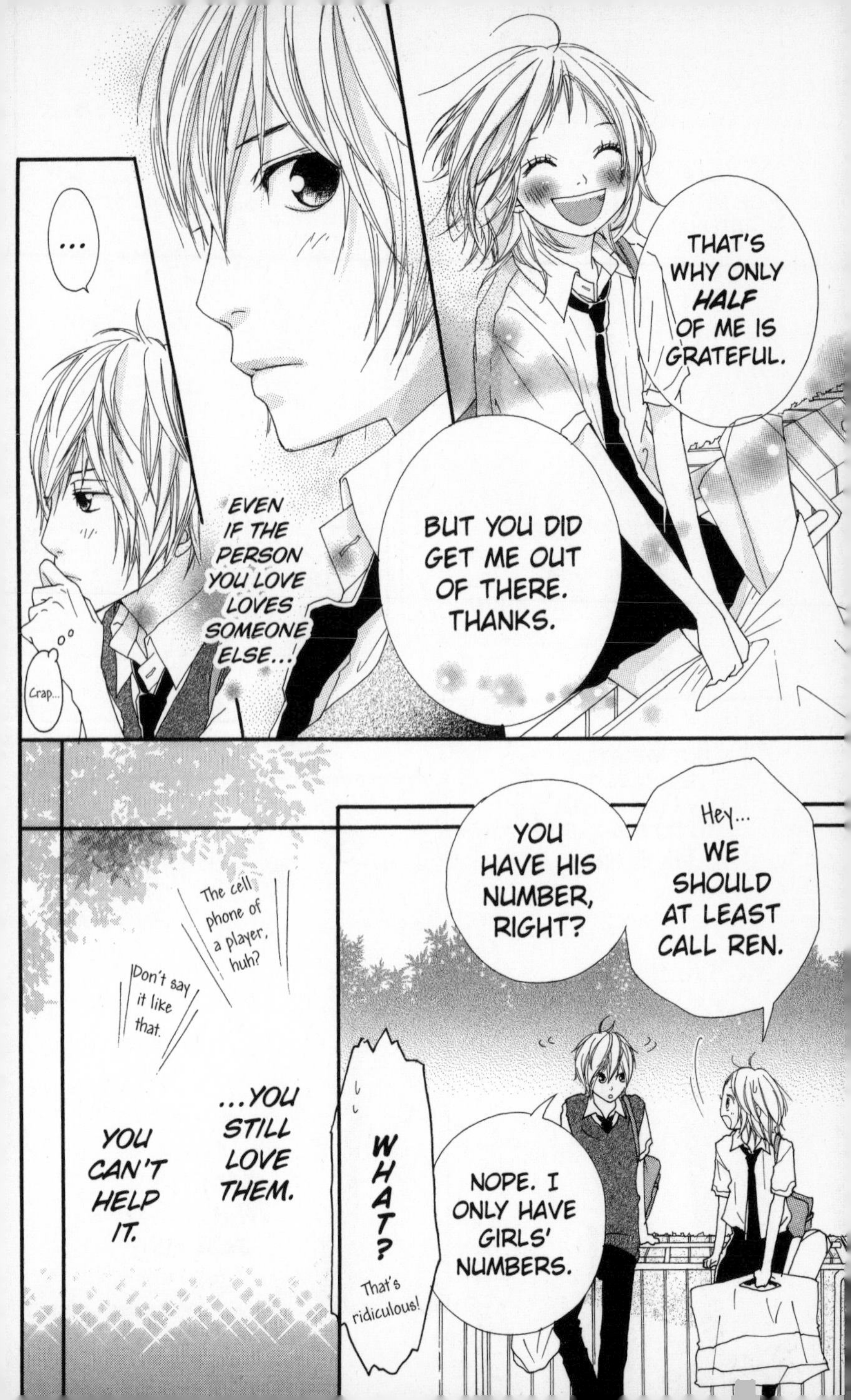
THAT'S WHY ONLY HALF OF ME IS GRATEFUL.
BUT YOU DID GET ME OUT OF THERE. THANKS.
EVEN IF THE PERSON YOU LOVE LOVES SOMEONE ELSE...
...
Crap...
Hey... WE SHOULD AT LEAST CALL REN.
YOU HAVE HIS NUMBER, RIGHT?
NOPE. I ONLY HAVE GIRLS' NUMBERS.
WHAT?
That's ridiculous!
The cell phone of a player, huh?
Don't say it like that.
...YOU STILL LOVE THEM.
YOU CAN'T HELP IT.

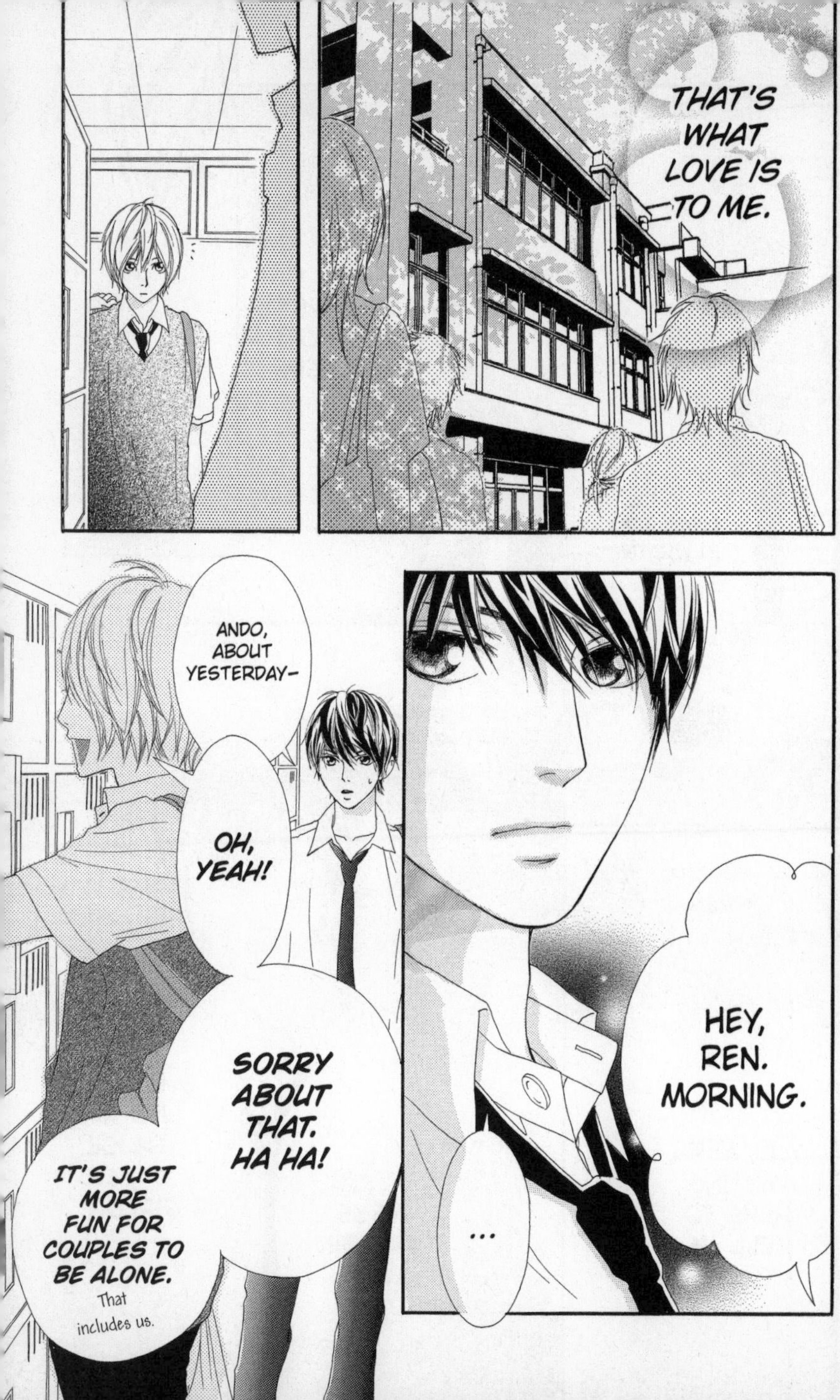
THAT'S WHAT LOVE IS TO ME.
HEY, REN. MORNING.
...
ANDO, ABOUT YESTERDAY–
OH, YEAH!
SORRY ABOUT THAT. HA HA!
IT'S JUST MORE FUN FOR COUPLES TO BE ALONE.
That includes us.

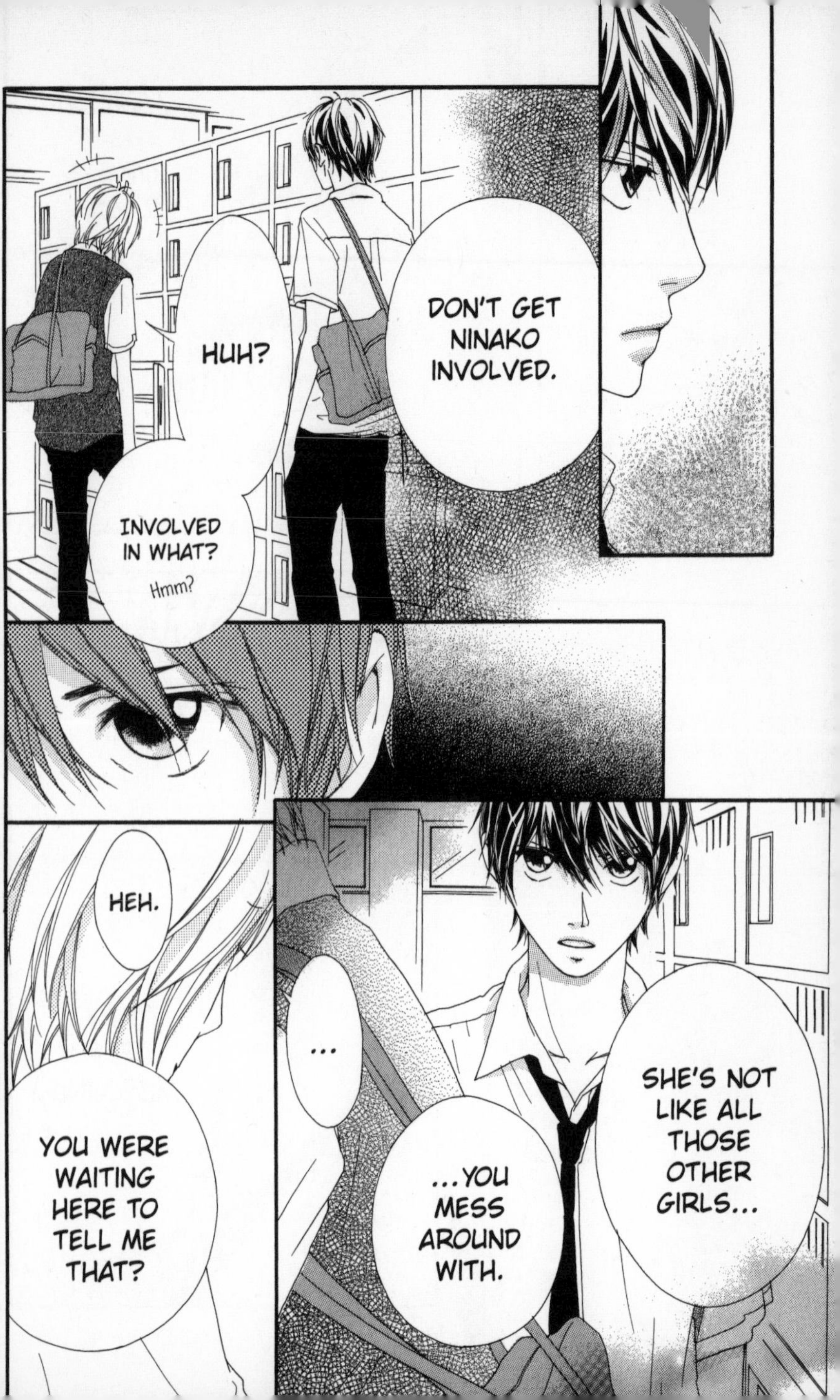
DON'T GET NINAKO INVOLVED.
HUH?
INVOLVED IN WHAT?
Hmm?
SHE'S NOT LIKE ALL THOSE OTHER GIRLS...
...YOU MESS AROUND WITH.
...
HEH.
YOU WERE WAITING HERE TO TELL ME THAT?

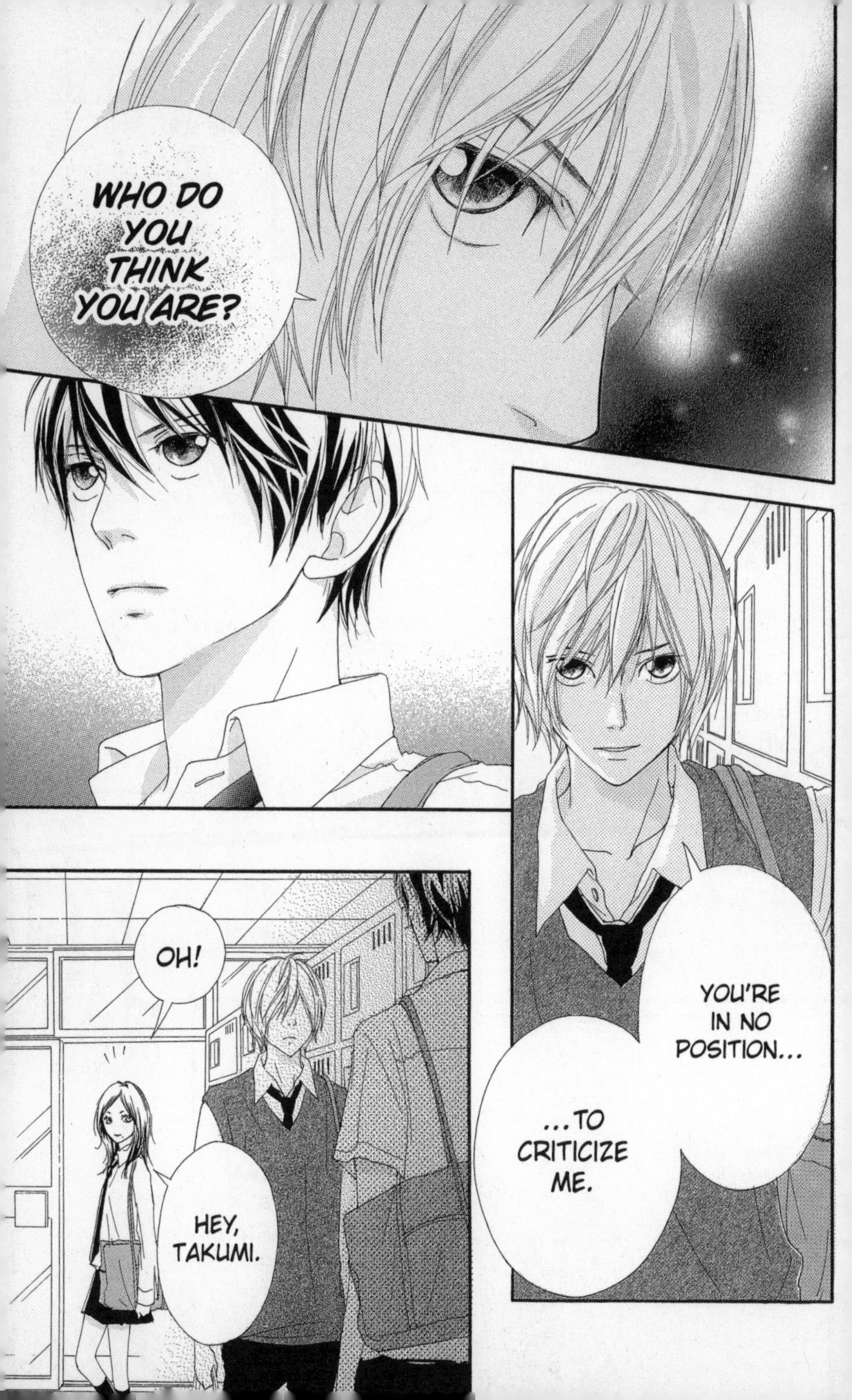
WHO DO YOU THINK YOU ARE?
YOU'RE IN NO POSITION...
...TO CRITICIZE ME.
OH!
HEY, TAKUMI.

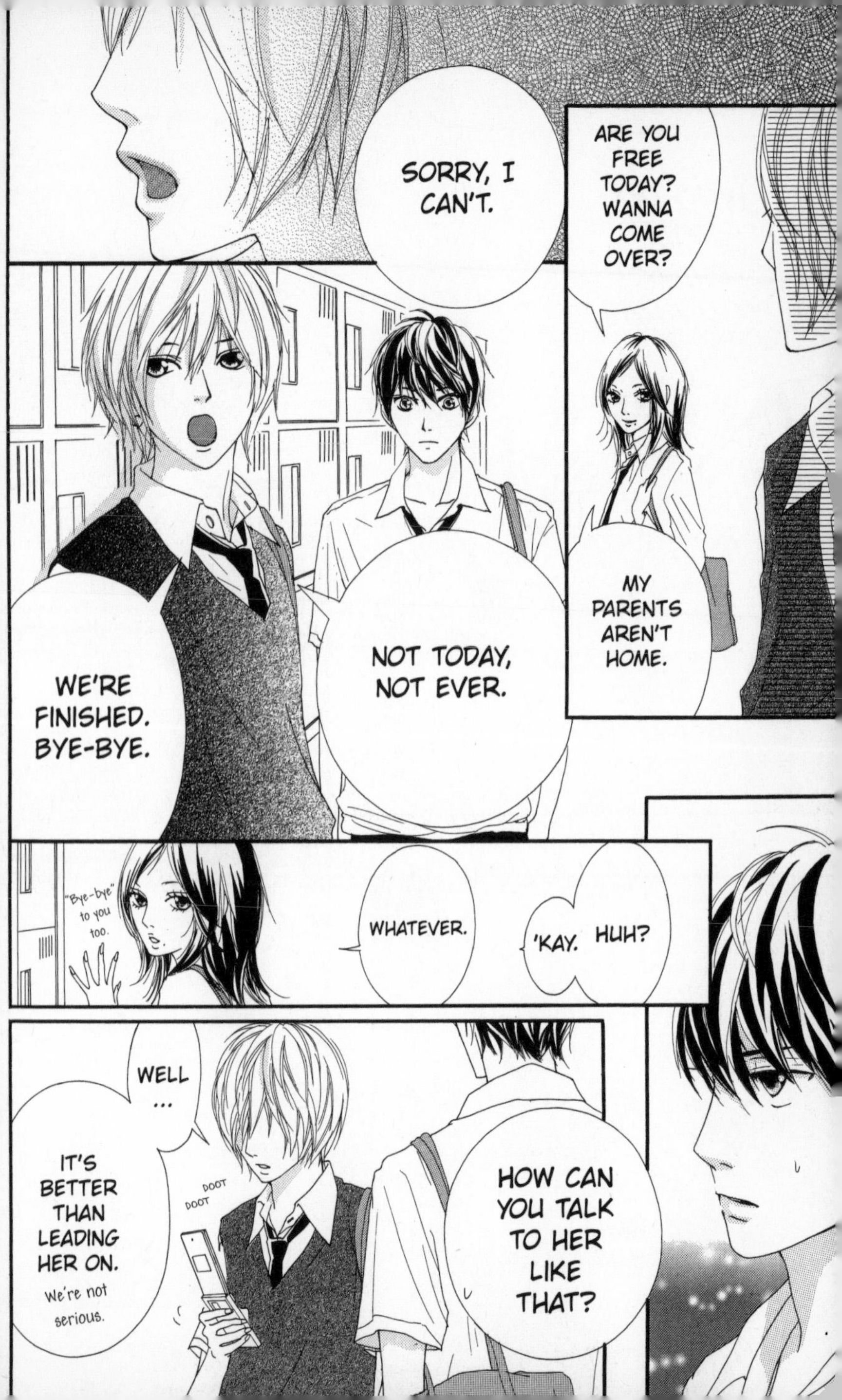
ARE YOU FREE TODAY? WANNA COME OVER?
MY PARENTS AREN'T HOME.
SORRY, I CAN'T.
NOT TODAY, NOT EVER.
WE'RE FINISHED. BYE-BYE.
HUH?
'KAY.
WHATEVER.
"Bye-bye" to you too.
HOW CAN YOU TALK TO HER LIKE THAT?
WELL ...
IT'S BETTER THAN LEADING HER ON.
We're not serious.
DOOT DOOT

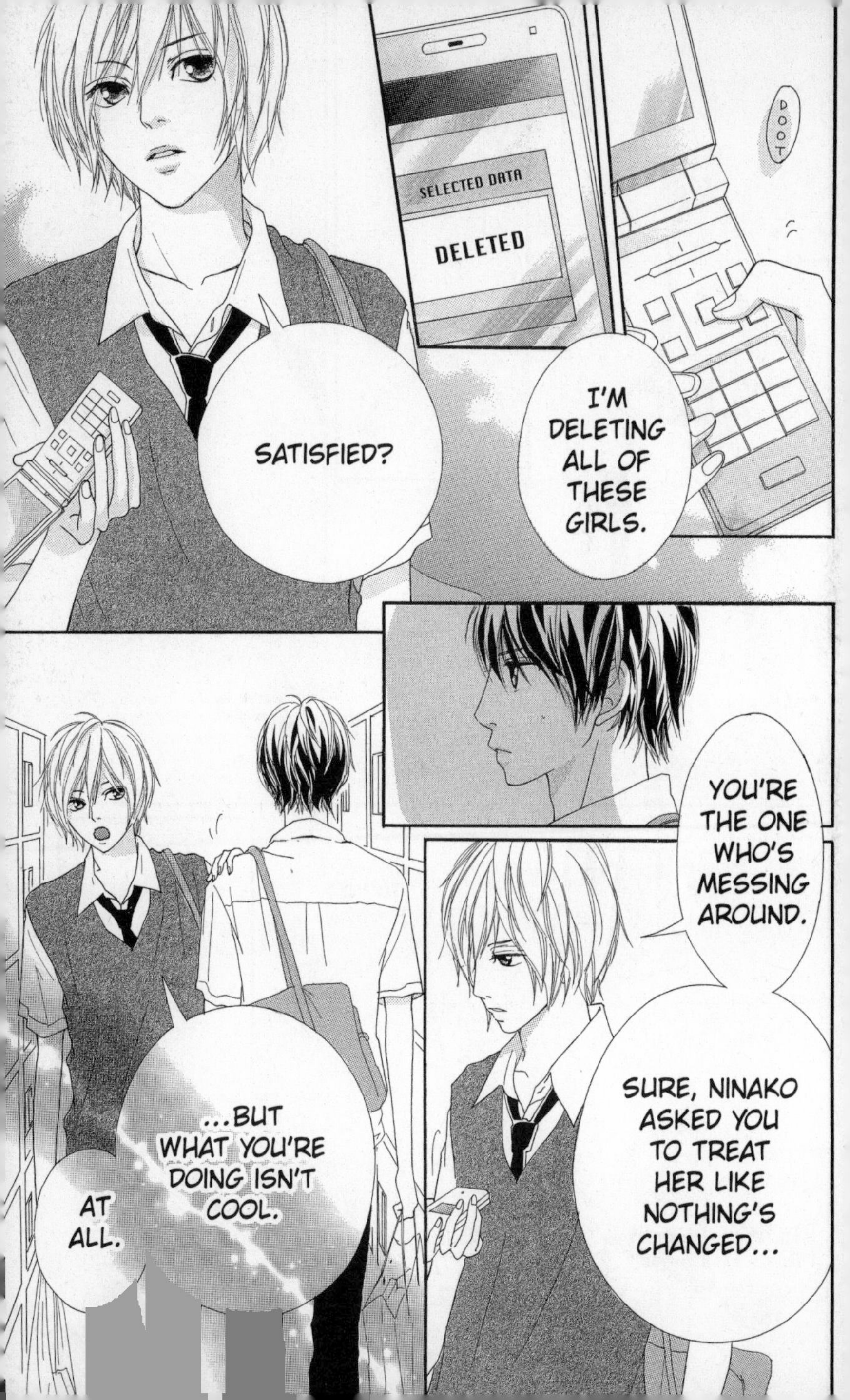
DOOT
SELECTED DATA
DELETED
I'M DELETING ALL OF THESE GIRLS.
SATISFIED?
YOU'RE THE ONE WHO'S MESSING AROUND.
SURE, NINAKO ASKED YOU TO TREAT HER LIKE NOTHING'S CHANGED...
...BUT WHAT YOU'RE DOING ISN'T COOL.
AT ALL.

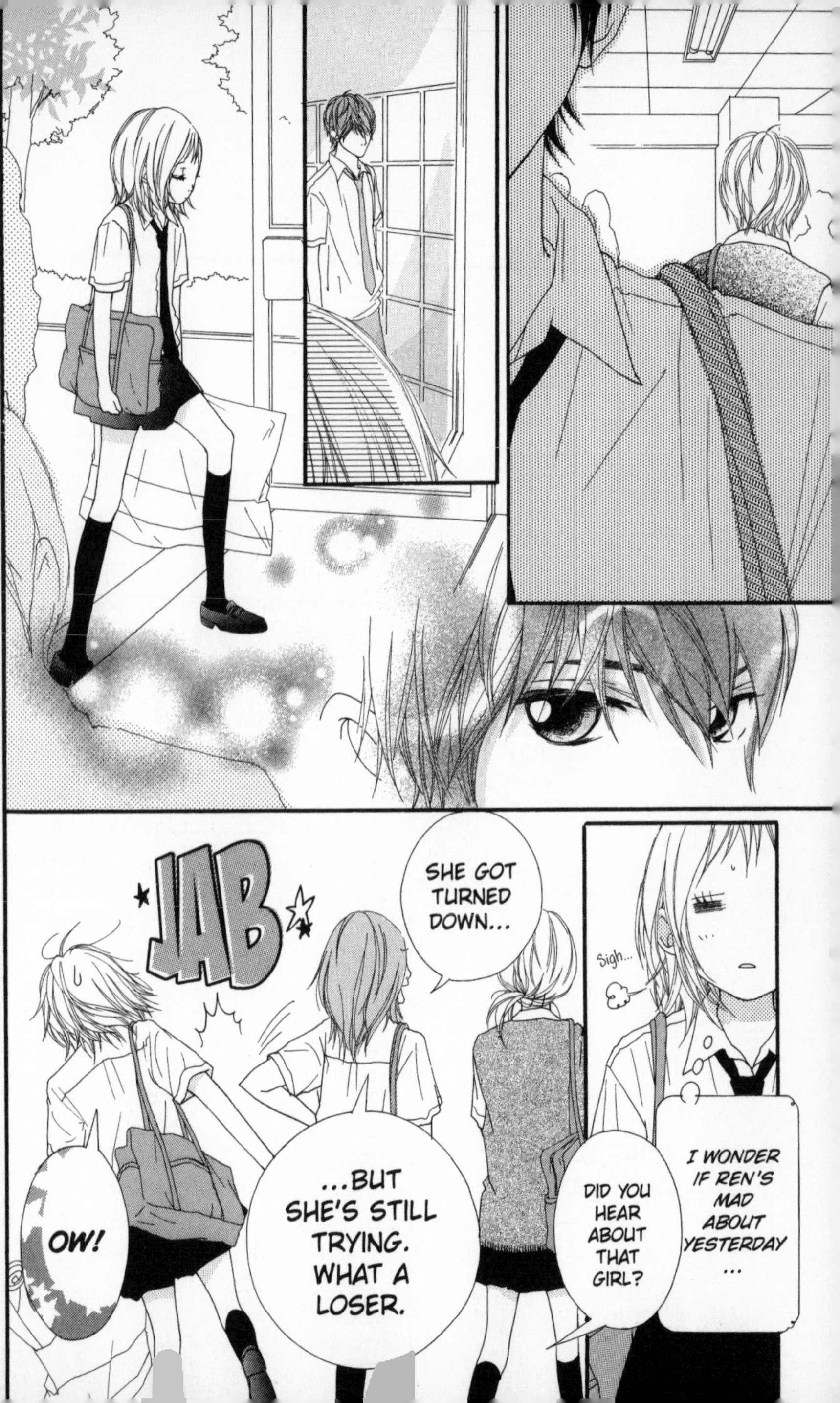
Sigh...
I WONDER IF REN'S MAD ABOUT YESTERDAY...
DID YOU HEAR ABOUT THAT GIRL?
SHE GOT TURNED DOWN...
...BUT SHE'S STILL TRYING. WHAT A LOSER.
JAB
OW!

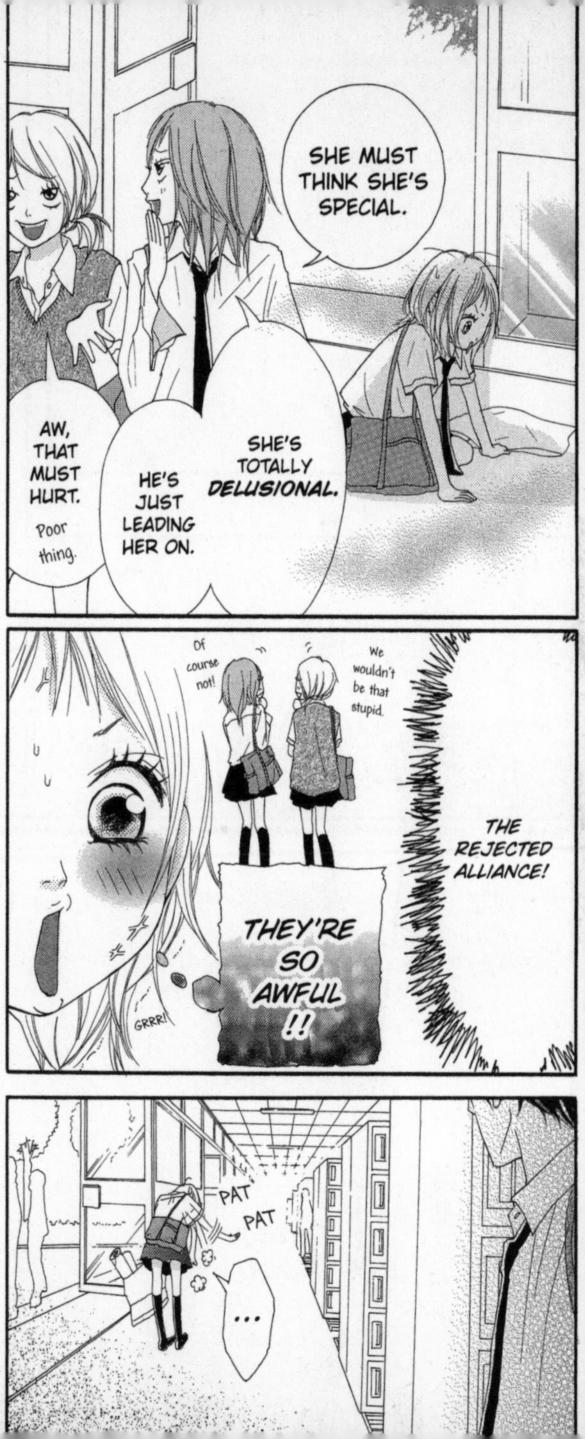
SHE MUST THINK SHE'S SPECIAL.
SHE'S TOTALLY DELUSIONAL.
HE'S JUST LEADING HER ON.
AW, THAT MUST HURT.
Poor thing.
THE REJECTED ALLIANCE!
We wouldn't be that stupid.
Of course not!
THEY'RE SO AWFUL!!
GRRR!
PAT
PAT
...

WANNA GO FOR A DRIVE? ③

I had to skip a whole month of driving school because of work, but I finally got my license! I even got it on my first try, just like I'd planned. But I still can't park properly. You know why? Because there's no guiding pole like the one at the driving school. And why would there be? So I can drive just fine, but without being able to park, I can't go out by myself. Surprise! How inconvenient!

So I've become a driver in name only. My mother must be disgusted. Sorry, Mom. I'll visit you by bus or train. I'm trying to be environmentally friendly, anyway...

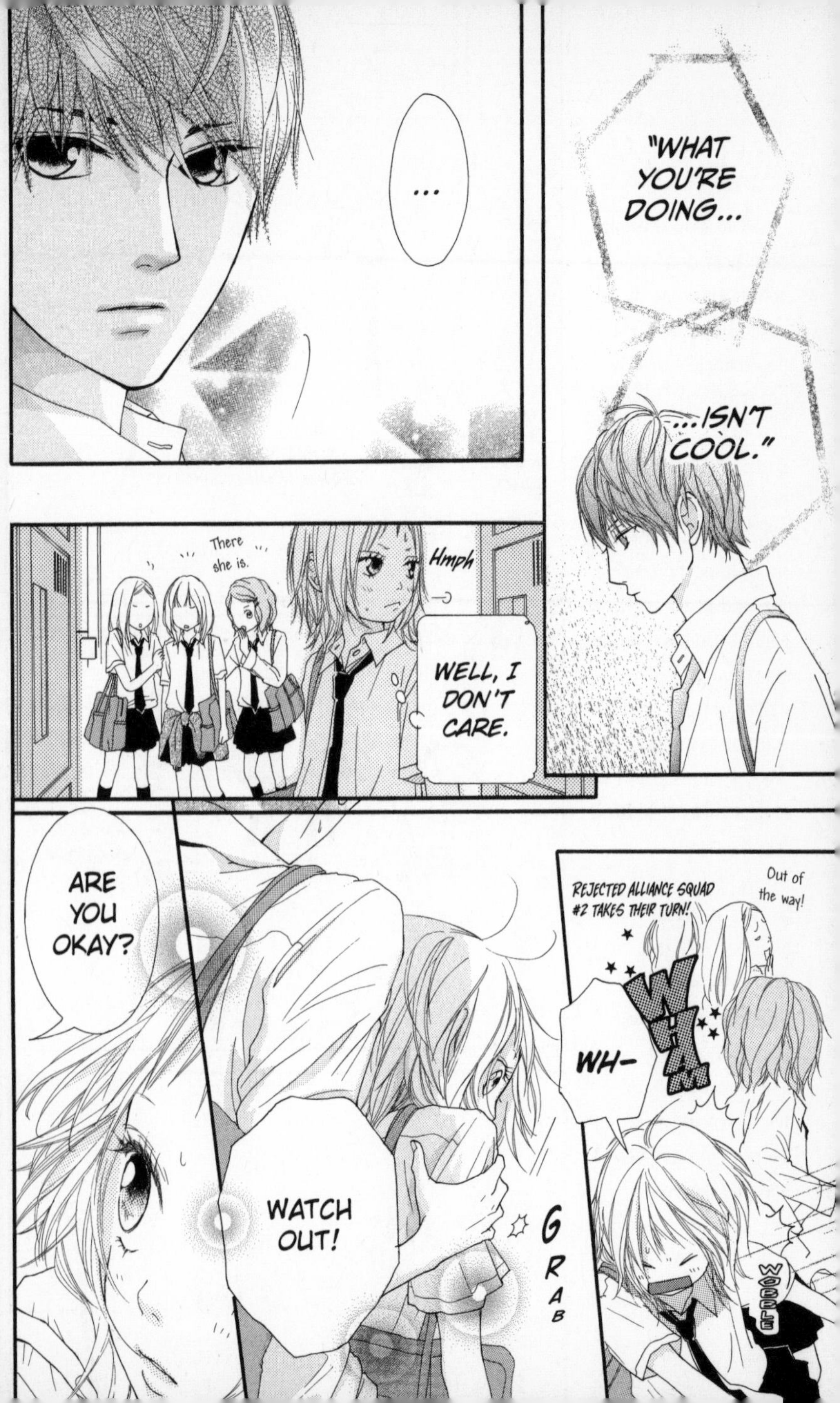
"WHAT YOU'RE DOING...
...ISN'T COOL."
...
There she is.
Hmph
WELL, I DON'T CARE.
Out of the way!
REJECTED ALLIANCE SQUAD #2 TAKES THEIR TURN!
WHAM
WH-
WOBBLE
ARE YOU OKAY?
WATCH OUT!
GRAB

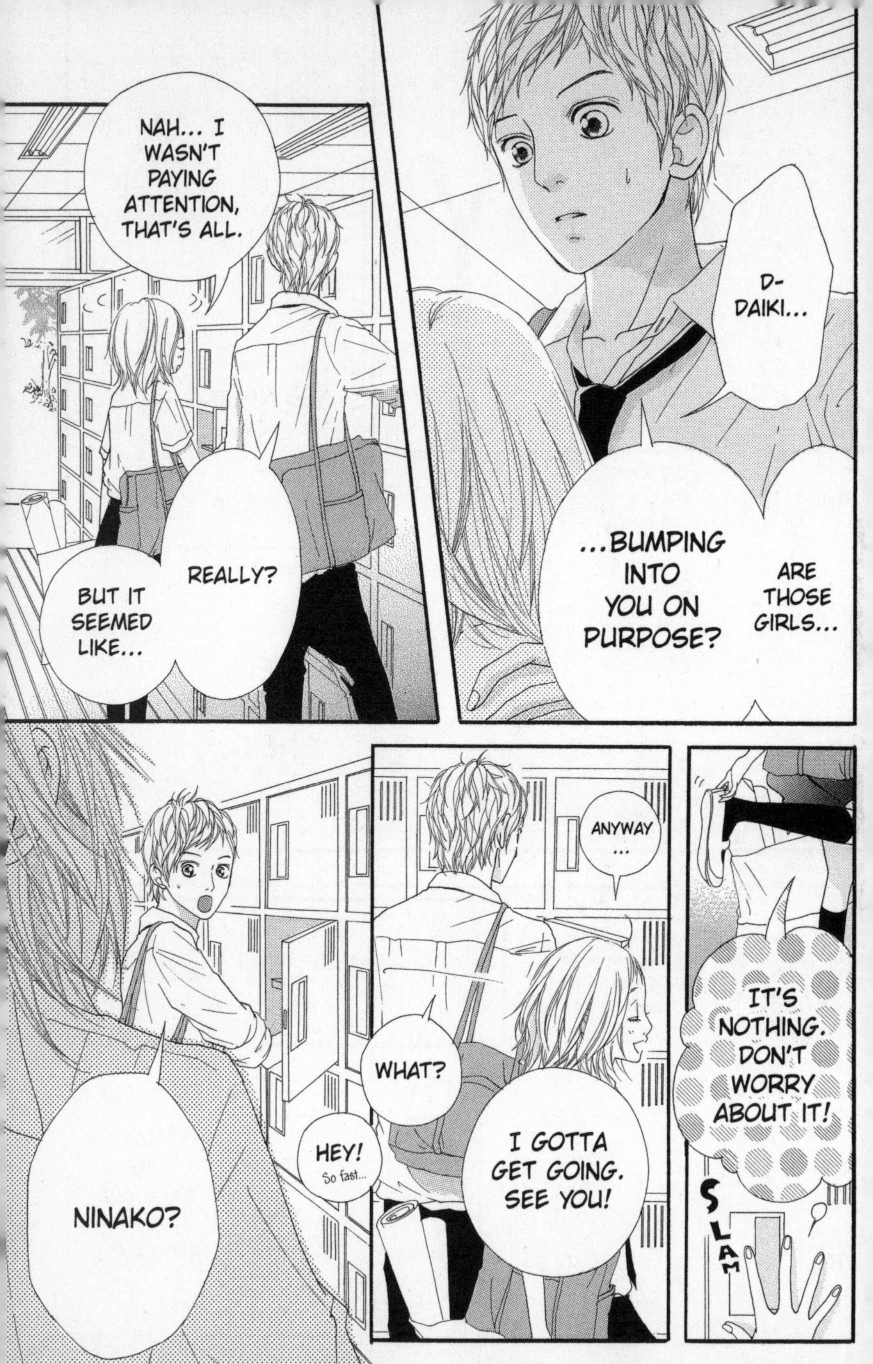
D-
DAIKI...
ARE THOSE GIRLS...
...BUMPING INTO YOU ON PURPOSE?
NAH... I WASN'T PAYING ATTENTION, THAT'S ALL.
REALLY?
BUT IT SEEMED LIKE...
IT'S NOTHING. DON'T WORRY ABOUT IT!
SLAM
ANYWAY ...
I GOTTA GET GOING. SEE YOU!
WHAT?
HEY! So fast...
NINAKO?

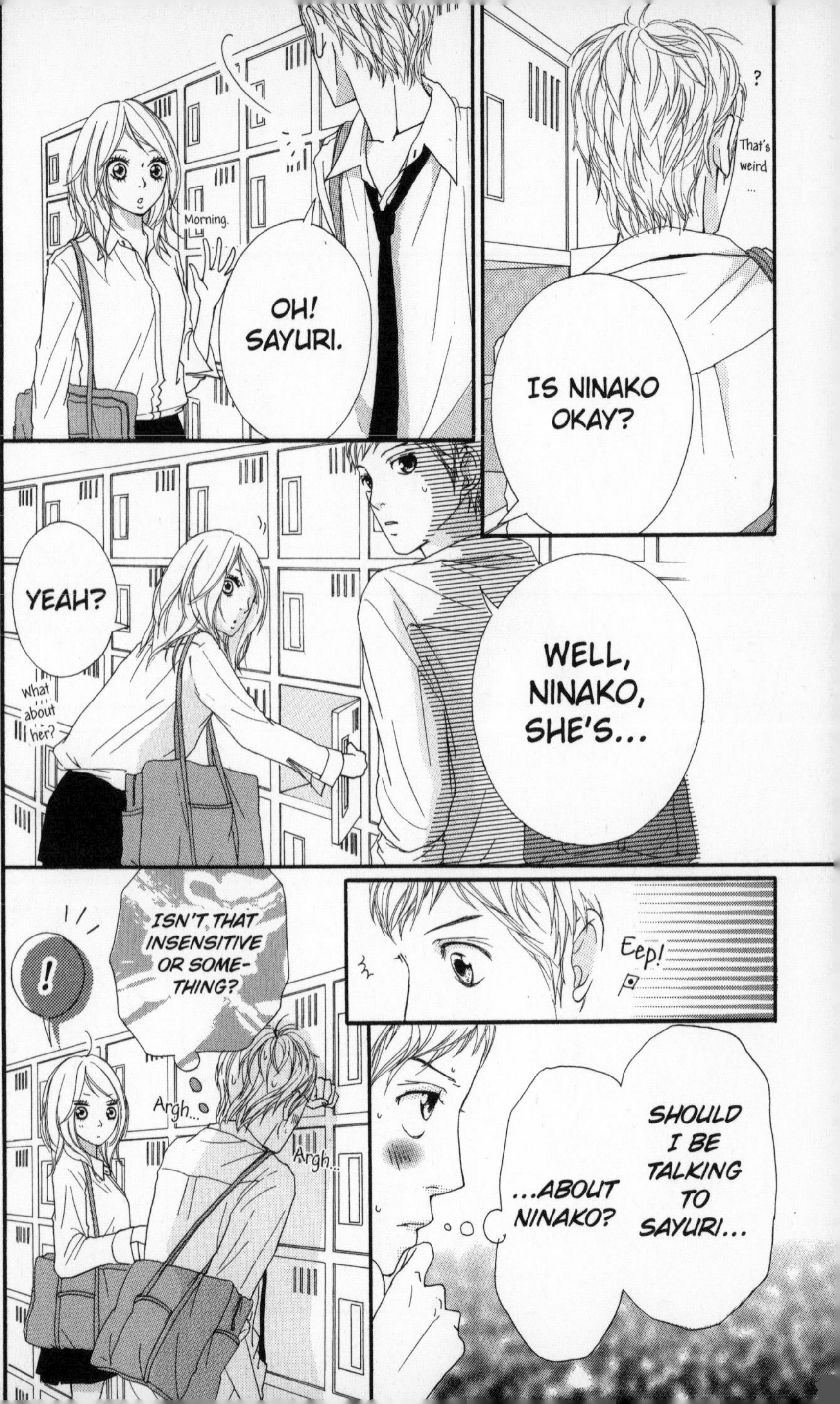
?
That's weird...
IS NINAKO OKAY?
Morning.
OH! SAYURI.
WELL, NINAKO, SHE'S...
YEAH?
What about her?
Eep!
SHOULD I BE TALKING TO SAYURI...
...ABOUT NINAKO?
!
ISN'T THAT INSENSITIVE OR SOME-THING?
Argh...
Argh...

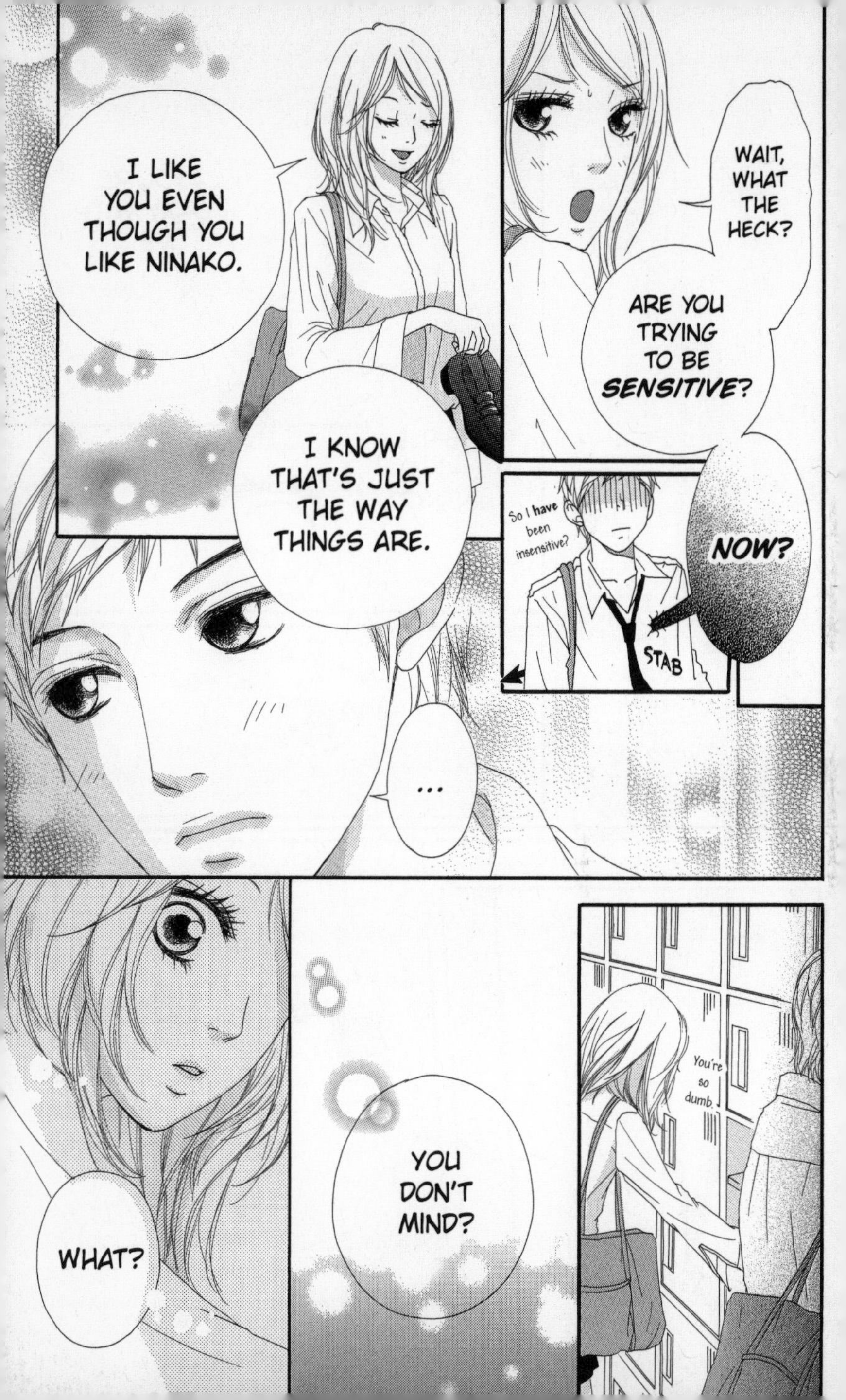
WAIT, WHAT THE HECK?
ARE YOU TRYING TO BE *SENSITIVE*?
I LIKE YOU EVEN THOUGH YOU LIKE NINAKO.
NOW?
So I **have** been insensitive?
STAB
I KNOW THAT'S JUST THE WAY THINGS ARE.
...
You're so dumb.
YOU DON'T MIND?
WHAT?

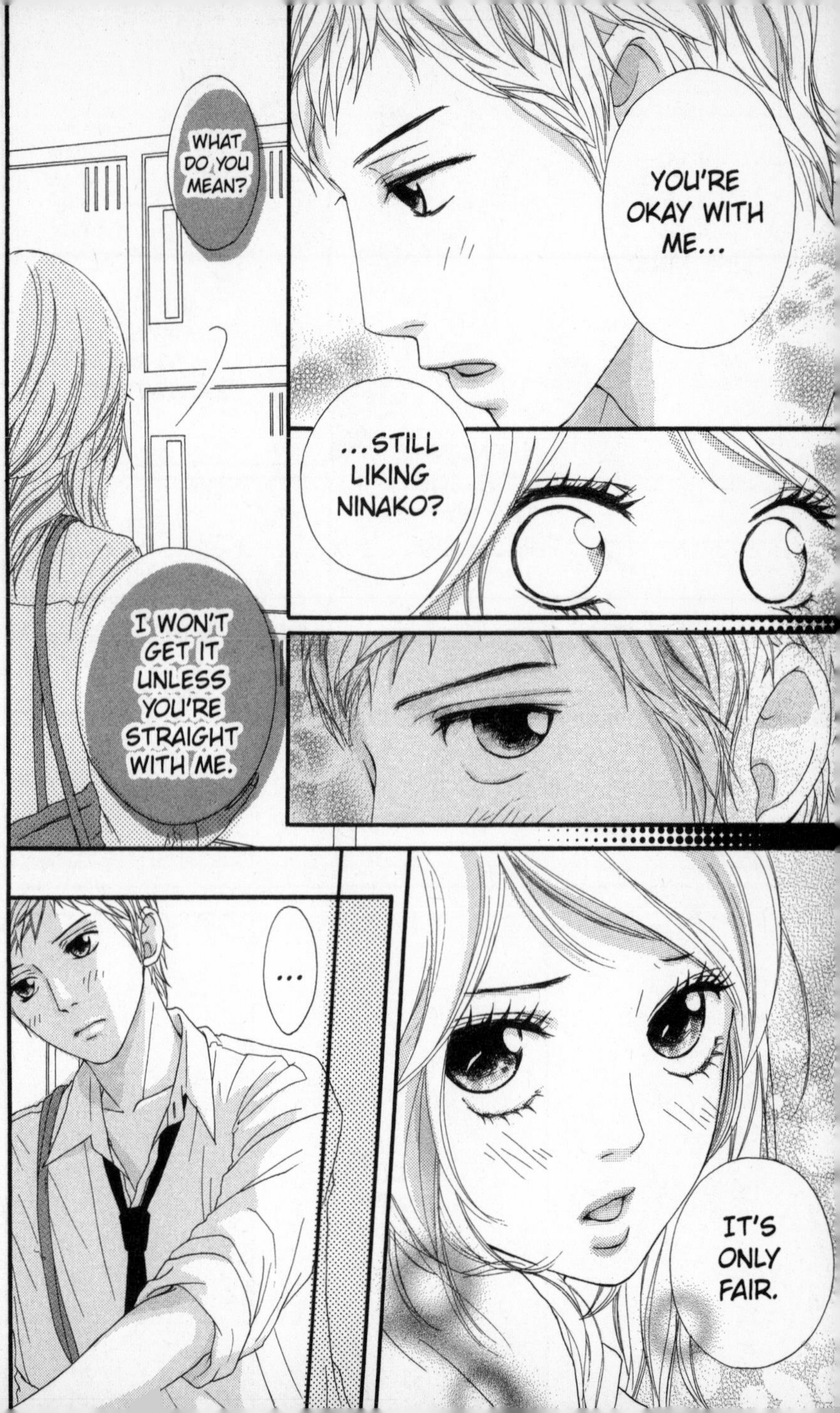
YOU'RE OKAY WITH ME...
...STILL LIKING NINAKO?
WHAT DO YOU MEAN?
I WON'T GET IT UNLESS YOU'RE STRAIGHT WITH ME.
IT'S ONLY FAIR.
...

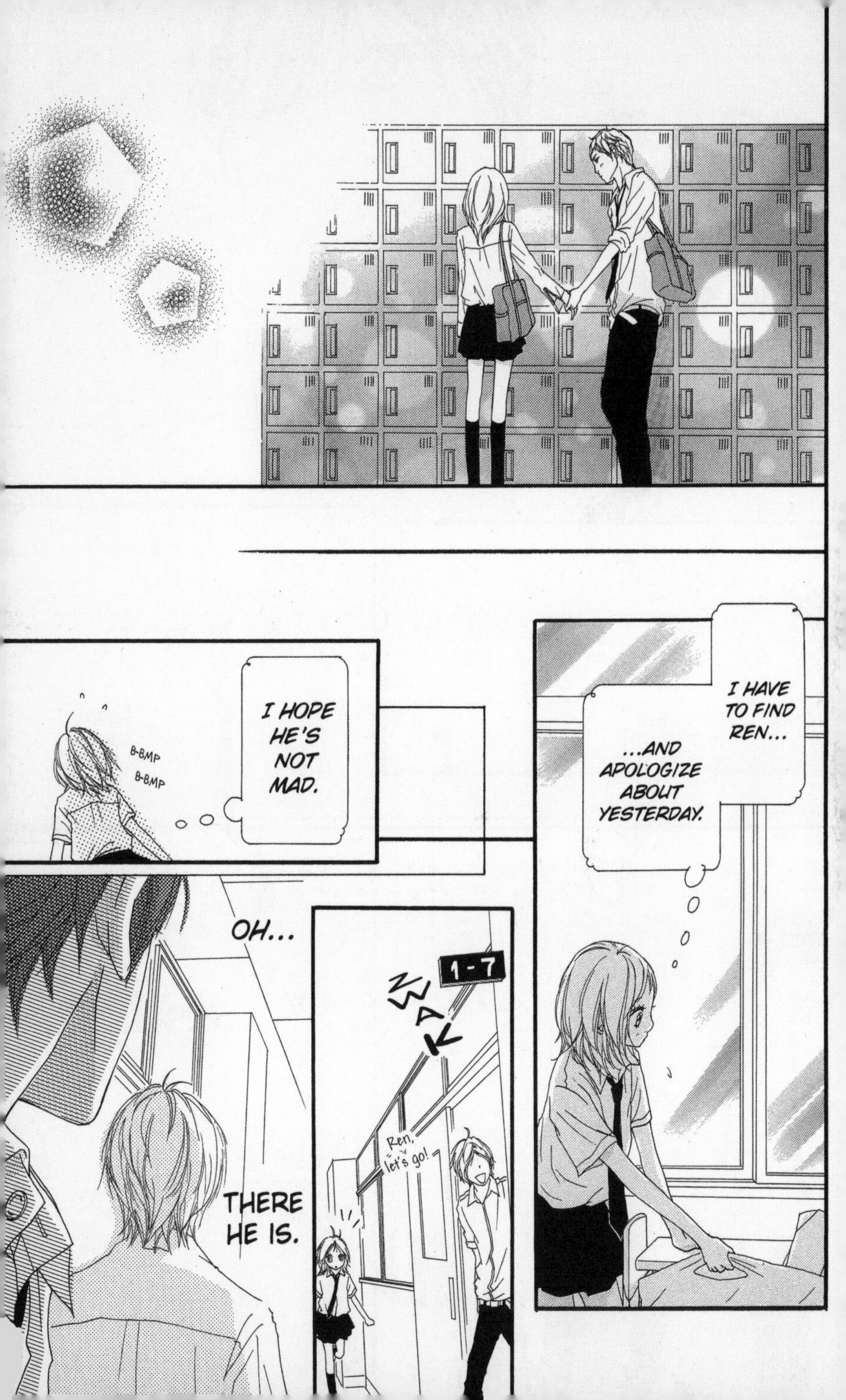
I HAVE TO FIND REN...
...AND APOLOGIZE ABOUT YESTERDAY.
I HOPE HE'S NOT MAD.
B-BMP
B-BMP
1-7
ZWAK
Ren, let's go!
OH...
THERE HE IS.

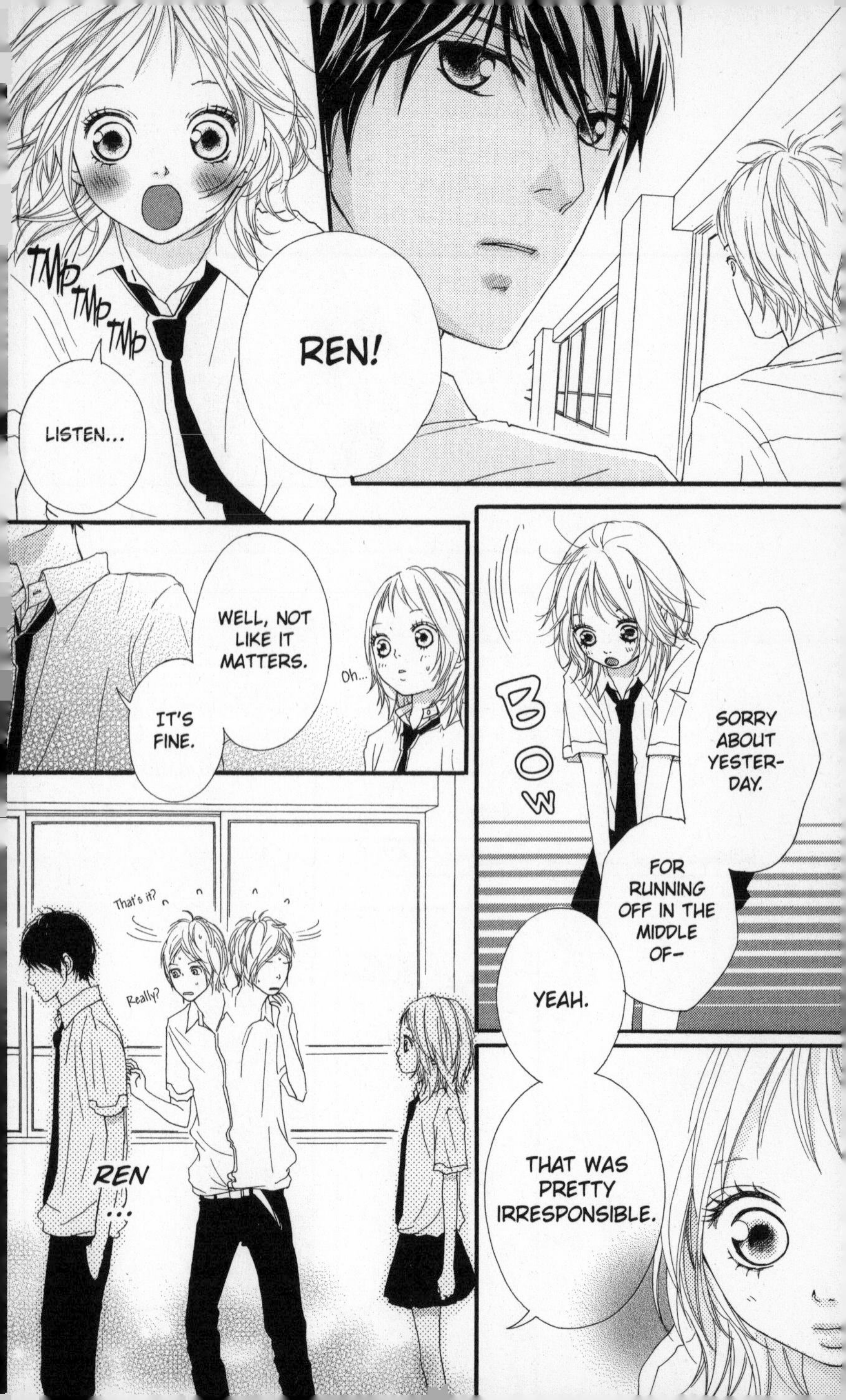
TMP TMP TMP
REN!
LISTEN...
BOW
SORRY ABOUT YESTER-DAY.
FOR RUNNING OFF IN THE MIDDLE OF-
YEAH.
THAT WAS PRETTY IRRESPONSIBLE.
WELL, NOT LIKE IT MATTERS.
IT'S FINE.
Oh...
That's it?
Really?
REN...

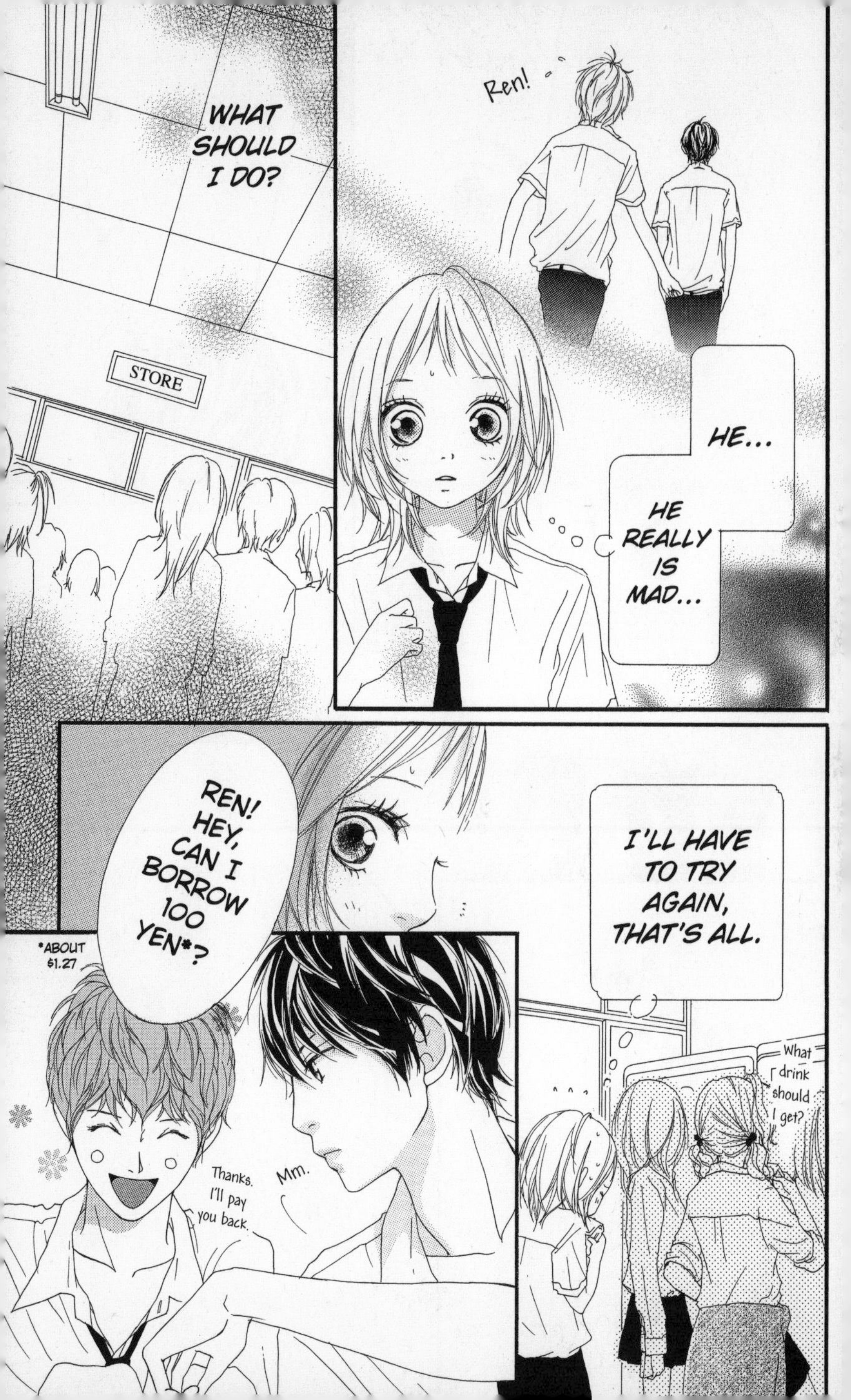
Ren!
HE...
HE REALLY IS MAD...
WHAT SHOULD I DO?
STORE
I'LL HAVE TO TRY AGAIN, THAT'S ALL.
What drink should I get?
REN! HEY, CAN I BORROW 100 YEN*?
*ABOUT $1.27
Mm.
Thanks. I'll pay you back.

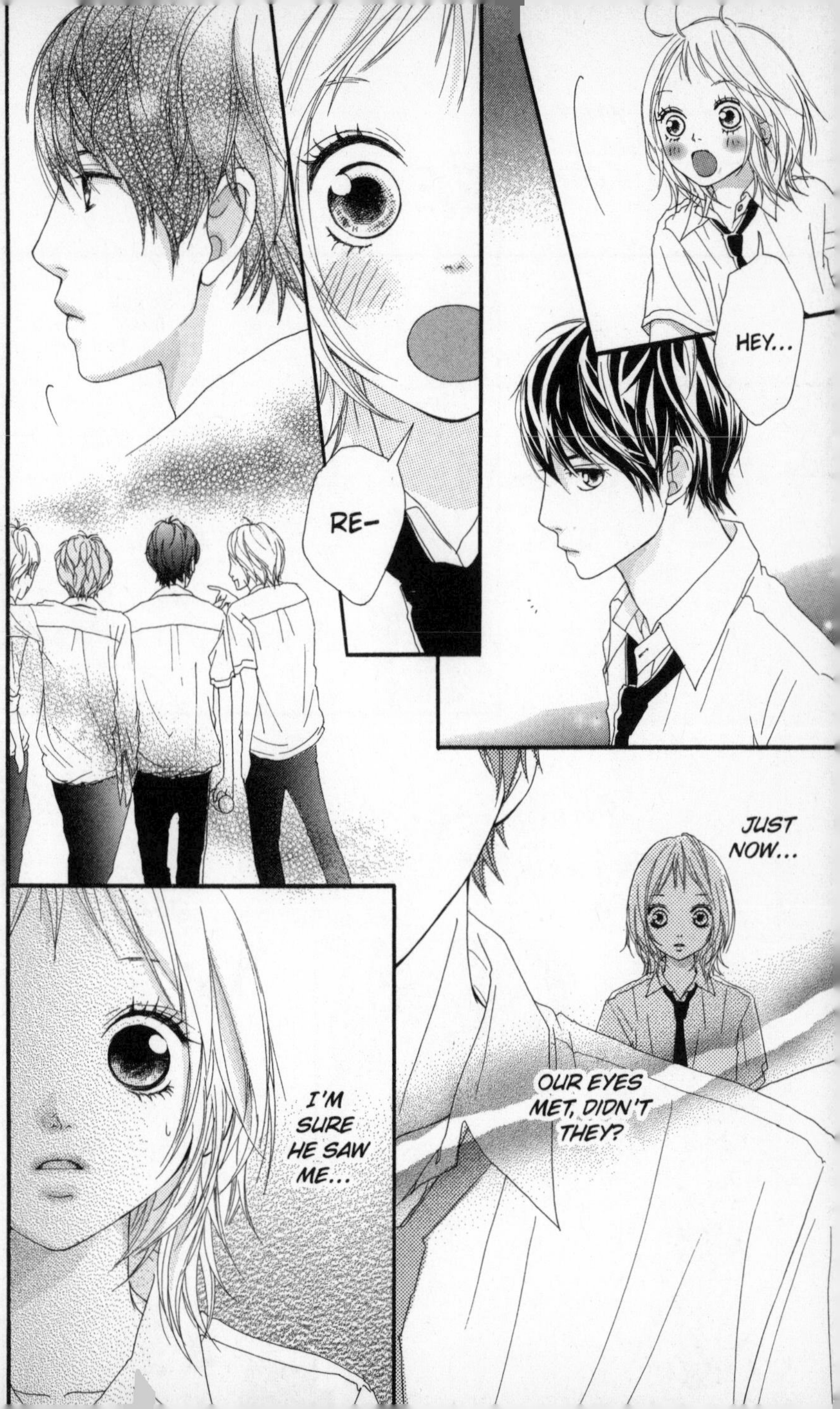
HEY...
RE-
JUST NOW...
OUR EYES MET, DIDN'T THEY?
I'M SURE HE SAW ME...

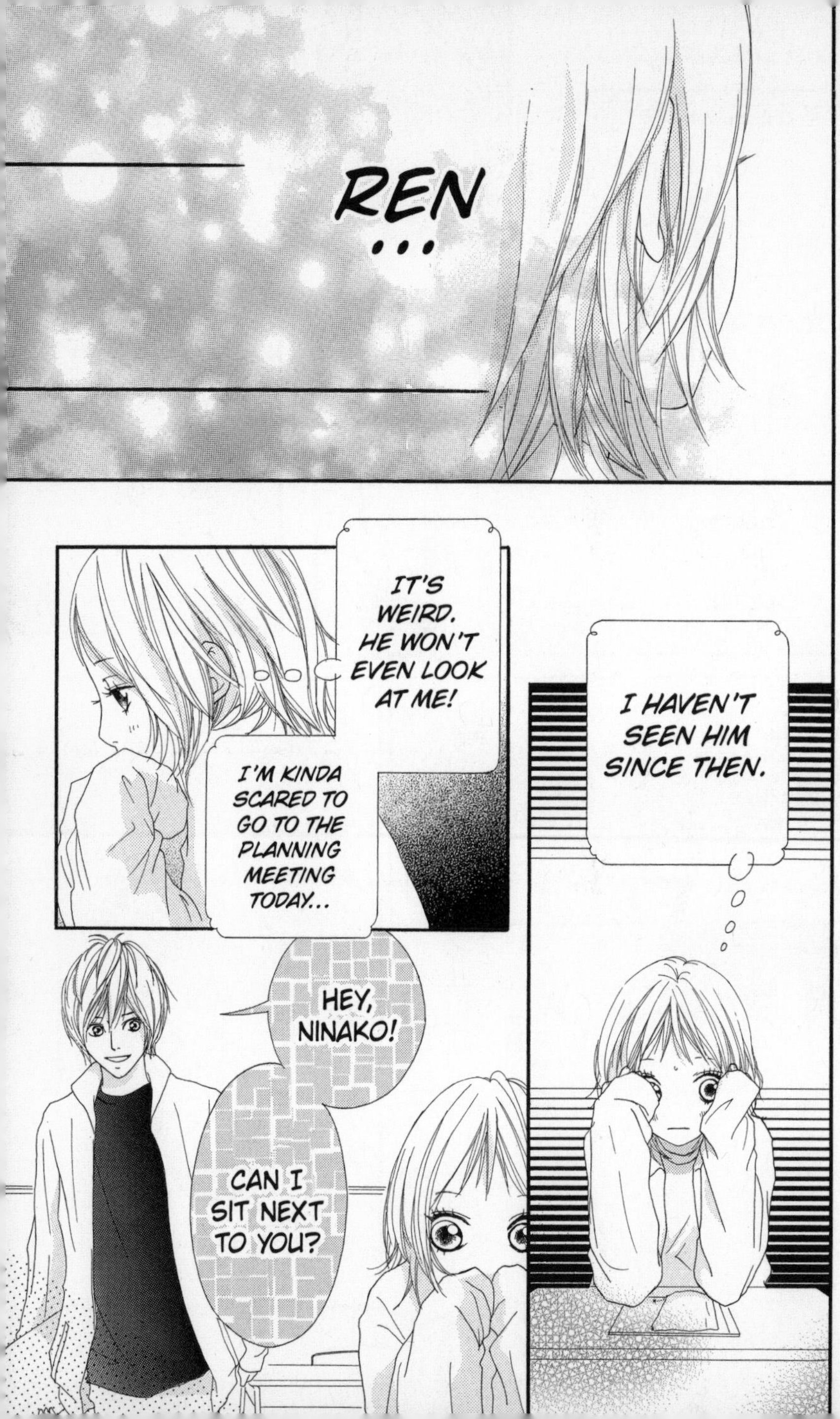
REN...
I HAVEN'T SEEN HIM SINCE THEN.
IT'S WEIRD. HE WON'T EVEN LOOK AT ME!
I'M KINDA SCARED TO GO TO THE PLANNING MEETING TODAY...
HEY, NINAKO!
CAN I SIT NEXT TO YOU?

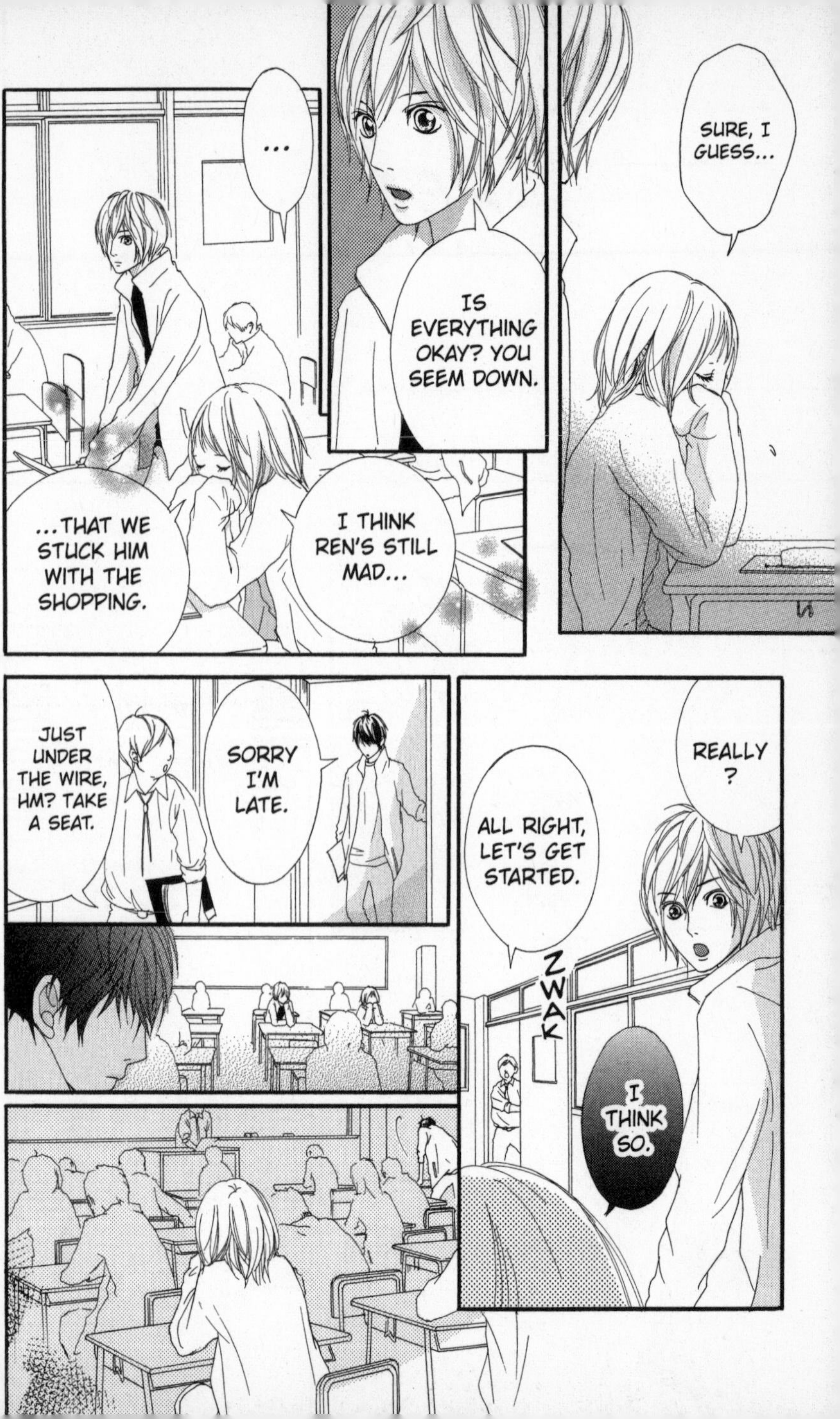
SURE, I GUESS...
IS EVERYTHING OKAY? YOU SEEM DOWN.
...
I THINK REN'S STILL MAD...
...THAT WE STUCK HIM WITH THE SHOPPING.
REALLY?
ALL RIGHT, LET'S GET STARTED.
ZWAK
I THINK SO.
SORRY I'M LATE.
JUST UNDER THE WIRE, HM? TAKE A SEAT.

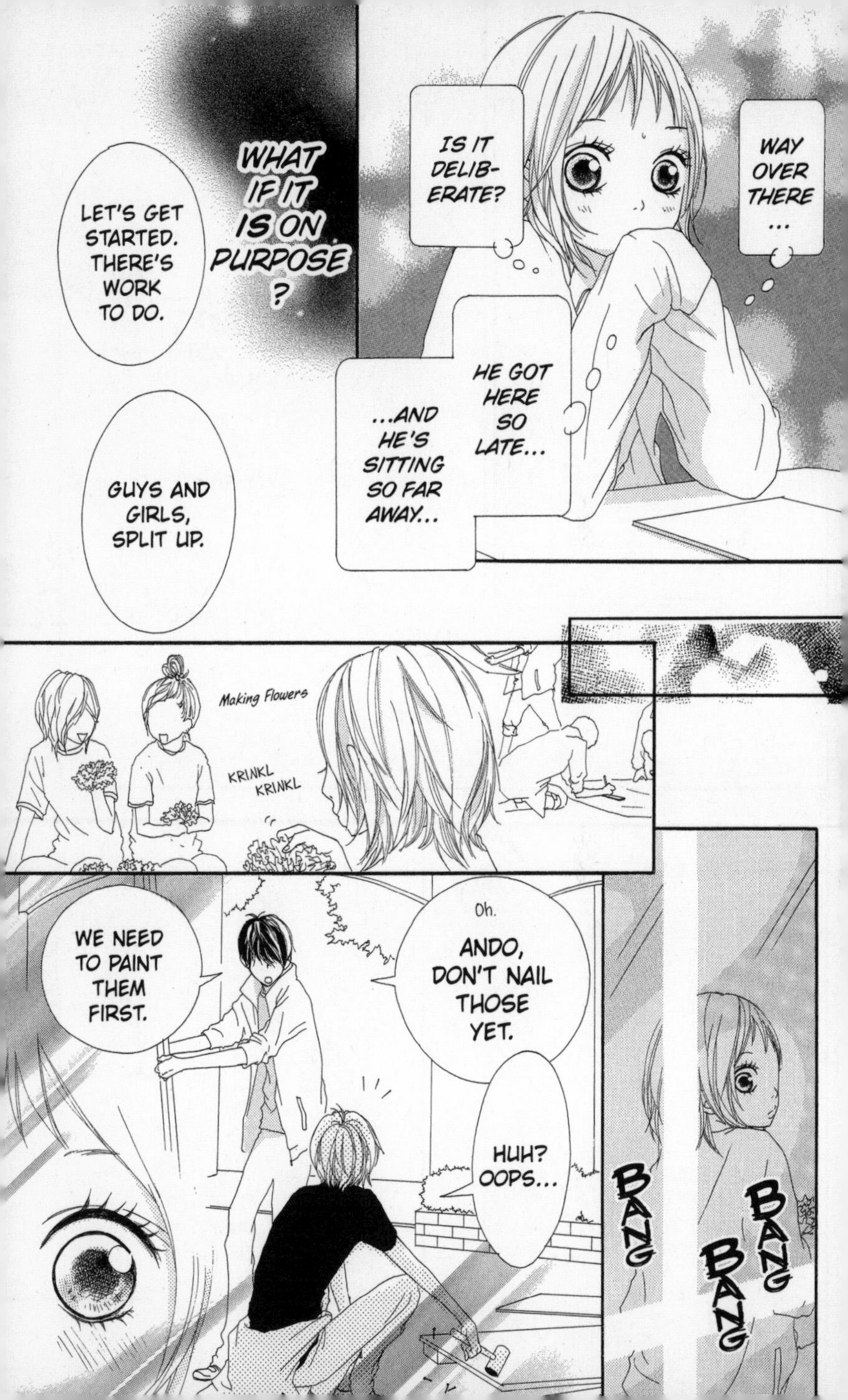
WAY OVER THERE ...
IS IT DELIB-ERATE?
HE GOT HERE SO LATE...
...AND HE'S SITTING SO FAR AWAY...
WHAT IF IT IS ON PURPOSE?
LET'S GET STARTED. THERE'S WORK TO DO.
GUYS AND GIRLS, SPLIT UP.
Making Flowers
KRINKL KRINKL
BANG
BANG
BANG
Oh.
ANDO, DON'T NAIL THOSE YET.
WE NEED TO PAINT THEM FIRST.
HUH? OOPS...

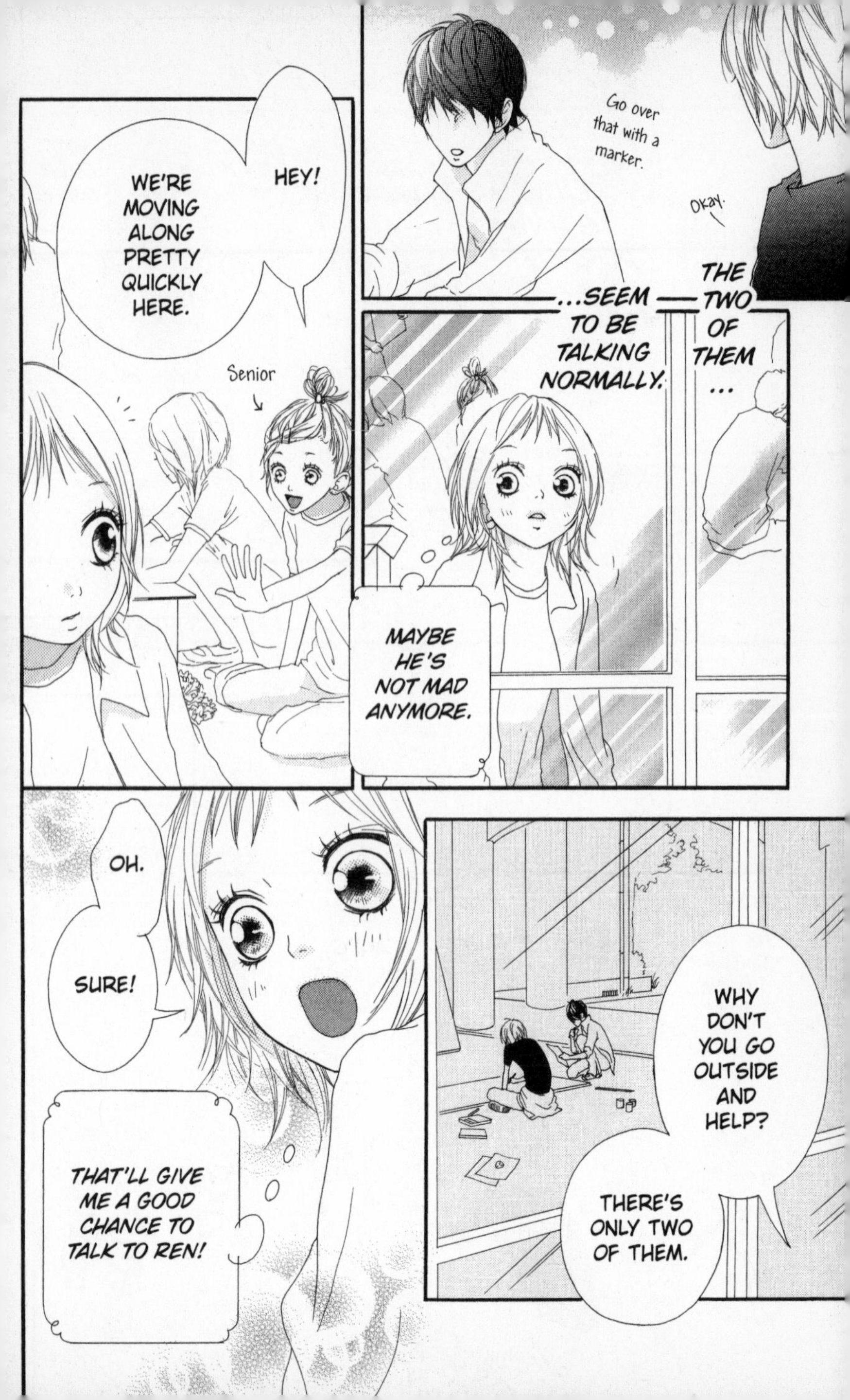
Go over that with a marker.
Okay.
THE TWO OF THEM...
...SEEM TO BE TALKING NORMALLY.
MAYBE HE'S NOT MAD ANYMORE.
HEY!
WE'RE MOVING ALONG PRETTY QUICKLY HERE.
Senior
WHY DON'T YOU GO OUTSIDE AND HELP?
THERE'S ONLY TWO OF THEM.
OH.
SURE!
THAT'LL GIVE ME A GOOD CHANCE TO TALK TO REN!

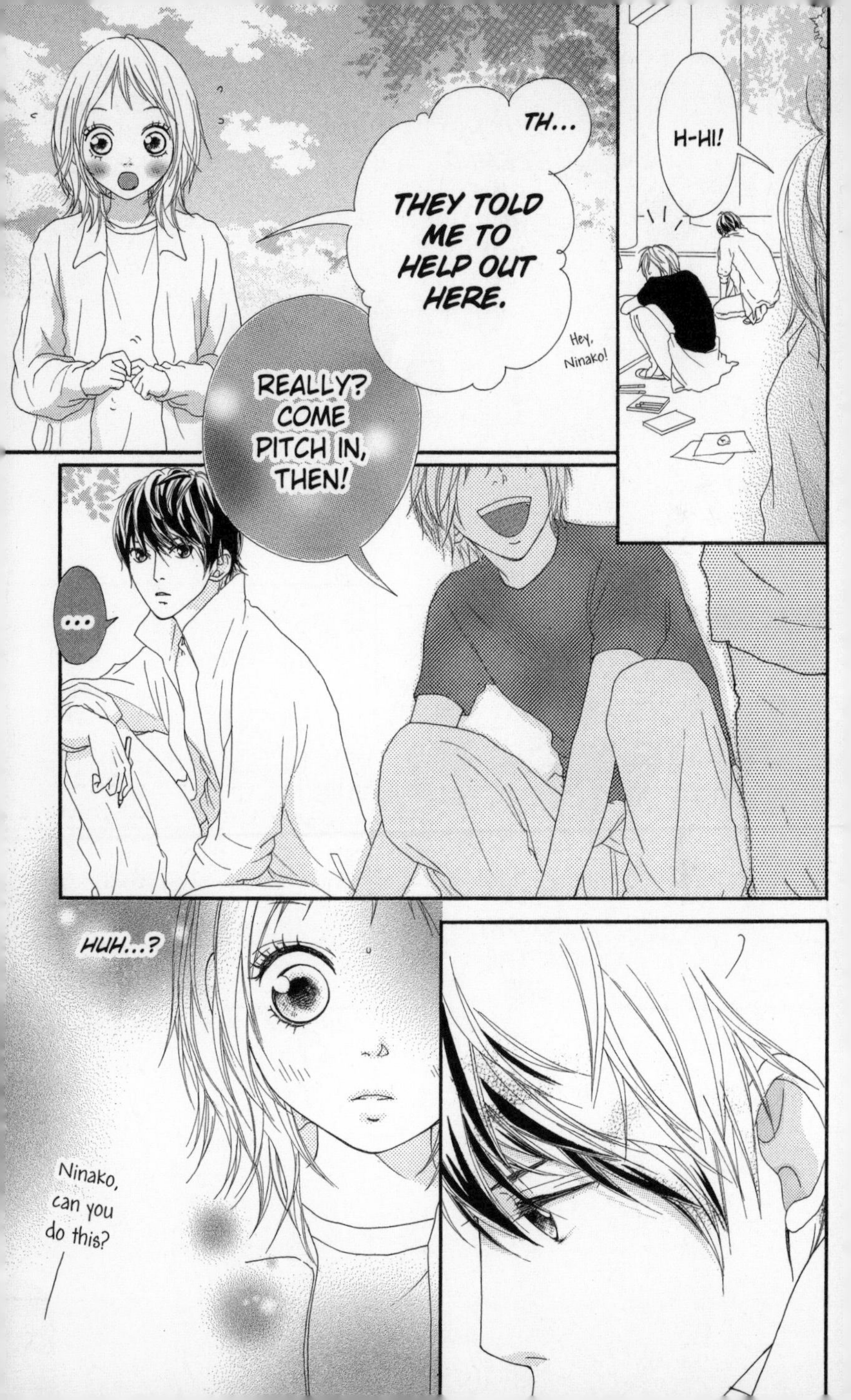
H-HI!
Hey, Ninako!
TH...
THEY TOLD ME TO HELP OUT HERE.
REALLY? COME PITCH IN, THEN!
...
HUH...?
Ninako, can you do this?

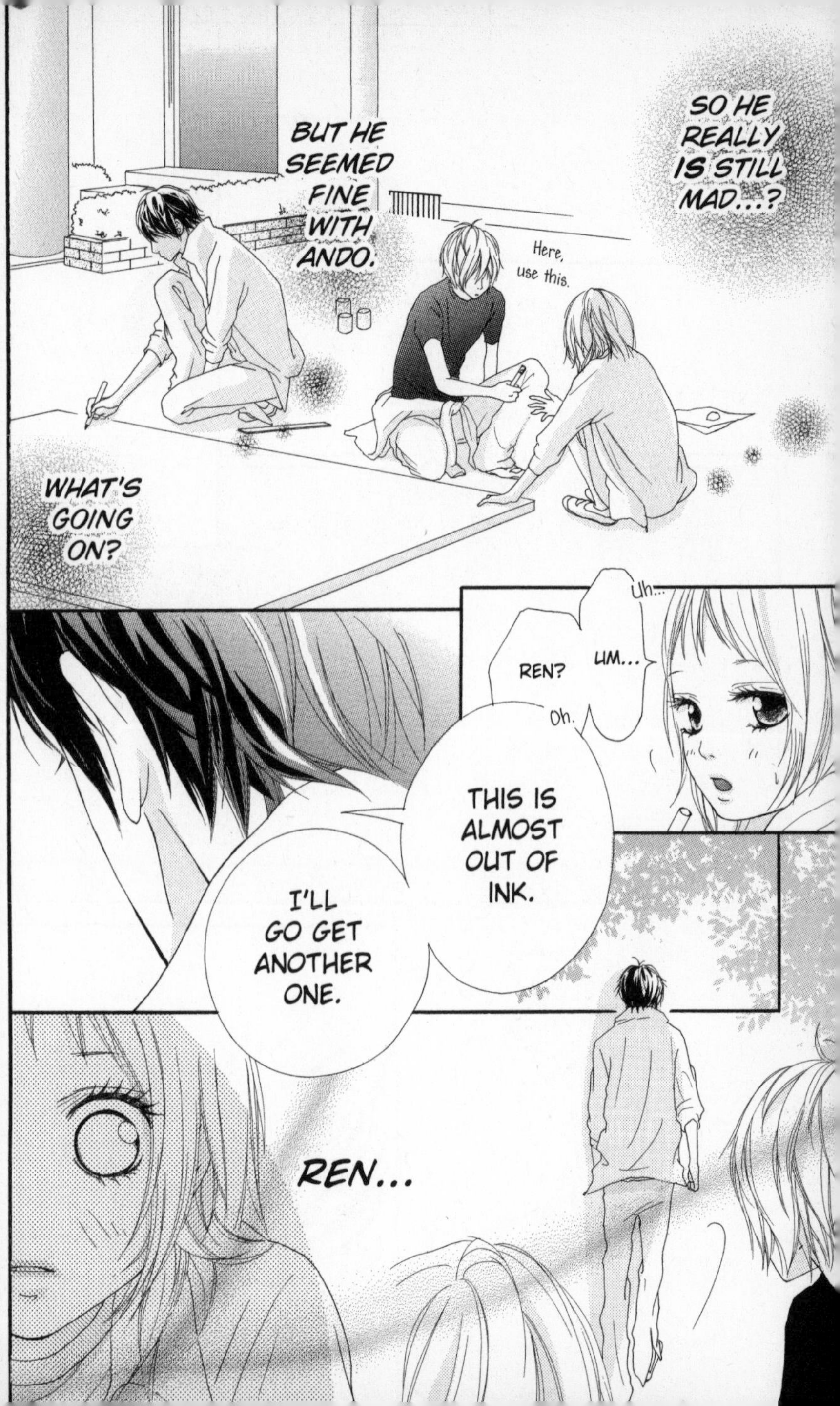
SO HE REALLY IS STILL MAD...?
Here, use this.
BUT HE SEEMED FINE WITH ANDO.
WHAT'S GOING ON?
Uh...
UM...
REN?
Oh.
THIS IS ALMOST OUT OF INK.
I'LL GO GET ANOTHER ONE.
REN...

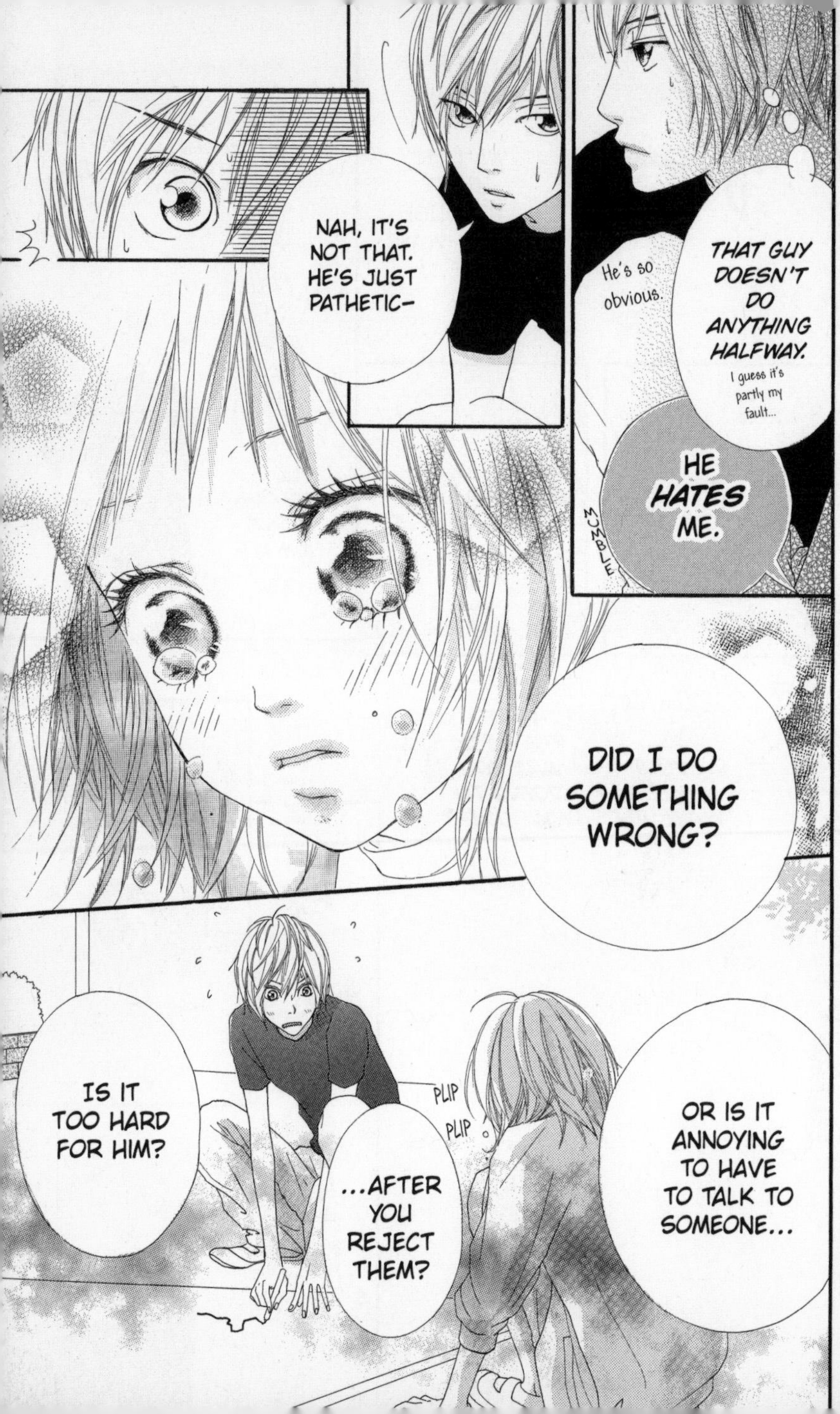
THAT GUY DOESN'T DO ANYTHING HALFWAY.
I guess it's partly my fault...
He's so obvious.
HE HATES ME.
MUMBLE
NAH, IT'S NOT THAT. HE'S JUST PATHETIC-
DID I DO SOMETHING WRONG?
OR IS IT ANNOYING TO HAVE TO TALK TO SOMEONE...
PLIP
PLIP
...AFTER YOU REJECT THEM?
IS IT TOO HARD FOR HIM?

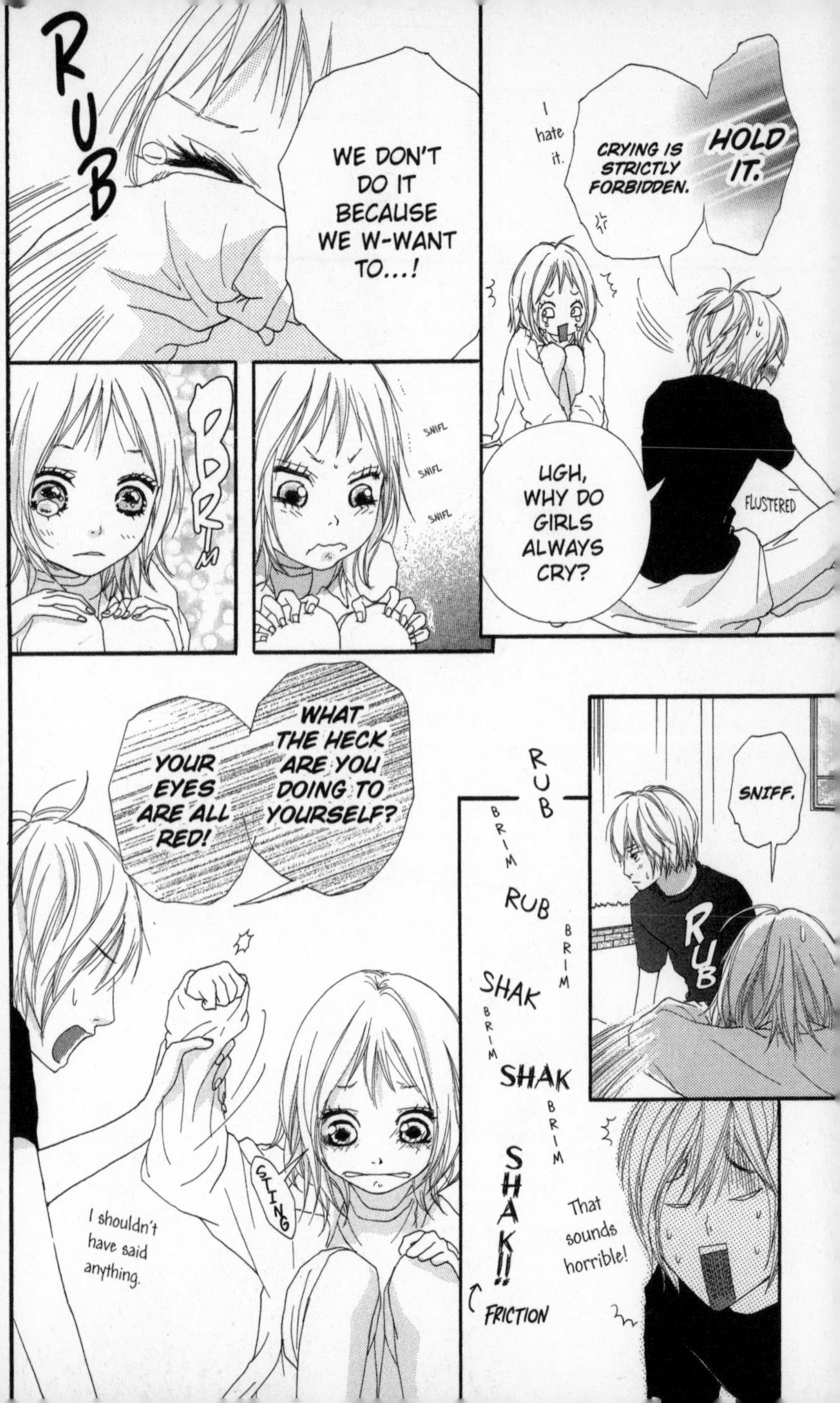
HOLD IT.
CRYING IS STRICTLY FORBIDDEN.
I hate it.
UGH, WHY DO GIRLS ALWAYS CRY?
FLUSTERED
RUB
WE DON'T DO IT BECAUSE WE W-WANT TO...!
SNIFL
SNIFL
SNIFL
BRIM
SNIFF.
RUB
RUB
BRIM
RUB
BRIM
SHAK
BRIM
SHAK
BRIM
SHAK!!
FRICTION
That sounds horrible!
WHAT THE HECK ARE YOU DOING TO YOURSELF?
YOUR EYES ARE ALL RED!
STING
I shouldn't have said anything.

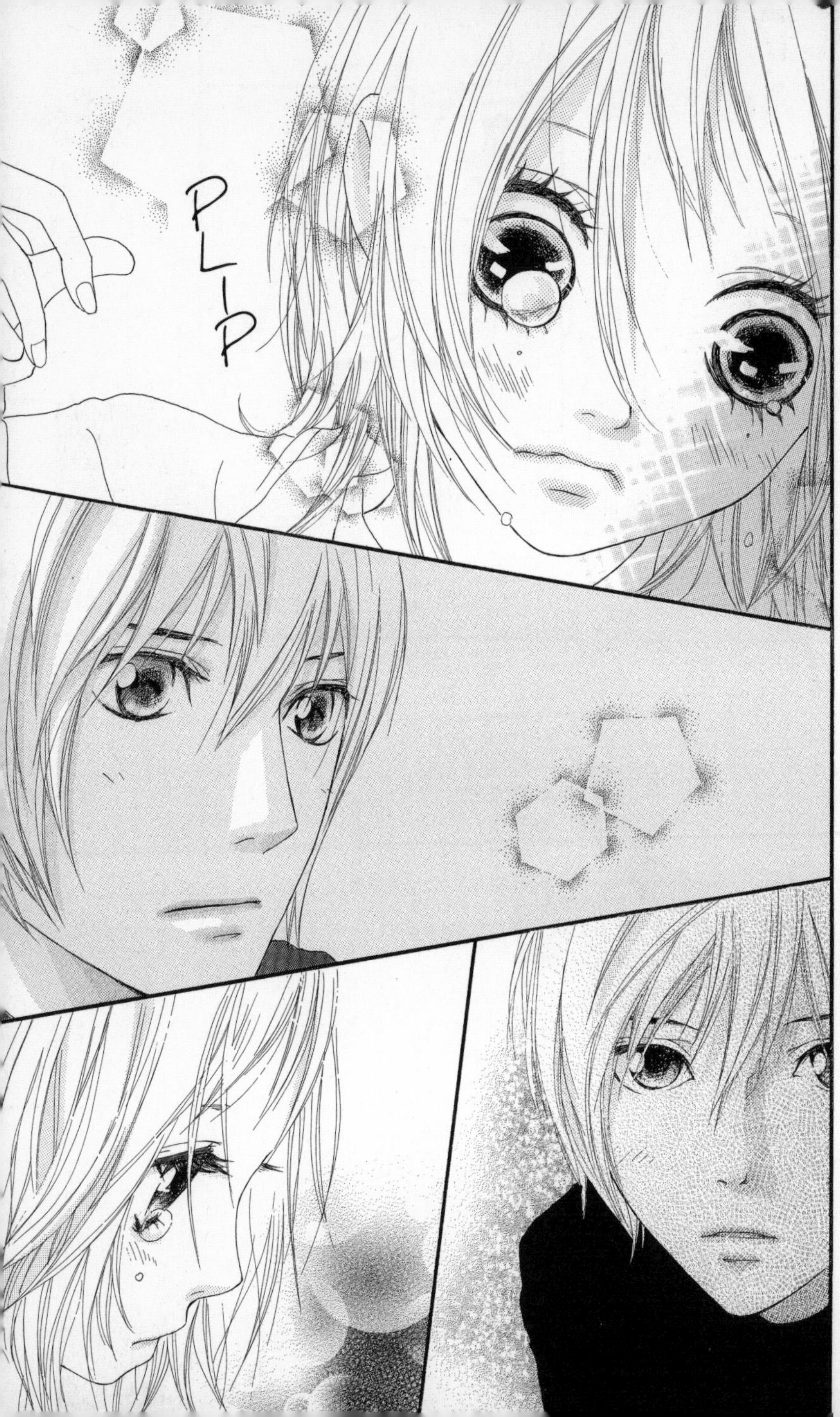
PLIP

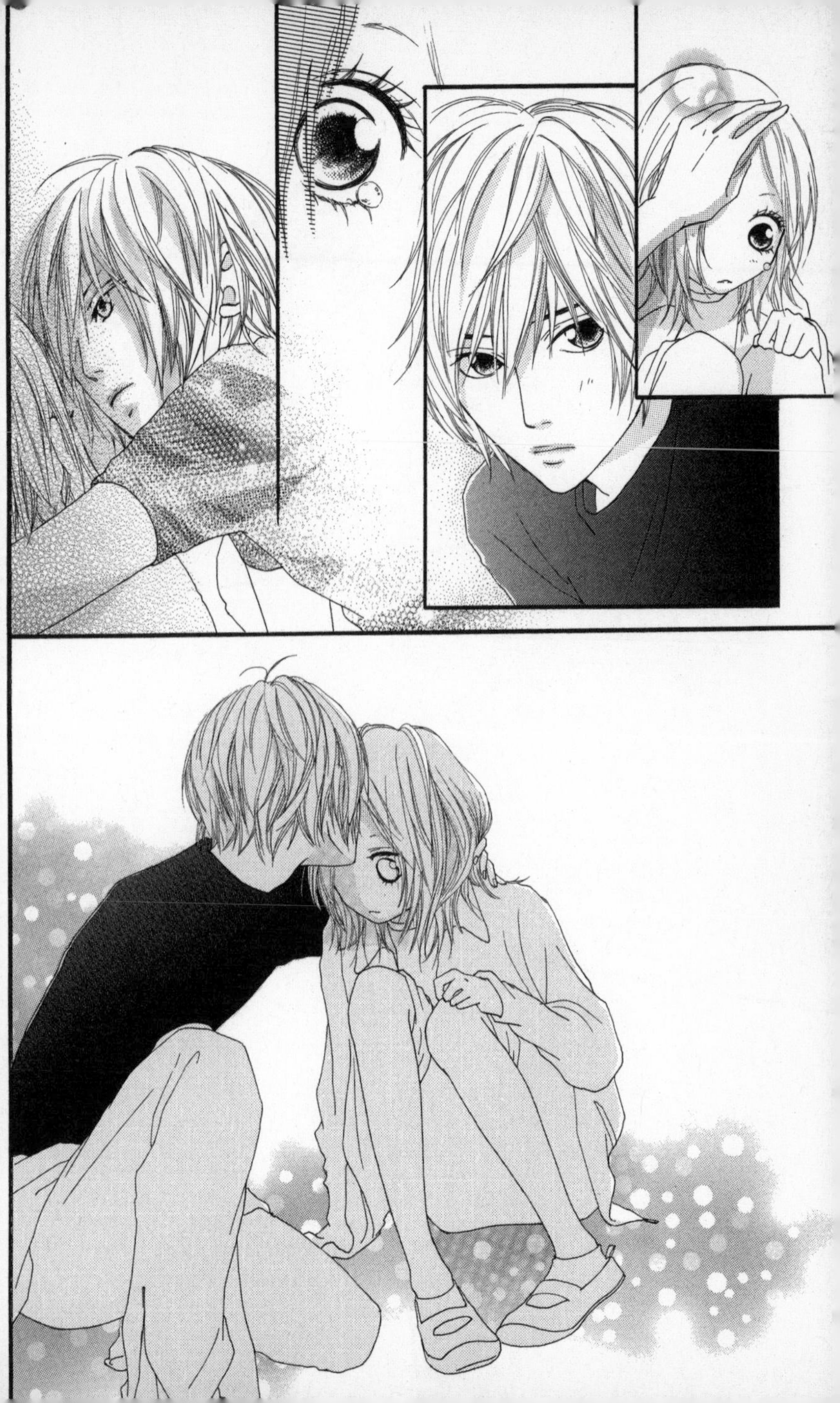

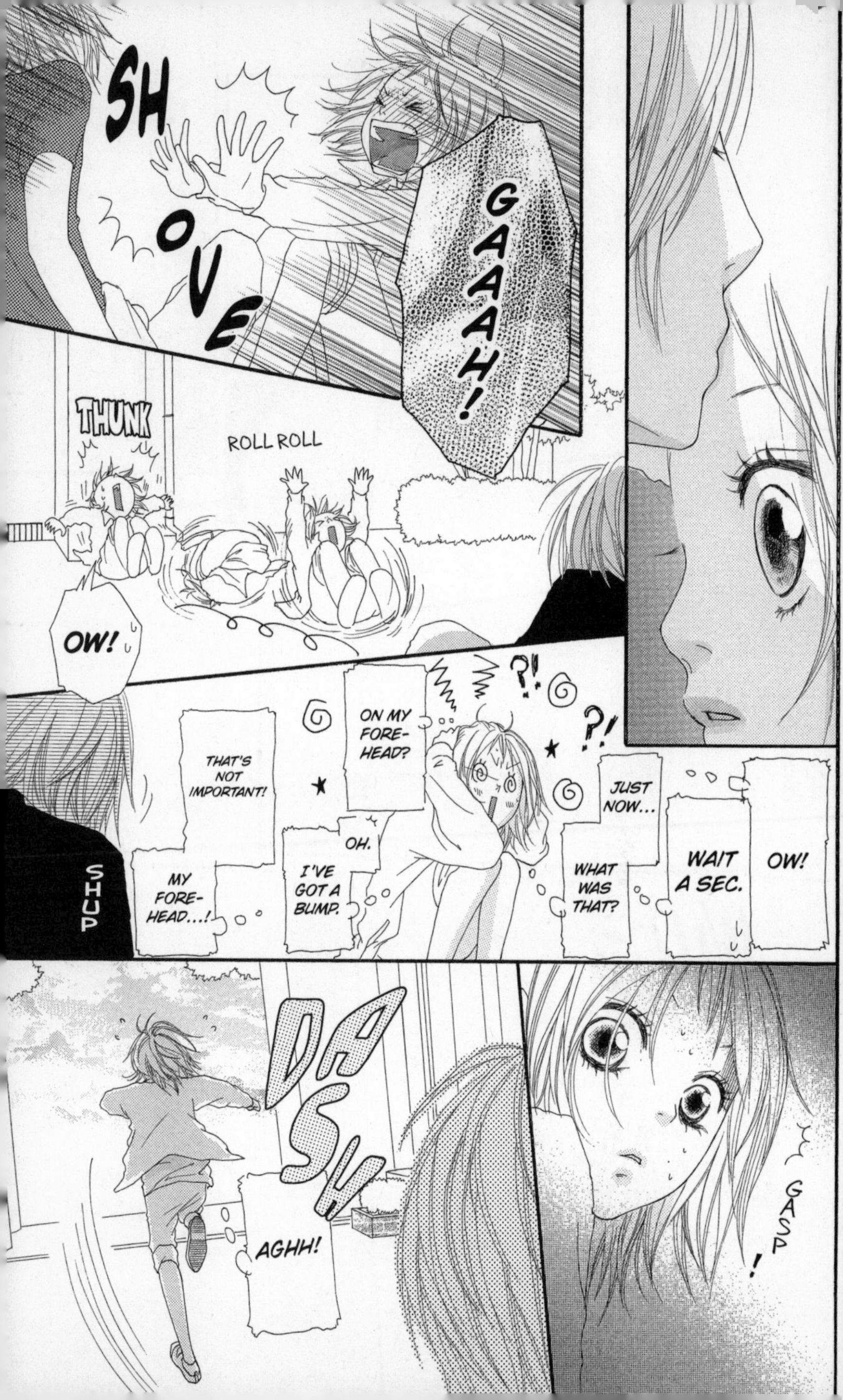
GAAAH!
SHOVE
ROLL ROLL
THUNK
OW!
OW!
WAIT A SEC.
JUST NOW...
WHAT WAS THAT?
ON MY FORE-HEAD?
OH.
I'VE GOT A BUMP.
THAT'S NOT IMPORTANT!
MY FORE-HEAD...!
SHUP
GASP!
DASH
AGHH!

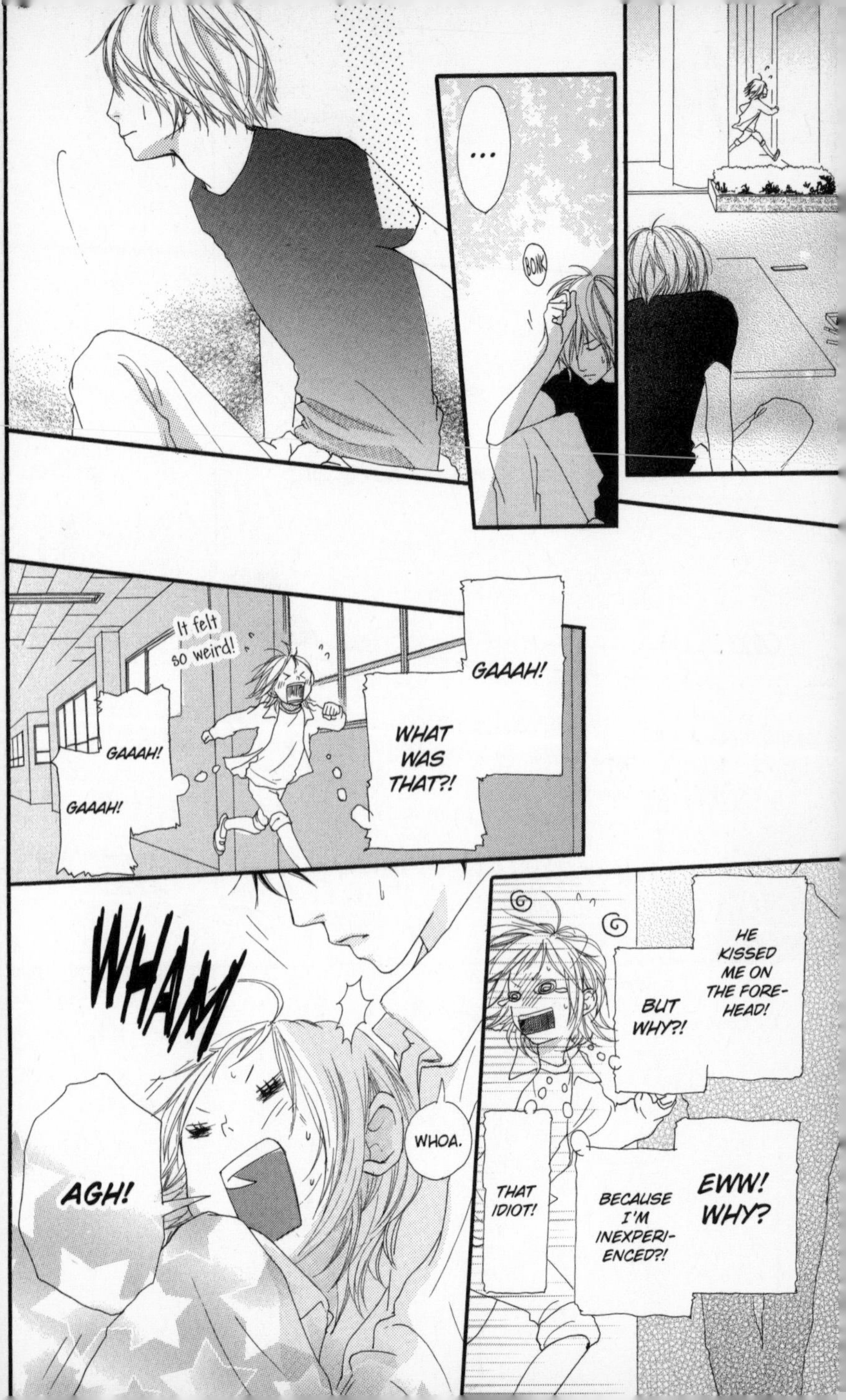

...
BONK
GAAAH!
WHAT WAS THAT?!
It felt so weird!
GAAAH!
GAAAH!
HE KISSED ME ON THE FOREHEAD!
BUT WHY?!
EWW! WHY?
BECAUSE I'M INEXPERIENCED?!
THAT IDIOT!
WHAM
WHOA.
AGH!

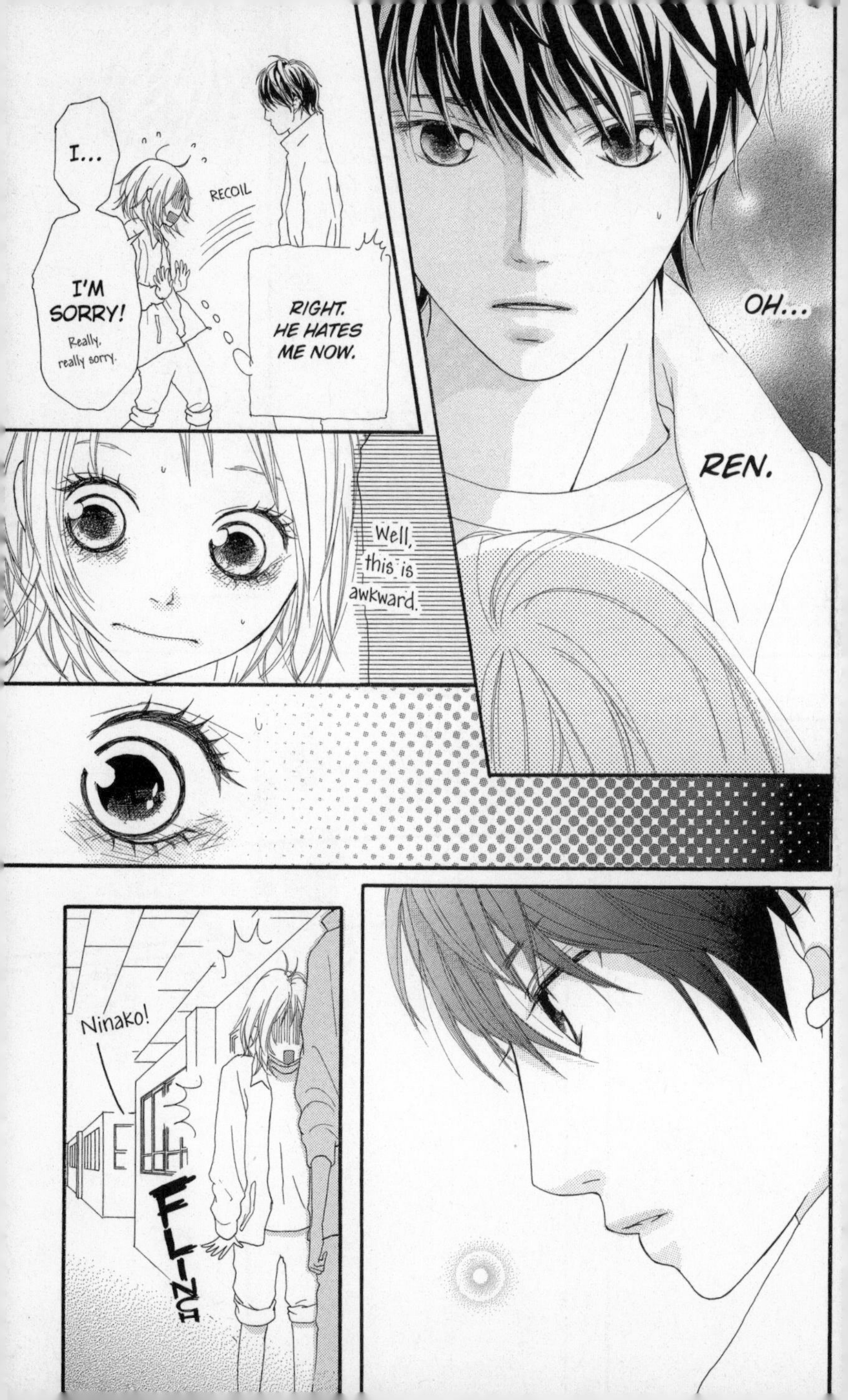
OH...
REN.
RIGHT. HE HATES ME NOW.
RECOIL
I... I'M SORRY!
Really, really sorry.
Well, this is awkward.
Ninako!
FLI-NCH

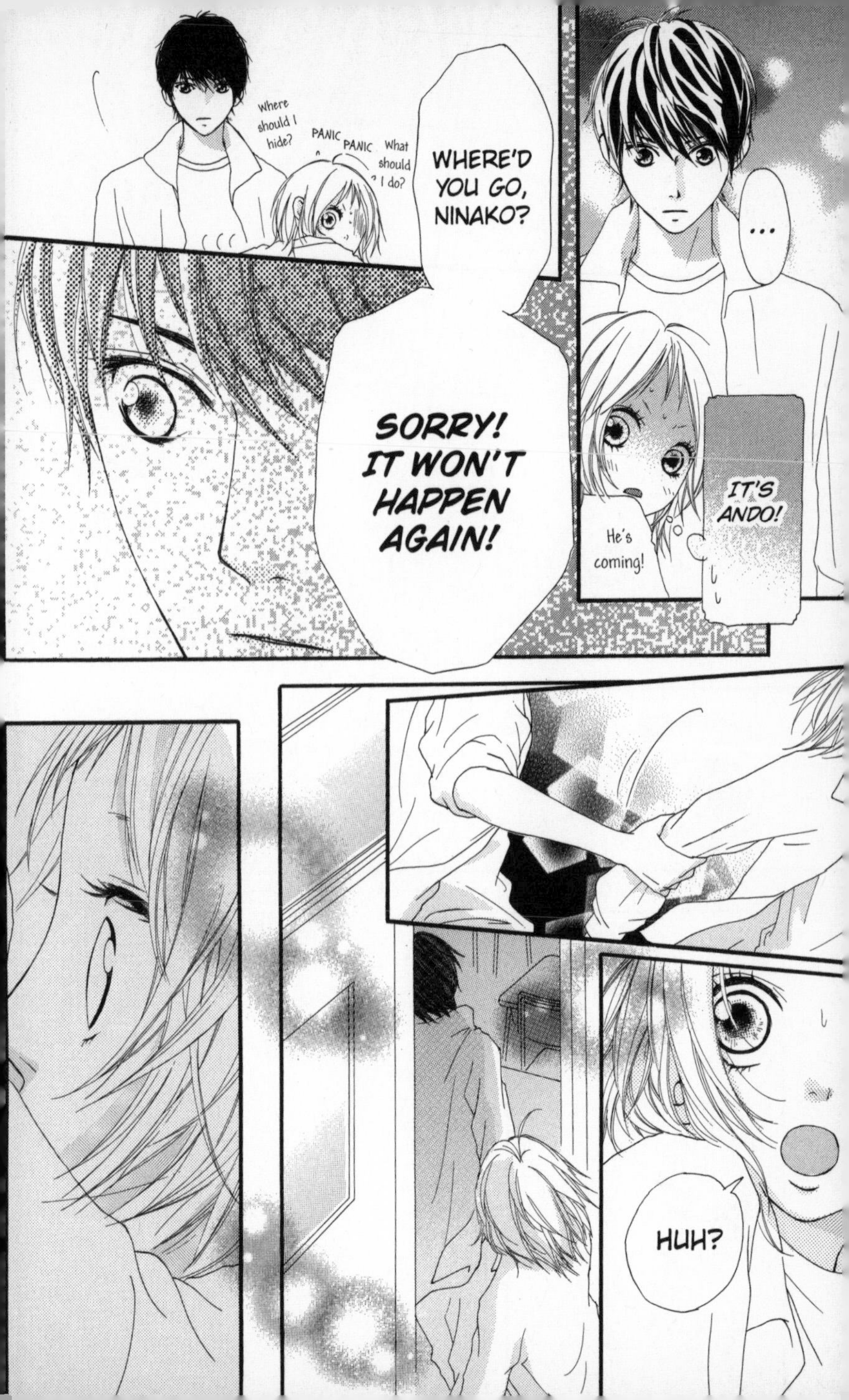
...
IT'S ANDO!
He's coming!
WHERE'D YOU GO, NINAKO?
What should I do?
PANIC PANIC
Where should I hide?
SORRY! IT WON'T HAPPEN AGAIN!
HUH?

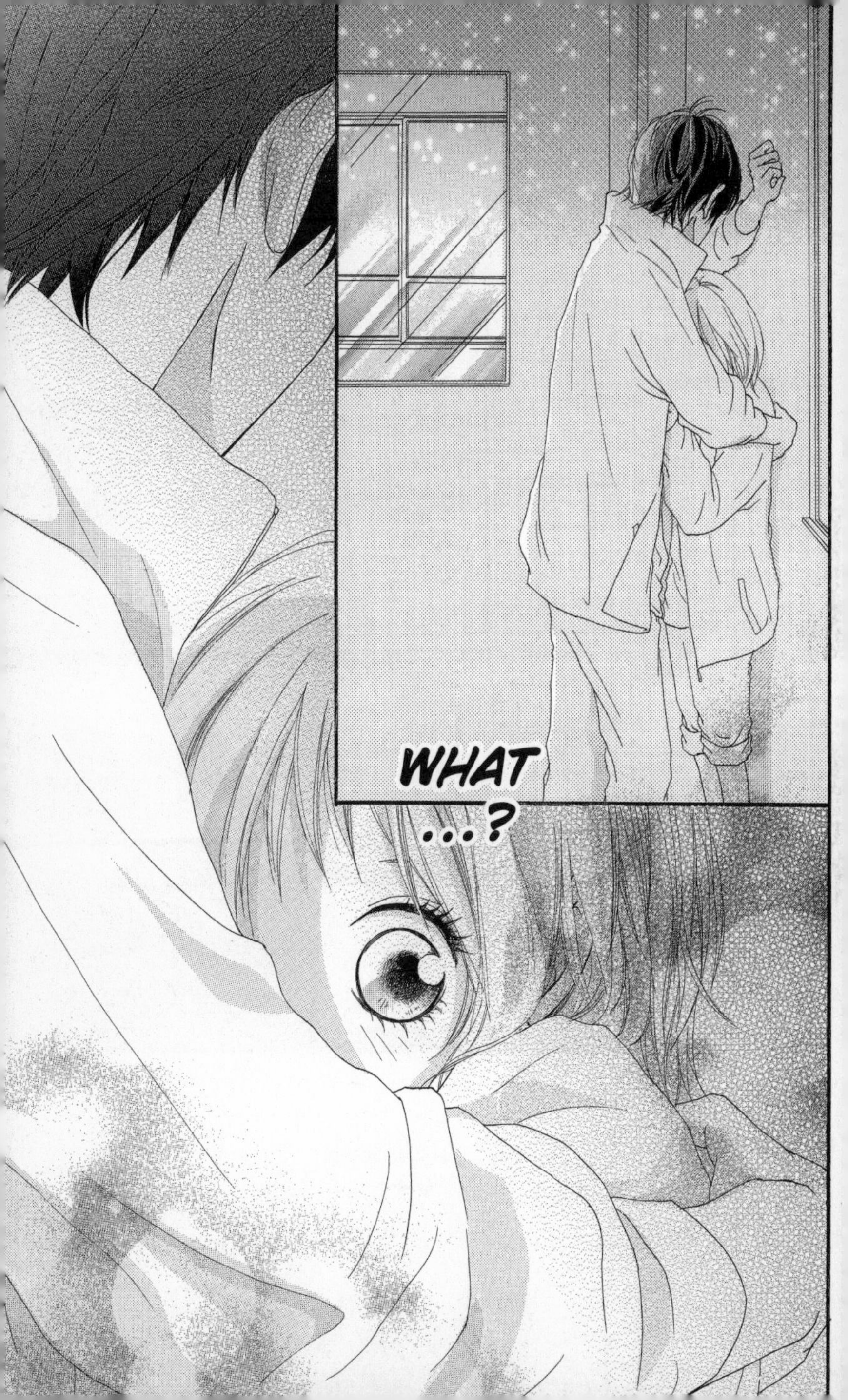
WHAT ...?

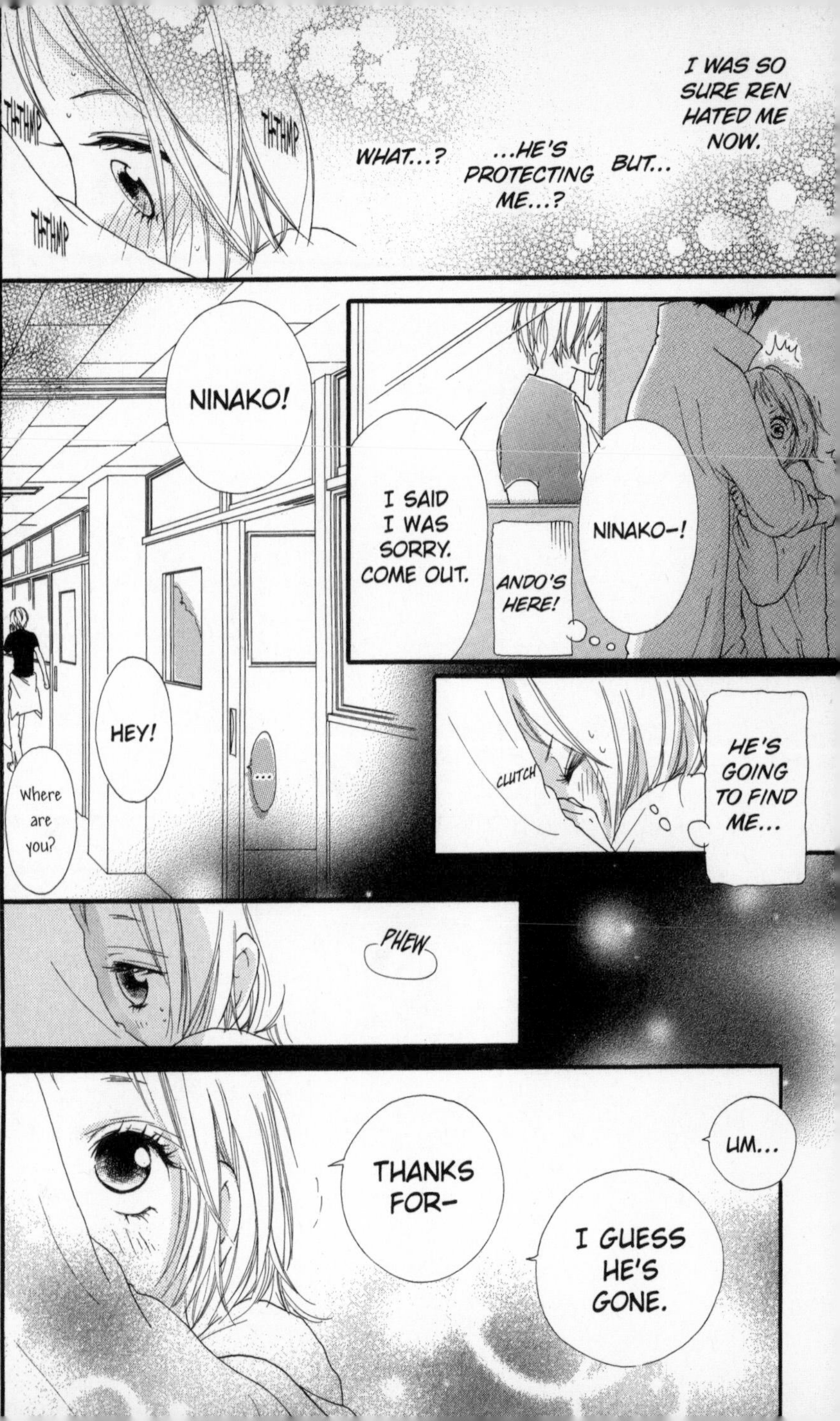
I WAS SO SURE REN HATED ME NOW.
BUT...
...HE'S PROTECTING ME...?
WHAT...?
THTHMP
THTHMP
THTHMP
NINAKO-!
ANDO'S HERE!
I SAID I WAS SORRY. COME OUT.
HE'S GOING TO FIND ME...
CLUTCH
NINAKO!
HEY!
...
Where are you?
PHEW
UM...
I GUESS HE'S GONE.
THANKS FOR-

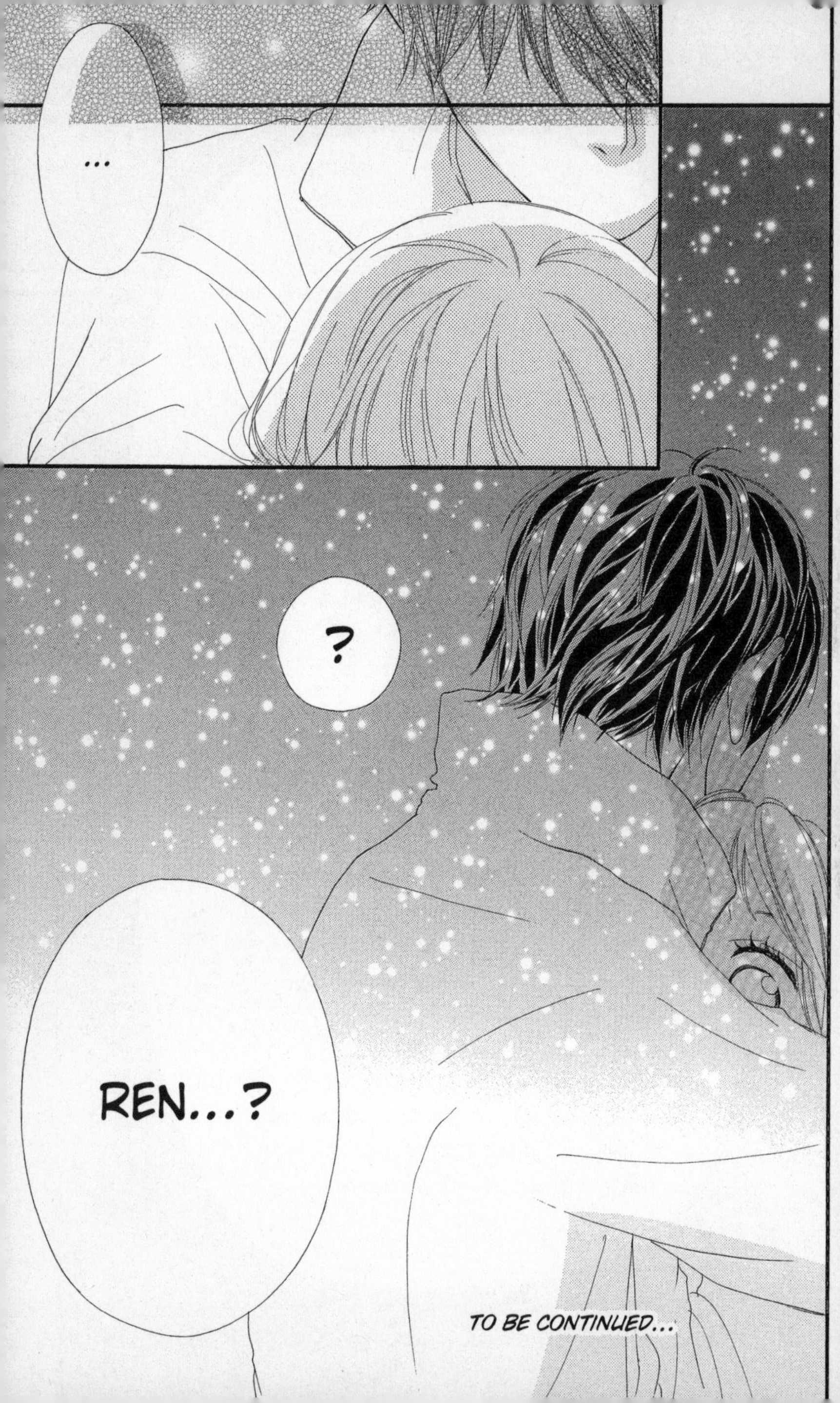
...
?
REN...?
TO BE CONTINUED...

I know this is totally random, but I'm a towel blanket aficionado. I don't just drape one over myself when I go to sleep—I roll it into a ball and put it by my face so I can enjoy the feel of it on my cheek and hands as I drift off.

I'm not really fond of new ones. Personally, I think the older they are, the better, because they get so soft. But on the other hand, as they get old they also get threadbare. Sometimes they rip. But I use them anyway! I don't get a new one until the old one's in tatters, so I've actually only had three of them my entire life.

Hooray!

WANDER WANDER

How do they give me such a feeling of security...? Sometimes I wrap it around my neck or head even when it's not bedtime. But my family gets mad when I wander around with my blanket around my neck, so I only do it when I'm alone. I remember that I went to sleep over at Aruko's house once and brought my trusty towel blanket with me.

I believe there are many other towel blanket aficionados out there who use them the same way. It makes me so happy. Why don't you join the club? New members are always welcome!

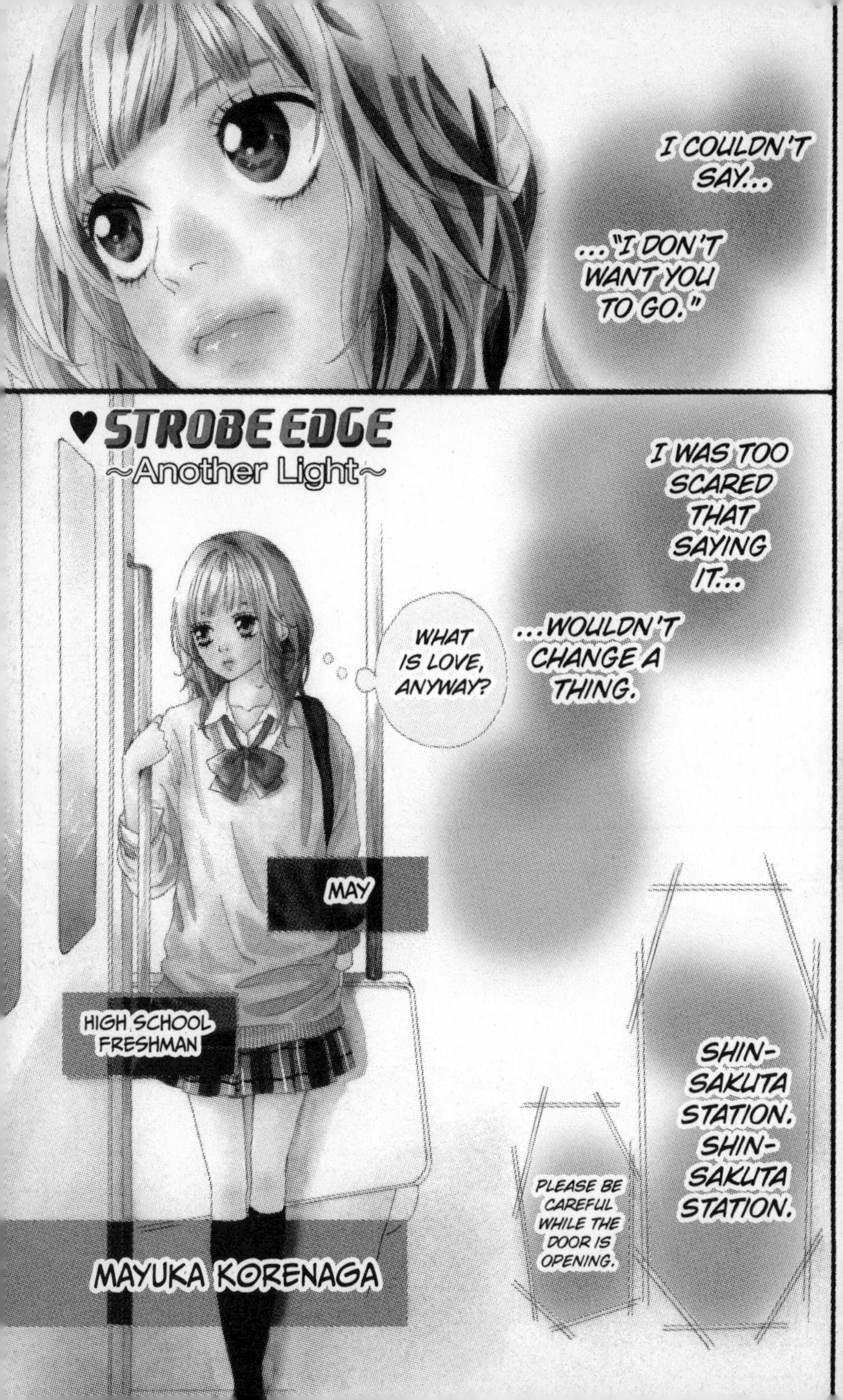
I COULDN'T SAY...
..."I DON'T WANT YOU TO GO."
I WAS TOO SCARED THAT SAYING IT...
...WOULDN'T CHANGE A THING.
STROBE EDGE
~Another Light~
WHAT IS LOVE, ANYWAY?
MAY
HIGH SCHOOL FRESHMAN
SHIN-SAKUTA STATION. SHIN-SAKUTA STATION.
PLEASE BE CAREFUL WHILE THE DOOR IS OPENING.
MAYUKA KORENAGA

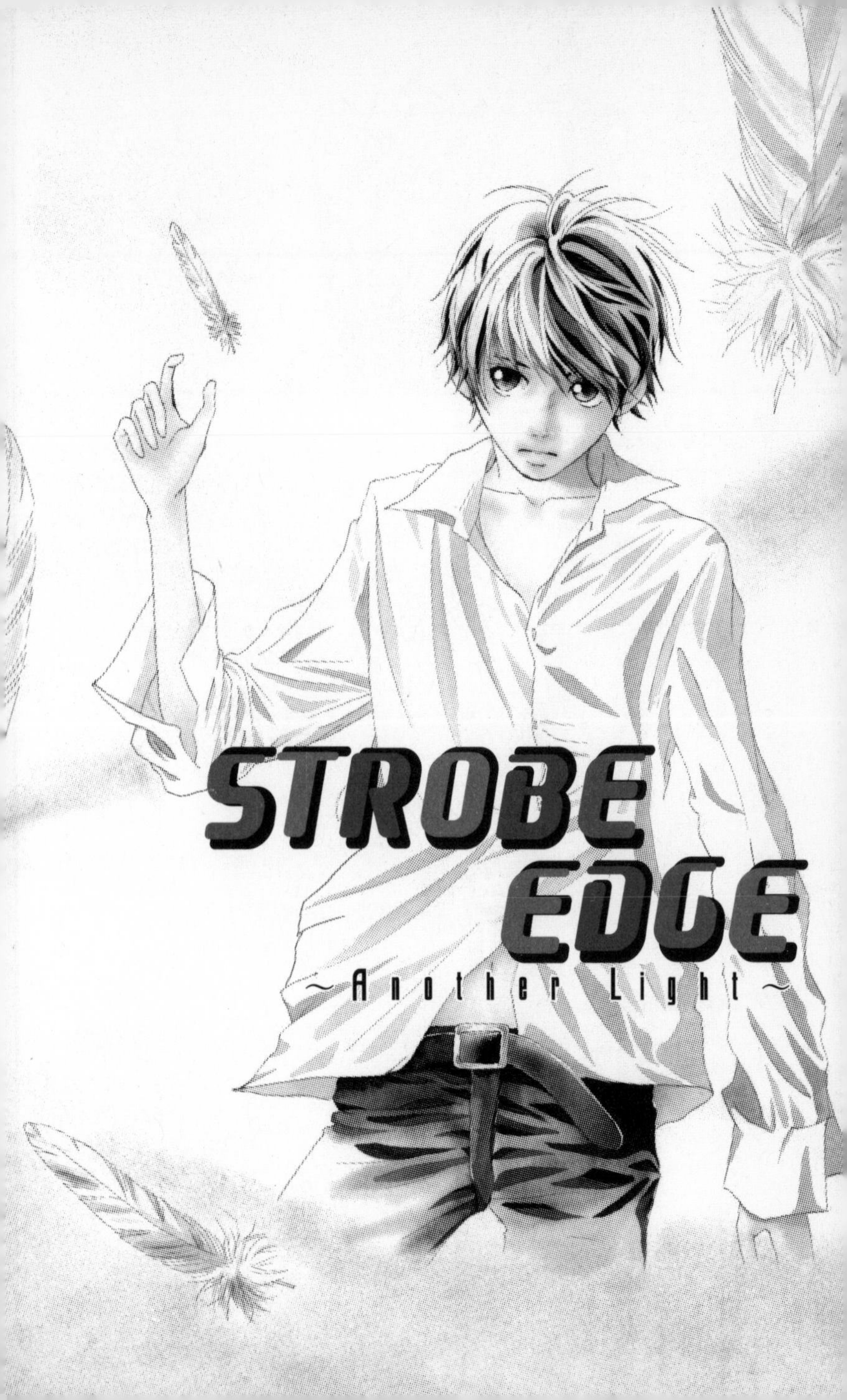
STROBE EDGE
~Another Light~

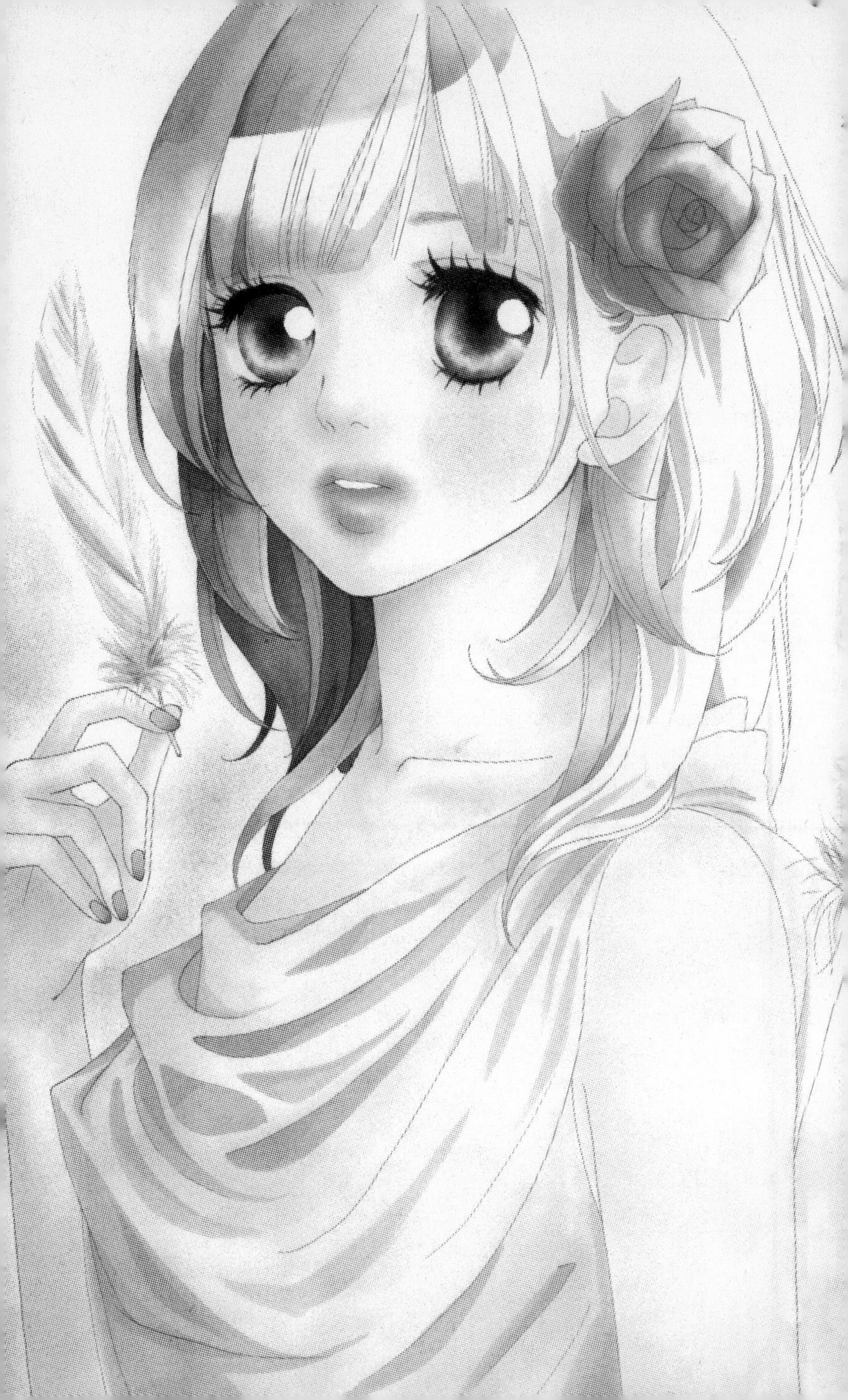

Strobe Edge – Bonus Chapter

About "Another Light"

This bonus story takes place two years before *Strobe Edge* begins. It's the story of how Ren and Mayuka met.

When I first started *Strobe Edge*, the premise was that the guy the heroine falls in love with isn't always available. I wanted to establish early on that Ren already had a girlfriend—and not only that, but a girlfriend that everyone would be jealous of. She had to be someone who would make the heroine, Ninako, feel intimidated. So I made the girlfriend a model and also decided she'd be Daiki's older sister.

So that was all decided before I started working on *Strobe Edge*. I knew there wouldn't be an opportunity to really develop Ren and Mayuka's story, but I'd already planned out how they met, what was going through Mayuka's mind, and so on. So when we decided to add this bonus story, it was pretty easy to just put it all together.

The thing is, there's no obvious "bad guy" in this story. That's what makes things so hard sometimes.

At least, that's what I think.

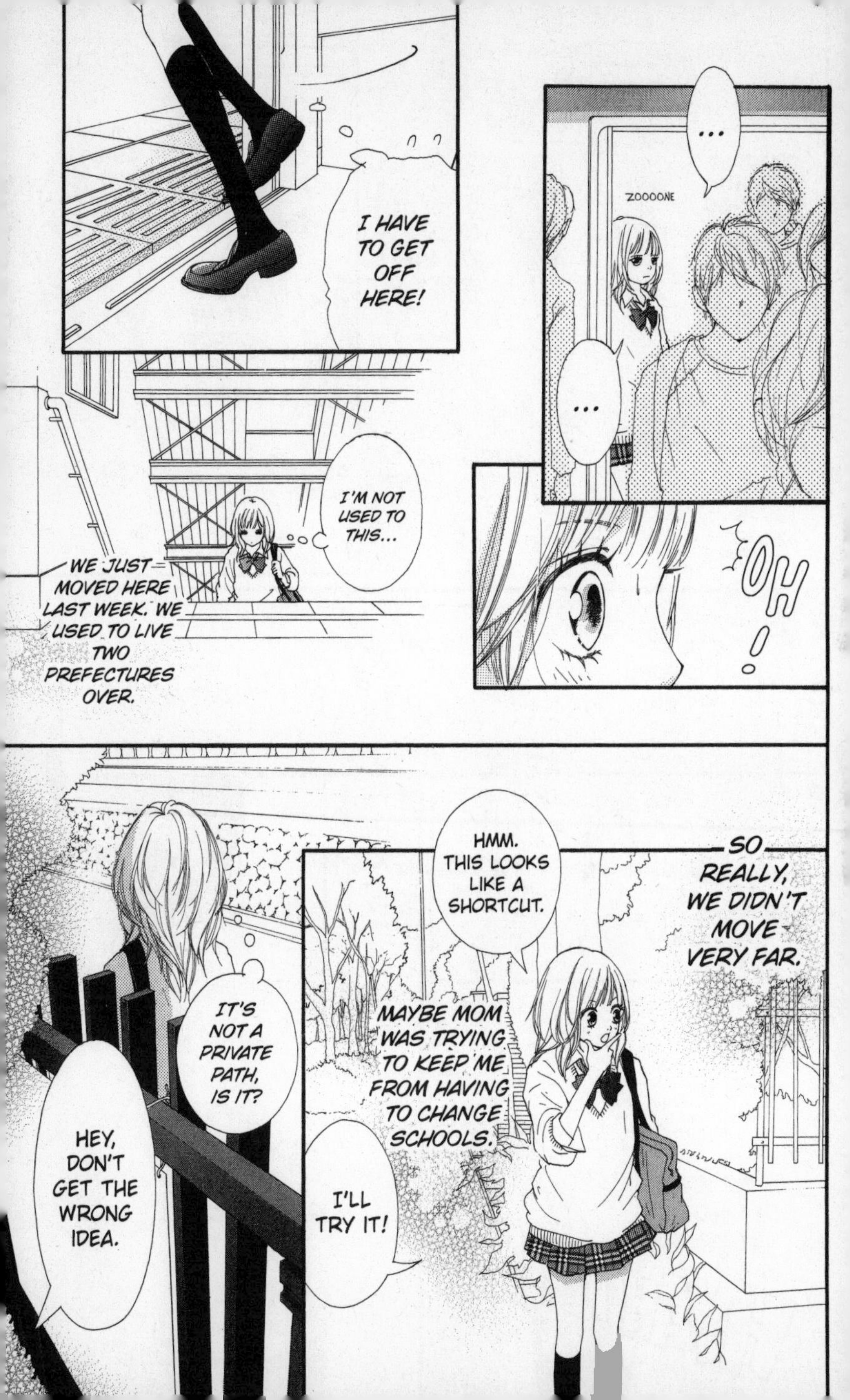
...
ZOOOONE
...
I HAVE TO GET OFF HERE!
OH!
I'M NOT USED TO THIS...
WE JUST MOVED HERE LAST WEEK. WE USED TO LIVE TWO PREFECTURES OVER.
SO REALLY, WE DIDN'T MOVE VERY FAR.
HMM. THIS LOOKS LIKE A SHORTCUT.
MAYBE MOM WAS TRYING TO KEEP ME FROM HAVING TO CHANGE SCHOOLS.
I'LL TRY IT!
IT'S NOT A PRIVATE PATH, IS IT?
HEY, DON'T GET THE WRONG IDEA.

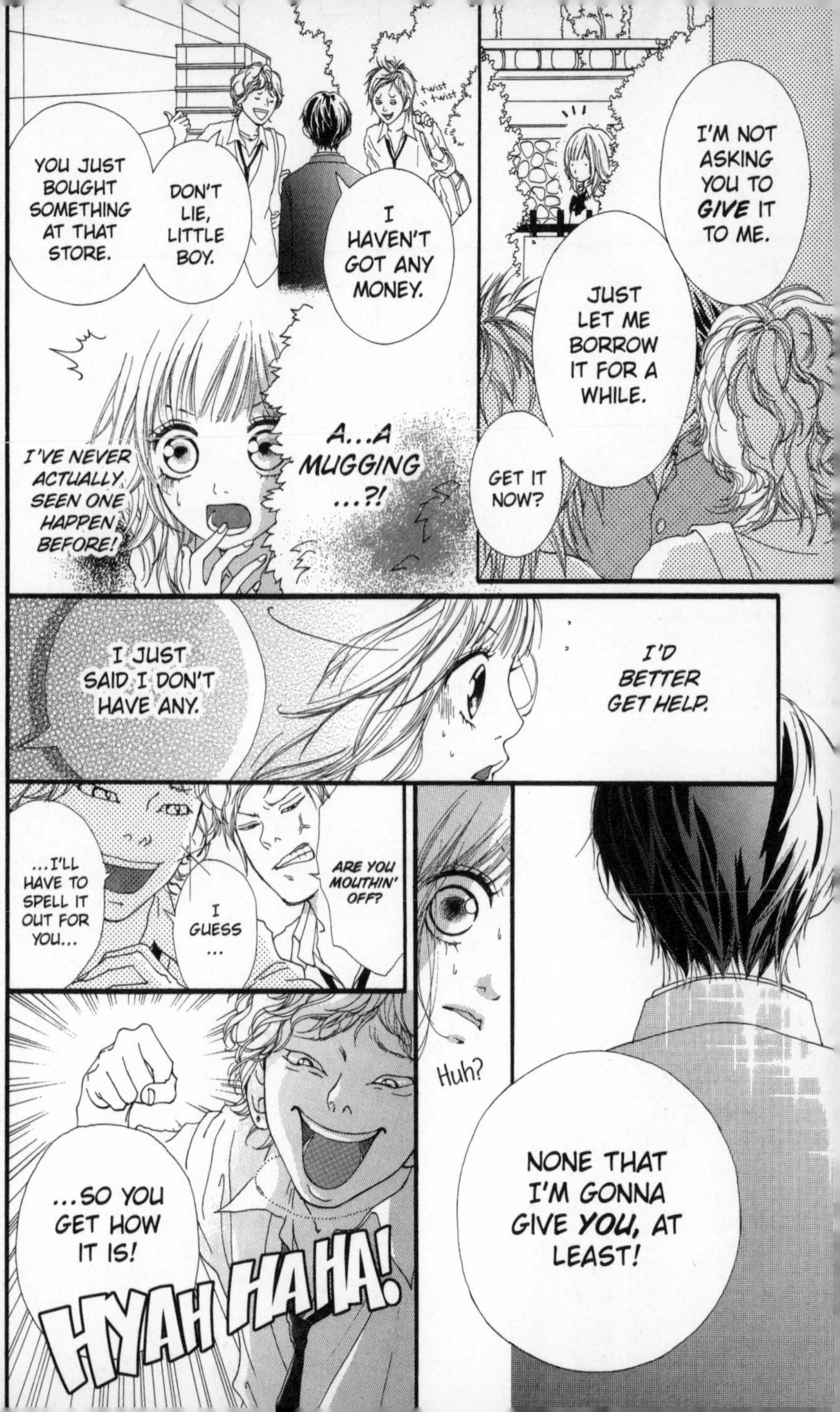
I'M NOT ASKING YOU TO GIVE IT TO ME.
JUST LET ME BORROW IT FOR A WHILE.
GET IT NOW?
twist twist
I HAVEN'T GOT ANY MONEY.
DON'T LIE, LITTLE BOY.
YOU JUST BOUGHT SOMETHING AT THAT STORE.
A...A MUGGING ...?!
I'VE NEVER ACTUALLY SEEN ONE HAPPEN BEFORE!
I'D BETTER GET HELP.
I JUST SAID I DON'T HAVE ANY.
NONE THAT I'M GONNA GIVE YOU, AT LEAST!
Huh?
ARE YOU MOUTHIN' OFF?
I GUESS ...
...I'LL HAVE TO SPELL IT OUT FOR YOU...
...SO YOU GET HOW IT IS!
HYAH HAHA!

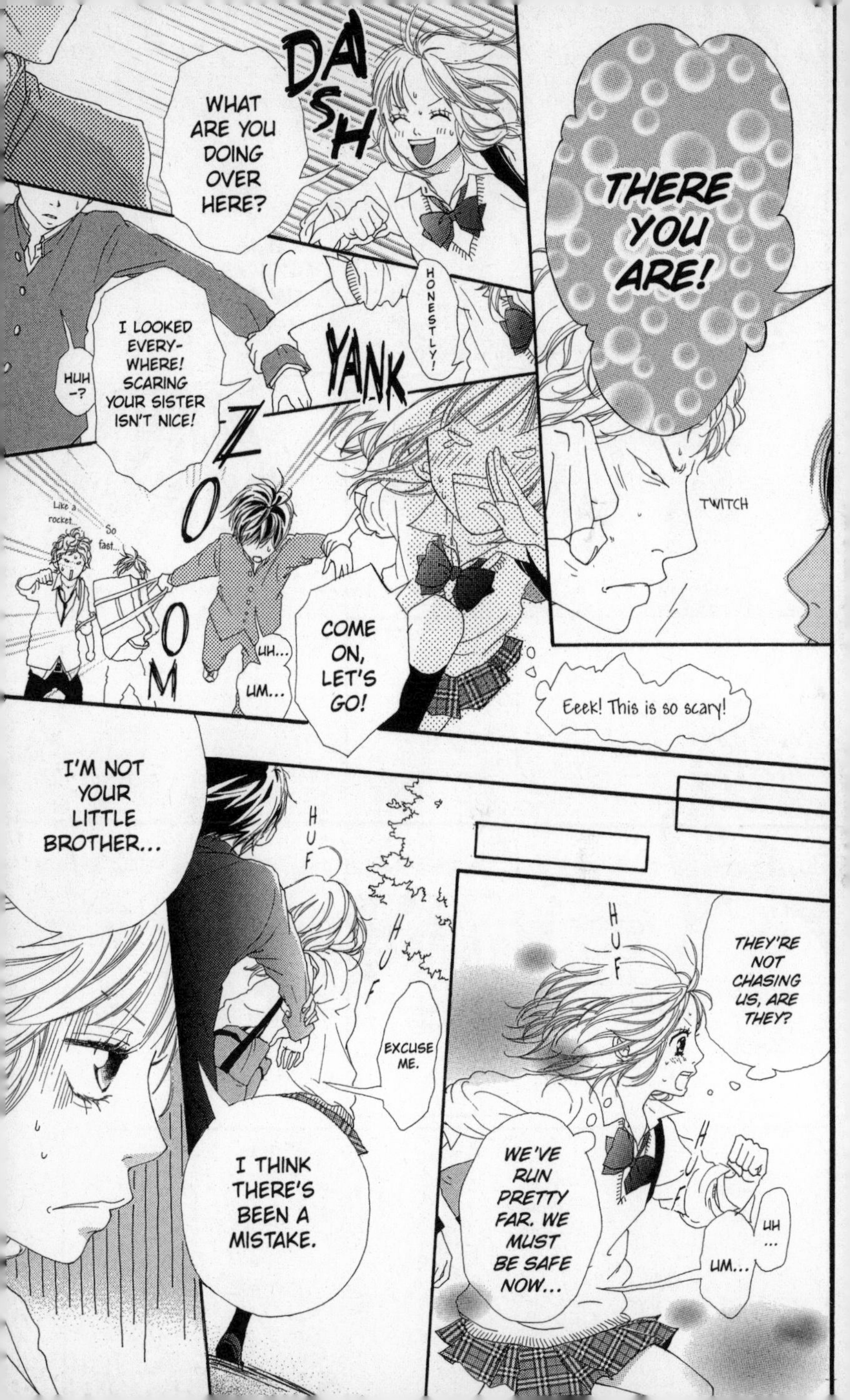
THERE YOU ARE!
TWITCH
DASH
WHAT ARE YOU DOING OVER HERE?
HONESTLY!
YANK
I LOOKED EVERY-WHERE! SCARING YOUR SISTER ISN'T NICE!
HUH-?
ZOOM
Like a rocket...
So fast...
COME ON, LET'S GO!
UH...
UM...
Eeek! This is so scary!
HUF
THEY'RE NOT CHASING US, ARE THEY?
WE'VE RUN PRETTY FAR. WE MUST BE SAFE NOW...
HUF
UH...
UM...
HUF
HUF
EXCUSE ME.
I'M NOT YOUR LITTLE BROTHER...
I THINK THERE'S BEEN A MISTAKE.

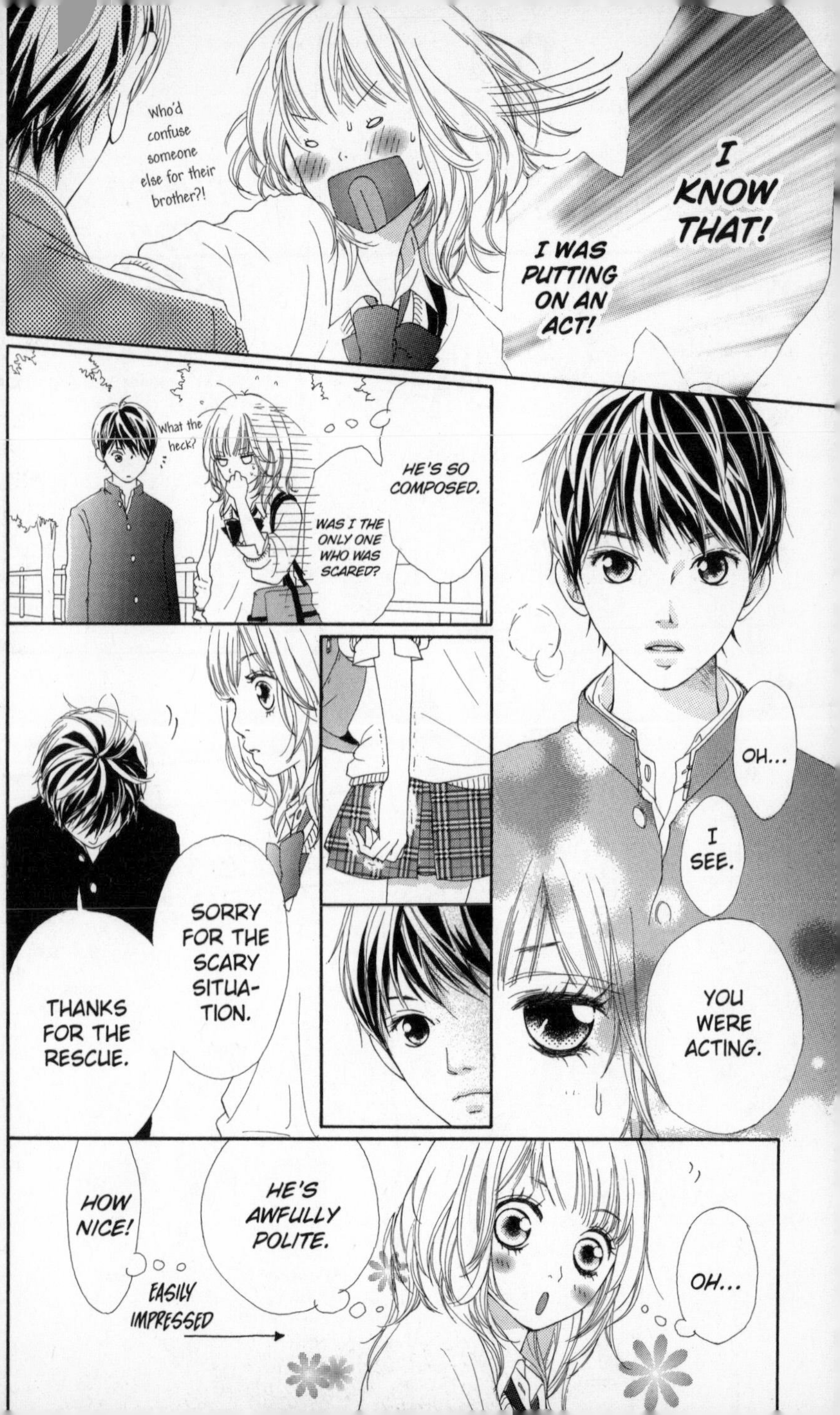
I KNOW THAT!
I WAS PUTTING ON AN ACT!
Who'd confuse someone else for their brother?!
OH... I SEE.
YOU WERE ACTING.
HE'S SO COMPOSED.
WAS I THE ONLY ONE WHO WAS SCARED?
What the heck?
SORRY FOR THE SCARY SITUATION.
THANKS FOR THE RESCUE.
OH...
HE'S AWFULLY POLITE.
HOW NICE!
EASILY IMPRESSED

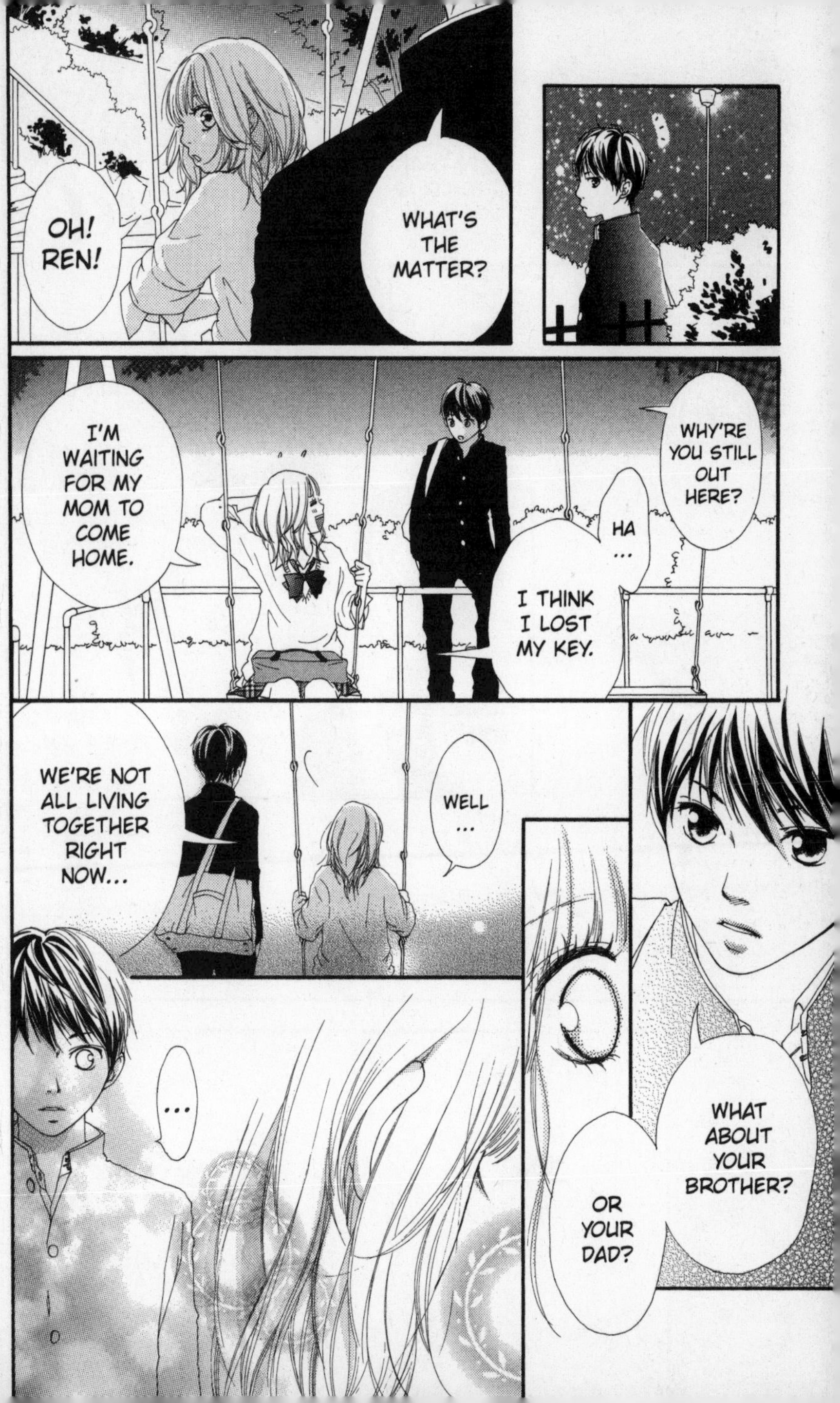
WHAT'S THE MATTER?
OH! REN!
WHY'RE YOU STILL OUT HERE?
HA...
I THINK I LOST MY KEY.
I'M WAITING FOR MY MOM TO COME HOME.
WHAT ABOUT YOUR BROTHER?
OR YOUR DAD?
WELL...
WE'RE NOT ALL LIVING TOGETHER RIGHT NOW...
...

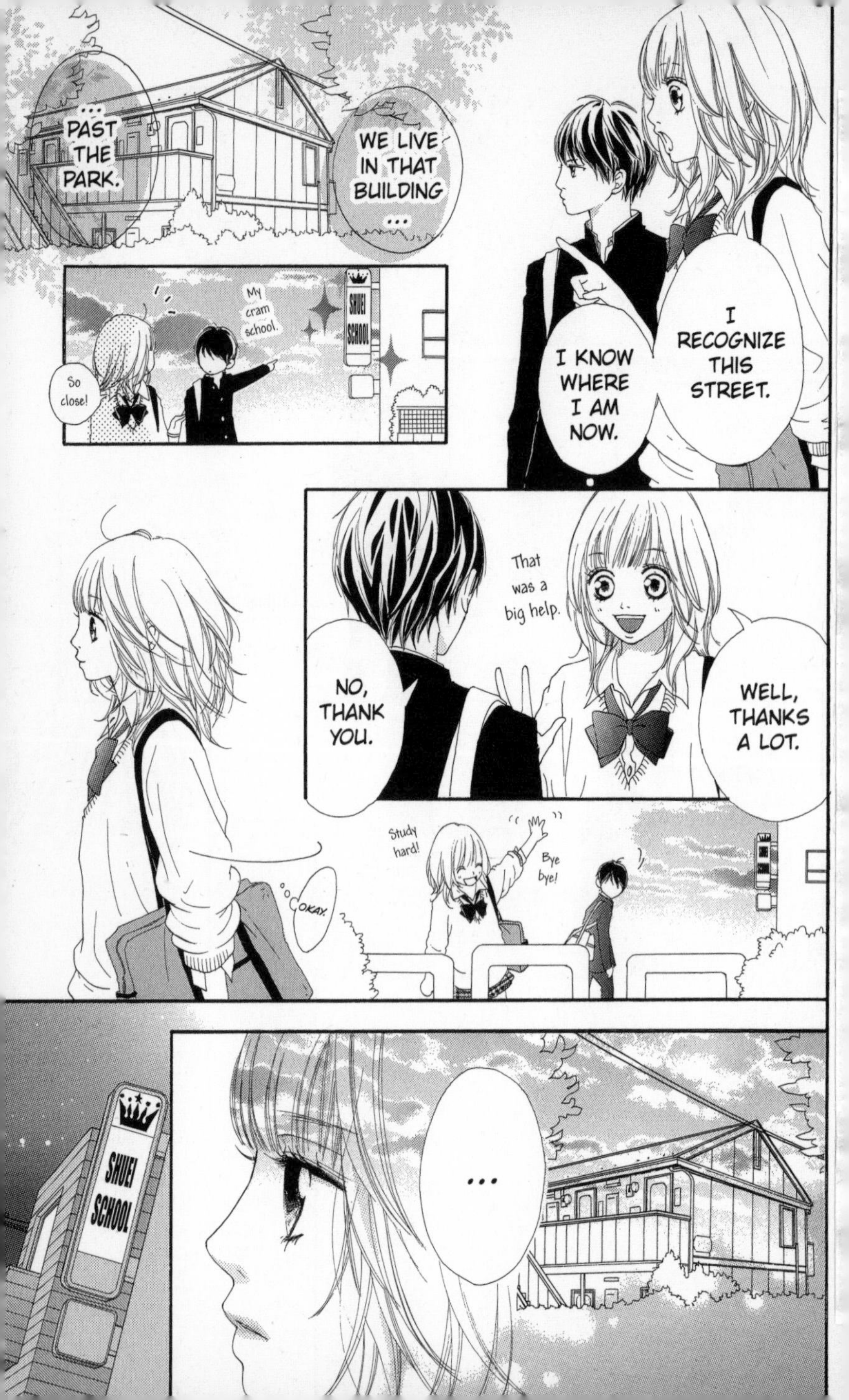
I RECOGNIZE THIS STREET.
I KNOW WHERE I AM NOW.
WE LIVE IN THAT BUILDING ...
... PAST THE PARK.
My cram school.
SHUEI SCHOOL
So close!
WELL, THANKS A LOT.
That was a big help.
NO, THANK YOU.
Bye bye!
Study hard!
OKAY.
SHUEI SCHOOL
...

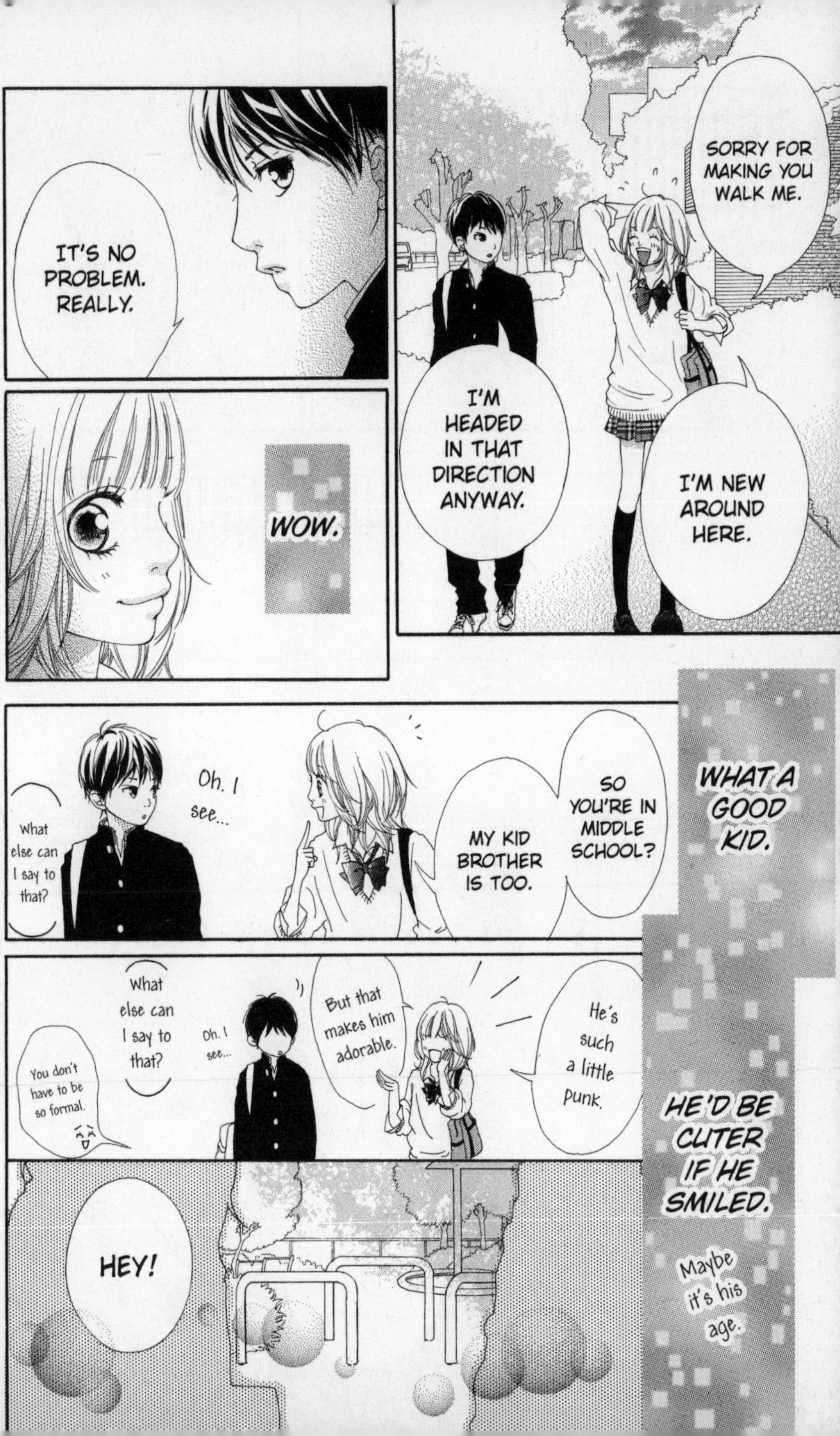
SORRY FOR MAKING YOU WALK ME.
I'M NEW AROUND HERE.
I'M HEADED IN THAT DIRECTION ANYWAY.
IT'S NO PROBLEM. REALLY.
WOW.
WHAT A GOOD KID.
SO YOU'RE IN MIDDLE SCHOOL?
MY KID BROTHER IS TOO.
Oh. I see...
What else can I say to that?
HE'D BE CUTER IF HE SMILED.
Maybe it's his age.
He's such a little punk.
But that makes him adorable.
Oh. I see...
What else can I say to that?
You don't have to be so formal.
HEY!

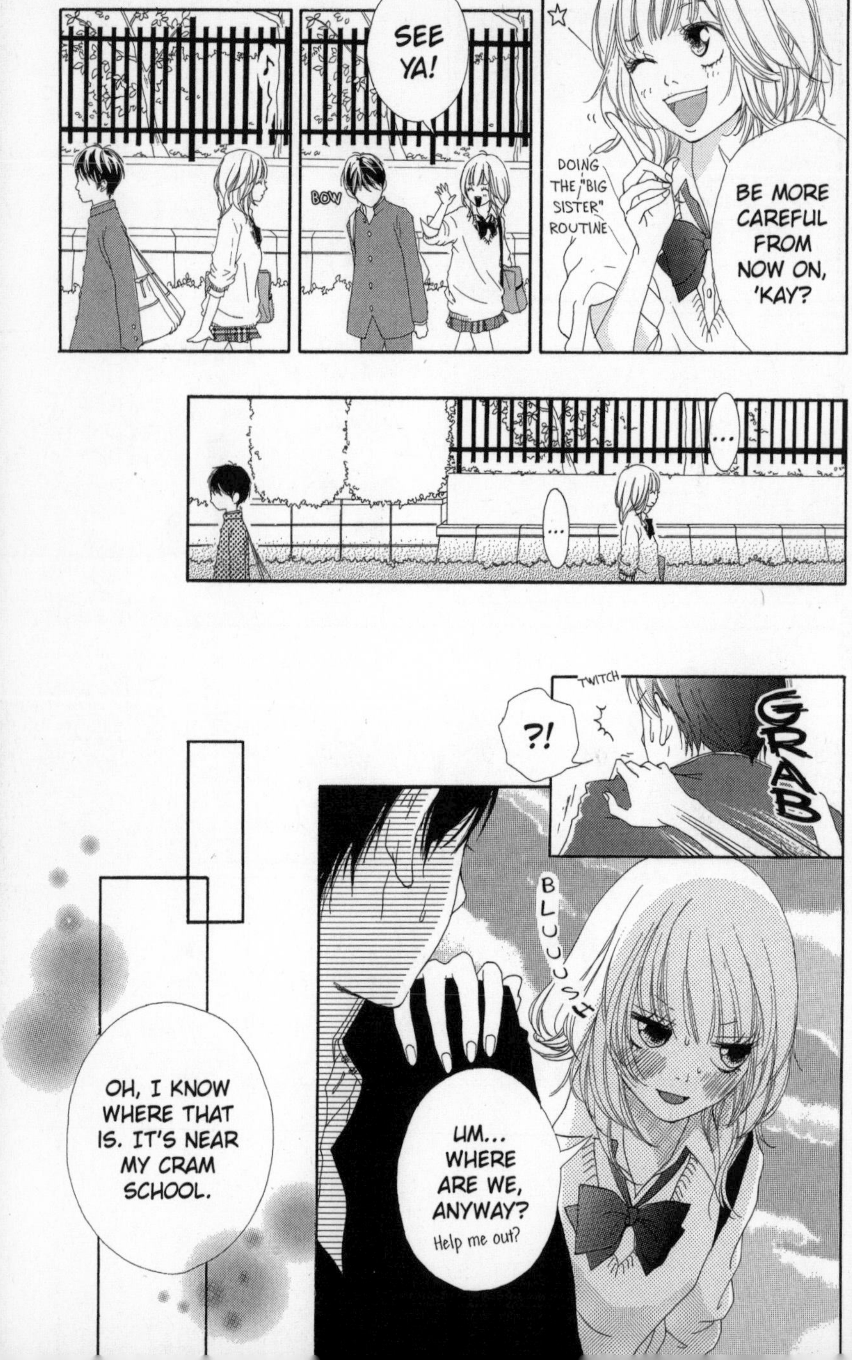
BE MORE CAREFUL FROM NOW ON, 'KAY?
DOING THE "BIG SISTER" ROUTINE
SEE YA!
BOW
...
...
TWITCH
?!
GRAB
BLUUUSH
UM... WHERE ARE WE, ANYWAY?
Help me out?
OH, I KNOW WHERE THAT IS. IT'S NEAR MY CRAM SCHOOL.

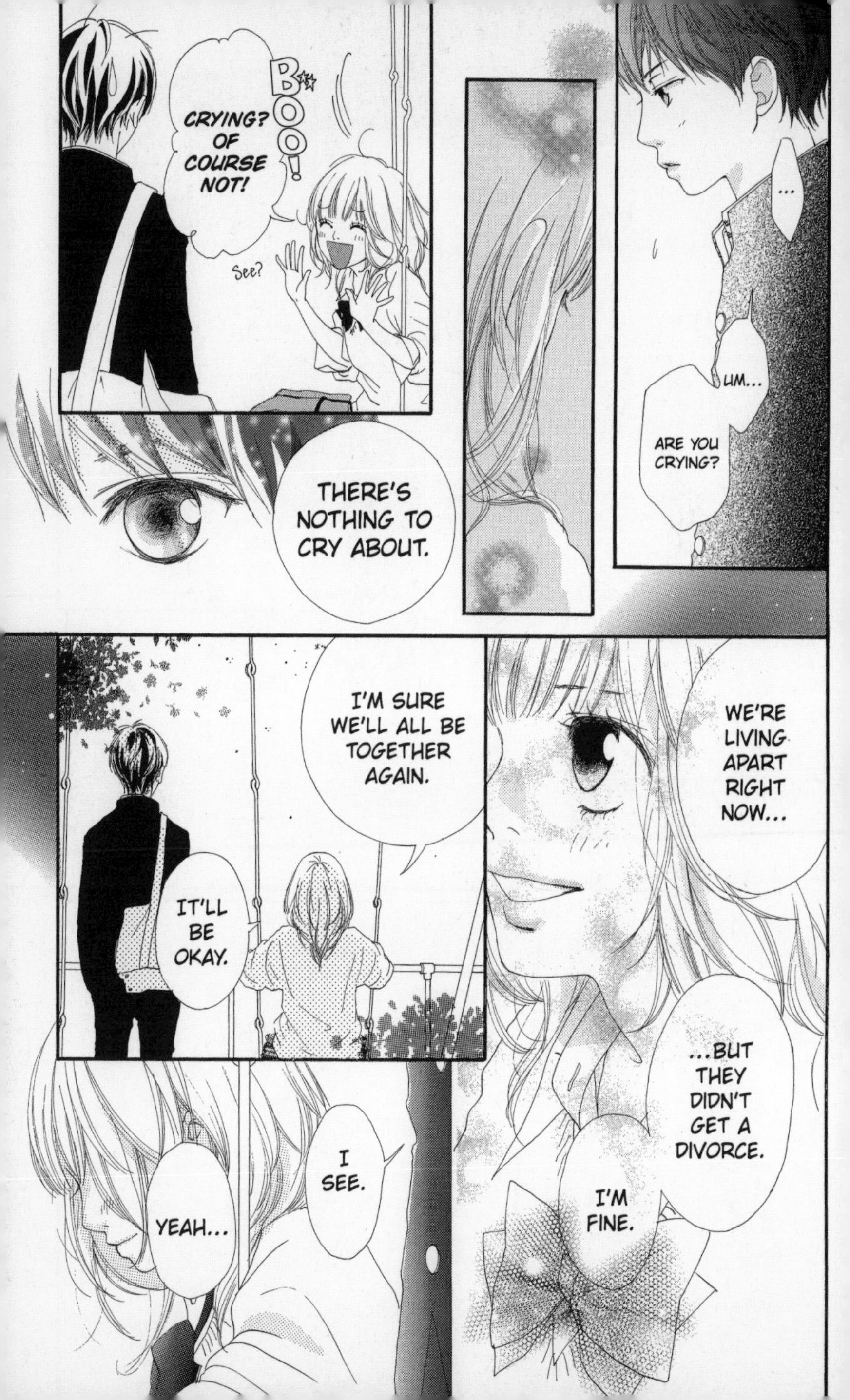
...
UM...
ARE YOU CRYING?
CRYING? OF COURSE NOT!
BOO!
See?
THERE'S NOTHING TO CRY ABOUT.
WE'RE LIVING APART RIGHT NOW...
...BUT THEY DIDN'T GET A DIVORCE.
I'M FINE.
I'M SURE WE'LL ALL BE TOGETHER AGAIN.
IT'LL BE OKAY.
I SEE.
YEAH...

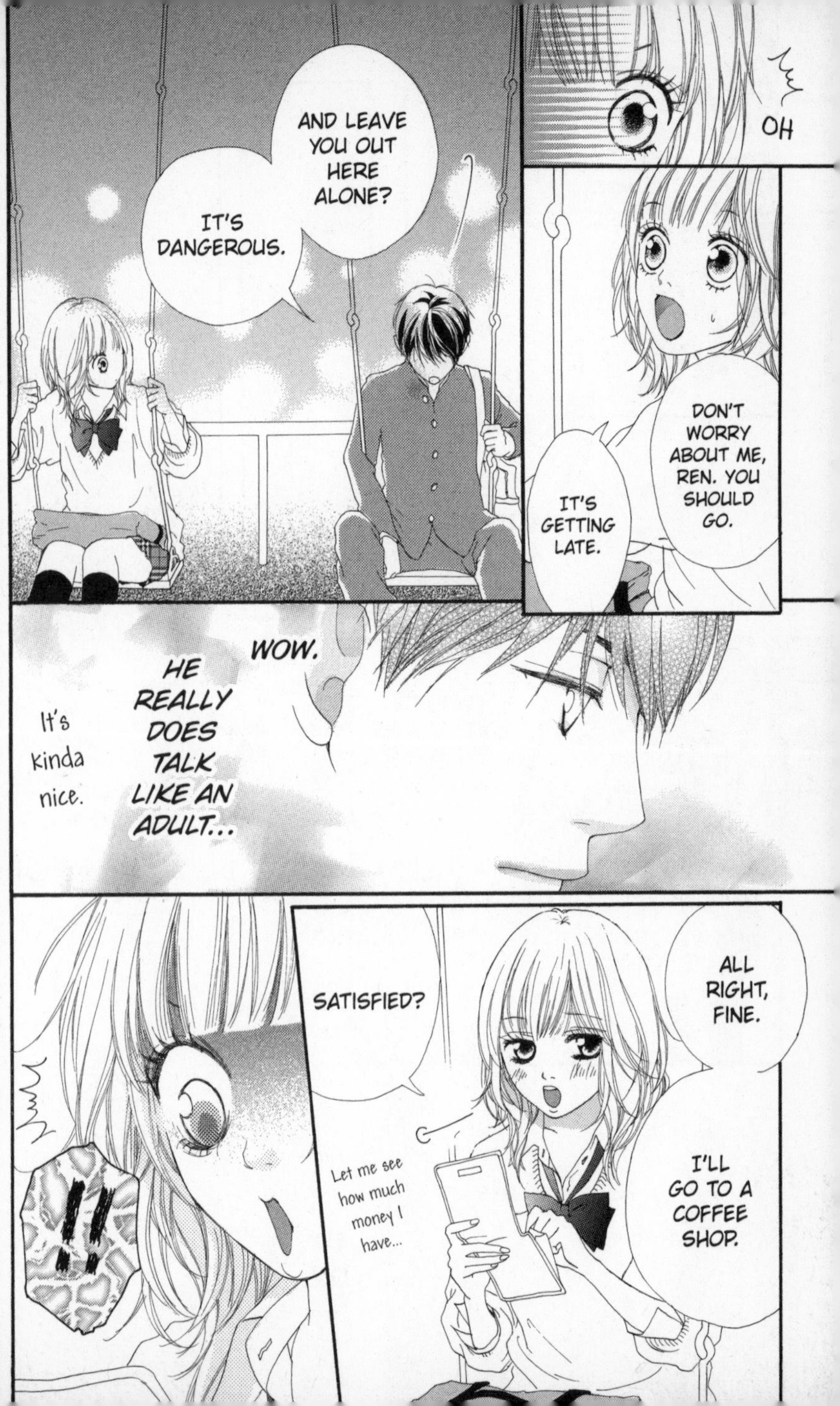
OH
DON'T WORRY ABOUT ME, REN. YOU SHOULD GO.
IT'S GETTING LATE.
AND LEAVE YOU OUT HERE ALONE?
IT'S DANGEROUS.
WOW.
HE REALLY DOES TALK LIKE AN ADULT...
It's kinda nice.
ALL RIGHT, FINE.
I'LL GO TO A COFFEE SHOP.
Let me see how much money I have...
SATISFIED?
!!

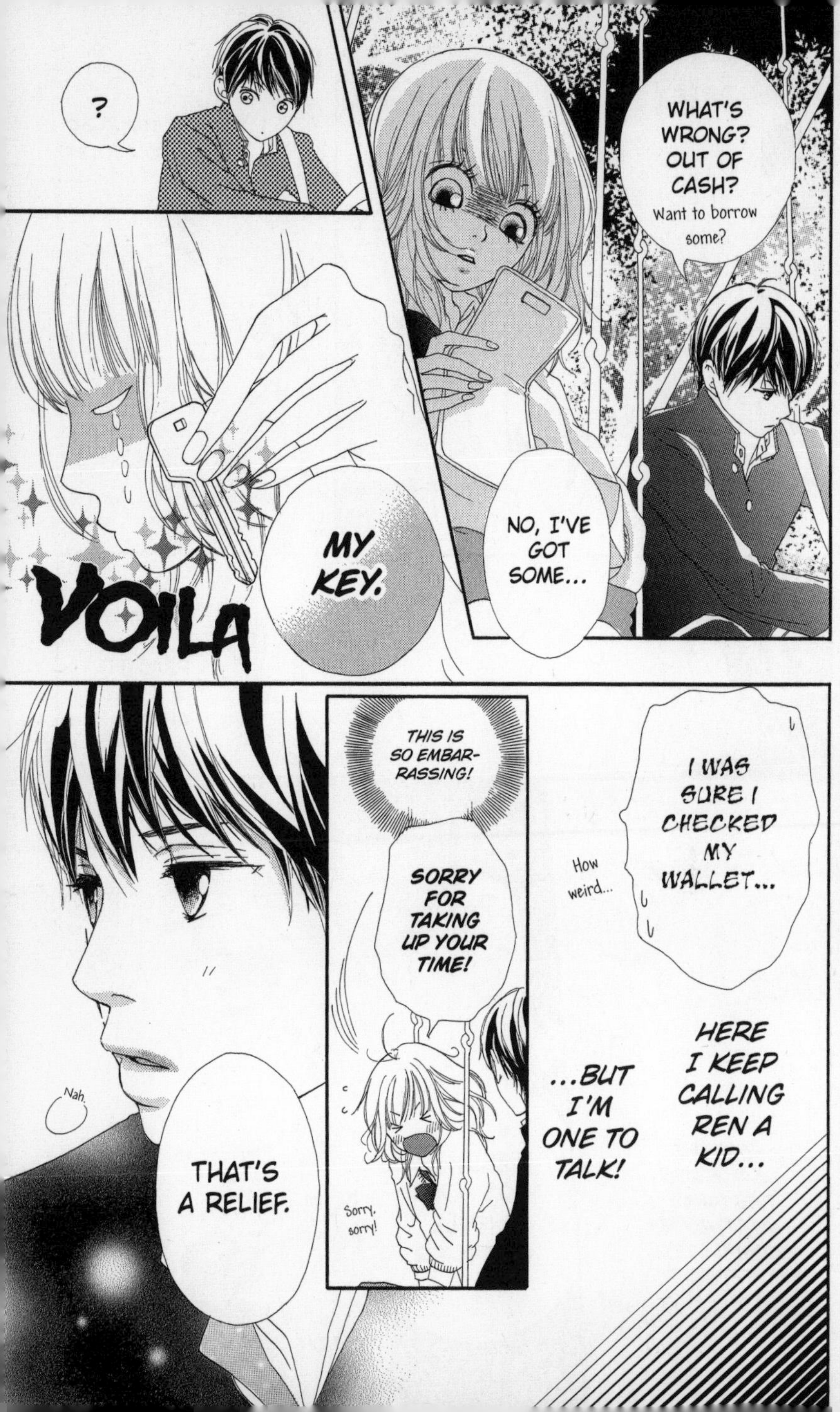
WHAT'S WRONG? OUT OF CASH?
Want to borrow some?
NO, I'VE GOT SOME...
?
MY KEY.
VOILA
I WAS SURE I CHECKED MY WALLET...
How weird...
HERE I KEEP CALLING REN A KID...
...BUT I'M ONE TO TALK!
THIS IS SO EMBARRASSING!
SORRY FOR TAKING UP YOUR TIME!
Sorry, sorry!
THAT'S A RELIEF.
Nah.

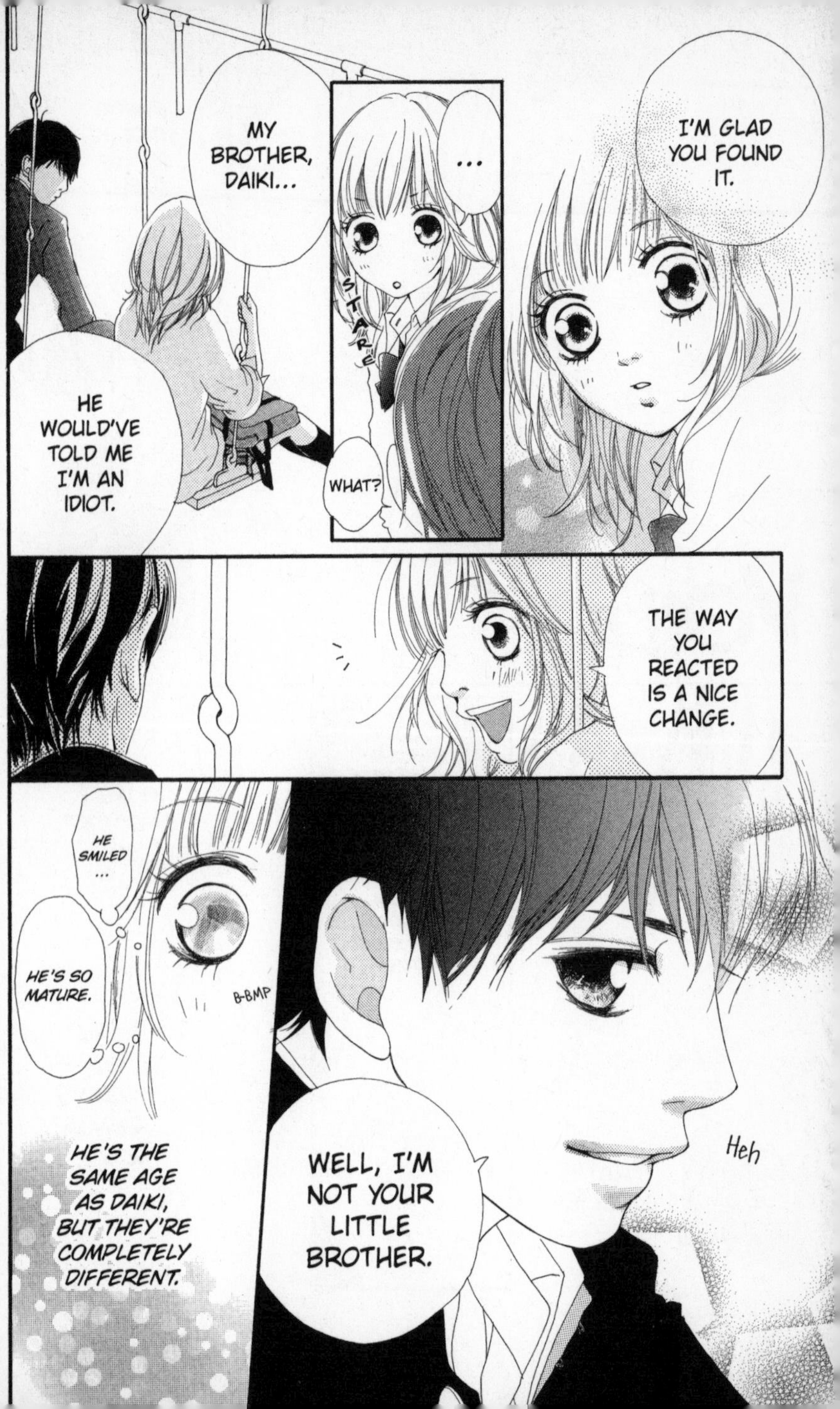
I'M GLAD YOU FOUND IT.
...
STARE
WHAT?
MY BROTHER, DAIKI...
HE WOULD'VE TOLD ME I'M AN IDIOT.
THE WAY YOU REACTED IS A NICE CHANGE.
HE SMILED...
HE'S SO MATURE.
B-BMP
Heh
WELL, I'M NOT YOUR LITTLE BROTHER.
HE'S THE SAME AGE AS DAIKI, BUT THEY'RE COMPLETELY DIFFERENT.

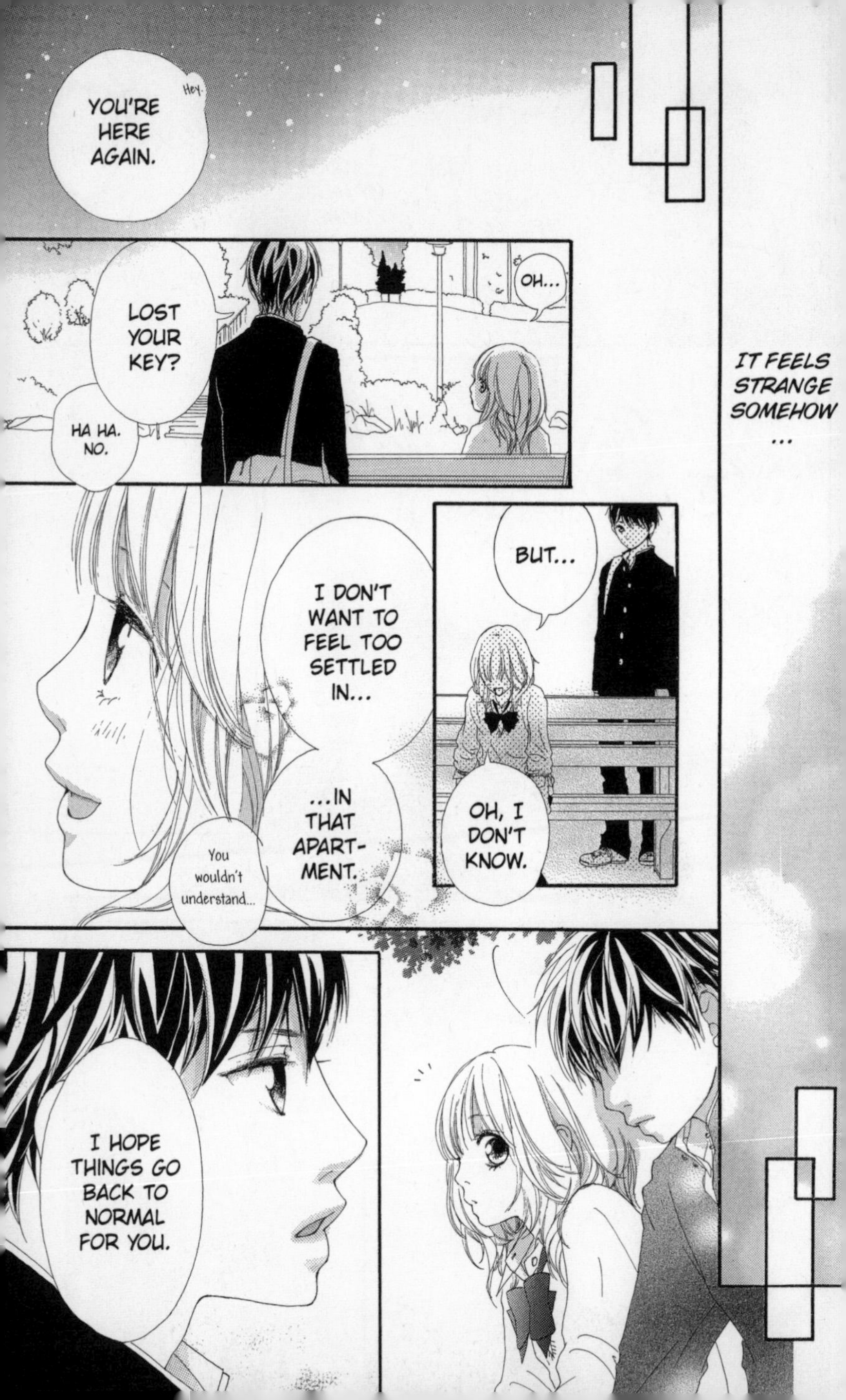
Hey.
YOU'RE HERE AGAIN.
IT FEELS STRANGE SOMEHOW...
OH...
LOST YOUR KEY?
HA HA. NO.
BUT...
OH, I DON'T KNOW.
I DON'T WANT TO FEEL TOO SETTLED IN...
...IN THAT APARTMENT.
You wouldn't understand...
I HOPE THINGS GO BACK TO NORMAL FOR YOU.

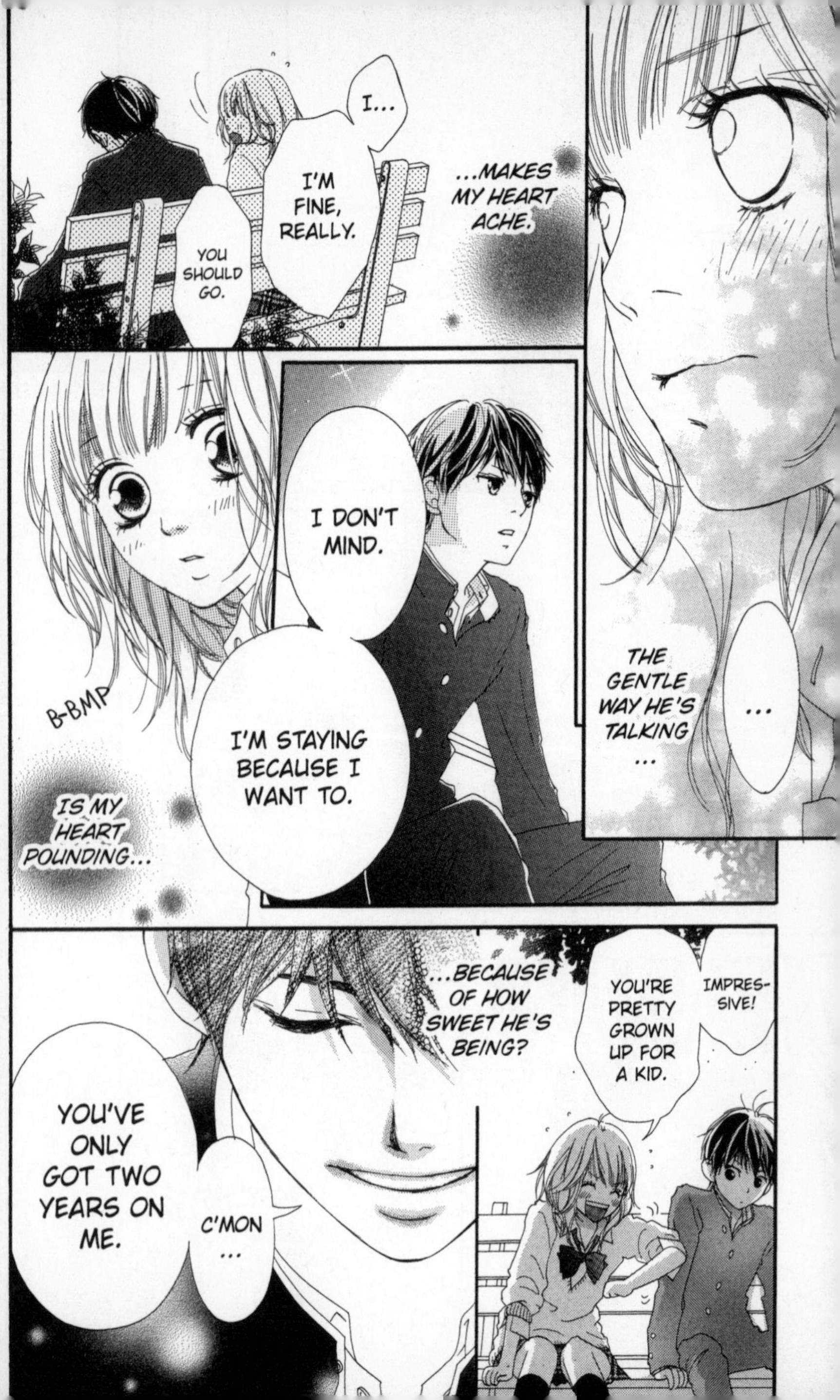
...
THE GENTLE WAY HE'S TALKING ...
I...
I'M FINE, REALLY.
YOU SHOULD GO.
...MAKES MY HEART ACHE.
I DON'T MIND.
I'M STAYING BECAUSE I WANT TO.
B-BMP
IS MY HEART POUNDING...
IMPRESSIVE!
YOU'RE PRETTY GROWN UP FOR A KID.
...BECAUSE OF HOW SWEET HE'S BEING?
C'MON ...
YOU'VE ONLY GOT TWO YEARS ON ME.

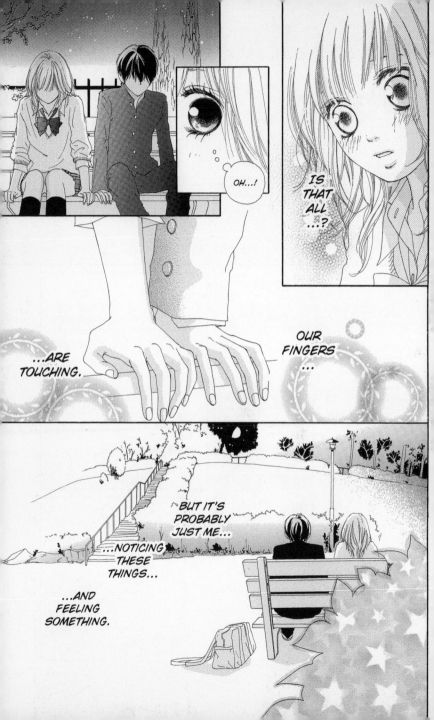

OH...!

IS THAT ALL ...?

OUR FINGERS...

...ARE TOUCHING.

BUT IT'S PROBABLY JUST ME...

...NOTICING THESE THINGS...

...AND FEELING SOMETHING.

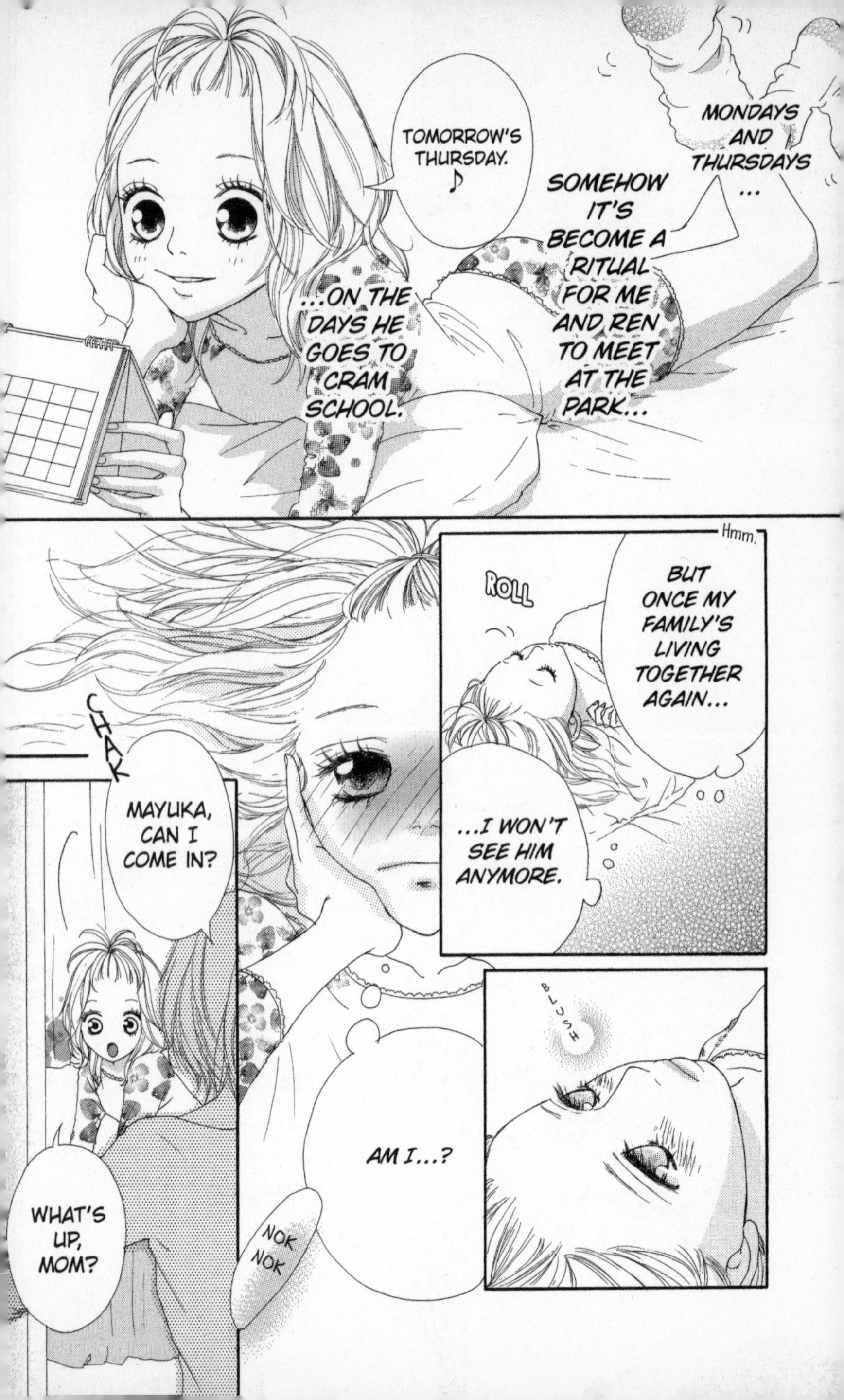
MONDAYS AND THURSDAYS...
SOMEHOW IT'S BECOME A RITUAL FOR ME AND REN TO MEET AT THE PARK...
...ON THE DAYS HE GOES TO CRAM SCHOOL.
TOMORROW'S THURSDAY. ♪
Hmm.
ROLL
BUT ONCE MY FAMILY'S LIVING TOGETHER AGAIN...
...I WON'T SEE HIM ANYMORE.
BLUSH
AM I...?
NOK NOK
CHAK
MAYUKA, CAN I COME IN?
WHAT'S UP, MOM?

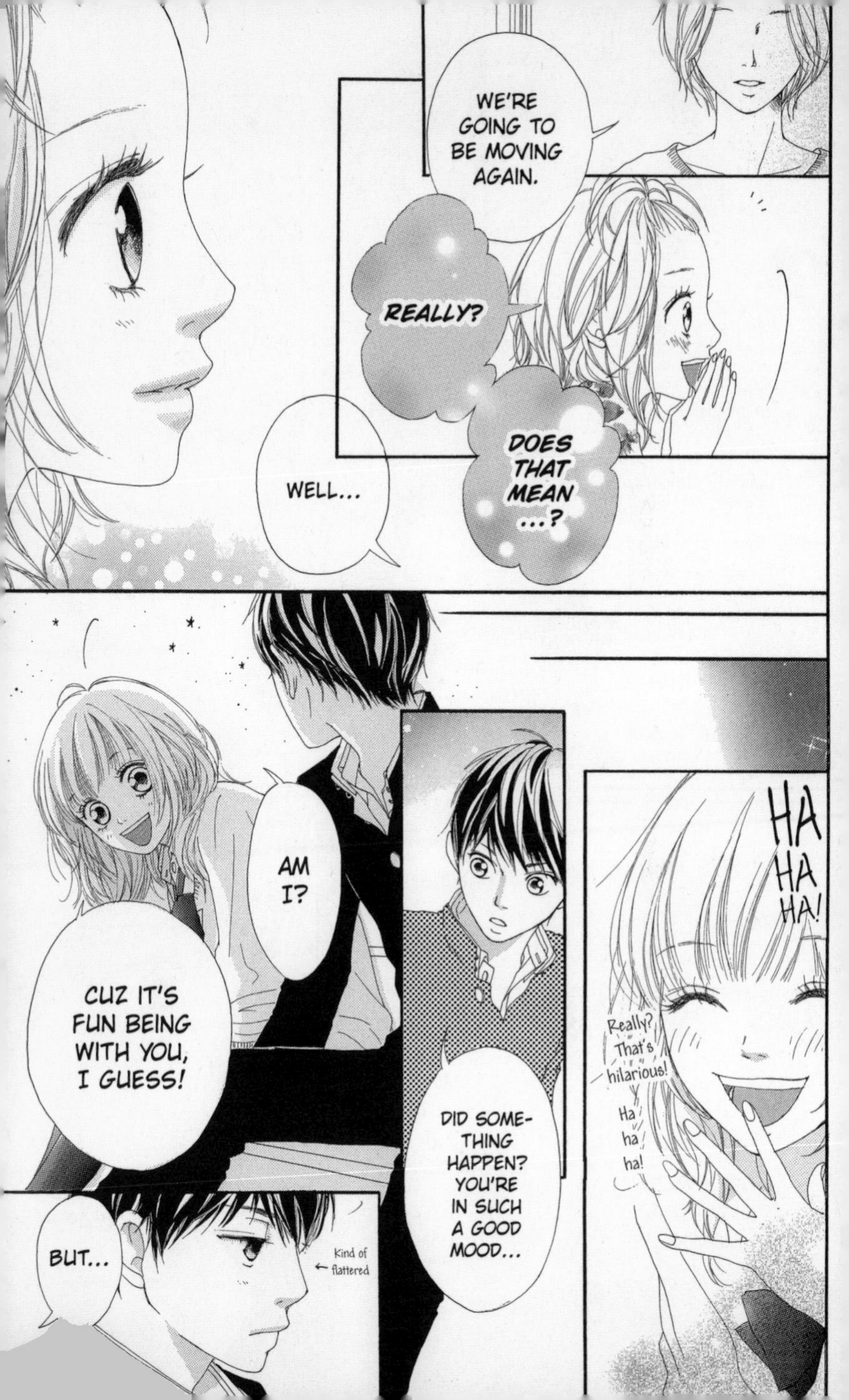
WE'RE GOING TO BE MOVING AGAIN.
REALLY?
DOES THAT MEAN ...?
WELL...
HA HA HA!
Really? That's hilarious!
Ha ha ha!
DID SOME-THING HAPPEN? YOU'RE IN SUCH A GOOD MOOD...
AM I?
CUZ IT'S FUN BEING WITH YOU, I GUESS!
BUT...
Kind of flattered

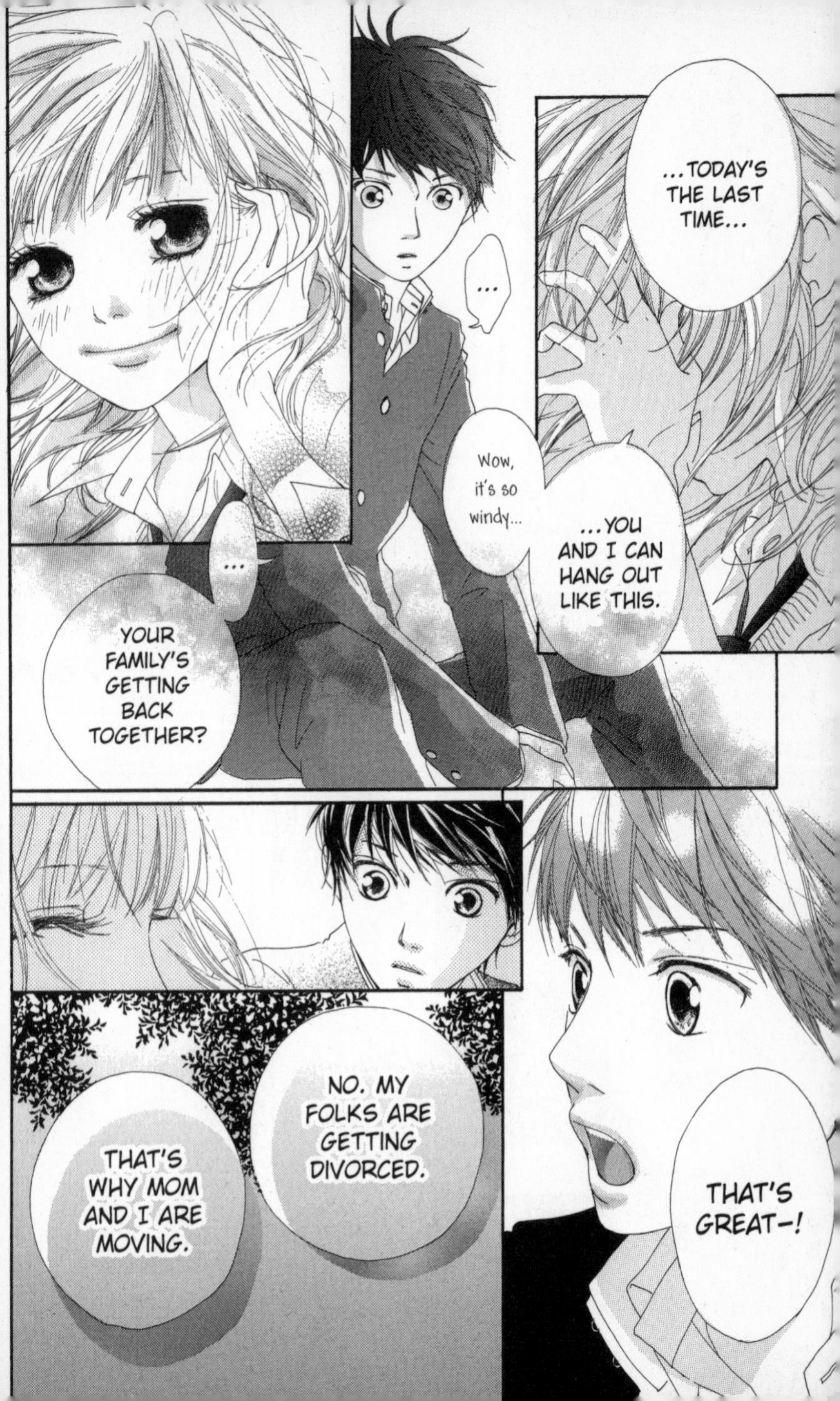
...TODAY'S THE LAST TIME...
...YOU AND I CAN HANG OUT LIKE THIS.
...
Wow, it's so windy...
...
YOUR FAMILY'S GETTING BACK TOGETHER?
THAT'S GREAT-!
NO. MY FOLKS ARE GETTING DIVORCED.
THAT'S WHY MOM AND I ARE MOVING.

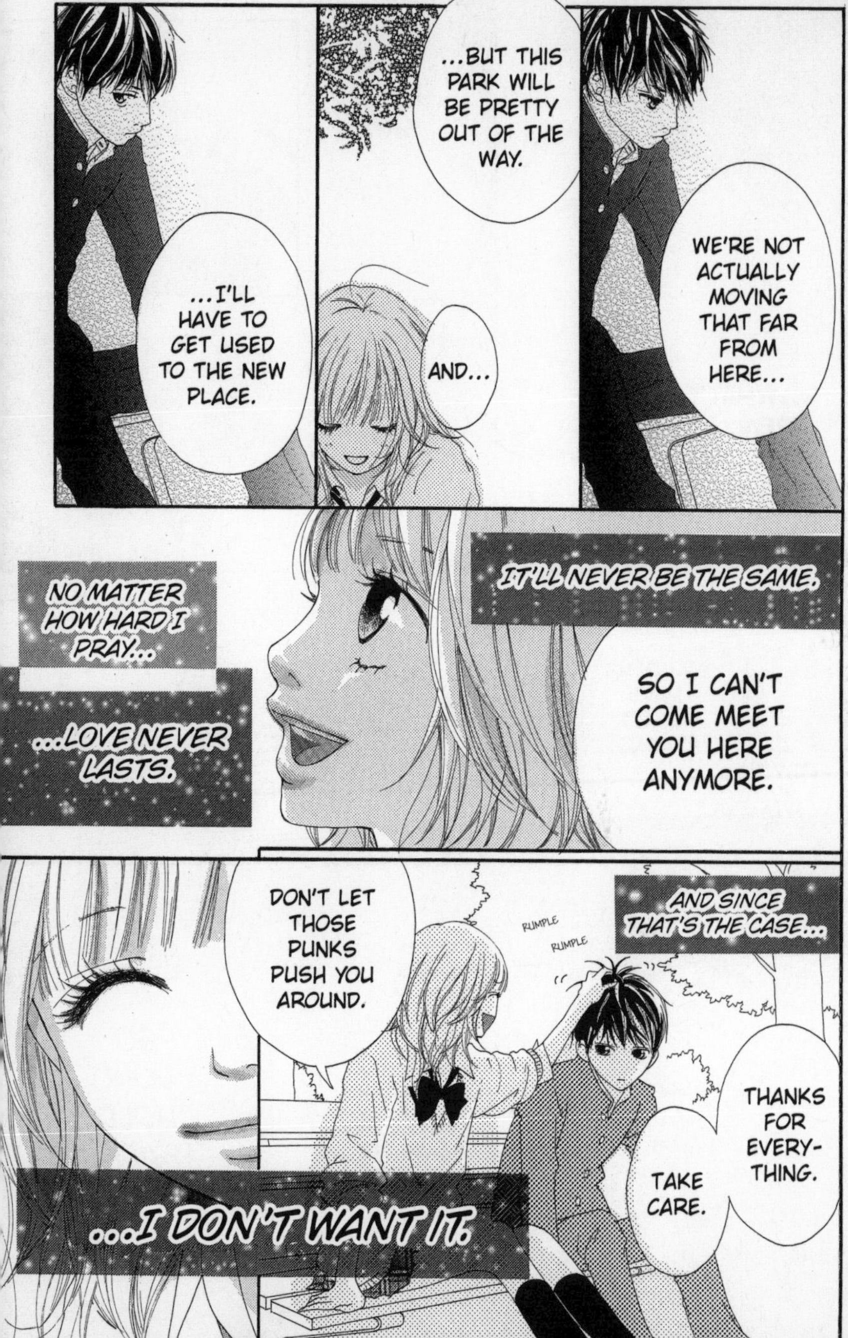
WE'RE NOT ACTUALLY MOVING THAT FAR FROM HERE...
...BUT THIS PARK WILL BE PRETTY OUT OF THE WAY.
AND...
...I'LL HAVE TO GET USED TO THE NEW PLACE.
IT'LL NEVER BE THE SAME.
SO I CAN'T COME MEET YOU HERE ANYMORE.
NO MATTER HOW HARD I PRAY...
...LOVE NEVER LASTS.
AND SINCE THAT'S THE CASE...
THANKS FOR EVERYTHING.
TAKE CARE.
RUMPLE
RUMPLE
DON'T LET THOSE PUNKS PUSH YOU AROUND.
...I DON'T WANT IT.

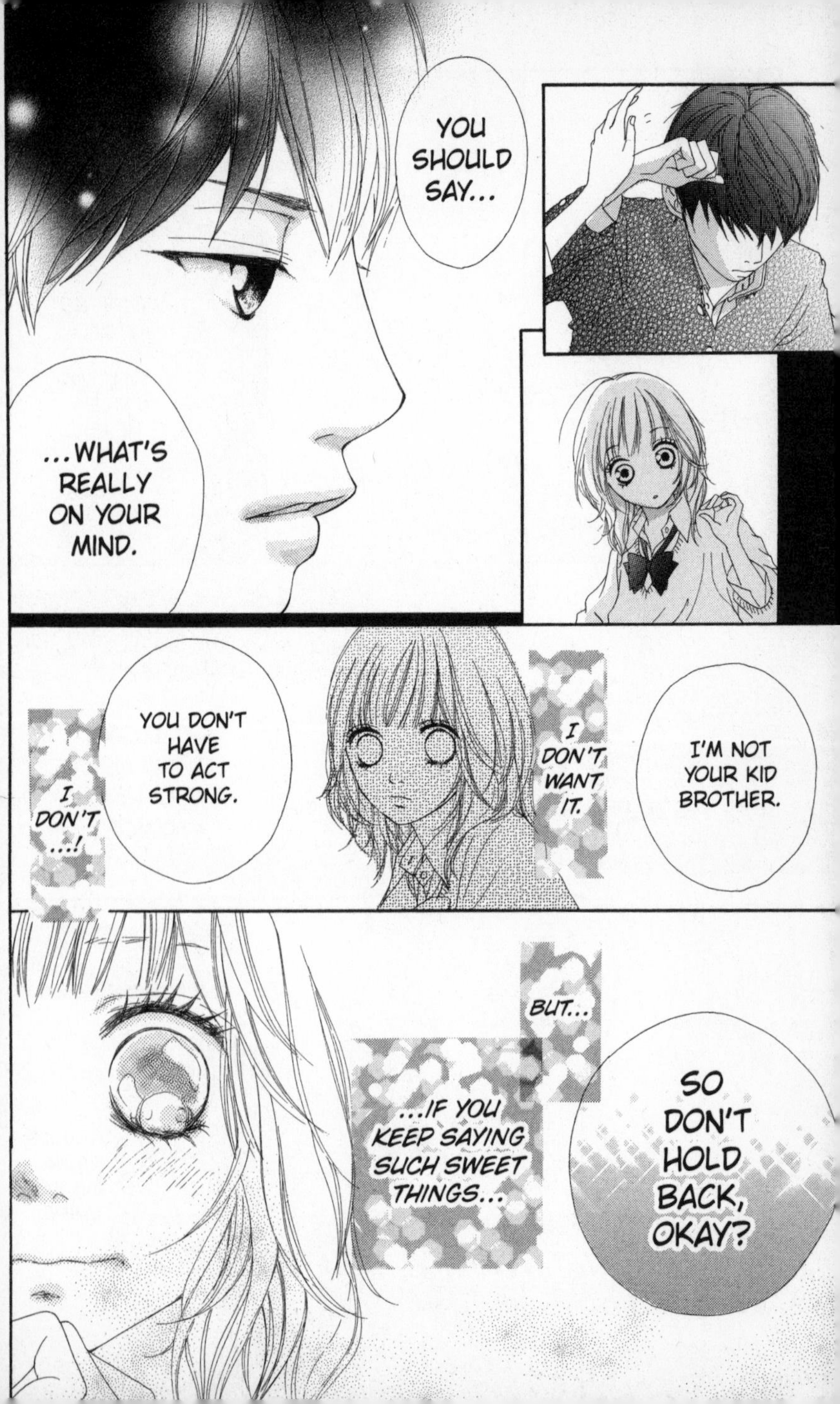
YOU SHOULD SAY...
...WHAT'S REALLY ON YOUR MIND.
I'M NOT YOUR KID BROTHER.
I DON'T WANT IT.
YOU DON'T HAVE TO ACT STRONG.
I DON'T ...!
SO DON'T HOLD BACK, OKAY?
BUT...
...IF YOU KEEP SAYING SUCH SWEET THINGS...

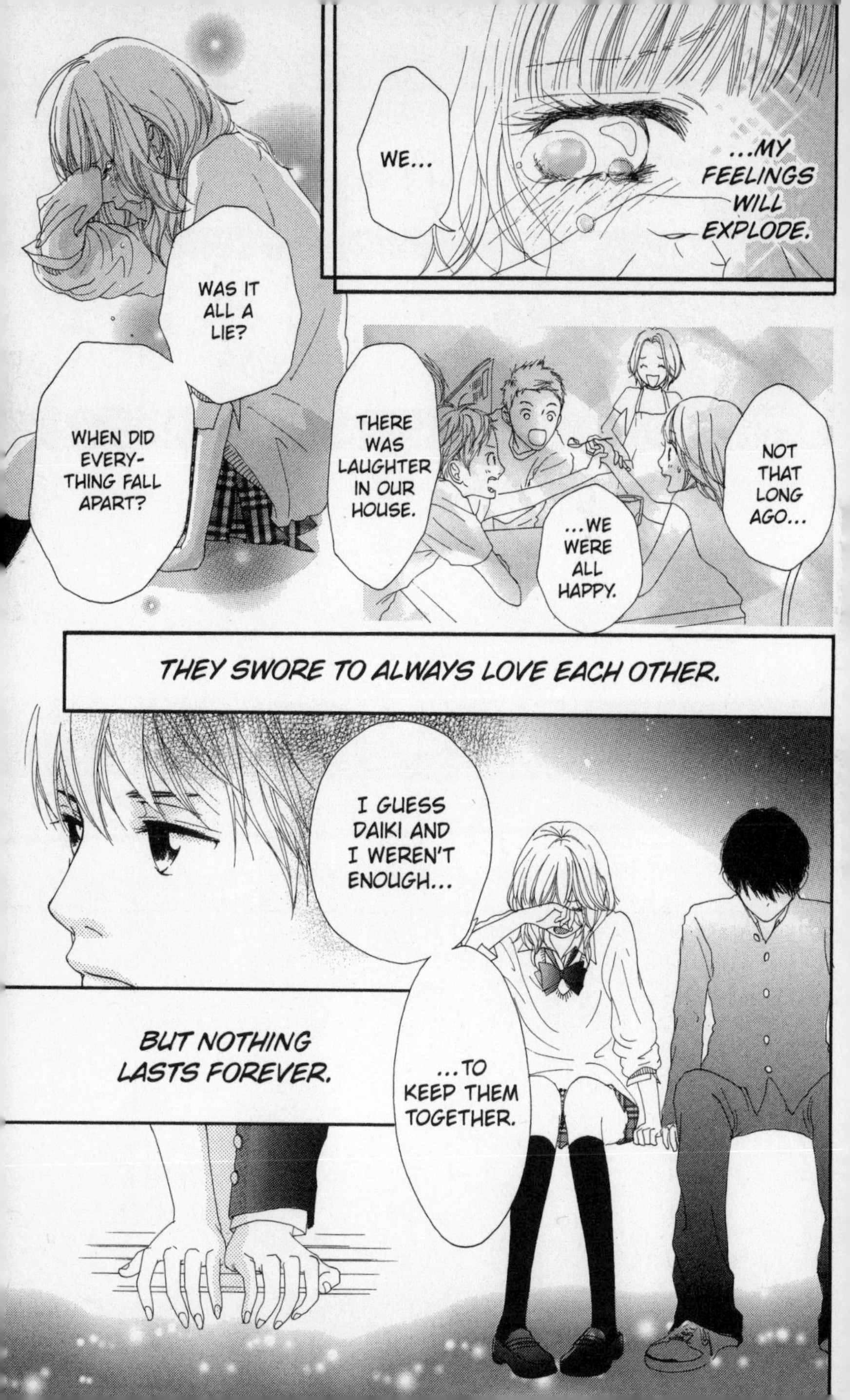
...MY FEELINGS WILL EXPLODE.
WE...
NOT THAT LONG AGO...
...WE WERE ALL HAPPY.
THERE WAS LAUGHTER IN OUR HOUSE.
WAS IT ALL A LIE?
WHEN DID EVERY-THING FALL APART?
THEY SWORE TO ALWAYS LOVE EACH OTHER.
I GUESS DAIKI AND I WEREN'T ENOUGH...
...TO KEEP THEM TOGETHER.
BUT NOTHING LASTS FOREVER.

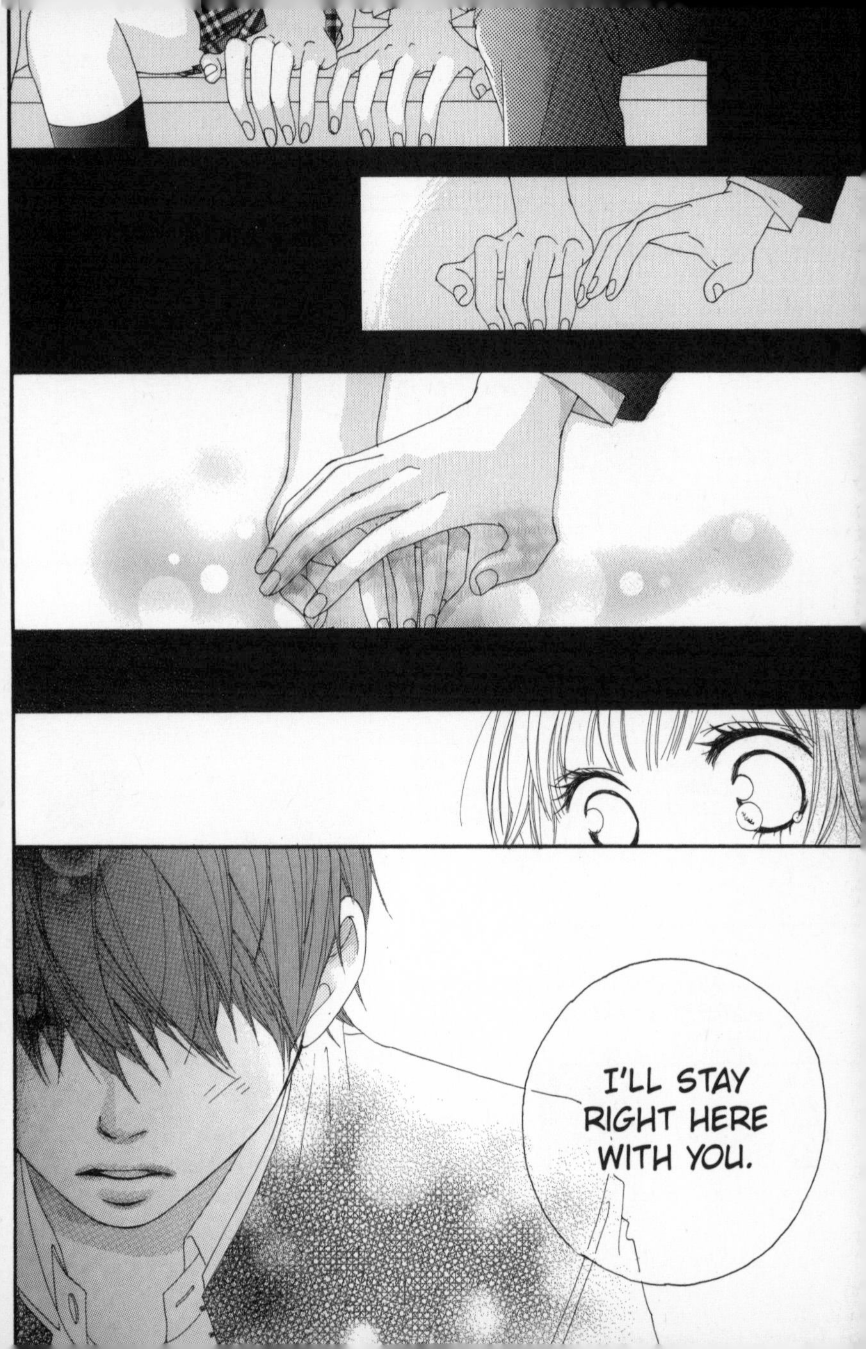
I'LL STAY RIGHT HERE WITH YOU.

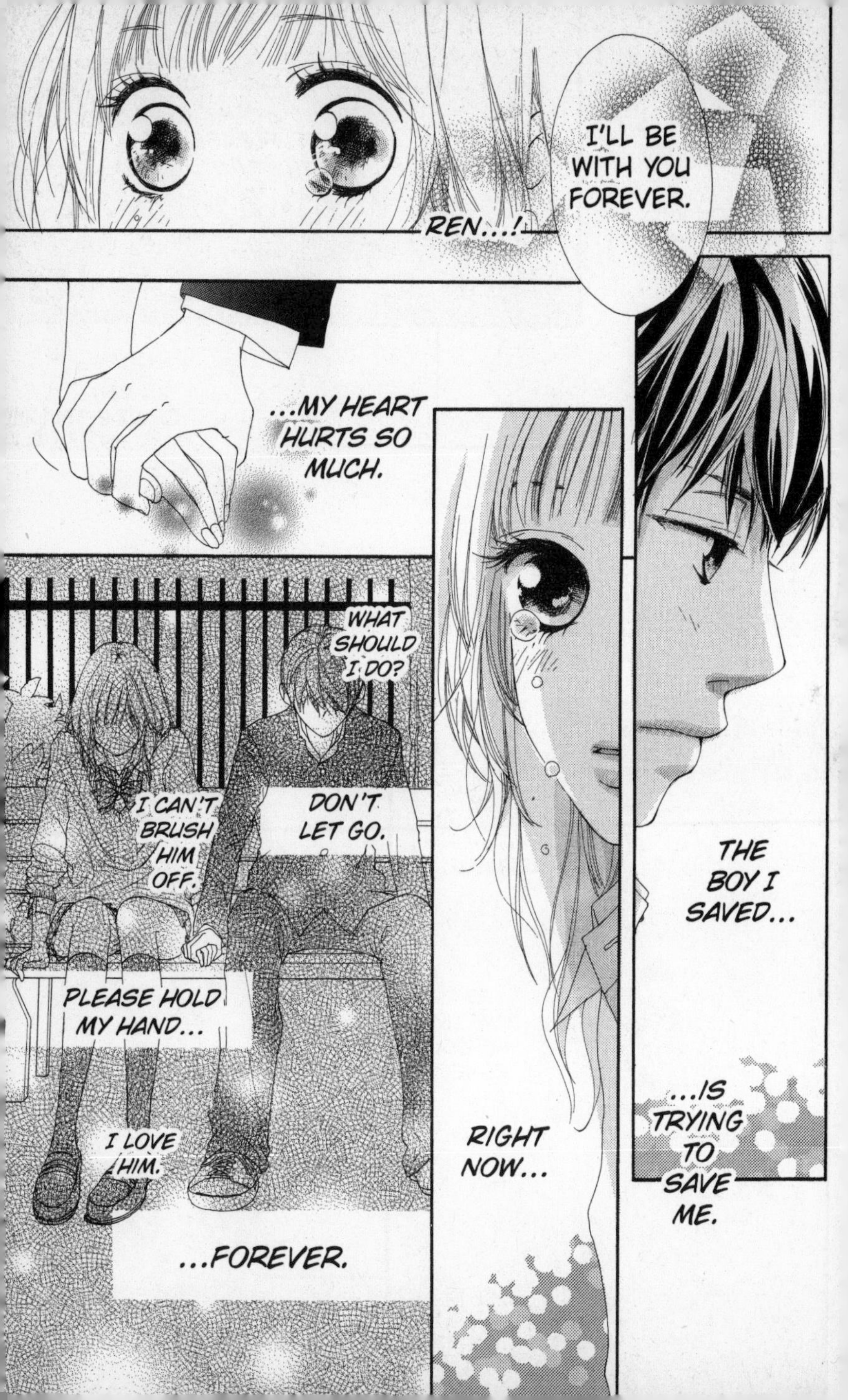
I'LL BE WITH YOU FOREVER.
REN...!
THE BOY I SAVED...
...IS TRYING TO SAVE ME.
RIGHT NOW...
...MY HEART HURTS SO MUCH.
WHAT SHOULD I DO?
DON'T LET GO.
I CAN'T BRUSH HIM OFF.
PLEASE HOLD MY HAND...
I LOVE HIM.
...FOREVER.

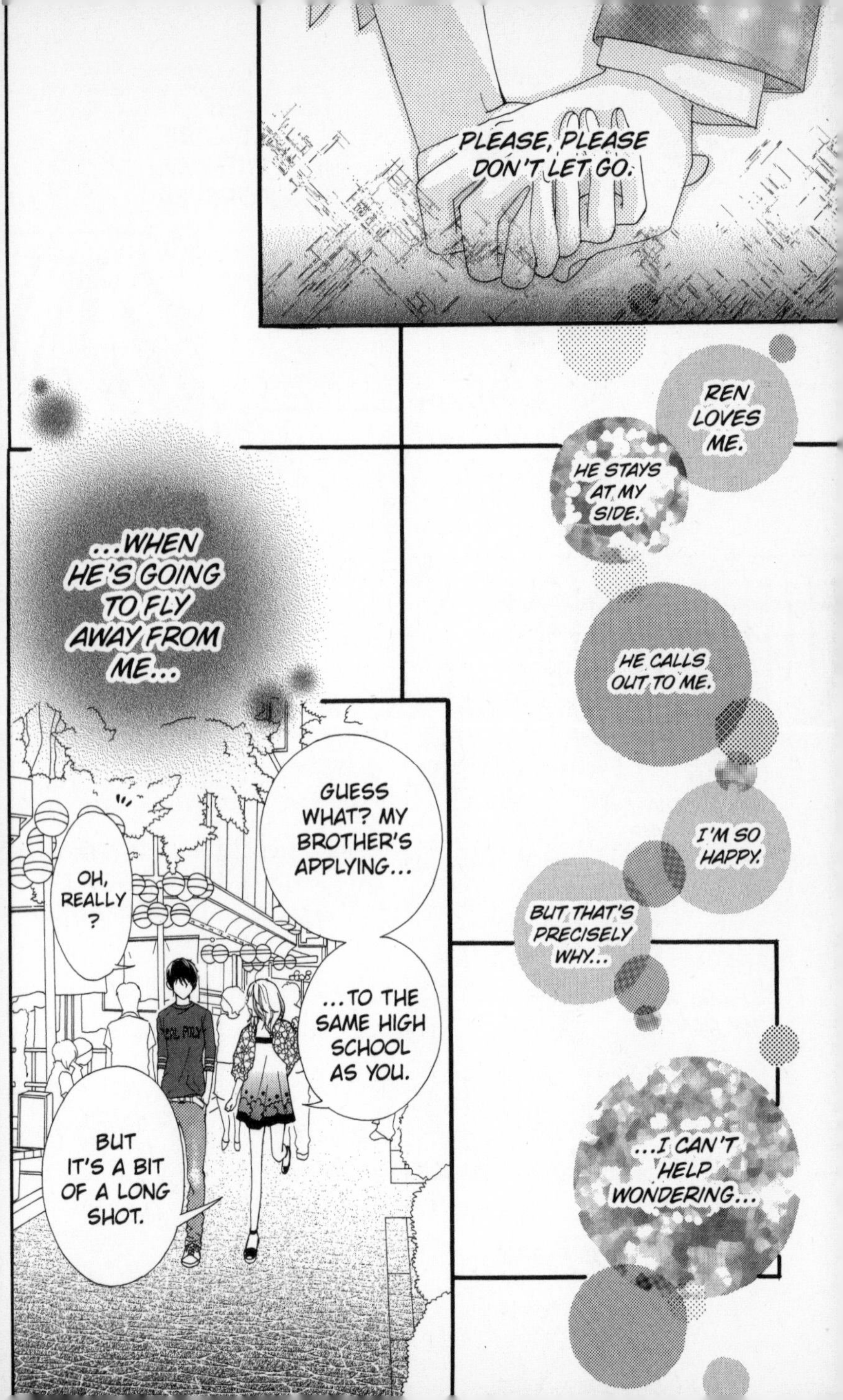
PLEASE, PLEASE DON'T LET GO.
REN LOVES ME.
HE STAYS AT MY SIDE.
HE CALLS OUT TO ME.
I'M SO HAPPY.
BUT THAT'S PRECISELY WHY...
...I CAN'T HELP WONDERING...
...WHEN HE'S GOING TO FLY AWAY FROM ME...
GUESS WHAT? MY BROTHER'S APPLYING...
...TO THE SAME HIGH SCHOOL AS YOU.
OH, REALLY?
BUT IT'S A BIT OF A LONG SHOT.

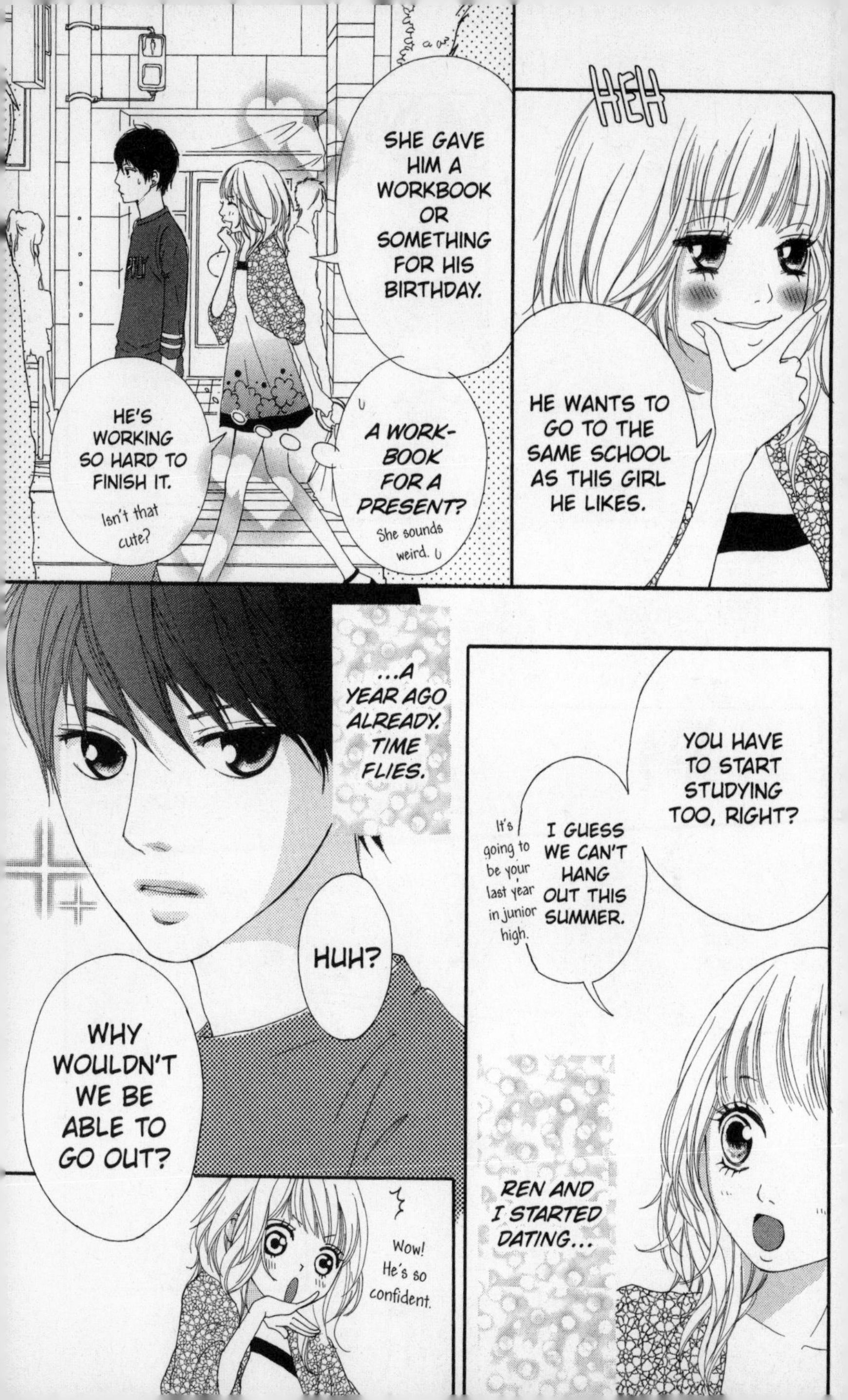
HEH
HE WANTS TO GO TO THE SAME SCHOOL AS THIS GIRL HE LIKES.
SHE GAVE HIM A WORKBOOK OR SOMETHING FOR HIS BIRTHDAY.
A WORK-BOOK FOR A PRESENT?
She sounds weird.
HE'S WORKING SO HARD TO FINISH IT.
Isn't that cute?
YOU HAVE TO START STUDYING TOO, RIGHT?
I GUESS WE CAN'T HANG OUT THIS SUMMER.
It's going to be your last year in junior high.
REN AND I STARTED DATING...
...A YEAR AGO ALREADY. TIME FLIES.
HUH?
WHY WOULDN'T WE BE ABLE TO GO OUT?
Wow! He's so confident.

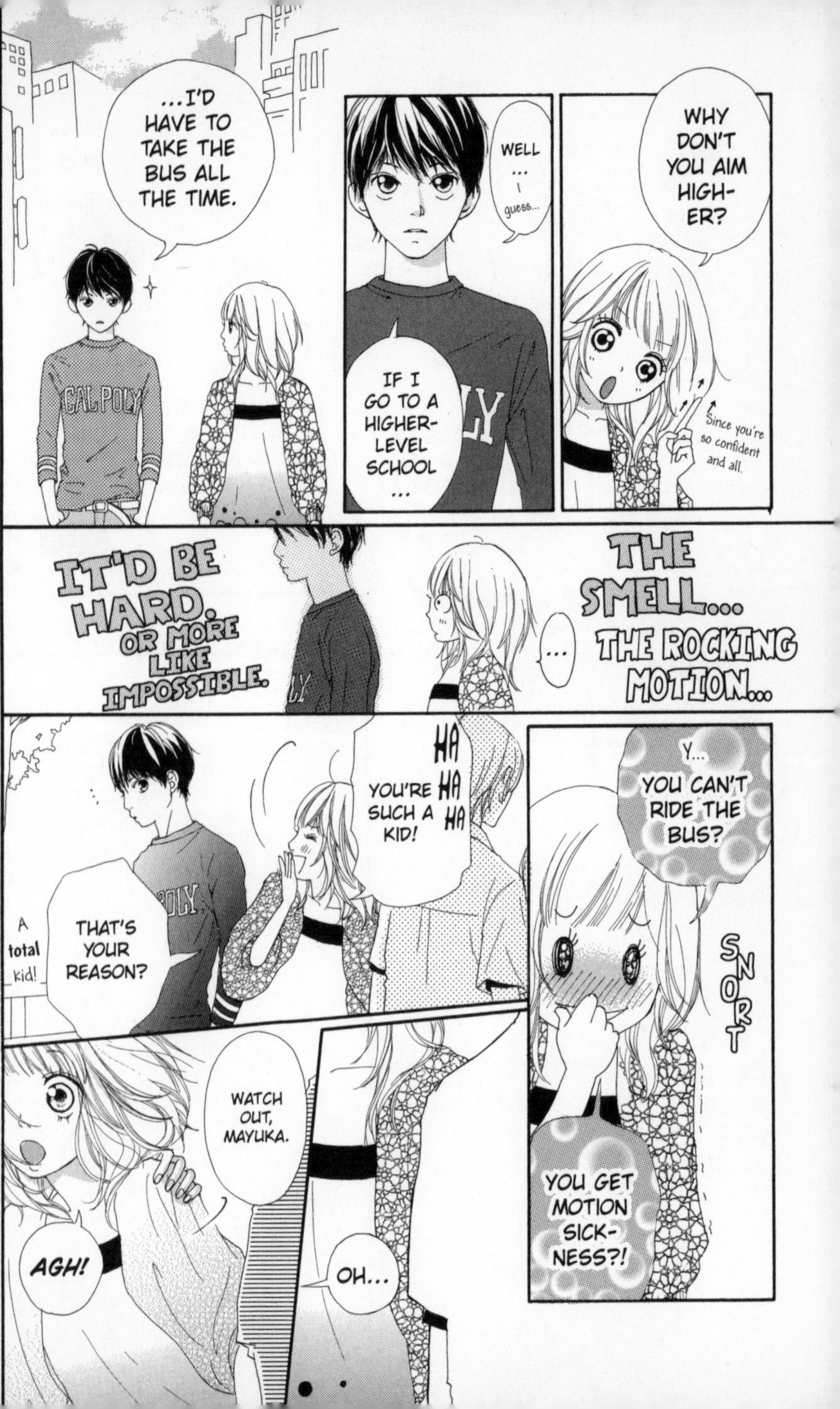
WHY DON'T YOU AIM HIGHER?
Since you're so confident and all.
WELL... I guess...
IF I GO TO A HIGHER-LEVEL SCHOOL...
...I'D HAVE TO TAKE THE BUS ALL THE TIME.
THE SMELL... THE ROCKING MOTION...
...
IT'D BE HARD. OR MORE LIKE IMPOSSIBLE.
Y... YOU CAN'T RIDE THE BUS?
SNORT
YOU GET MOTION SICKNESS?!
HA HA HA
YOU'RE SUCH A KID!
THAT'S YOUR REASON?
A total kid!
WATCH OUT, MAYUKA.
OH...
AGH!

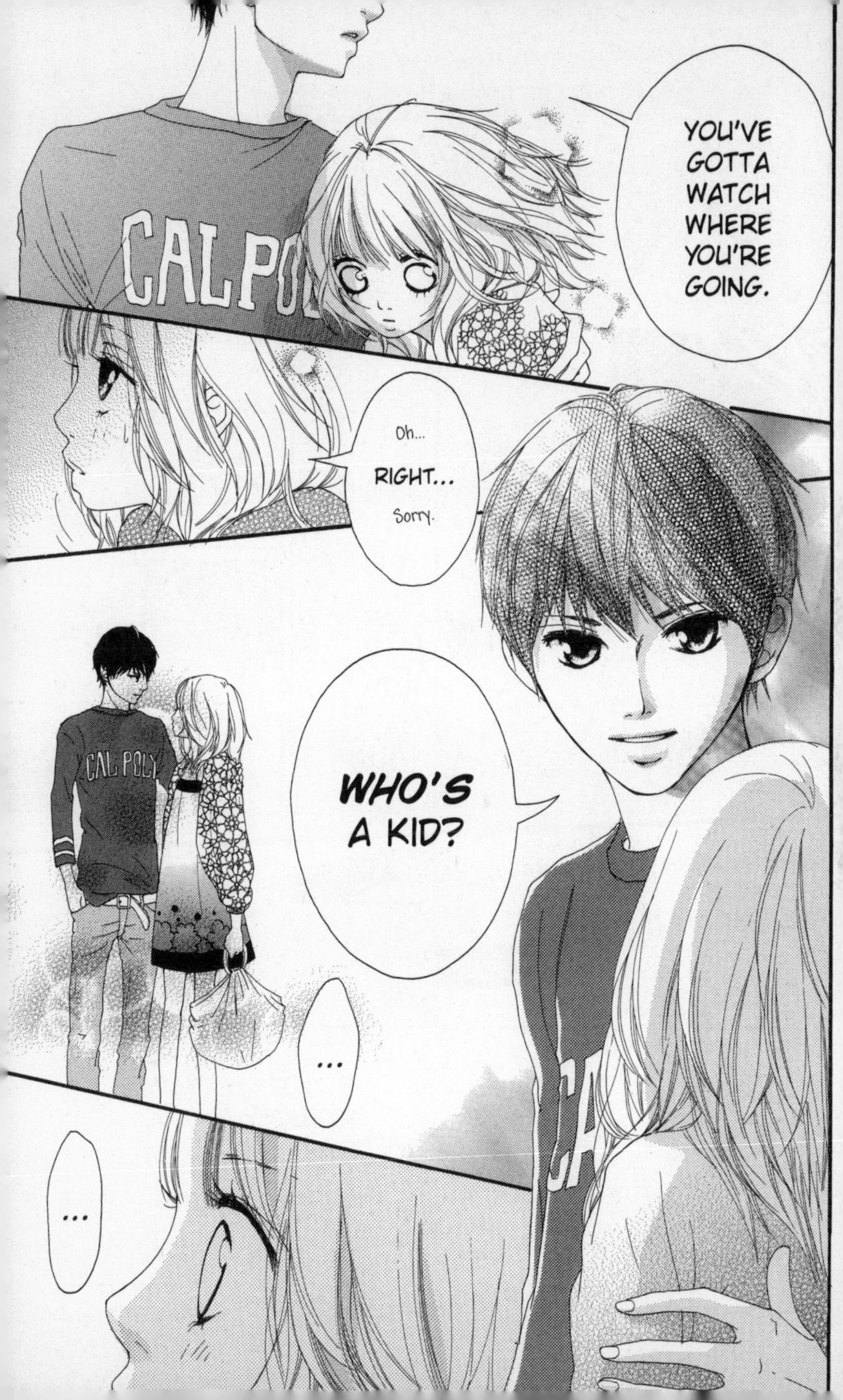
YOU'VE GOTTA WATCH WHERE YOU'RE GOING.
Oh... RIGHT... Sorry.
WHO'S A KID?
...
...

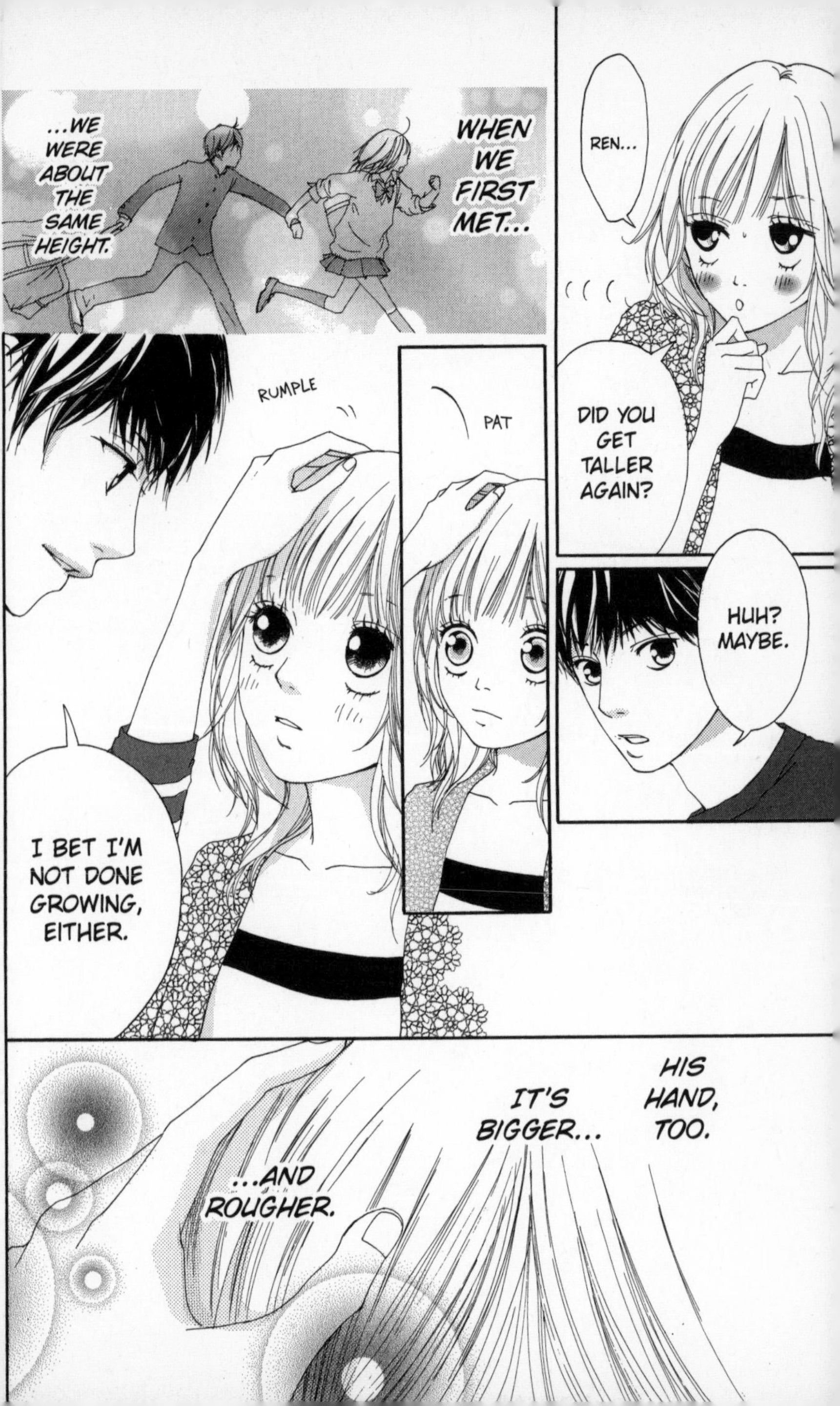
REN...
DID YOU GET TALLER AGAIN?
WHEN WE FIRST MET...
...WE WERE ABOUT THE SAME HEIGHT.
HUH? MAYBE.
PAT
RUMPLE
I BET I'M NOT DONE GROWING, EITHER.
HIS HAND, TOO.
IT'S BIGGER...
...AND ROUGHER.

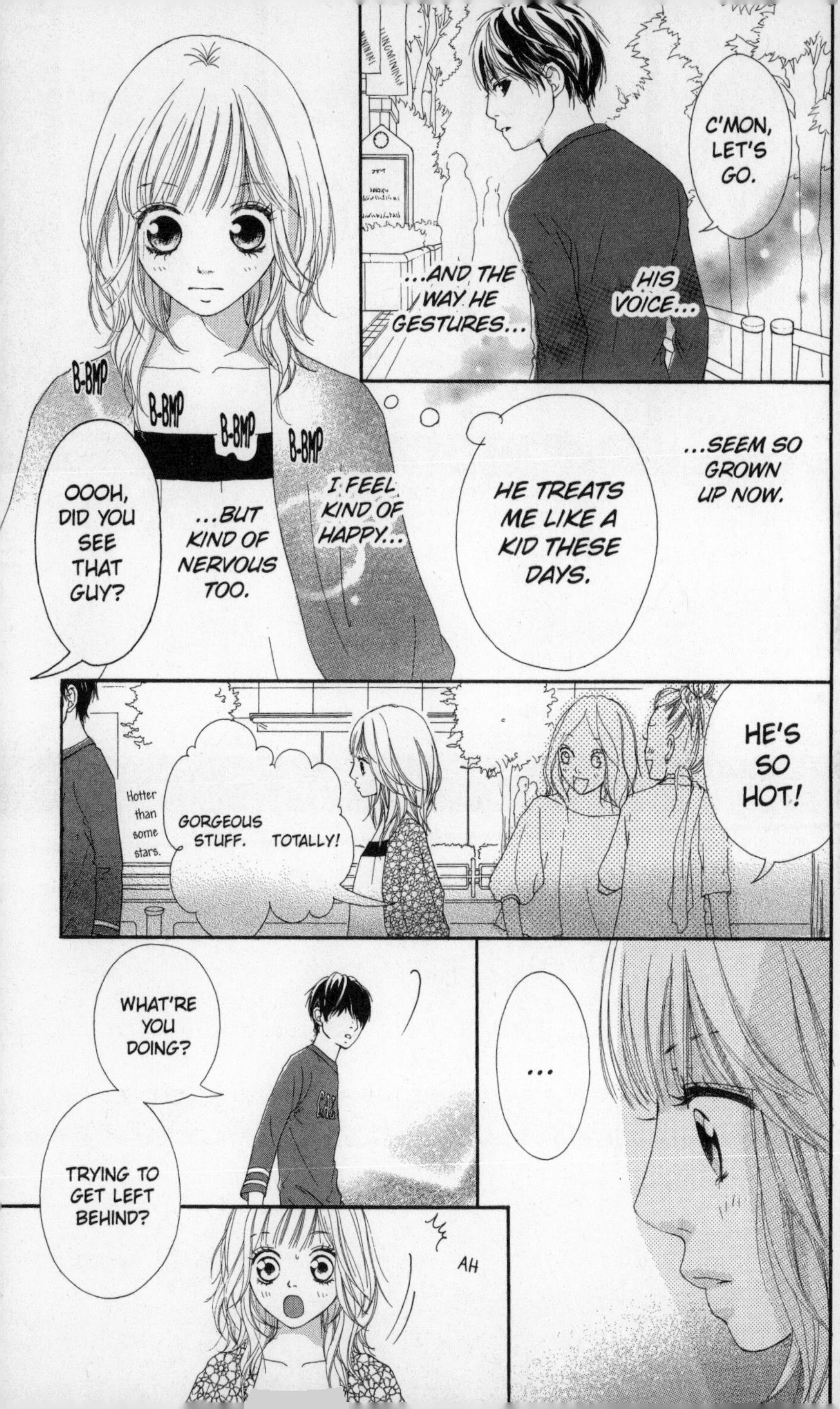
C'MON, LET'S GO.
HIS VOICE...
...AND THE WAY HE GESTURES...
...SEEM SO GROWN UP NOW.
HE TREATS ME LIKE A KID THESE DAYS.
B-BMP
B-BMP
B-BMP
B-BMP
I FEEL KIND OF HAPPY...
...BUT KIND OF NERVOUS TOO.
OOOH, DID YOU SEE THAT GUY?
HE'S SO HOT!
TOTALLY!
GORGEOUS STUFF.
Hotter than some stars.
...
WHAT'RE YOU DOING?
TRYING TO GET LEFT BEHIND?
AH

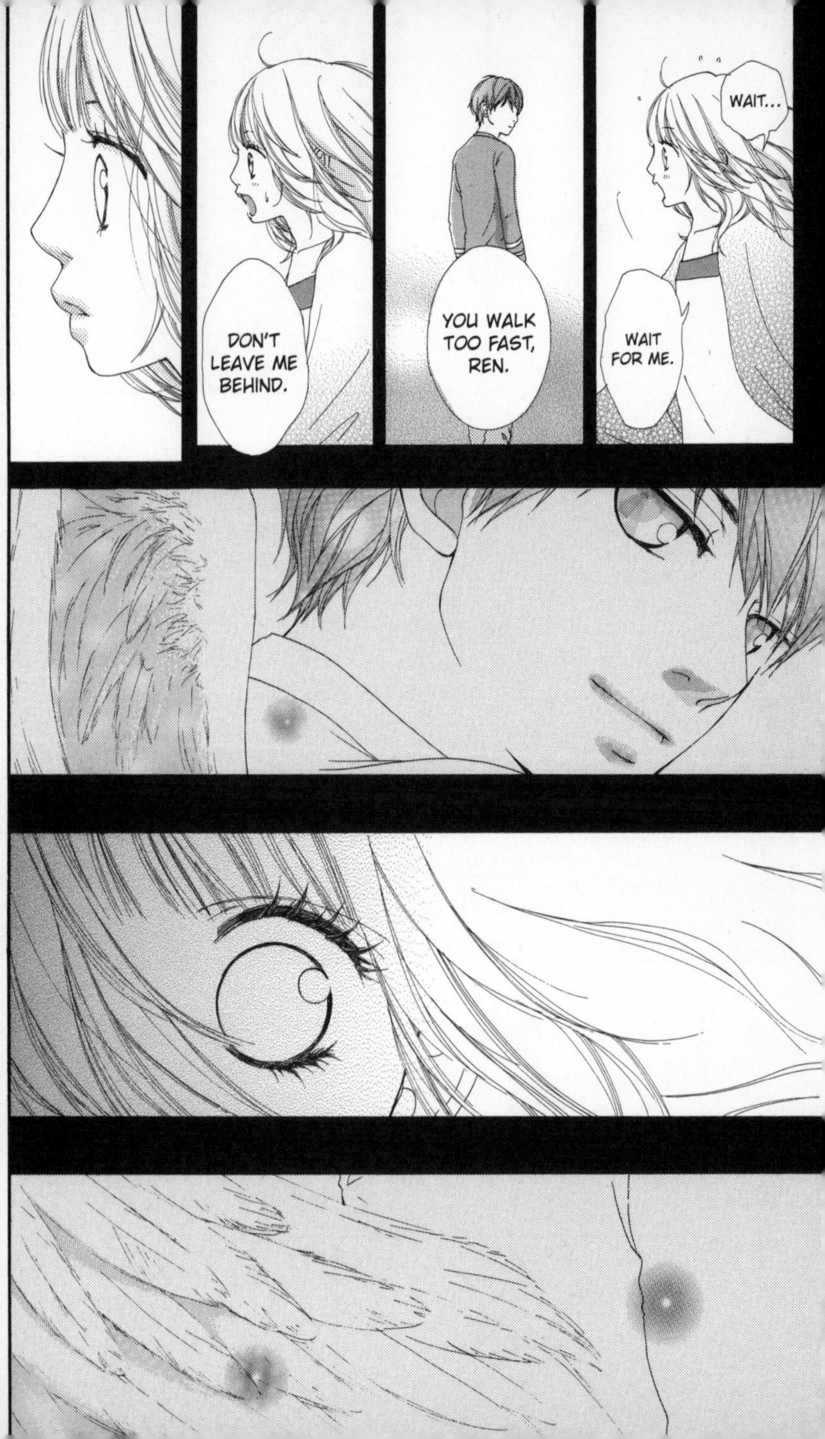
WAIT...
WAIT FOR ME.
YOU WALK TOO FAST, REN.
DON'T LEAVE ME BEHIND.

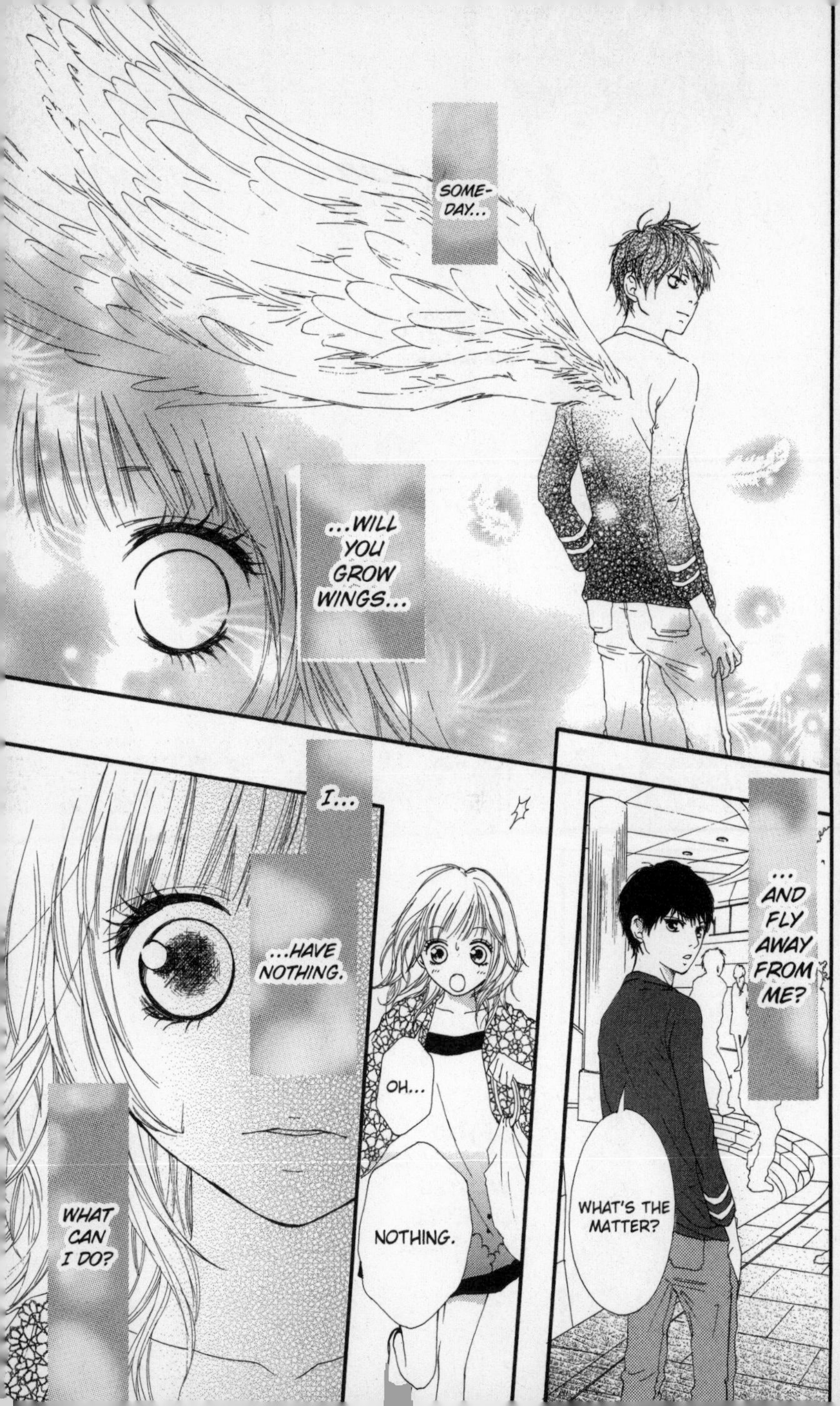
SOME-DAY...
...WILL YOU GROW WINGS...
...AND FLY AWAY FROM ME?
WHAT'S THE MATTER?
OH...
NOTHING.
I...
...HAVE NOTHING.
WHAT CAN I DO?

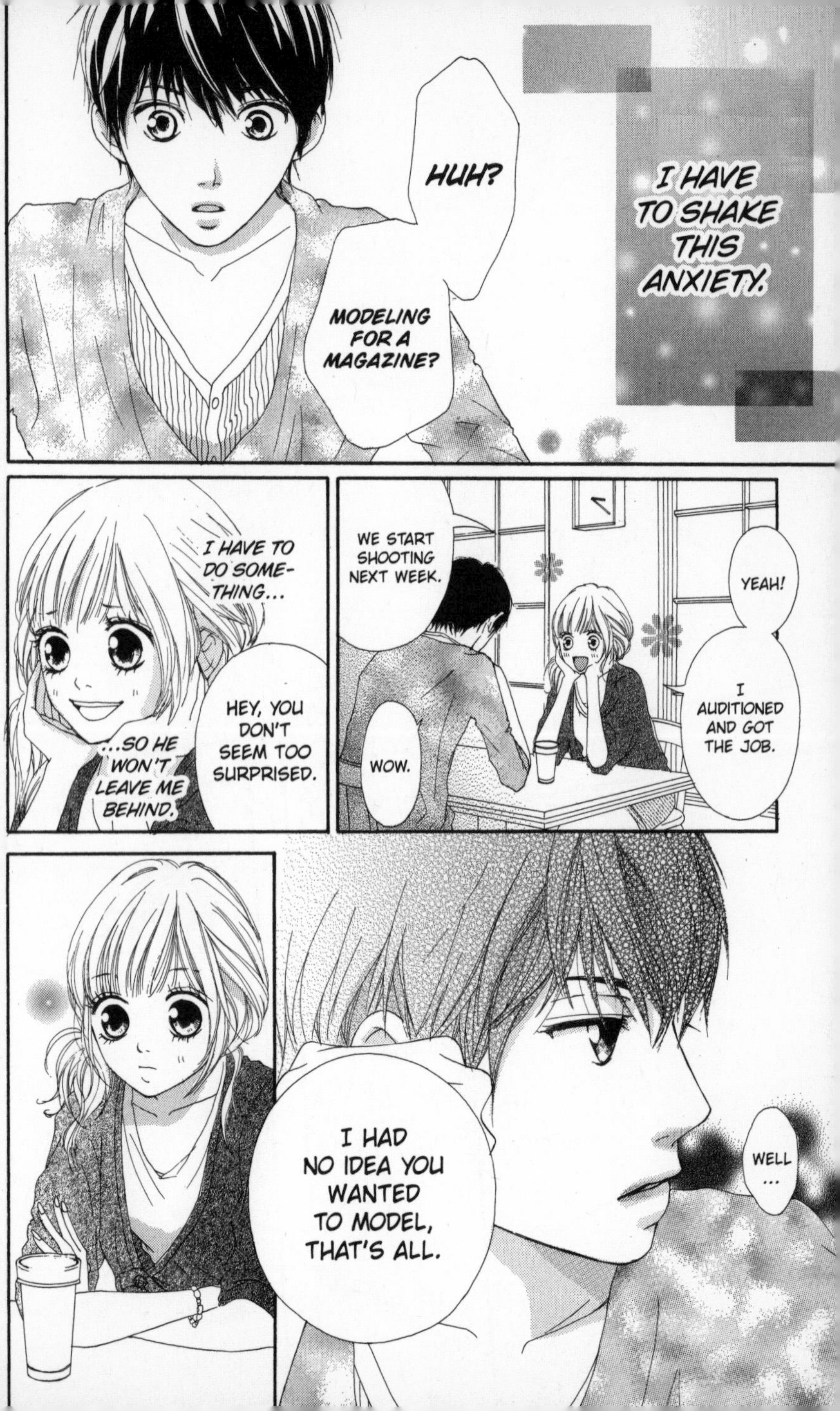
I HAVE TO SHAKE THIS ANXIETY.
HUH?
MODELING FOR A MAGAZINE?
YEAH!
I AUDITIONED AND GOT THE JOB.
WE START SHOOTING NEXT WEEK.
WOW.
HEY, YOU DON'T SEEM TOO SURPRISED.
I HAVE TO DO SOME-THING...
...SO HE WON'T LEAVE ME BEHIND.
WELL...
I HAD NO IDEA YOU WANTED TO MODEL, THAT'S ALL.

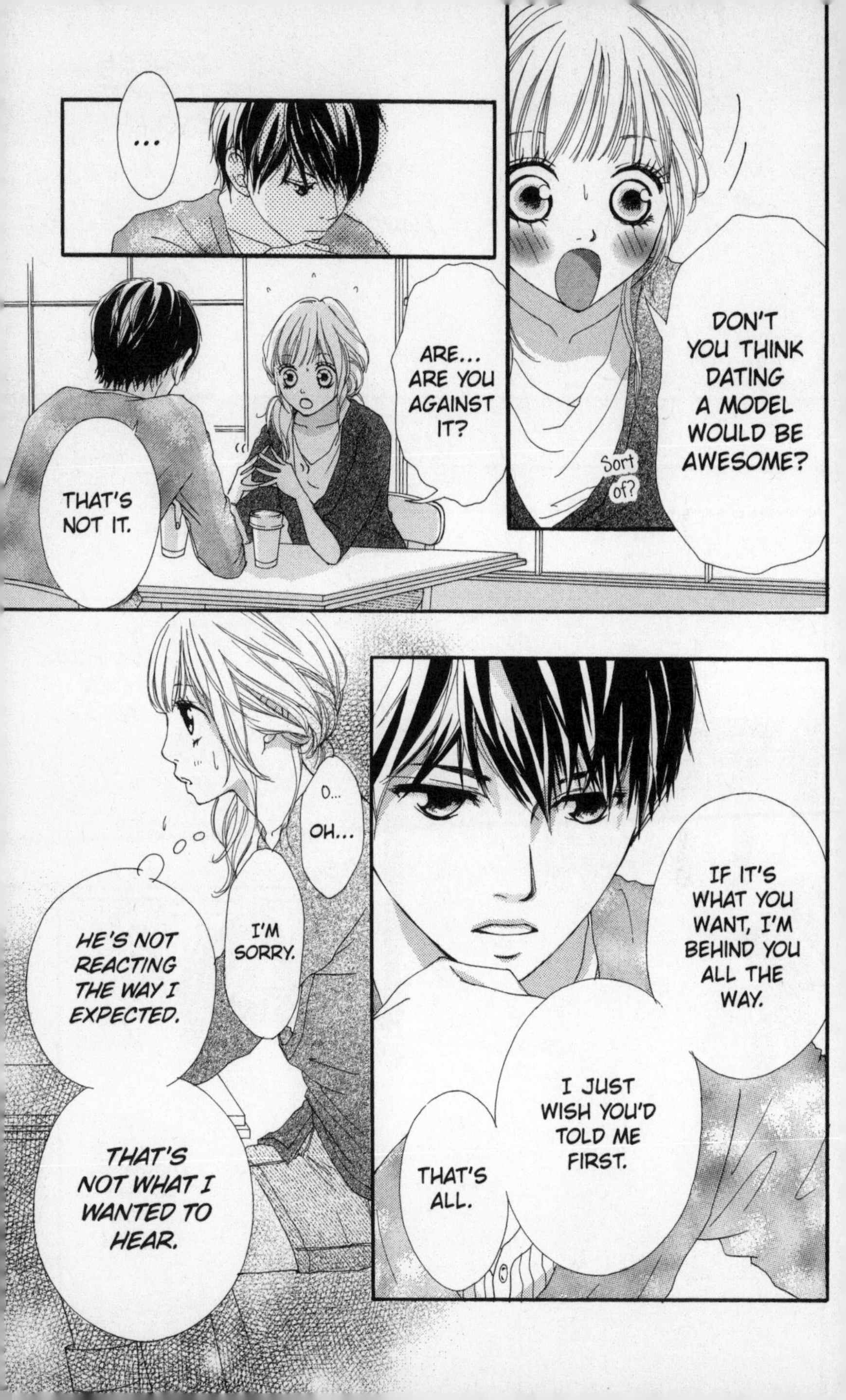
DON'T YOU THINK DATING A MODEL WOULD BE AWESOME?
Sort of?
...
ARE... ARE YOU AGAINST IT?
THAT'S NOT IT.
IF IT'S WHAT YOU WANT, I'M BEHIND YOU ALL THE WAY.
I JUST WISH YOU'D TOLD ME FIRST.
THAT'S ALL.
O... OH...
I'M SORRY.
HE'S NOT REACTING THE WAY I EXPECTED.
THAT'S NOT WHAT I WANTED TO HEAR.

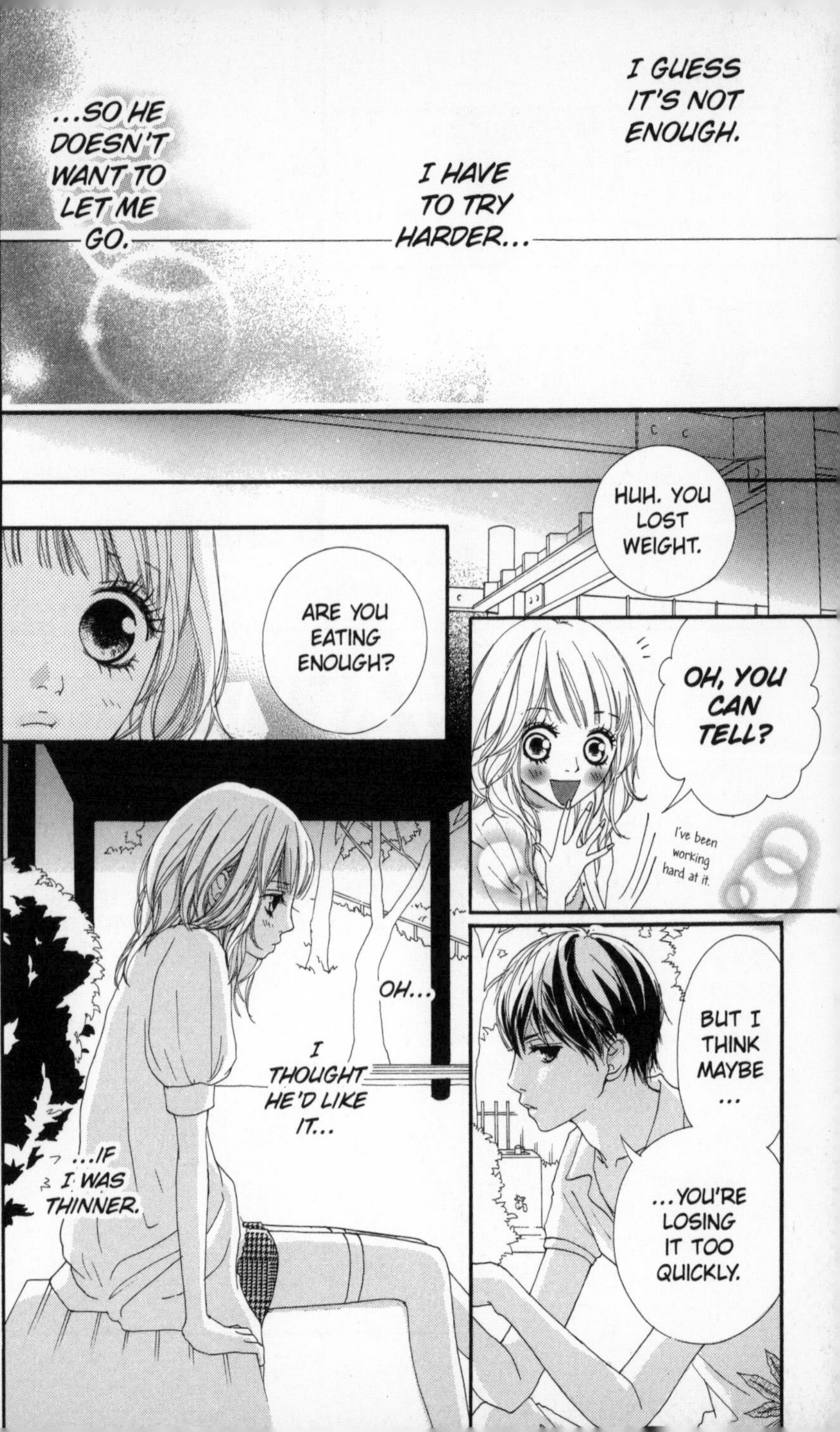
I GUESS IT'S NOT ENOUGH.
I HAVE TO TRY HARDER...
...SO HE DOESN'T WANT TO LET ME GO.
HUH. YOU LOST WEIGHT.
OH, YOU CAN TELL?
I've been working hard at it.
ARE YOU EATING ENOUGH?
BUT I THINK MAYBE...
...YOU'RE LOSING IT TOO QUICKLY.
OH...
I THOUGHT HE'D LIKE IT...
...IF I WAS THINNER.

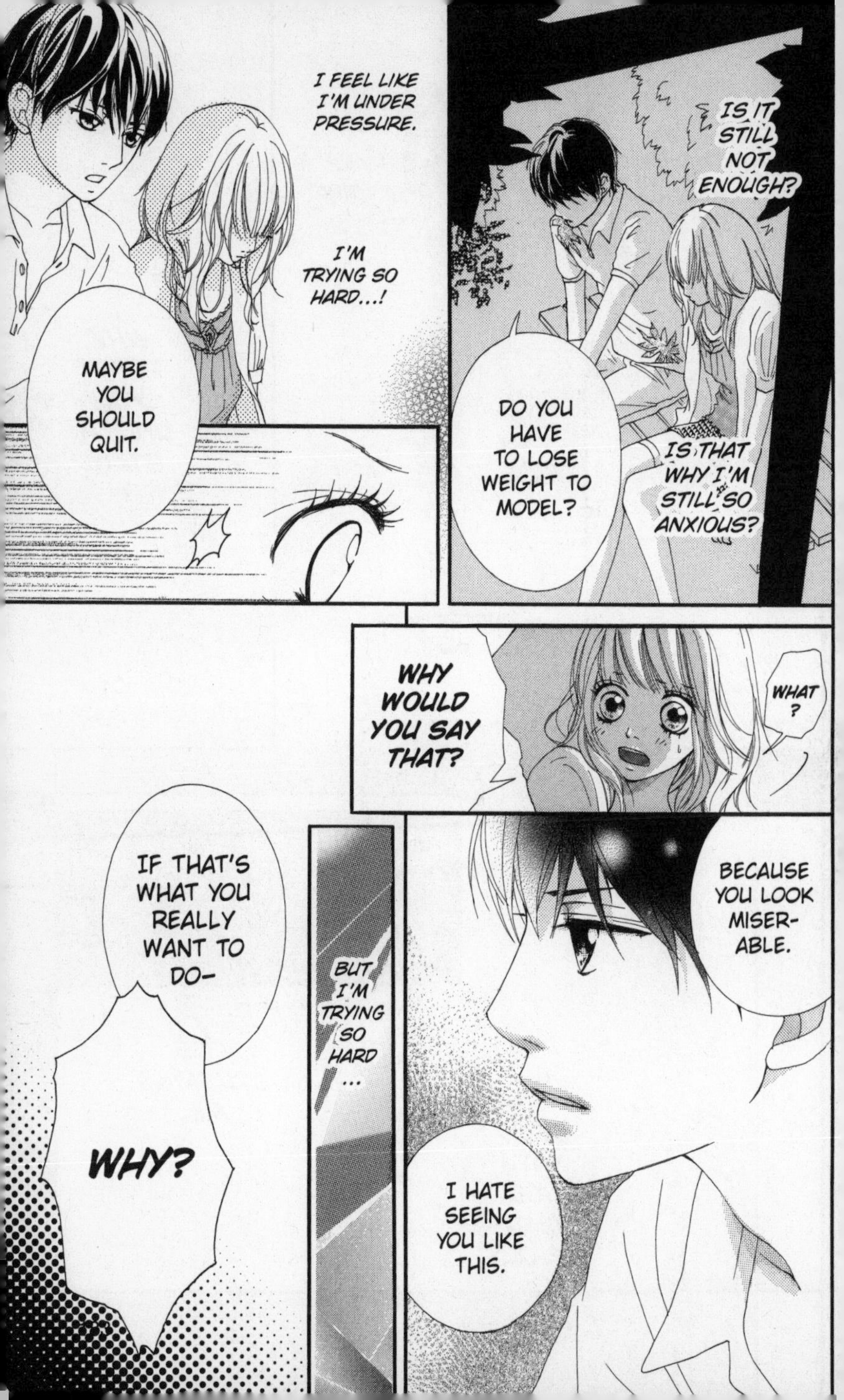
IS IT STILL NOT ENOUGH?
IS THAT WHY I'M STILL SO ANXIOUS?
DO YOU HAVE TO LOSE WEIGHT TO MODEL?
I FEEL LIKE I'M UNDER PRESSURE.
I'M TRYING SO HARD...!
MAYBE YOU SHOULD QUIT.
WHAT?
WHY WOULD YOU SAY THAT?
BECAUSE YOU LOOK MISER-ABLE.
I HATE SEEING YOU LIKE THIS.
BUT I'M TRYING SO HARD...
IF THAT'S WHAT YOU REALLY WANT TO DO-
WHY?

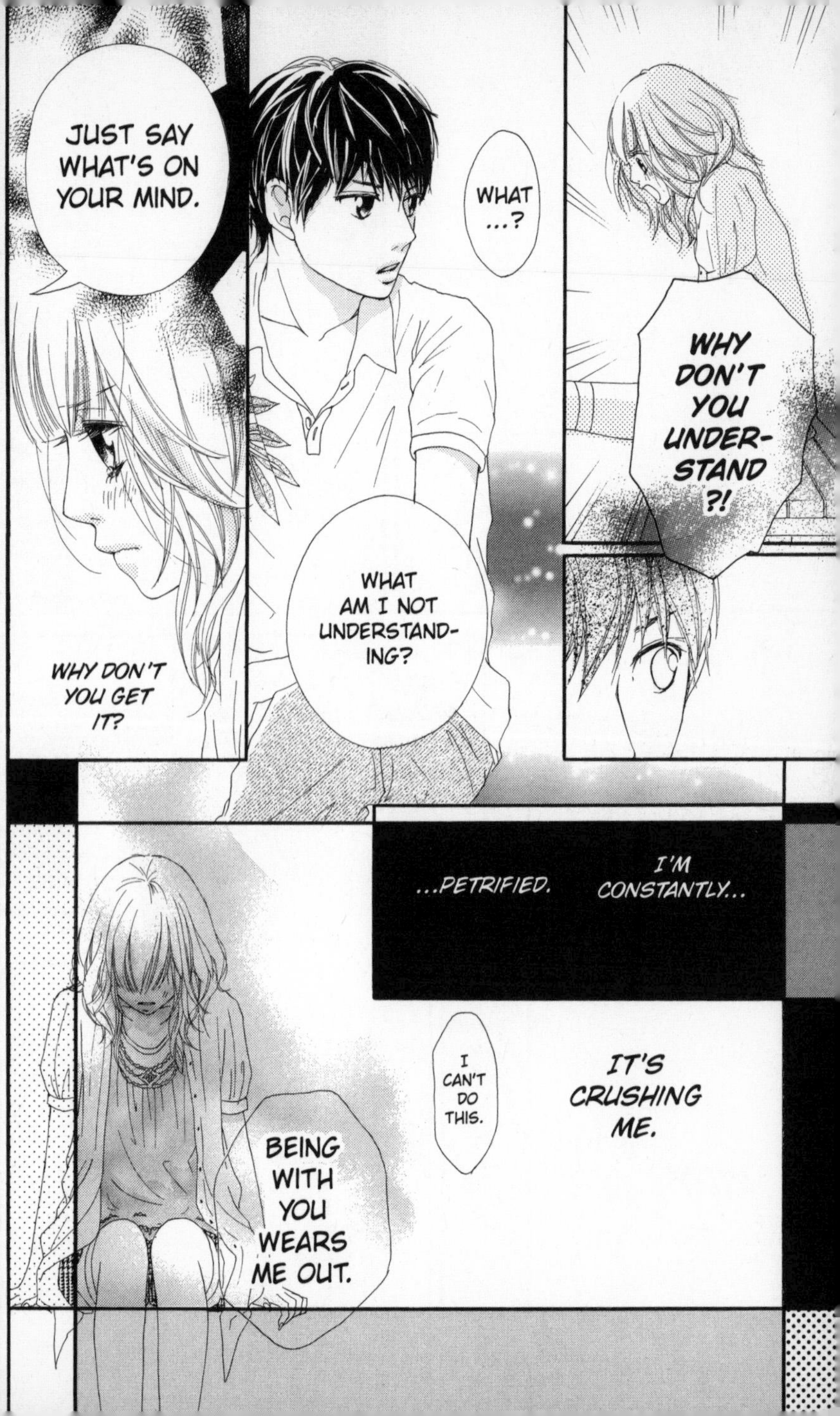
WHY DON'T YOU UNDERSTAND?!
WHAT ...?
WHAT AM I NOT UNDERSTANDING?
JUST SAY WHAT'S ON YOUR MIND.
WHY DON'T YOU GET IT?
I'M CONSTANTLY...
...PETRIFIED.
IT'S CRUSHING ME.
I CAN'T DO THIS.
BEING WITH YOU WEARS ME OUT.

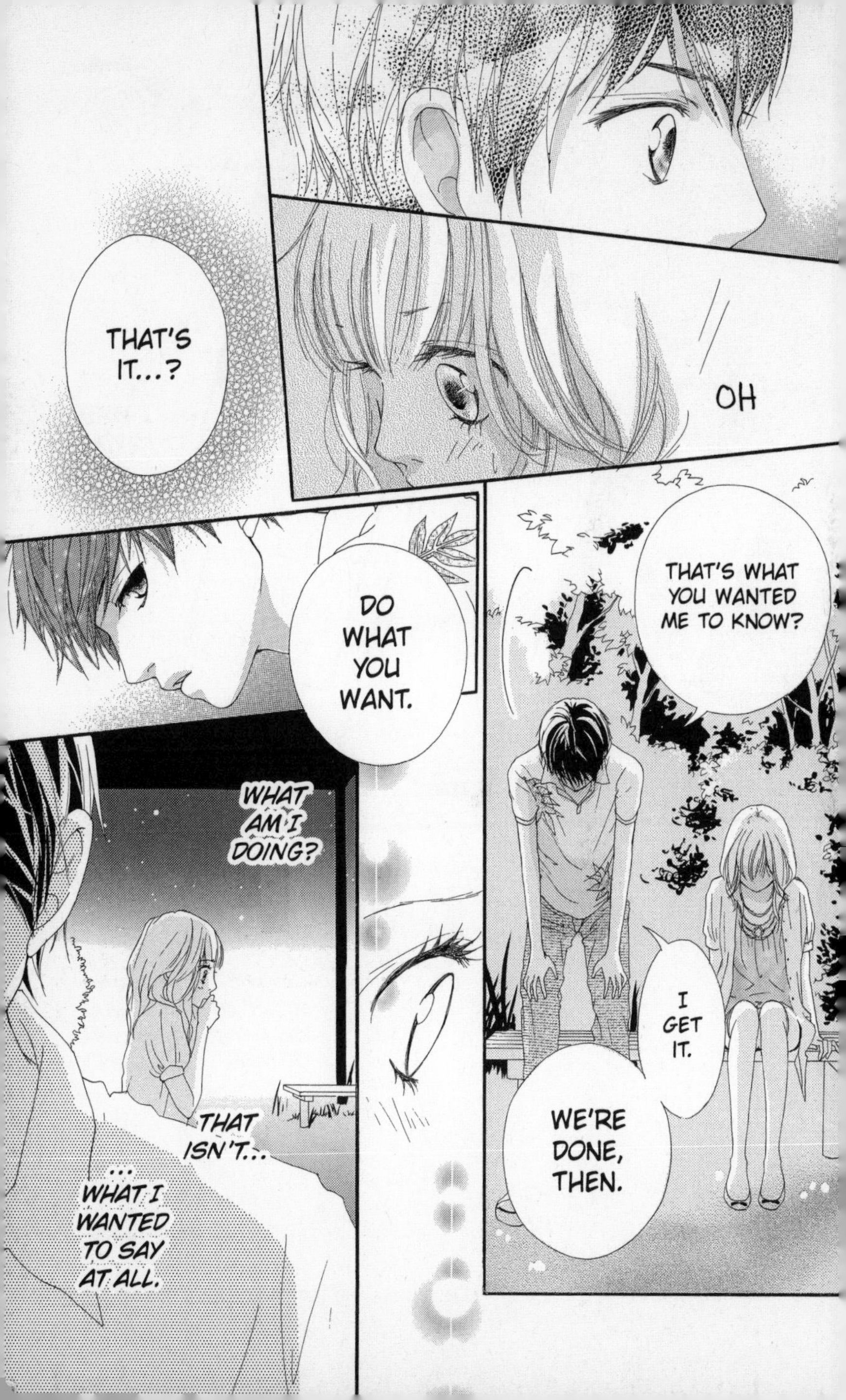
OH
THAT'S IT...?
THAT'S WHAT YOU WANTED ME TO KNOW?
I GET IT.
WE'RE DONE, THEN.
DO WHAT YOU WANT.
WHAT AM I DOING?
THAT ISN'T...
...WHAT I WANTED TO SAY AT ALL.

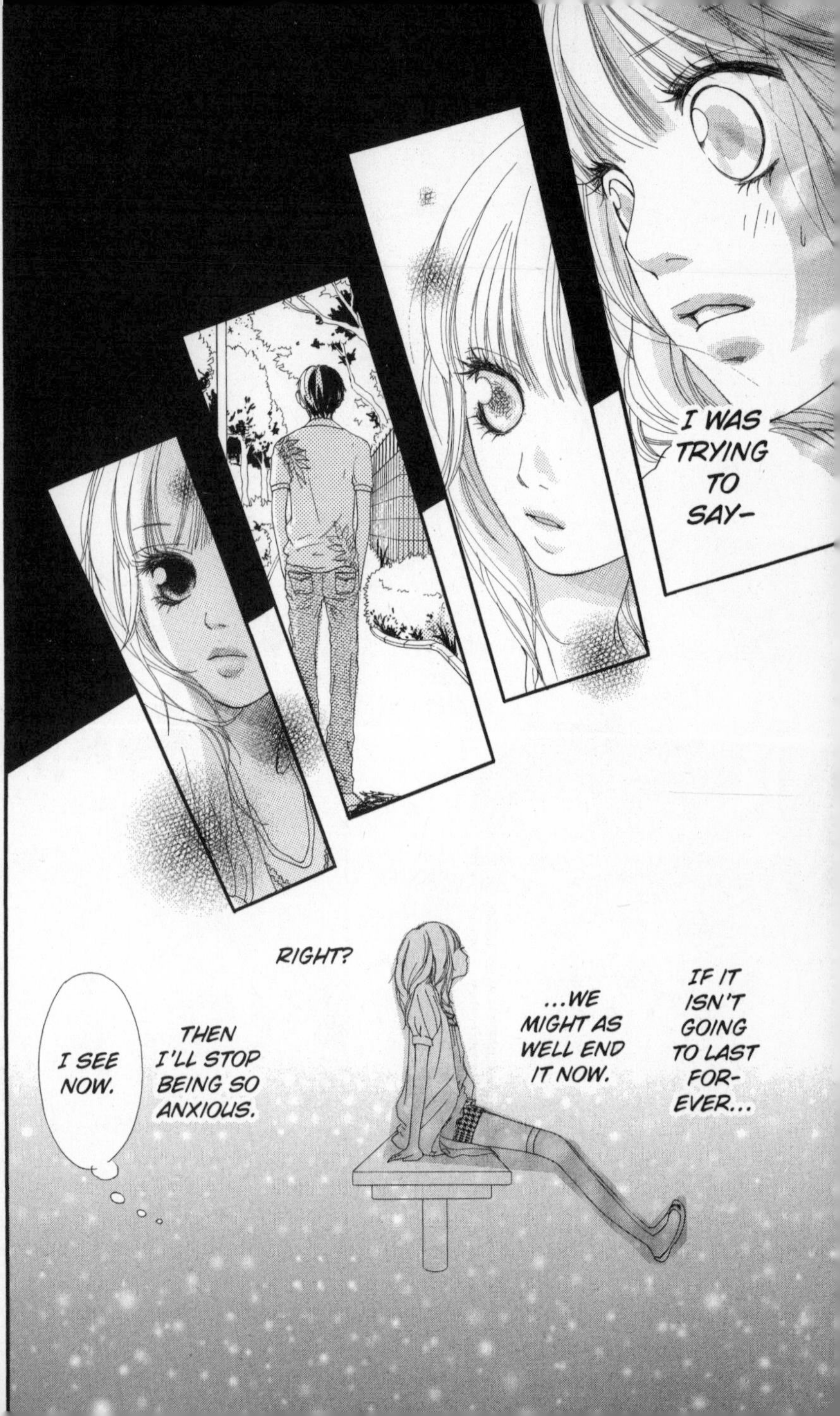
I WAS TRYING TO SAY-
IF IT ISN'T GOING TO LAST FOR-EVER...
...WE MIGHT AS WELL END IT NOW.
RIGHT?
THEN I'LL STOP BEING SO ANXIOUS.
I SEE NOW.

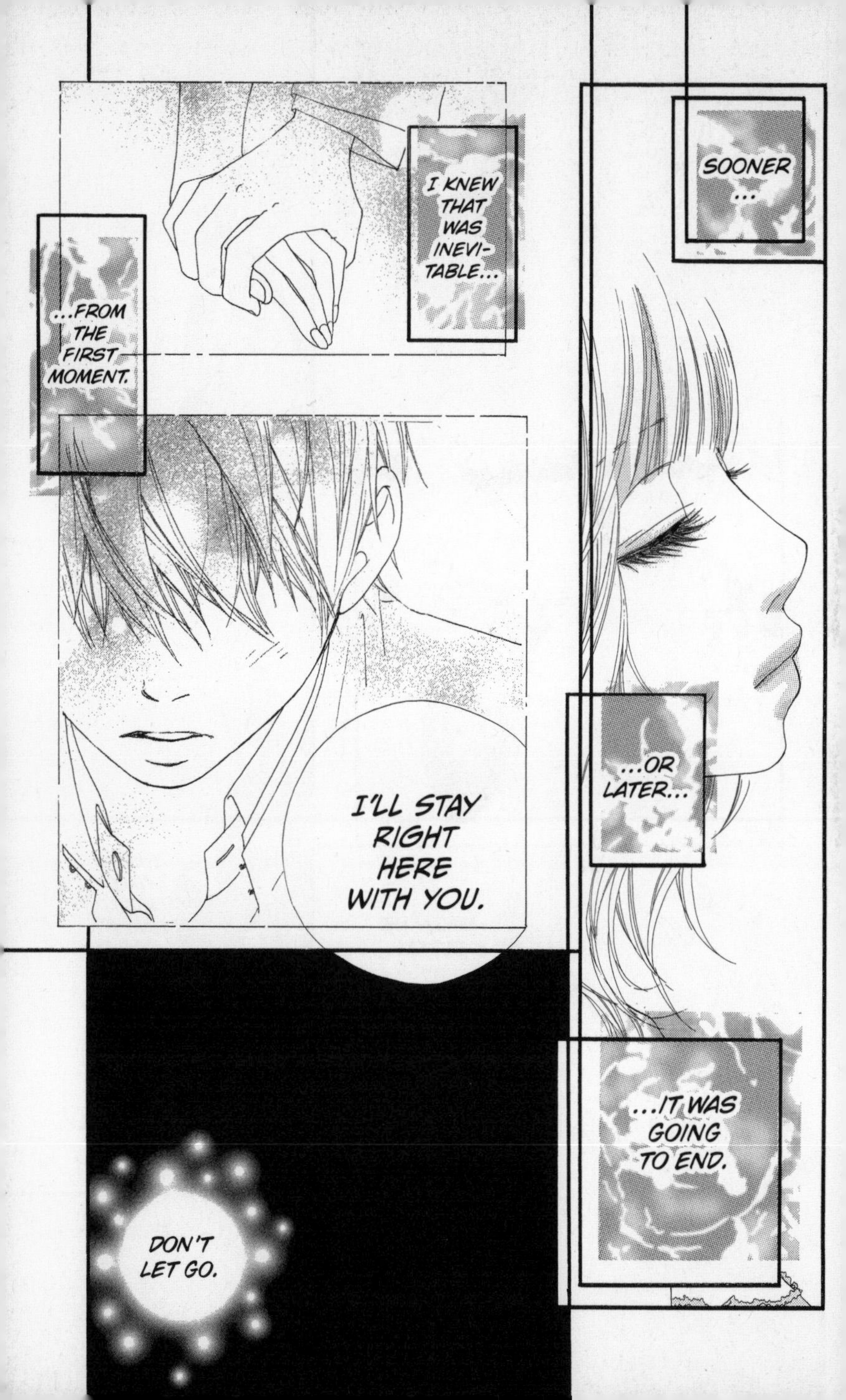
SOONER ...
...OR LATER...
...IT WAS GOING TO END.
I KNEW THAT WAS INEVI-TABLE...
...FROM THE FIRST MOMENT.
I'LL STAY RIGHT HERE WITH YOU.
DON'T LET GO.

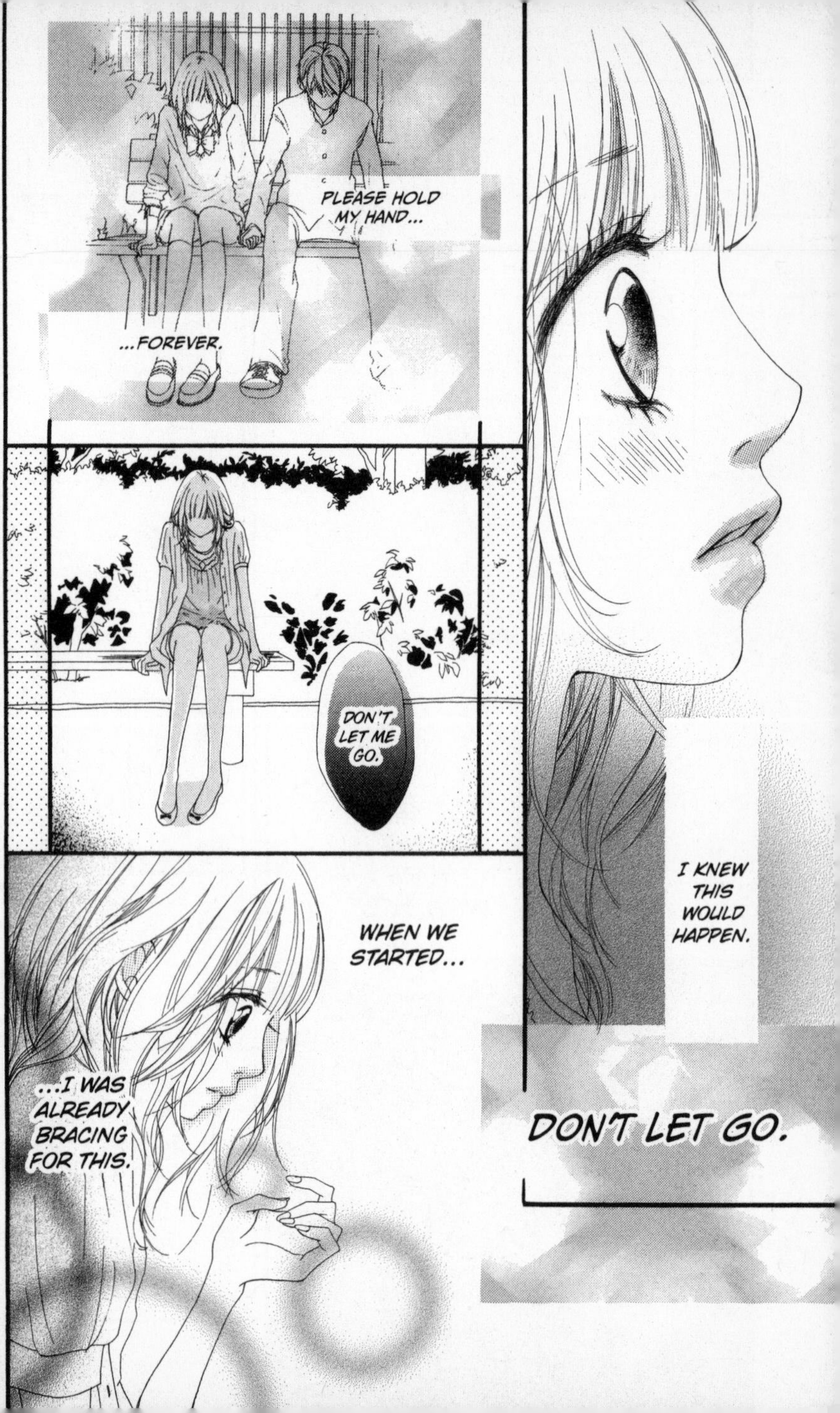

I KNEW THIS WOULD HAPPEN.
DON'T LET GO.
PLEASE HOLD MY HAND...
...FOREVER.
DON'T LET ME GO.
WHEN WE STARTED...
...I WAS ALREADY BRACING FOR THIS.

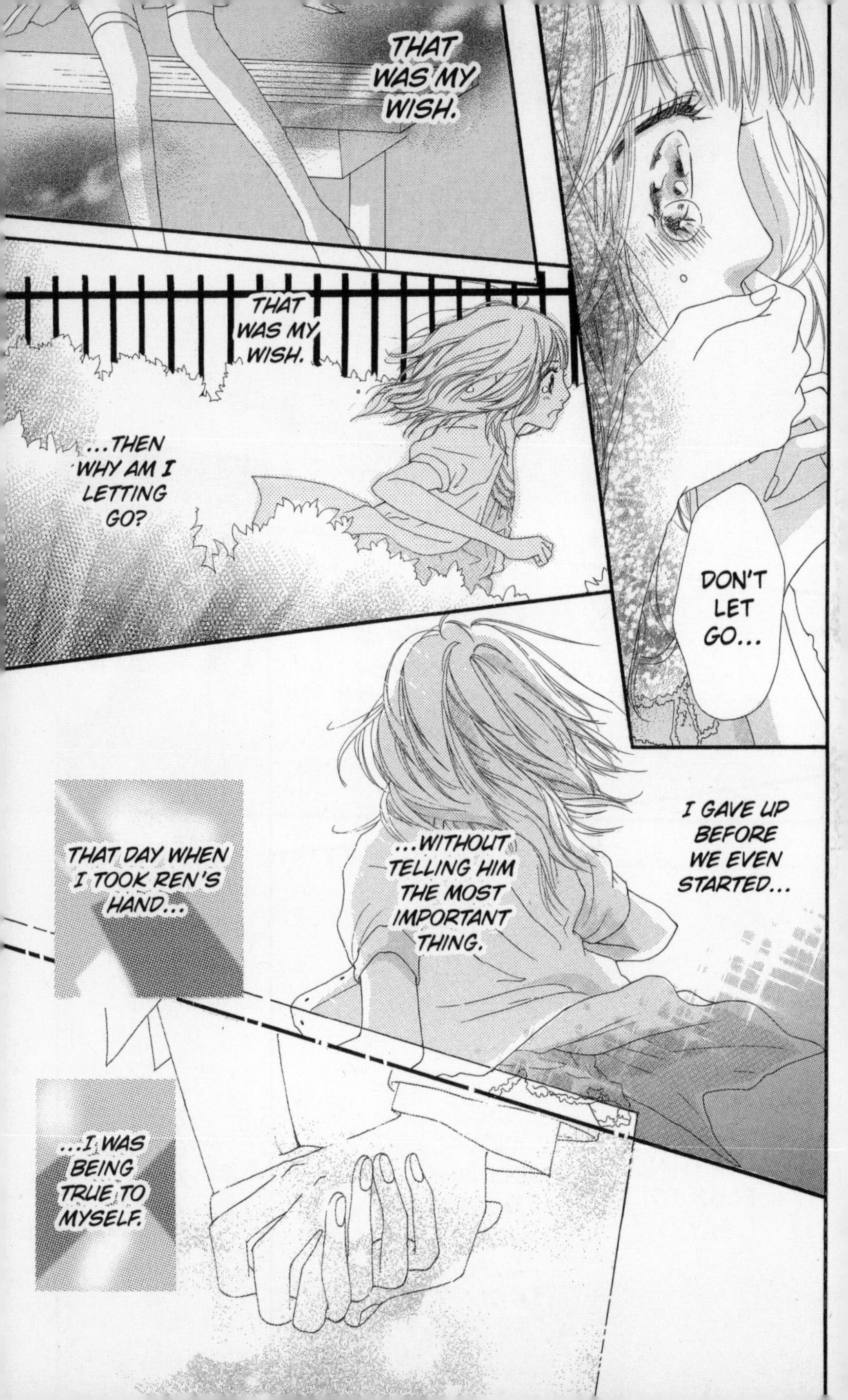
DON'T LET GO...
THAT WAS MY WISH.
THAT WAS MY WISH.
...THEN WHY AM I LETTING GO?
I GAVE UP BEFORE WE EVEN STARTED...
...WITHOUT TELLING HIM THE MOST IMPORTANT THING.
THAT DAY WHEN I TOOK REN'S HAND...
...I WAS BEING TRUE TO MYSELF.

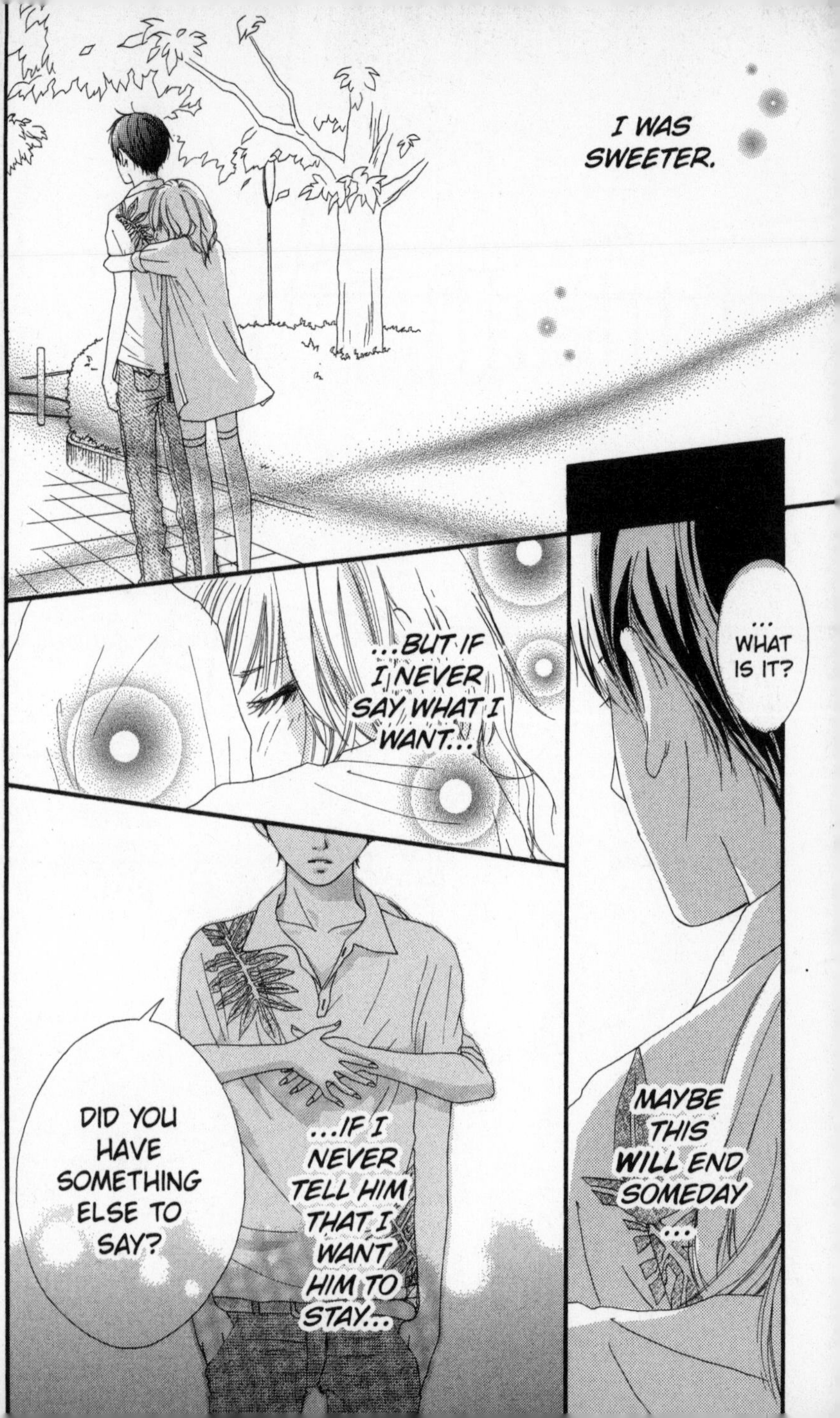
I WAS SWEETER.
...WHAT IS IT?
MAYBE THIS WILL END SOMEDAY...
...BUT IF I NEVER SAY WHAT I WANT...
...IF I NEVER TELL HIM THAT I WANT HIM TO STAY...
DID YOU HAVE SOMETHING ELSE TO SAY?

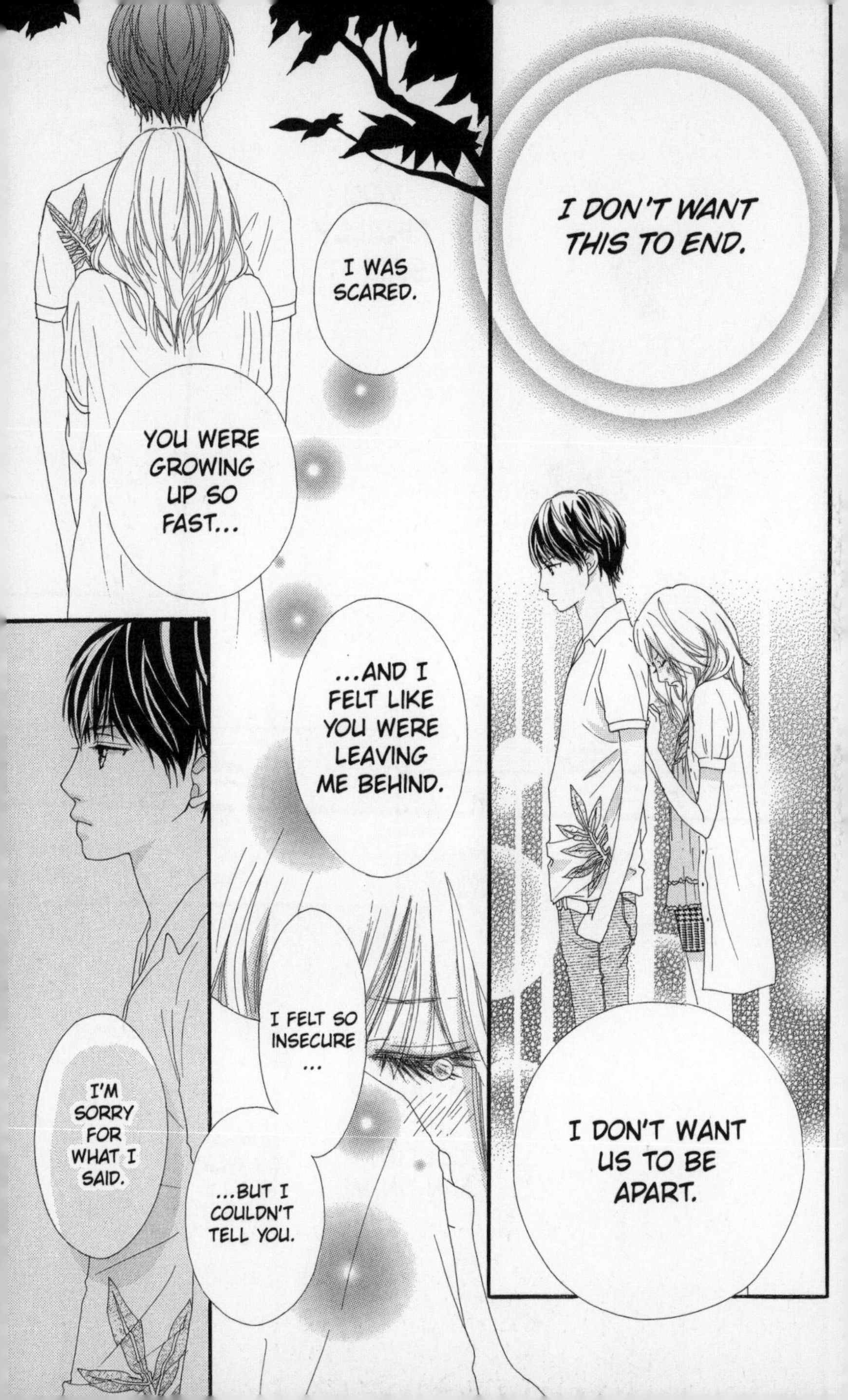
I DON'T WANT THIS TO END.
I DON'T WANT US TO BE APART.
I WAS SCARED.
YOU WERE GROWING UP SO FAST...
...AND I FELT LIKE YOU WERE LEAVING ME BEHIND.
I FELT SO INSECURE...
...BUT I COULDN'T TELL YOU.
I'M SORRY FOR WHAT I SAID.

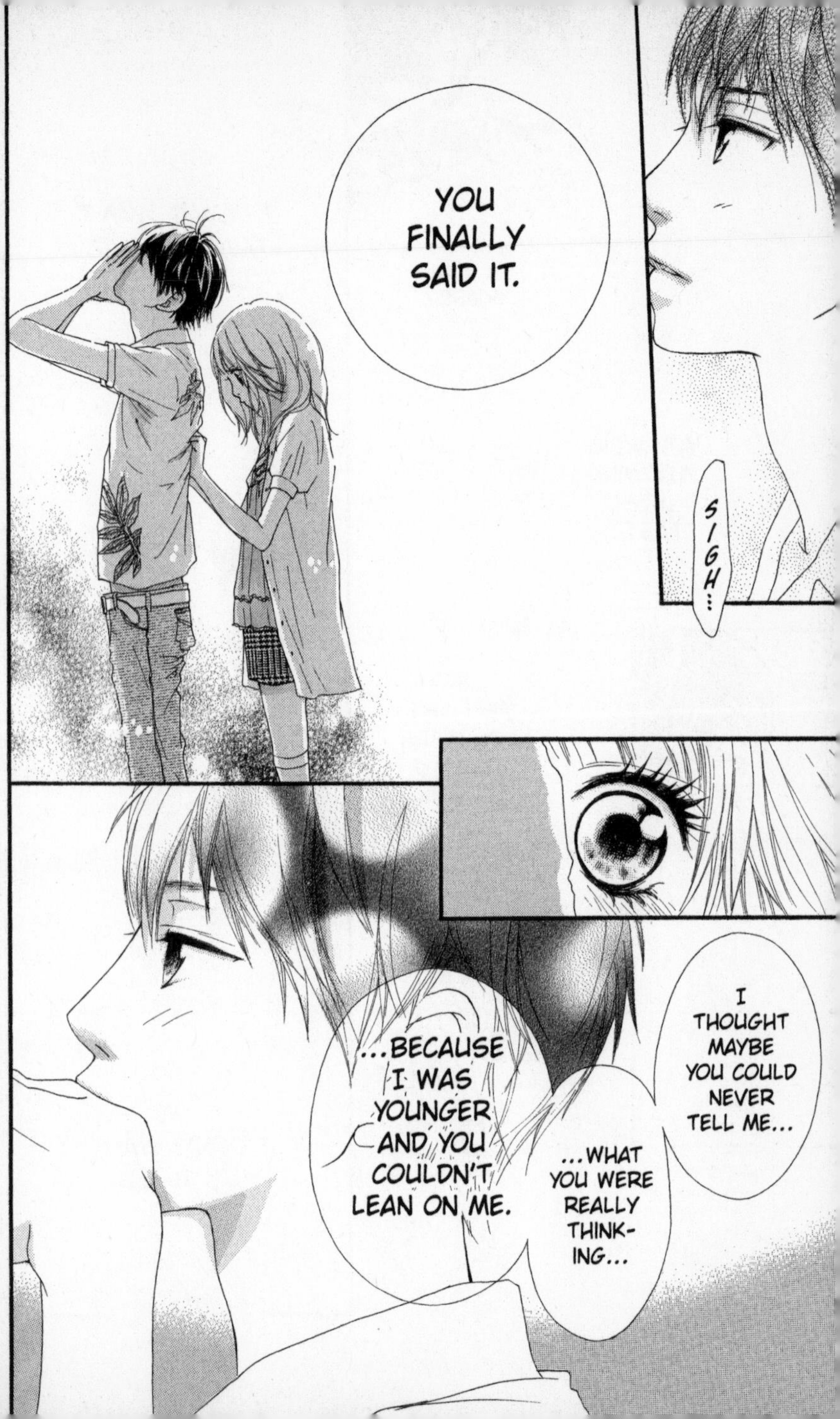
SIGH...
YOU FINALLY SAID IT.
I THOUGHT MAYBE YOU COULD NEVER TELL ME...
...WHAT YOU WERE REALLY THINKING...
...BECAUSE I WAS YOUNGER AND YOU COULDN'T LEAN ON ME.

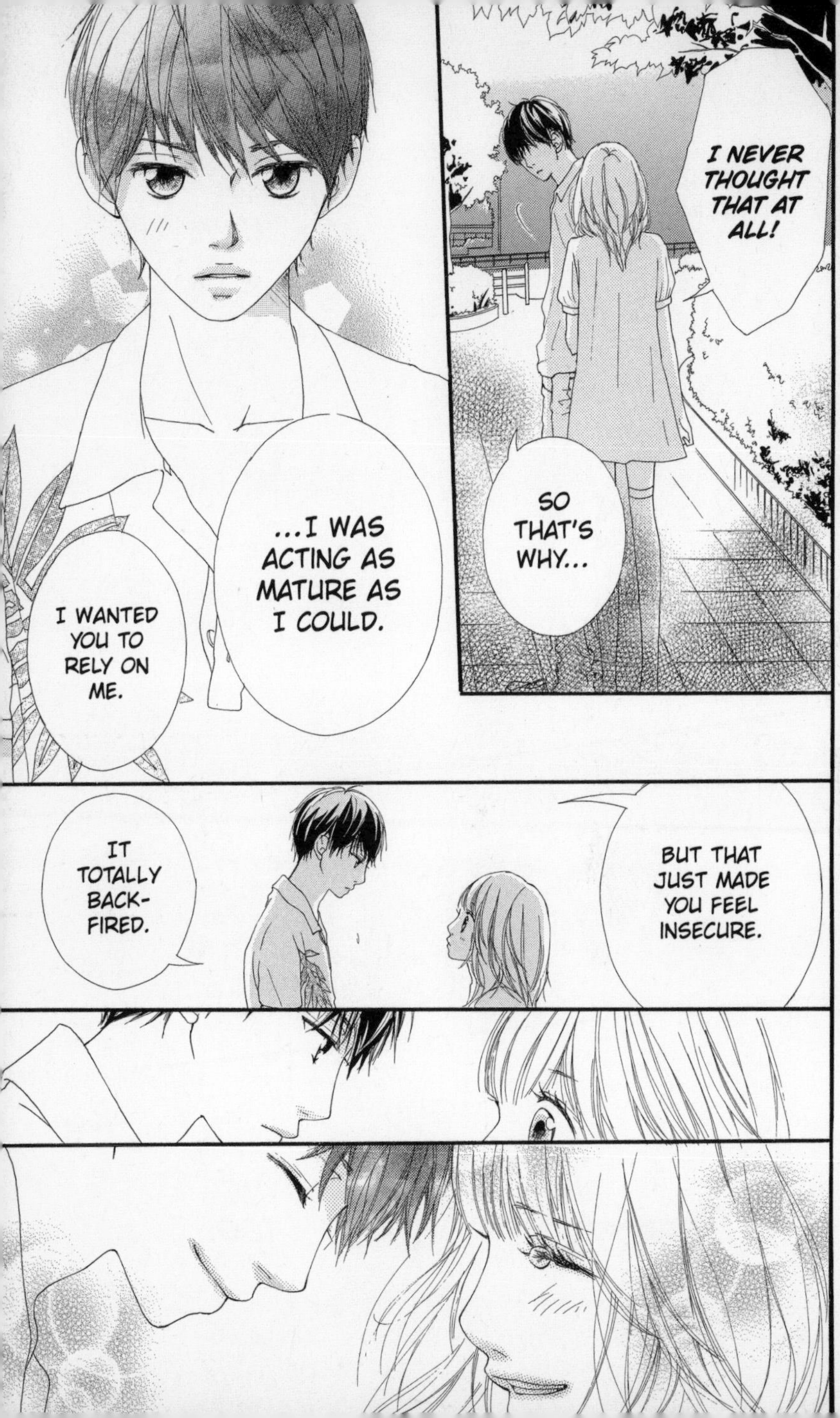
I NEVER THOUGHT THAT AT ALL!
SO THAT'S WHY...
...I WAS ACTING AS MATURE AS I COULD.
I WANTED YOU TO RELY ON ME.
BUT THAT JUST MADE YOU FEEL INSECURE.
IT TOTALLY BACK-FIRED.

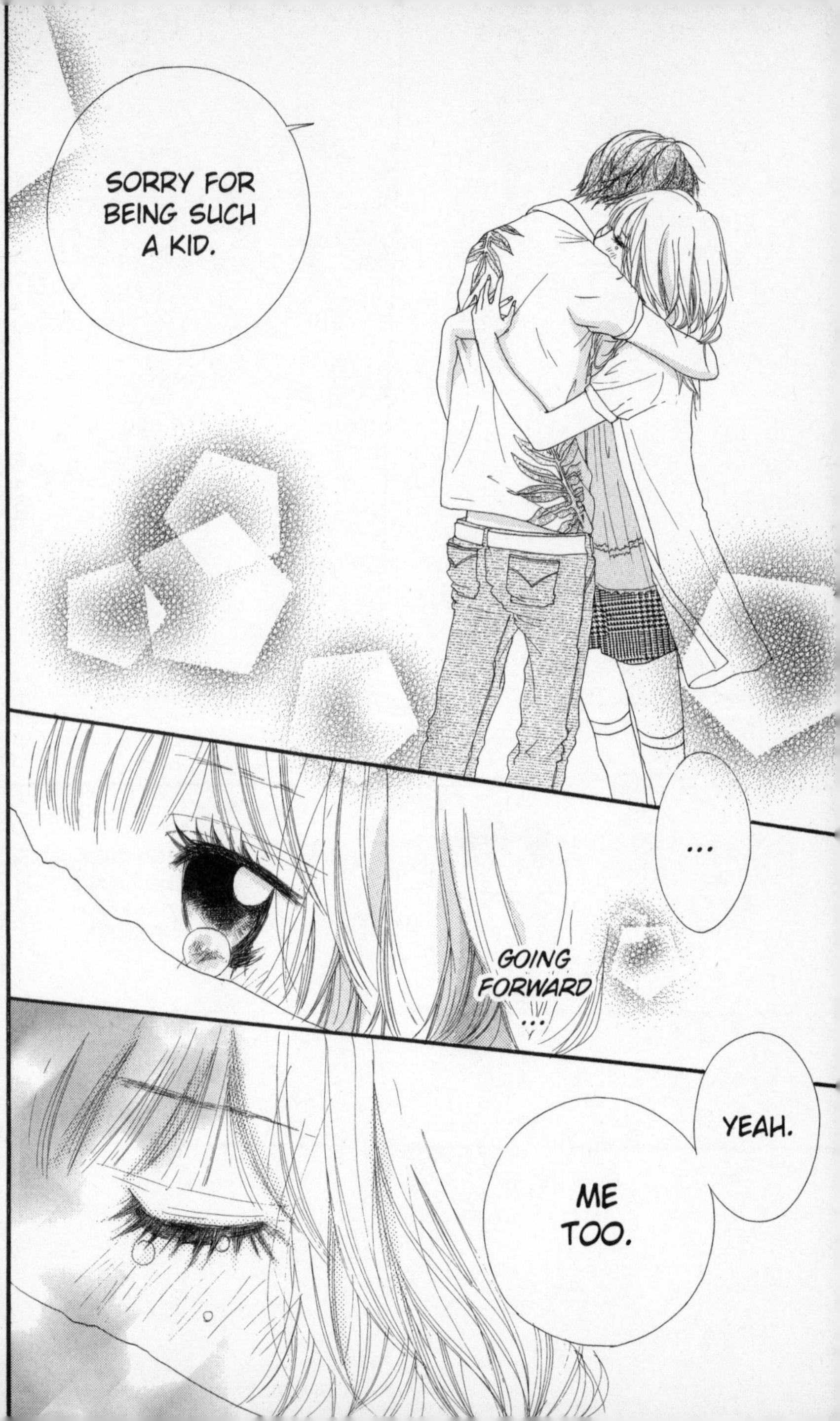
SORRY FOR BEING SUCH A KID.
...
GOING FORWARD ...
YEAH.
ME TOO.

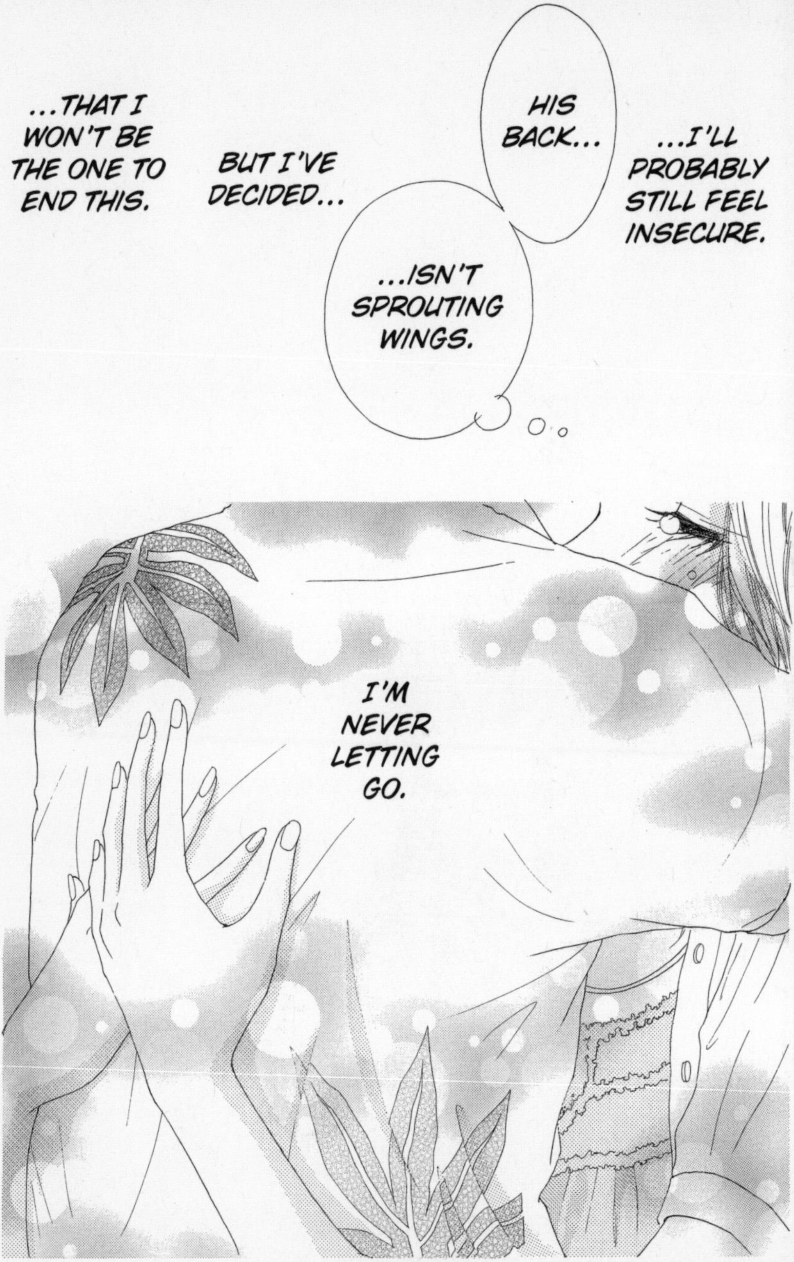
...I'LL PROBABLY STILL FEEL INSECURE.
HIS BACK...
...ISN'T SPROUTING WINGS.
BUT I'VE DECIDED...
...THAT I WON'T BE THE ONE TO END THIS.
I'M NEVER LETTING GO.
THE END

AFTERWORD

Thank you for reading all the way to the end!

When I'm creating manga, I often lose my way and don't feel very confident. But thanks to you, my readers, I always manage to think positively again. I could never do this on my own. I'm only able to be who I am because of you. I wish there was a device that could measure my gratitude...

But if nothing else, I can pour that gratitude into my manga! It may be kind of intense. Is that scary?

Anyway!

I hope that you can all feel at least a fraction of how grateful I am!!

 Io Sakisaka

To be continued...

...in volume 3!

Doing a serialized title is causing me to become more of a recluse. This has everything to do with how slow I am at drawing manga. I thought that if I gained more experience, I could draw faster, but I realized that I'm getting slower. Why? I need to go outside for a bit so I can stimulate my brain. I'm going to do my best!

—Io Sakisaka

Born on June 8, Io Sakisaka made her debut as a manga creator with *Sakura, Chiru*. Her works include *Call My Name*, *Gate of Planet*, and *Blue*. Her current series, *Ao Haru Ride*, is currently running in *Bessatsu Margaret* magazine. In her spare time, Sakisaka likes to paint things and sleep.

STROBE EDGE
Vol. 2
Shojo Beat Edition

STORY AND ART BY
IO SAKISAKA

English Adaptation/Ysabet MacFarlane
Translation/JN Productions
Touch-up Art & Lettering/John Hunt
Design/ Yukiko Whitley
Editor/Amy Yu

STROBE EDGE © 2007 by Io Sakisaka
All rights reserved.
First published in Japan in 2007 by SHUEISHA Inc., Tokyo.
English translation rights arranged by SHUEISHA Inc.

The rights of the author(s) of the work(s) in this publication to be so identified
have been asserted in accordance with the Copyright, Designs and Patents Act 1988.
A CIP catalogue record for this book is available from the British Library.

The stories, characters and incidents mentioned in this publication are
entirely fictional.

No portion of this book may be reproduced or transmitted in any form or
by any means without written permission from the copyright holders.

Printed in the U.S.A.

Published by VIZ Media, LLC
P.O. Box 77010
San Francisco, CA 94107

10 9 8 7 6 5 4 3 2 1
First printing, January 2013

www.viz.com   www.shojobeat.com

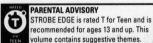

Surprise!

You may be reading the wrong way!

It's true: In keeping with the original Japanese comic format, this book reads from right to left—so action, sound effects, and word balloons are completely reversed. This preserves the orientation of the original artwork—plus, it's fun! Check out the diagram shown here to get the hang of things, and then turn to the other side of the book to get started!